THE OLD SERVICE

Here is the first extensive study of the men who served as regimental colonels in the armies of Charles I during the English Civil War of 1642–46. In following the king's cause these colonels faced likely death in battle and many never survived to greet the restored monarchy. Their enduring and toughened loyalty to the Royalist cause lies at the centre of this book. P. R. Newman examines why this high-profile group of Royalists took the risks they did and explores how their role in the Civil Wars is an important key to our understanding of the wider questions of Royalist ideology and allegiance.

The impression of the Royalist military commander has too often been shaped by familiarity with a far from representative few. This study breaks new ground in subjecting to analysis more than six hundred Royalist colonels and offering a series of new perspectives on the nature of armed Royalism. It deals with the social pattern of regimental command as well as the religious dimensions of Royalism. It examines the principles which underlay armed support for Charles I, and looks also at the reality behind the mythical figure of the Cavalier. There are new insights into familiar Civil War figures and fresh approaches to problems of historical interpretation.

There has been a curious imbalance in Civil War historiography with extensive work on Parliament and its armies and yet a relative paucity of in-depth analyses of Royalists. This book seeks to redress the balance and it will fill a notable gap in Civil War studies. The book constitutes invaluable reading for historians of the English Civil War and early modern political, ideological and military history.

For Bronwen Vickers
with affection and profound respect

The old service

Royalist regimental colonels and the Civil War, 1642–46

P. R. Newman

MANCHESTER
UNIVERSITY PRESS
Manchester and New York

*distributed exclusively in the USA
and Canada by St Martin's Press*

Copyright © P. R. Newman 1993

Published by Manchester University Press
Oxford Road, Manchester M13 9PL, UK
and Room 400, 175 Fifth Avenue, New York, NY 10010, USA

Distributed exclusively in the USA and Canada
by St Martin's Press, Inc., 175 Fifth Avenue, New York,
NY 10010, USA

British Library Cataloguing-in-Publication Data
A catalogue record for this book is available from the British Library

Library of Congress Cataloging-in-Publication Data
Newman, P. R.
    The old service : Royalist regimental colonels and the Civil War,
1642–46 / P.R. Newman.
        p. cm.
    ISBN 0–7190–3752–2 (hard)
        1. Great Britain—History—Civil War, 1642–1649.   2. Royalists–
–Great Britain—History—17th century.   3. Great Britain.   Army–
–Officers.   I. Title.
DA415.N49   1993
941.06′2—dc20   93–14678
                                                                        CIP

ISBN 0 7190 3752 2 *hardback*

Photoset in Linotron Baskerville
by Northern Phototypesetting Co. Ltd, Bolton
Printed in Great Britain by
Bookcraft (Bath) Ltd

CONTENTS

MAPS AND TABLE

Maps

Table

PREFACE

Charles Rosecarrock of St Neot's in Cornwall was twenty-six when the Civil War broke out in 1642. His mother Dorothy came of the Thynnes of Wiltshire, a Royalist family from the outbreak of the war. His wife, Margaret, was the aunt of Warwick third Lord Mohun, who commanded a regiment under Charles I. Rosecarrock himself was a commissioned officer from 1642 until 1646. In 1648 he joined the attempted rising, although where he fought is unclear. As spring wore on in 1651 he was informed against to the Council of State in London as one 'ready for new action'. By September he was serving as a lieutenant-colonel in the forces raised on behalf of King Charles II. The Council of State had been warned against Rosecarrock: his record was such that his future actions were predictable. He was 'one that was formerly in the old service all along'. He was, in short, a diehard Royalist fighting man.

The Council of State's informant, whether he knew it or not, by his choice of the term 'the old service' pitched upon the very essence of armed Royalism. Rosecarrock's indefatigable loyalty to the Stuarts was, by 1651, bidding fair to become an anachronism. But for him, and countless others, involvement in the 'old service' – in the cause of King Charles I – had fixed them more firmly still in that obedience which had drawn them into arms in the first place.

Whenever men like Rosecarrock chose to justify their actions, whether publicly or privately, in the heat of war or in the wake of their defeat, the concept of service to the Crown was a common and constant theme. It mattered more, to some of them, than any reservations which they may have had concerning the policies pursued by Charles I prior to 1642, or in the course and after-math of the war. They experienced a sense of personal obligation and commitment to a personalised monarchy, a dedication to a man as much as to an institution, that of the monarchy. This idea of service more clearly conveys the thinking of Royalists in arms than any other term which historians may choose to employ. It embodies both the principle of obedience in a true subject, and the fundamentals of a patriarchal view of society. It is the element which sustained devotion during the years of the Republic and which in part made possible the Restoration of 1660.

Men such as Rosecarrock saw no shame in representing themselves as the King's servants, a view that Royalist clergy and army chaplains hammered home in countless sermons. Without a clear understanding of the concept of the 'old service' our understanding of the forces that made civil war possible must be imperfect.

A study of the men who exercised regimental command during the time when the 'old service' took on profound meaning is a study of a distinctive group of Royalists whose actions were eloquent of service. In obedience to their king, they put their economic security, their political future, their families and their reputations on the line. More than this, they hazarded their lives. They may be considered, for the purposes of this study, the foremost proponents of that traditional expression of their loyalty, the shouldering of the burden of an old service.

P. R. Newman
St William's College
York, 1992

ACKNOWLEDGEMENTS

My editor at Manchester, Jane Thorniley-Walker, invited me to write this book. She proved herself to be the most painstaking and conscientious editor I have ever dealt with. I hope the finished work does her justice. I must thank the British Academy for their financial help in the preliminary stages of this study. It came at a time when even the notion of a book was barely formed in my mind. Colonel Edward York of Hutton Wandesley Hall I had always presumed to count as a friend. He gave more than sufficient evidence that this was so, and my thanks go to him. It is also true to say that without A. V. R. this book would have fallen short of the goal I had set for it: and she well knows the pressures of writing, always self-induced.

Originally this book was to be dedicated to Catherine Mary Phillimore and Lucy Sealey, for reasons obvious only to a few. Events in March 1993 caused me to alter that dedication, but I cite them here very happily. As for the input of other historians into what follows, it has been marginal. That is the consequence of pursuing an unfashionable course of research. That said, I owe a debt to many scholars, living and dead, which requires me to say that I hope this book confirms their support for me. Those I count among my friends will know who they are, and if I do not name them, they may escape blameless from association with the arguments advanced in what follows. I do not intend to allow Norman Dore, Malcolm Grattan, Gordon Blackwood, and John Morrill to escape the fact of my respect for them and their work. Each of them has given me cause to think and think again.

How many hundreds of times former pupils express their ongoing gratitude to G. E. Aylmer I'd hate to imagine. Since this is in some ways a book about obligation, however, I see no reason not to cite my own to the example of a great scholar.

INTRODUCTION

This book is a study as diverse as the sources permit of Royalist regimental colonels during the Civil War of 1642–46. It is concerned with both group and individual characteristics. It sets out to answer a straightforward historical question: who and what were the men, beyond the fact of their military role, who prosecuted the King's war against his Parliament? We know much concerning the war itself, its campaigns, its impact upon the national, regional and local communities. Its causes and its consequences continue to be the subject matter of scholarly debate. We are familiar enough with certain leading personalities, some of whom – Cromwell, Rupert, Fairfax, for example – remain household names 350 years on. Yet we still know little enough about the vast majority of men, of either side, who fought that war and upon whose efforts and achievements great reputations were founded.

Study of the armies of the Parliament, especially of the radically chic New Model, have been prolific in comparison with studies of those raised by the King. Even scholars who set out to examine the Royalist war effort have abandoned the field in pursuit of other historical quarry, or are dead and their work unfinished. This book sets out to help make good that deficit in scholarship, and to break with traditional generalisations about the Cavaliers.

I have attempted to offer far more than a straightforward group analysis of the Royalist colonels even though that in itself would be both novel and valuable. Questions of motivation have also to be considered and there must be discussion of what it was that these men saw themselves as fighting for. To restore to them even a small part of their crucial role in the years 1642–46 it is necessary to accord to them serious consideration of their principles. I recognise the limitations of the evidence, yet I have sought to bring to the forefront of this study men whose very names may be largely forgotten. It is my contention that the Parliament's victory in arms in 1646, so long coming (even after massive Scottish help in 1644) and never to be seen as inevitable until after Naseby in June 1645, must be set against the achievements and merits of its enemies. I insist upon the quality of the King's commanders, and if that quality is acknowledged, Parliament's victory becomes all the more famous. I intend that this study should go some way towards a truer assessment of the merits of the King's men.

Where motivation is concerned, this study will argue that, where the evidence permits us to judge, Royalist fighting commanders claimed or, as in the case of Gervase Lucas, demonstrated a profound sense of personal loyalty to Charles I as man and king. Whereas many Parliamentarians made a show of juggling with the notion of the King's two bodies, the man apart from the office, the Royalists for the most part evinced little sign of such philosophical perplexity. They entertained few doubts as to the inherent rightness of what they were doing, reserving their debate for more pragmatic issues. They regarded as 'odious and ridiculous' (to quote Sir Richard Grenvile) what they saw as the exculpatory arguments of enemy polemicists. A fighting commander with the lives of men entrusted to his judgement cannot afford much in the way of inward dispute as to the rightness of the work in hand. Parliament perceived the wretched consequences of political ambivalence in its Grandee commanders, and inaugurated a purge out of which came the steel-hard commanders of the New Model. The Royalist armies required no such 'new modelling', for, give or take a faint heart here and there, the kind of commanders the King needed to wage his war were in place long before Fairfax replaced the Earl of Essex as commanding general of the enemy.

I will argue that, if the Civil War is to be seen as a war of religion, only one side in it possessed anything approaching crusading zeal. Whereas Parliament was concerned, if not to change men's beliefs, then at least to create the conditions for change commencing with the stripping away of the structure of an hierarchical church, the Royalists saw themselves as defenders of that structure. If anything, the King's armies were most impressive in their apparent Laodicean indifference to the very factors which gave to their enemies a sense of the crusade. Parliamentarians and subsequent historians were puzzled and alarmed by the way in which Protestants and Roman Catholics could fight side by side. Parliamentarians explained it away as part of the popish conspiracy: historians have been less able to endorse such a view. Yet the alliance of two diametrically opposed groups of believers is wholly explicable if the religious factor is recognised as subservient to the cause of the defence of the Crown. The predilection of some historians for seeing the Civil War as the confrontation of opposed religious viewpoints has led some of them to play down and undervalue the Catholic role in the Royalist party. They have professed to see the anti-Catholicism of Parliament's propaganda as a necessary ploy not necessarily related to the true threat from Catholicism, and have chosen to regard the Catholic Royalist as a propaganda construct. Now that most historians are persuaded that the Catholic commitment to Charles I was significant and long-lasting, they are obliged to try to explain such an unexpected response to decades of centralised though spasmodic persecution. In 1642, for the Royalists, what a man believed in matters of religion mattered a good deal less than his willingness to serve the King. It is that fact which alarmed the Parliament and its supporters far more than any long-imagined Popish plot.

Clearly, the attitude of the Royalists, their motivation and their fighting spirit were not enough to overcome the King's enemies. They fought long and hard and were worn down until they suffered overwhelming military defeat in 1646. It is arguable that the true spirit of Cavalierism perished in that collapse. What came after was a series of hitherto unthinkable alliances between former enemies, political and religious compromises and the breakdown of what passed for consensus in the Parliamentarian camp. Although many individual survivors of the old service continued to threaten the Parliament and the Interregnum regimes, politics had moved on and left them behind. The broken, bankrupted Cavalier of the 1660s was a stock figure then as now, a reminder of bad times:

> Like an old almanack, I now but represent
> How long since Edgehill fight or the rising was in Kent.
> [Lamentation of a Bad Market, 1660]

Where the King's regimental colonels were concerned, not so many of them survived to see the Restoration. Many died in the field before 1646 or in other fights in later years. Some succumbed to camp fever, tuberculosis, dysentery or sheer exhaustion. Some died in prison, or on the scaffold. Many ended their lives in exile in Europe, perhaps in the service of foreign princes and foreign powers. Those that did survive often found their worldly fortunes impaired, not least by their expenditure in the war years, with the engagement of their credit, and the legalised plundering of their estates by a Parliament out for money and revenge. The regimental colonels drew upon themselves not only the bullets, blades and round shot of their enemies, but the full and rigorous implementation of state-sanctioned sequestration.

In a country without a professional army, regiments were raised by and identified with their commanding colonels. Each was known by its commander's name. Such commanders therefore stepped directly into national notoriety, marching in the forefront of events and the glare of publicity even as they commanded their men from the front in countless hand-to-hand engagements: the brutal, hacking fights into which set-piece battles degenerated. Their example and sometimes their sacrifice could make victory possible: Slanning and Trevanion at Bristol, Bevil Grenvile at Lansdown. The deaths of some of them (when death was still novel and frightening) were made the subject matter of panegyrics and eulogies, showing spotless or reformed lives leading to martyrs' deaths. In death, too, Royalist fighting commanders could be exemplars.

This study, many years in the making, offers a comprehensive examination of Charles I's regimental commanders. It is concerned less with their martial exploits than with their origins, their motives and those factors which led them into regimental command in the first place. It is a contribution towards our fuller understanding of the nature of support for the King, and may go some way towards showing where that support came from upon which Charles relied in his war against his Parliament. The thread of armed Royalism is apparent from 1639/40, and was no new phenomenon of 1642. It did not arise, then, from nowhere, but was present in the Army Plots, the Incident, the attempt on the Five Members and the abortive Kingston on Thames muster in January 1642. The men of the old service were always there; it is just that there were a great many more of them from the summer of 1642 onwards.

The King's regimental commanders are mostly men without an historical voice. Surviving documentation, whilst it is able to tell us who they were and at least some of the things they did, rarely offers insights into their personalities or beliefs. Some few of them declared their minds openly in public print, during and after hostilities, or else they spoke their minds freely in letters to family or friends: Frank Wortley, first and for a time most notorious of them; Charles Dallison, the Lincolnshire lawyer impatient with religion; Henry Slingsby, the taciturn man of conscience; and Bevil Grenvile, apparently seeking and finding honourable death. These and others have partially bared their minds. They thus communicate directly with us, and their principles and values display a not surprising unanimity. They may indeed represent many, if not all, of their voiceless comrades in arms.

The degree of commitment amongst these men is revealed by the attitude and measures which Parliament adopted towards and against them. Someone like Robert Brandling in Yorkshire could successfully negotiate a change of sides in 1644, and lead the remnant of his regiment thenceforth under Parliament's colours. Others scorned to look for favour, and some would not have found it had they sought it. The merciless hounding of many commanders – the 'skellum' Richard Grenvile, Colonel Harry Lingen (Harry for the King) and poor John Scrope, for example – is clear proof that such men were known as bitter and implacable enemies of the Parliament, or the Parliament as it had become. Sir John Stawell, formerly an MP, refused to kneel at the bar of the Commons' House, was marked for death, and was confined many years in prison. His well documented case is by no means unique. There was at work in the minds of many Royalist commanders an enduring and toughened sense of loyalty to the King that overrode all else.

Of course this study is necessarily partisan in so far as it is based upon a belief that any study of those who fought in the old service can only enhance our understanding of the Civil War; that such a study is as necessary and important as any devoted to the fighting men of the 'good old cause'. Many years ago Dr John Morrill, in reviewing my *Royalist Officers in England and Wales, 1642–1660* (New York, 1981), observed that the 'unthinkable' was happening, that we were beginning to know more about the Royalists than about the Parliamentarians. Dr Morrill was characteristically generous, yet his remark was justified, for there has not been a balance in historical scholarship. My *Royalist Officers* and this present work will, I hope, further broaden the historical horizon. There have been biographies of Royalist figures. George Digby (who also features in this study) has been examined. Sir Edward Nicholas, Sir John Berkenhead, Viscount Falkland, Robert Filmer, Edward Hyde and others have demanded attention. Military commanders, of which number George Digby was disastrously one, have also attracted biographers. Bevil and Richard Grenvile, Marmaduke Langdale, the valuable study of Ralph Hopton by Edgar and, most written about of all, Prince Rupert, who to this day remains immortalised as the archetypal Cavalier. On no very good grounds. Yet such studies are few: if all the biographies of Oliver Cromwell were piled one upon another, it might be possible to peer over them by standing on a pile of published biographies of leading Royalists, Charles I and his nephew included. Countless Royalist commanders pass too fleetingly before the reader, alluded to and passed over. Even the works of familial piety so beloved of the nineteenth and twentieth centuries offer little in the way of depth. One looks in vain for the Gerards, the Lunsfords, the Comptons, the Slingsbys, the Stradlings. Our impression of the Royalist military leader, the Cavalier, has been determined by a narrow perspective and to this day remains coloured by the lies, distortions and allegations of those who wrote as journalists at the time when such men flourished. We cannot know how representative was the allegedly brutal Francis Doddington, the severe and partisan Marmaduke Langdale, the quiet and almost self-effacingly loyal Henry Slingsby. This study may be an exercise in collective biography, but it is necessary to begin the process of redressing the balance of our knowledge.

The men under scrutiny were vital to the King's proceedings, and this work seeks to restore them to the forefront of events and to accord them that importance which, however transitory, they enjoyed in their time. It is based upon the view that what William Heylin did as a commissioned officer was more immediately important, briefly, than what Peter Heylin the Royalist thinker pondered upon and wrote of. Parliament itself regarded the King's fighting men with fear and animosity: the punishments meted out to them prove that. That Parliament had been obliged to fight a war at all was due to men such as William Heylin who, in their thousands, chose to commit themselves to the King's service.

Historiography has passed over that contemporary truth, and has thereby relegated these men to the sidelines and footnotes of scholarly enquiry.

This study has its origins more than twenty years ago when I began research towards a doctoral thesis under the supervision of Dr Gerald Aylmer. My work then, on the King's armies north of the Trent, developed into an enquiry into the personnel of those armies. I recognised then that what men were was as significant as what they did, and that to explain their actions it was necessary to try to understand their attitudes and inclinations. I came to the conclusion then, and have seen no reason to change it, that 'attitudes' and 'inclinations' are more commonly to be met with than 'principles' and 'beliefs' but that the latter may well arise from testing of the former. After the completion of my thesis I commenced a study of the King's officer corps on a nationwide basis. In that new work, limited for practical reasons to a survey of field officers commissioned between 1642 and 1660, I set about gathering information on as many individual officers as could be accounted for. The *Royalist Officers* of 1981 drew together those data, and was offered very much as a research aid rather than as a completed study in itself. In papers and articles I assessed the data and endeavoured to present some conclusions from them. Historians reviewing that work, and in the course of correspondence and conversation with me, made a strong case for treating the period of the First Civil War, 1642–46, as quite distinct from what came after it. Since alterations and amendments to *Royalist Officers* were inevitable, a study of the regimental commanders of the First Civil War seemed to provide an opportunity both to offer wide-ranging analysis and to amend the lacunae of the original work.

It perhaps needs to be explained why this present study is more limited in scope than that of 1981. Even in the case of regimental colonels there yet remain cases of insoluable identification problems. However, in the context of this concentration upon regimental command, rather than upon field officers in general, such instances are not sufficient in number to affect any overall conclusions which may be drawn. They also possess some significance in themselves. Had this present work attempted to encompass all field officers the proportion of the known to the unknown might have rendered some conclusions at best tentative. There is ample evidence for the colonels to permit discussion in depth, and to relate that where possible to historical debate.

Some historians have inclined to the belief that the Civil War was fought largely by amateurs, whilst others (and particularly where the King's armies are concerned) have claimed everywhere to see the imprint of the mercenary, the soldier of fortune. We must be extremely careful in choosing terminology: often the terms 'soldier of fortune' and 'mercenary' are used lazily, and the word 'professional' is inadequately defined. It has, for example, been felt that 'professionalism' might be attributed to any officer who, prior to 1642, had experience of actual war in a command rank. Rightly, recent historians have questioned whether such experience in the Bishops' Wars alone could be any guide to true professionalism. Clearly, it cannot have been on a par with experience in the Thirty Years War in Europe, which many English and Welsh gentlemen played sometimes important parts in. The first distinction to be kept in mind is that professionalism in things military, arising from direct experience, was an additional accomplishment for many landed gentlemen or Grandees. It was a desirable attribute. As John Ferne wrote in 1586, 'so necessarye then, is the profession of Armes, that no common-weale, no citie, no common societie, can dure without them'. The Earl of Lindsey, the King's commanding general, who died at Edgehill in October 1642, exemplifies the Grandee distinguished from others by his knowledge of war, which recommended him to the King for high command quite apart from his social status. The way in which the Royalist party in arms reflected the distinctions of peacetime society is known: but the attributes of the gentry which recommended them for employment included knowledge of war, and many of them, at all levels of gentry society, possessed such knowledge. The way in which they exercised their authority showed their professionalism. To limit the application of the word 'professional' to persons earning their living from war is to miss a salient point about mid-seventeenth-century gentry society. At least 184 of the King's colonels commissioned or promoted between 1642 and 1646 had sufficient experience of war to be regarded as professional in their duties. That is a little under one-third of all identified colonels. Those who came into command rank for the first time in their lives in 1642, or subsequently, either acquired professionalism within a short space of time or were no use to anyone.

It is also essential that the equation of 'professional' with 'mercenary' should be abandoned in any study of the Royalist armies. The true mercenary, one who made his living by drifting into other people's wars, shifting allegiance as his pocket dictated, was a rarity in Civil War England. This is true of both rival armies. A mere sprinkling of such men may be found at various levels in each, but their impact was localised and their group significance minimal. Charles I was no Tudor despot seeking foreign soldiery to suppress rebellion because he could not rely upon his own people in a crisis. A king in search of soldiers he may have been in the summer of 1642: he found them in every shire of England and every county of Wales.

Yet the equation of 'professional' with 'mercenary' is no new error of judgement. Edward Somerset Lord Herbert of Raglan, as diehard a Royalist as any, accused the Earl of Forth of being a mere 'soldier of fortune', a polite euphemism for mercenary. Yet it is evident that Forth made a choice of conscience when he accepted a command in the King's armies, turning his back on his fellow Scots and their League and Covenant. He took a risk, he made a brave decision: a man of his calibre must have had alternatives open to him in Europe, and there was precious little guarantee of enrichment out of England's civil war. Forth was, of course, a professional: long years of campaigning in Europe had taught him the trade of soldiering, and had made of him a competent and efficient general who was motivated by military considerations above all else. What Lord Herbert perceived and took exception to was the difference between a career soldier and a soldier for the working day, impelled by necessity. The true career soldier such as Lord Forth had lost many of the niceties and constraints of civilian life which might restrain him in the exercise of his duty. For Lord Herbert, such constraints were natural: the morality he brought to war was a civilian morality. Yet this difference between them no more made the one a mercenary than it made the other merely an amateur.

As has been said, the newcomer to military rank in 1642–46, if he intended to make good his command, was obliged to become at least outwardly professional. Two or three years on from 1642, many a country gentleman turned commander was either a veteran or was wholly useless. Deaths, wounds, defeats and responsibility for the lives of men either instilled professionalism or broke the unprofessional. Historians who insist upon the specious argument that the Civil War was fought by gentlemen amateurs, and was therefore in some degree less intensively prosecuted than the wars of Europe, have missed the point by a mile. To take an example familiar enough, and from the Parliament's side, Oliver Cromwell was new to soldiering in 1642. What he did as Marston Moor in 1644 was sheer professionalism. In that respect, at least, he was no different from hundreds of his fellow countrymen.

In what follows I have chosen to dispense with the use of the terms 'mercenary' and 'soldier of fortune' and have alternatively categorised colonels of experience as either professional or career soldiers. The distinction does not, I think, need to be drawn further. Men such as Lord Forth, James King, Marmaduke Langdale and others were professionals: Forth and King were also career soldiers. For them, the military life was predominant. To Langdale and many country gentlemen like him, it was an adjunct to their other accomplishments, and one into which they could slip as conveniently as into their riding boots. Even novice commanders who took the field against the Scots in 1639/40 were learning the duties of a soldier under the most trying of circumstances, that of defeat. Those that went into Ireland against the Catholic rebels acquired professionalism in particularly brutal warfare. The practice of employing experienced men as subordinate field officers in the regiments of novice commanders from 1642 assisted the colonel's transition from civilian to soldier, and imparted professional organisational abilities to newly levied companies and troops. It takes little wit to perceive that within a short time the King's commanders, and those of the Parliament, became real soldiers if they were not already so. If that fact is accepted, the view taken of the Civil War must necessarily reflect it: perception of the gaudy trappings of seventeenth-century command too often obscures the bloody business that war was. Dr Hutton, among many services to scholarship, has introduced us to the notion of the English gentry turned feral: men in whom the process of brutalisation went very far indeed.

What angered Lord Herbert about Lord Forth was the latter's apparent disregard for the well-being of civilians. Lord Herbert, whose own period of command was not particularly successful, but who poured much wealth into the King's coffers, was alarmed at the way in which standards of behavioural decency declined in the face of warfare. Lord Forth was not a brutal man, but he was a realist, and knew how war must be waged to be effective. Hutton's feral gentry were men who thought like Forth and went further than he did. Herbert's attitude, which also had its partakers, though laudable in itself was rendered irrelevant by war. Nevertheless, it is wise to keep in mind that Forth and Herbert represented two aspects of Royalism in arms: that which both men felt profoundly was their sense of loyalty to the person of their king, but the nature of their experience determined how they sought to serve him.

The rank of colonel, like any military rank, betokened authority and was also a title of honour. Since, as a title of honour, military rank came well down in the scale of things, there is a real problem in determining who was and who was not a colonel. For if such a man happened also to be a knight, baronet or peer, then it was by the distinction 'Sir' or his other title that he would tend to be known. This was common usage, and requires that the sources be examined closely for evidence of precise military rank. A colonel elevated socially subsequent to his military commission, to knighthood or hereditary honour, likewise became subsumed within such common usage. In such cases, of course, the evidence of rank is clearer, since it antedated other elevations. However, in a few cases I have been obliged to exercise my judgement, applying what Alfred Burne would have called Inherent Military Probability, as to whether or not a knight or other titled commander was a regimental colonel. Wherever the uncertainty defied such efforts I chose to omit such a person from inclusion in a study which is concerned solely with regimental colonels.

A further difficulty in arriving at precise rank arises from the way in which (and this is as true now as then), unless precision was essential, common usage conflated 'colonel' and 'lieutenant colonel' into 'colonel'. The same careful scrutiny of the sources as must be used to identify the rank of titled commanders has been applied in this case also. It follows that some have been omitted because, the evidence itself being inconclusive, there was no justification for assuming full regimental command.

In short, every precaution has been taken to ensure that those upon whom this study is based, and such of them as figure in the text, were full colonels by commission or promotion between 1642 and 1646. Most of them are cited in my *Royalist Officers*, which is quoted frequently as the source for what may be said of them. However, since its publication in 1981 additional work on many officers has occasionally required me to alter my earlier judgement, or has enabled me either to identify a man positively or in some way to amplify what is known of his career. Where there is reason to cite such a case the references for what is said are given distinct from the published work. Some colonels – though, perhaps surprisingly, very few of them – remain mere names or the subject of conflicting identities. The fact of their rank requires their inclusion in the study. But wherever, by virtue of inadequate information they must be omitted from analysis, that is made clear in the text. I am confident that only a tiny handful of full colonels will never ultimately be identifiable: the omission of those and of other problem cases from assessment of group characteristics cannot materially affect the overall findings.

Identification must involve the establishment of a colonel's social status at the time of his commission or promotion. It was the factor which, more than any other, led to regimental command. I have opted for a broad categorisation in this respect. There seems to me to be little value in trying to establish minute distinctions between mere gentlemen, gentlemen and esquires, although I am aware that much emphasis has been placed upon these fine distinctions (not least by myself in earlier published work). Instead, I choose to recognise plebeians; individuals distinguished by profession, vocation or trade; and, for the upper strata of society, to adhere to what used to be called the *nobiles minores/nobiles majores* distinction. The *nobiles minores*, the untitled gentry, encompass gentlemen and esquires, and here again I have declined to distinguish the one from the other. It was not unusual then for a man insistent upon his entitlement to be known as 'armiger', or esquire, to find himself to be but a mere gentleman when the subsidy man knocked. Whilst we may well look for and find consistent usage of social distinction in certain cases, it is spasmodically rewarding research at best. To follow a simplified model of untitled as against titled gentry appears more practical. I am aware that knighthood belongs to the classification of the *nobiles minores*, a personal honour carrying with it no hereditary right. Knighthood could be bestowed upon deserving plebeians with ease, since society was not obliged to recognise the issue of such distinguished men or to show them the courtesy due their fathers. Many Royalists knighted between 1642 and 1646 – social advancement which, like all others, Parliament declined to recognise – not infrequently included men of small means. For some, of course, it was a first step upwards, and knighthood an indicator of social mobility, but knighthoods were not passed round indiscriminately, by any means. There is no evidence of any real inflation of honours during the war years among the King's military supporters.

In practical terms it made very little difference that a knighthood conferred in the field brought with it precedence over the baronetage (the lowest grouping of the *nobiles majores*), for this was not a precedence that could be passed on. In this study knights are therefore considered, properly, as the leading element within the *nobiles minores*, though with this caveat: that because knighthood in the field was so singular a mark of honour, whether bestowed by the King himself or by a delegated viceroy such as Lord Newcastle, recipients of such an honour should be distinguished from their fellow knights. In 1642 Charles I quite generously, and before hostilities, bestowed knighthoods as an inducement to future service or acknowledgement of loyal service done. Not a few potential colonels were thus encouraged before they received a commission. Such knighthoods often recognised local, regional or county standing, which might be crucial in the evolution of Royalist armies. Such pre-war distribution was far higher than wartime distribution amongst fighting men.

Above the *nobiles minores* were the holders of hereditary titles, the baronetage and the peerage. There were wartime creations in both the peerage and the baronetage for serving colonels, but not on any very significant scale, as will be shown. King Charles did not swamp the land with ennobled Royalists, which would have aroused jealousies and given offence. He rarely used titles to buy support, though there are some instances of it, after war had broken out: he was more inclined to do it in the process of creating his party.

There is, within the peerage, a group that requires some distinguishing preliminary remarks, the younger sons and brothers of peers. Historians have tended to see such younger men as prime material for army service and command, the Civil War offering an alternative to trade, the church or adventuring in Europe. In some ways that remains a fair assessment, but it would be wrong to adduce from it that peerage families sought to safeguard property and well-being by token gestures of dispensable cadets. The frequency with which heads of families as well as their heirs appear in arms, and at all command levels, shows that side-taking in the Civil War demanded a high degree of commitment in familial terms. This should tell us that something very important was seen to be at stake by contemporaries, even if inclination rather than strict principle led many to assert themselves.

The younger sons and brothers of the nobility cannot be classified as a group distinct from the peerage: not a few were married, heads of their own families, living apart from the main familial seat, though perhaps annuitants. They were recognised as a distinct part of the *nobiles majores*, by custom, usage and the rules of the Heralds. Untitled for the most part, they were nonetheless potential heirs to titles. James I by decree gave precedence to the younger sons of viscounts and barons (the lowest ranks of the peerage) over his newly created order of baronets and thus not only fixed them clearly in the order of precedence but, in the somewhat muddled laws pertaining to that order, defined them. He both affirmed their status and decreed their quality. Whilst this is not the place for a discussion of issues of precedence in early modern England, where status consciousness was habitual, where Heralds then as now lived off their fees, I must make the point. In this study I choose to allow the term *nobiles majores* to embrace and include all untitled younger sons and brothers of the peerage, the consequence of which is set out clearly in Chapter Two.

If social status might be critical in the selection of a man for regimental command, his religious beliefs were less so, even though the King affected to prefer Protestants. I have already said that the Royalist army was characterised by a remarkable lack of religious bigotry and contrasts strongly with the Parliament's forces in this respect. Nevertheless, the role of the Roman Catholic Royalist requires that some attempt be made to define Royalist colonels according to their religion. Certain general remarks can be made to preface, as it were, the discussion in Chapter Four. Then as now, the Anglican church was a broad church, encompassing within itself all shades of religious opinion and learning by virtue of its monopoly as state church. Those who stood beyond its wide catchment did so not because they were excluded but because they distanced themselves. The Catholics excluded themselves by refusing to conform to the rites and liturgy of a Protestant church, but it was the state which penalised them more effectively than the church courts. Their stance was seen as essentially political. The Catholics were an identifiable minority within the nation, with areas of localised predominance. Catholicism was, moreover, a religion of the gentry, and the King's sweep for commanders inevitably embraced them not because of their religion, but in spite of it.

Puritans unable to worship according to the requirements of the Laudian reform merely inherited a tradition of alienation and dissent well established by the 1630s. They excluded themselves, as did the Catholics, although sharing a common ethic of Protestantism with their mainstream Anglican neighbours. They were a force for disruption within the state church which Catholics were not. Just as there were Catholic Royalists (or, to put the emphasis where it belongs, Royalists who were also Catholics) so, too, there appear to have been Royalists who were Puritans. It remains hard to prove exactly who they were, at least where army command is concerned. It is clear that the first Civil War is distinct from what came after it, not least in the observable shift after 1646 of 'Puritans' towards the Crown. Between 1642 and 1646 few identifiable Puritans appear also to have been Royalists, though they might profess their allegiance to the institution of monarchy. It would be hard to see how any Puritan, even if he were prepared to accept a modified episcopacy, could side with a cause one of the fundamental tenets of which was the maintenance of the bishops and the church's ancient hierarchical structure. That hardly mattered to Catholics, who had no legitimate interest in the Protestant church anyway. But Puritanism, as Gerald Aylmer has observed, was a frame of mind rather than an ideology, and a rigorous Puritanism in matters of worship did not preclude service to the King in time of war.

Yet categorisation of Royalist colonels according to religious belief is not straightforward. I have chosen to assume that an individual was a communicating member of the Anglican church unless positive evidence – not mere accusation or hearsay – indicates otherwise. Thus comprised within that almost amorphous body may well be men of Puritan inclination whose opinions are wholly lost to us. There were also, if the way in which terms of abuse like 'papist' and 'popish' were thrown around, a body of communicating Anglicans hankering after something older, far older than their present state church.

Roman Catholic colonels may be defined by evidence of recusancy prior to 1642 and, if necessary, subsequent to 1646; by coming from families with strong recusancy traditions; and, though less reliably, by what contemporaries said of them. That some Catholics may have been communicants of the Anglican church, outwardly conforming, is possible. I do not, however, hold much truck with the notion that Catholics began to flock to church in 1642 to enable themselves to qualify for rank and command in the coming war. If 'church papist' means anything it may well apply in the same sense as 'papist' and 'popishly affected', denoting Anglicans, Protestants, favourable to Laudian reform and opposed to Puritanical doctrines. Historians run a risk of complementing the work of Parliamentarian pamphleteers by accepting terms such as those as indicative of some Catholic consensus approaching a conspiracy. The very idea of a domestic Catholic intrigue against the state and church embracing laymen and women is a nonsense. One wonders how many of those who propagated the idea really believed in it. If they did, the least that can be said is that there was something distinctly unpleasant in the psyche of many of the King's enemies.

I have attempted to isolate the 'popish' and 'papist' from the defined Roman Catholic, and have distinguished them also from the mainstream of Anglican conformity. Evidently, men who had used against them words of opprobrium such as 'papist' must have been known to their contemporaries for their specific leanings in matters of worship. I suggest it is indicative of commitment to Laudianism. Accusations of popishness were flung regularly at all Royalists, but where the charge is levelled against particular Royalists it must be treated as a guide to belief. Sir Henry Slingsby, who favoured episcopacy but not Laudianism, was never accused of popishness, even though at the Restoration some Catholic writers liked to pretend he was of their faith. On the other hand, Sir Thomas Aston, a prominent and outspoken champion of the bishops, was condemned as popish because of it. Between Slingsby and Aston there were differences in emphasis, but Slingsby clearly belongs to the mainstream of the church and Aston to its Laudian reforming wing. He was, in Puritan terms, a popish Protestant.

However, in terms of army command the number of cases involving individuals accused of popishness is small enough, and the large majority of the King's colonels, if they had any religious leanings at all, were probably indifferent to theological niceties whilst loyal to established forms. That is the essence of innate conservatism, and the Royalist party as a whole was rooted in such instinctual, emotive social political and religious conservatism.

The roots of armed Royalism will be discussed more fully in Chapter One, where the motives which lay behind men's resort to arms will be considered. In that same discussion it will be argued that Royalism was a reactive force, fighting what its proponents largely thought of as a defensive war against an ambitious element of the Lords and Commons. This is not contrary to what ought to be wholly apparent, the fact that the King was the begetter of war and, in strict terms, Parliament was on the defensive. In its struggle to fend off and ultimately to beat the King, Parliament skilfully used the religious weapon, against which the Royalists had very little to offer. Royalist chaplains quite as much as enemy polemicists denounced the ungodliness of Royalist armies, and observers of the time saw fit to attribute Royalist defeat to the want of edge in their proceedings, a want of religious fervour. Parliament consistently played the religious card because it was central to their view of themselves as guardians of the reformed church and the Protestant state. They appeared to offer eradication of popery and the completion of reform. Against this the Royalists offered at least temporary toleration of the old enemy, and little more than sincerely horrified reactions to the excesses of sectaries and madmen who appeared to people the Parliament's armies. The ease with which Roman Catholics fitted into the Royalist military machine alienated barely a handful of their fellow commanders who occasionally used the Catholic presence to justify their own defection to the enemy. It might also be noted here, however, that such as did do so went over to the Parliament when the King's affairs began to look black. Parliament seized upon the Catholic presence in the King's armies and did so from indisputable moral high ground against which Royalists could not prevail. How far the anti-Catholic sentiment sustained Parliament in the dark days of 1643 remains to be shown.

In Chapter Four I shall discuss the Catholic involvement in regimental command and also try to relate that to Catholic perceptions of what Catholics thought they were doing. I shall endeavour to show that, far from being a puzzling development, Catholic Royalism was a quite natural and predictable phenomenon. Religious differences mattered less to Catholics than a sense of duty and obligation which they shared with their Anglican neighbours. Further, the very nature of the King's trawl for support amongst the gentry drew to him Catholic gentlemen on precisely the same grounds as it drew Protestants: local significance and influence and reserves of material wealth. Royalist apologists felt constrained to explain and to defend a process induced of necessity, but it is one of the consequences of that necessity that the Royalist armies achieved what peacetime political processes never could: toleration to the extent of parity in opportunity. In that light, Parliament's attitude was socially divisive, intolerant and verging on the genocidal.

This study will also address itself to the geographical origins of the King's colonels, touched upon in Chapter Four and the theme of Chapter Five. A county-by-county survey covering England and Wales is not practical. Instead, I have chosen to examine county distribution in broad terms, and to examine in depth certain areas or regions, and sample counties. The armed forces available to the Crown and to the Parliament in 1642 were, without exception, county or city-based. This was as true of Trained Bands brought to their colours as of volunteer units formed for the waging of mobile warfare. As the war progressed all regiments to a greater or lesser degree found their county associations diluted. The pressing of recruits, the assimilation of captured enemy rank and file, the movement of officers of all ranks between regiments, and the ordinary process of recruitment broke down initial links. Nevertheless I will show that the county remained the fundamental source of soldiery and commanders. Both the King's Commission of Array and the Parliament's Militia Ordinance were directed to the county authorities: if anything exemplifies the way in which England was not a centralised society it is the way in which armies were raised in times of crisis. By the end of the war armies were more truly national than they had previously been, and contained within them men from Scotland, Ireland and European nations and states, but through it all ran a continuous thread of localism which could sometimes manifest itself in apparent contention with the direction of the war. The great Pontefract Castle relief raid of March 1645 could not have happened but for the strong north-country links of Langdale's Northern Horse brigades.

In Chapter Three I intend to look at the personalities and characters of as many officers as space permits. There is no analytical point to that, though some perhaps original conclusions will be drawn from it. It is instructive to attempt to come face-to-face, as it were, with the subject matter of group analyses. In many instances, of course, we are reliant upon what others said of certain individuals rather than upon self-evaluation. Yet by this means we come close, or as close as the passage of decades may permit, to once living men, and to the impact which they made upon their comrades in arms and upon their enemies (not all of whom were to be found in the Parliament's camp). If there is any poetry in history, as G. M. Trevelyan believed, then it lies, as he said,

in the quasi-miraculous fact that once, on this earth, once, on this familiar spot of ground, walked other men and women, as actual as we are today, thinking their own thoughts, swayed by their own passions, but now all gone, one generation vanishing after another, gone utterly as we ourselves shall shortly be gone, like ghosts at cock-crow.

I still consider it a primary task of history to get close to the minds of preceding generations and to seek to see as they saw. It may be beyond achievement, but it is nonetheless a worthy exercise, for all that. Analytical examinations of group characteristics are sterile if there is no attempt to approach at least some of those upon whom such analyses are based.

It will go without saying that I respect the cause which the subjects of this study served, as I hold in high regard many of its servants. Having said that much, I hope that in what follows I have smothered such subjective judgement. I have yet to come across an historian who studies where his sympathies are not in some way engaged.

'For the sake of our Publike Father'
The concept of obligation and the demands of service in Royalist thought

I

The epitome of Royalism, Professor Conrad Russell has recently urged, was a defence of 'at one and the same time, a religion, a way of life, and a corporate identity'.[2] Abraham Cowley, during his Royalist phase, said much the same thing:

> You fight things well establisht to defend;
> All ages past your pious armes commend.[3]

Both the modern historian of the period and the contemporary poetaster concur in seeing Royalism as essentially conservative and, by definition, reactionary. The Royalists reacted against the expanding authority of Parliament, where the House of Lords appeared to be led by an assertive Commons. Yet that reaction was violent, in a sense sudden, and sustained for some four years of civil war. Beyond 1646, resistance to the Parliament, and then to the Interregnum regimes, remained a matter of conscience for thousands of British men and women. Something far more profound than a general consensus that the *status quo* was under threat must have been at work in the hearts and minds of those who, by inclination, temperament and opportunity, actively espoused the Royalist cause.

Many Royalists in arms were sustained by a sense of personal loyalty to the King, an attitude which Charles I clearly recognised and encouraged. In September 1643 he acknowledged the considerable effort of the Cornish in his cause with an open letter intended to be read and displayed in perpetuity in the churches and chapels of that county. 'We are so highly sensible,' the King wrote, of the extraordinary Merit of Our County of Cornwall of their Zeal for the Defence of Our Person and the just Rights of Our Crown (in a time when We could contribute so little to Our Own Defence, or to their Assistance, in a time when not only no Reward appeared, but great and probable Dangers threatened Obedience and Loyalty . . .[4]

Sir Edward Walker, considering the commitment of the Cornish, attributed it not to 'a greater Measure of Judgement, or to more Humanity than others have, but unto that Obedience to their Superiours which the rest have cast off'.[5]

Both the King and Walker picked upon what they perceived to be the most vital element in the psyche of Royalists, the duty of obedience to the King, which was not simply mechanical but expressed itself in genuine committed loyalty to Charles I. There was little point in the King alluding to his professed intention to preserve the liberties and prerogatives of the Parliament once the war was over. He was addressing his soldiers, and speaking in clear-cut terms about the primary purpose of their labours: his, the King's, personal survival, with those prerogatives without which monarchy, guarantor of the liberties of the subject, would be but a cypher. As the King's Commissions of Array reach, perhaps deliberately, back into the medieval past, so the King drew upon an almost feudal sense of personal identification between monarch and subject. The Civil War of 1642–46 was, it is arguable, a confrontation between an old, personalised form of government and the emerging state, supported by its citizens. Perhaps this makes the Royalist cause archaic, even from 1649 (briefly, anyway), anachronistic. Royalism in arms was the pure expression of a traditional and learned commitment to patriarchal government on the part of a very large number of Englishmen and Welshmen. Whether many Royalists knew of or were able to express such sentiments as those of Henry Ferne – 'has not God put kings, fathers and masters all in one Commandment and enjoined this duty and reverence to them under one word, Honour?'[6] is not important. The sentiment was inherent in their actions, and their actions were eloquent. To fail to perceive the Royalist identification of personal interest with that of the King is to fail to feel the heat of the fire of Royalism.

To classify Royalism as a force rooted in the identification of the subject's well-being and security with those of the King is not to simplify it, although it is arguable that nothing like a Royalist ideology emerged between 1642 and 1646. That is probably because it would need the total overthrow of the institution and the execution of its head, as in 1649, to force upon Royalists a more profound consideration of what it was they intended to continue to fight for. Professor Kenyon goes too far towards the archetypal backwoodsman image of the Cavalier when he argues that Royalism was essentially 'gut loyalty',[7] for such a conclusion pre-empts the vital factor of identification of interest. It may be that it denies to the Royalist a concern with self-interest entirely, and makes his actions mechanical. Gut loyalty may be synonymous with a purely emotive response to the pressure of political events, but it precludes the working of conscience and, by definition, consideration of the abstract concept of honour. This is both Ferne's 'honour', due to the King by God's command, and the honour of individual integrity confronted by a perilous but unavoidable choice of actions.

There are two ways, for example, in which Sir Francis Wortley's action in April 1642 may be construed. In that month King Charles was denied entry (even with a much reduced entourage) into his port of Hull. The governor, a local Yorkshire gentleman, Sir John Hotham, in thus denying the King access to the military arsenal stored there, effectively put into practice the spirit of Parliament's Militia Ordinance. For many Royalists, the ordinance's frontal attack upon the most vital of the Crown's prerogatives, the right to levy and command armies, was an overt act of rebellion. Wortley[8] drew his sword in public, declared himself for the King, drew around him a following of like-minded and similarly armed gentlemen, and stepped into the forefront of events.

Wortley's action, or the news of it, spread rapidly around the country in a matter of days. In London his name was on as many lips as Hotham's: he was, it seems, the first Royalist hero to rival Parliament's darling. Attempts to dismiss what Wortley had done convey the impression that it was evidence of an excitable and unstable temperament, yet there is nothing in Wortley's career before 1642 or thereafter to suggest any pronounced volatility. What onlookers and observers nationwide actually understood from Wortley's gesture was something far more profound than the mere polarisation of opposing mobs in the city of London. Wortley's sword pointed unequivocally at a traitor, Hotham, and beyond him to the traitors at Westminster. Wortley's sword was drawn and raised against perceived, overt rebellion, and it cut clean through the Gordian knot of political negotiation and dissembling. If the reaction of some was to sneer at Wortley's histrionic gesture, their derision was nothing more than the expression of a sudden fear that the hour of the sword was upon them, and that deadlier hands than that of a Yorkshire baronet in his early fifties would wield it.

Wortley himself justified what he had done in a tract published in London in June entitled *A Declaration from York*, which, considering the hostility he had drawn upon himself, not least from the House of Commons, was far from conciliatory. His 'heart and conscience' excused him, he declared, and his social status obliged him ('being amongst others of my quality, the first in order of ranke') to do his 'Prince and Countrey that good service'. He was certainly a 'prime' and, for the Commons, a 'pernicious Royalist' because, in terms of armed support for the King in 1642, after the emergence of the Militia Ordinance, he was the first herald of what was to come.

Wortley's subsequent career as a Royalist swordsman did not live up to this initial promise, though he remained, in his own words, 'a well try'd loyall blade'.[9] He commanded as a colonel in his native county until his capture in 1644, and from then until his death in 1652 remained a prisoner in London, even though he was admitted to compound for his estate in 1649. His imprisonment for life, as it turned out, reflected his notoriety in the summer of 1642 and the service he performed for his king thereafter. Parliament's memory, being collective, was not faulty. His son and heir, a colonel fighting for the King elsewhere in England, surrendered himself in London in 1645, but remained active in conspiracy as late at 1659. Yet, unlike his father, Francis II experienced no prolonged periods of imprisonment, except a brief spell as a debtor in 1651.[10] Wortley's importance as an instigator of resistance to the Parliament in 1642 is, therefore, established.

Historians of the events leading to the outbreak of open war in 1642 have accorded far more importance to Hotham's action in Hull than to Wortley's defiance of it, although clearly what Wortley did was but the latest evidence of a factor which, in its earliest forms, has attracted scholarly interest. It would seem to be true that, before ever there was a Royalist party in political terms, there was Royalism in arms. It can be detected not merely through its manifestations as phenomena at particular times of crisis – the Army Plots of 1641, the attempted arrest of the Five Members, and the abortive muster at Kingston on Thames shortly thereafter – but in the personnel of those potentially violent ploys. In evidence heard in June 1641, for example, future Royalist field officers made their appearance. Henry Percy, Dan O'Neill, John Berkeley, George Goring, Henry Jermyn, Hugh Pollard, Henry Wilmot, William Ashburnham and William Davenant were all named.[11] All, without exception, served Charles I in arms from late 1642. Whilst there were other factors at work in 1641 apart from zeal for the King, it would be difficult to deny that these men were already the nucleus of a future Royalist military strength.

Not many of those who attended the King in his attempt to arrest the Five Members in January 1642 can be identified, but three at least were certainly with him. Thomas Lunsford, erstwhile Lieutenant of the Tower, was present.[12] He was subsequently a colonel of foot and taken at Edgehill.[13] The barrister William Mason, a Norfolk man, was active recruiting for the King at the Inns of Court, went with Charles to York, and from 1643 was a colonel in the army of the Earl of Newcastle.[14] Goddard Pemberton, from Rushton in Northamptonshire, was present also. From evidence laid against him[15] his forwardness singled him out in one street clash when 'God damn me, kill them' was alleged to have been his word of command to his following.[16] Pemberton rose to the rank of lieutenant-colonel in the King's army, and surrendered himself in 1646.[17]

After the attempt upon the Five Members, Lunsford and others rallied together at Kingston upon Thames. Ludovick 'Lodi' Lindsay, sixteenth Earl of Crawford in the Scottish peerage and a prime figure in the Incident of 1641,[18] was certainly there. The earl, a Roman Catholic with long military experience in the armies of Spain, was a colonel of horse and dragoons from November 1642, and served as major-general under the Earl of Hertford in 1643. He was one of but a handful of eminent Scottish soldiers who offered their services to Charles I against the Covenanters in 1639.[19] Alongside Lunsford and the earl was Fulk Hunks, a career soldier from Warwickshire who had been on the fringes of the Army Plot,[20] and who was to return from service in Ireland in 1643 to command a regiment for Charles I against the Parliament.[21] Also accused of being present at Kingston was Thomas Howard, younger son of the Earl of Berkshire. Although Howard denied involvement, the accusation conveys the suspicion with which Parliament regarded him. They were right to be wary of him. Howard was commissioned as a colonel of horse in September 1643, became governor of Malmesbury and fought at Naseby in 1645. He was to be an active conspirator throughout the 1650s, and died at a good old age in 1706 as Earl of Berkshire.[22]

To dismiss Wortley's action in April 1642 as aberrant behaviour, as some nervous contemporaries did, would be wrong. He clearly belongs to this line of committed Royalists who had emerged as supporters of the King before any real polarisation within society had begun. Wortley is the link between these men and the far more numerous Royalists of late 1642. They were men willing to act independently of the King in the King's interest as they perceived it, and willing also to be seen with him when Charles resorted to minimum force against the Five Members in January. Where most of these men differ from Wortley is in their backgrounds, for most of them had European military experience and were, to all intents and purposes, soldiers. Wortley's military experience had been as a Trained Band colonel in Yorkshire, and this fact adds to his significance. The perceived need to resort to arms in defence of Charles I passed in April 1642 from the soldiers to the civilians who would be soldiers. Wortley was the most forward of this rather more important body in society.

Wortley's watchwords were conscience and service, the one dictating the other. In the persona of *Mad Tom a Bedlam*, written in prison in 1648, Wortley persisted in his prayers for 'good king Charles' and 'The best of queens, queene Mary'. Extreme vicissitudes of fortune did not dampen the original ardour of 1642.

Royalists were persuaded of the rightness of their cause, and many of them looked upon military defeat as but a low point in the fortunes of their king and his party. Explanations of the way in which they perceived their relationship with King Charles underwent little change between 1642 and 1646. In the latter year Ralph Lord Hopton, militarily beaten but nonetheless unbowed, spoke plainly to Sir Thomas Fairfax and in a few words concisely summarised the prevalent Royalist attitude of the previous few years:

I am confident you have too much honour to expect from me [that] to avoyd any dainger, or to enjoy any worldly advantage, I will renounce my Masters House, to whom I am both a sworne Subject, and a sworne Servant; That I must professe I am resolved to undergoe all Fortunes with him, and, if there shall be cause, to suffer anything, rather then in the least poynt to taint my honour in that particular . . .[23]

King Charles is here represented as a patriarchal master, both of servants and of children, with both of which positions Hopton willingly identified himself. He found in willing subjection and in royal service a dignity integral to his sense of his personal honour. Hopton, whether he was familiar with the text or not, would have accepted Henry Ferne's strictures: 'as unto the first rule of fathers, the government of Kings did succeed, so unto kings is honour commanded under the name of fathers, that we might conceive the unnaturalness of war and forcible resistance against them'.[24] Fathers imposed a necessary discipline, as did kings, and for many Royalists resignation to obedience under such a discipline was as natural, as instinctive, as submission to a father as head of his family.

Moreover, that Hopton chose to identify his personal fortunes with those of the King was also crucial. 'Fortitude is a royal virtue; and though it be necessary in such private men as shall be soldiers, yet, for other men, the less they dare, the better it is both for the commonwealth and for themselves,' wrote Hobbes.[25] Hopton, as a soldier, qualified to share the fortitude of his master, just as he was required to fight for him and recognised an obligation to do so without reservation. Soldiering for the King was thus sanctioned by natural law as well as by the laws of the kingdom, upon which the Recorder of Lincoln, Charles Dallison, relied to justify his acceptance of a colonel's commission from Charles I in 1642. 'The Law expects from the servant,' Dallison wrote after the war, 'a personall assistance, to preserve his Master from violence or hurt; and in that regard, the Master being assaulted, the servant, by the Lawes of England, may justifie to resist the assailant, in defence of his Masters person.'[26] Dallison was a lawyer, Hopton a soldier as well as a country gentleman, yet both used the same imagery to represent themselves favourably, the relationship of servant to master. Hobbes understood that attitude of mind:

The virtue of a subject is comprehended wholly in obedience to the laws of the commonwealth. To obey the laws, is justice and equity, which is the law of nature, and, consequently, is civil law in all nations of the world; and nothing is injustice or iniquity, otherwise, than it is against the law. Likewise, to obey the laws, is the prudence of a subject; for without such obedience the commonwealth (which is every subject's safety and protection) cannot subsist.[27]

Thus Hopton could recognise in his enemy Sir Thomas Fairfax a sense of honour commensurate with Fairfax's social status and birth. The Parliamentarian's values, however, were aberrant in Hopton's view, and abhorrent, since for Hopton, Dallison and all Royalists rebellion was the most horrid of crimes and required of those opposed to it a firm assertion of the principles upon which they based their own actions; '. . . if there shall be cause', Hopton had said, he would 'suffer anything' rather than 'taint my honour'. Clearly, in Hopton's eyes Fairfax's honour was compromised and tainted, and he let his adversary know it.

Parliamentarians, or the most part of them, would have refuted the claim that they were disloyal to the King. The fiction that the Parliamentarians found necessary, that they fought for King and Parliament, was in fact a far more complex theory to grasp than the relative simplicity of the undiluted Royalism of men like Hopton. Hobbes let slip a point that more moderate Royalists would have had in common with Parliamentarians when he pronounced that the King 'commands the people in general but by a precedent law, and as a politic, not a natural person'.[28] Royalists, of course, recognised this, but recognised that the public authority which was as much the King as the King's own person required an identical demonstration of allegiance as that required, or shown, to the person of the King. Everyone understood that the King's authority could not solely prevail where he himself should chance to be, but must exist apart from his person. No Royalist, however, could conceive that the person of the King could at any time be distinct from the concept of his authority. Parliament had to deny that.

The idea of the King's 'double capacity', as defined, for

example, by Charles Herle in 1642,[29] and explained in the theory that the office of the magistrate was distinguishable from 'the person' of the magistrate, could not be countenanced by any thorough going Royalist, since it must necessarily deprive him of the sense of veneration for the King as a person. Later commentators reviewing the Royalist defeat in 1646 tended to argue, as will be shown later, that too many Royalists did in effect suffer from this awareness of the distinction between 'the man that hath the power' and 'the power of that man'. Seeking to account for Royalist defeat, such commentators could not avoid implying that, if the idea of the King's two bodies was truly entertained anywhere, it was amongst the Royalists themselves, whereas for their enemies it was but a convenient cover for their resolute rebellion. There is, however, this caveat to that view. The acceptance of the destructive notion of 'double capacity' tended to strangle the Royalist war effort at the very top, in the counsels of the King and his civilian advisers. Wherever Royalist military commanders expressed themselves, there is little evidence of subscription to that doctrine. Nor should there have been, if the war in the field was to be prosecuted with any degree of commitment. Many were later to feel that war in the field was hampered by the equivocation in the counsels of the King, that not all his enemies were to be found under Parliamentarian colours.

The erudite Dudley Digges, the gifted fellow of All Souls College, Oxford, produced one of the most important statements of the Royalist case ever written. His *The Unlawfulnesse of Subjects taking up Arms against their Sovereign, in What Case Soever*, published posthumously in 1644, is a complex mixture of political semantics and extremely accessible straight-talking. Digges's importance, which has only really been recognised in recent years,[30] lies chiefly in the pristine nature of the argument which it contains, written as it was before the spectre of failure seriously began to haunt the King and his supporters. Digges, of course, died before it might have been necessary for him to rewrite his masterpiece. His work may not have been unfamiliar to many Royalist commanders, who would have understood implicitly such direct passages as this:

by shooting at [the King], by attempting to kill him, they are lost temporally; their goods and chattels, lands and tenements, and lives are forfeited in law, and what is most lamentable, their souls are eternally ruined. Disloyalty to their king is disobedience to God. . . . They that resist shall receive to themselves damnation.

Digges the theoretician and Wortley the civilian turned soldier agreed entirely. Wortley perceived the risk to his eternal soul from offering to resist his King, as he made clear in 1646 when he sought to define what it was that made a true Cavalier:

[He] conceives the King to be the Head of the Church, as it is personall, not spirituall, and hath sworne him God's Deputy in Government. . . . He dares not question his Authority, who is onely answerable to God, but in his heart knows him as his Vice-regent, and knowes that to resist his power, is to resist him that gave it . . . He dares call his Soveraigne the Anointed of God . . . He conceives passive obedience always due to the power of the King.[31]

This is the kind of belief upon which men go willingly to fight, and it was widespread among Royalists. Theirs was a just and a right-eous cause for which they fought and died, and in which they killed and maimed, even though, in its strictest sense, obedience to the King did not in itself require that a subject should either understand or concur in that which the sovereign intended. Sir Robert Filmer made that wholly clear: '[It] may be said of the king's commanding a man to serve him in the wars. He may not examine whether the war be just or unjust, but must obey, since he hath no commission to judge of the . . . causes of war.' Nor, Filmer added, 'hath any subject power to condemn his King for breach of his own laws'.[32] This observation follows upon an exposition of the master/servant imagery which was widely familiar.

The sanctifying of the sabbath is a divine law, yet if a master command his servant not to go to church upon a sabbath day, the best divines teach us that the servant must obey this command, though it may be sinful and unlawful in the master; because the servant hath no authority or liberty to examine and judge whether his master sin or no in so commanding, for there may be a just cause for a master to keepe his servant from church as appears Luke XIV 5. Yet it is not fit to tie the master to acquaint his servant with his secrets, counsels or present necessity, and in such cases the servant's not going to church becomes the sin of the master and not of the servant.[33]

Filmer cannot really have been thinking of civil wars when he wrote this passage, even though his injunction to unquestioning obedience would have been appropriate and understood by many Royalists. The Civil War was marked time and time again by the printed justifications of either side, and the King's supporters probably knew more about his 'present necessity' than they had ever done in time of either peace or foreign war. The effectiveness of the Royalist war effort required that this should be so, and identification of interest between servant and master, subject and king, in the exigency of civil war, required an extraordinary confidence. Nor is it at all likely that any Royalist supposed that he could espouse the King's cause and that, if it all went wrong, he would be saved harmless by the other side's recognition that the sin lay in the master. Royalists, unless they were very poor or very lucky, did not escape punishment of their loyalty, for the Parliament reserved that loyalty, as has been said, for the authority of the King. This, from 1642 until 1646, they conceived to have remained at Westminster regardless of where the person of Charles Stuart might chance to be, and would remain there until Parliamentarian arms restored Charles to it. Thus the Royalists, as they sooner or later realised (had they been naive enough to have thought otherwise), were seen as fighters against the King's authority even as they fought for his person, and were thus malignants and disturbers of the peace.

The language of service was the common parlance of Royalists from 1642, and the identification of their interests with those of their king (and perhaps vice versa also) was fundamental. For such Royalists obedience was both natural and enjoined upon them by their understanding of the way in which society functioned. They could, in a sense, do no other than obey, but that did not mean that their obedience was merely a cold recognition of a familiar but resented state of subjection. On the contrary, the Civil War gave the subject an immediate importance for his king, and transformed years of grumbling acquiescence in the *status quo* into something far more dynamic. True and evident dependence of the subject upon the King, and of the King upon the obedience of his subjects, emerged with sharp definition in the Civil War. There was not only the positive injunction to oppose rebellion, but the necessity of the King which obliged him to make a direct, personal appeal to his people. Thousands answered it.

The Civil War made plain also the degree to which loyalty first and foremost to the person of the King had fallen away. 'The people in general,' wrote Hobbes, somewhat unfairly, 'were so ignorant of their duty, as that not one perhaps of ten thousand knew what right any man had to command him.'[34] There were those who found traditional expectations of loyalty meaningless, the King's power distinct from that of Peers and Commons in need of curtailment. If the old notion of obedience and loyalty was a burden, then those who shrugged it off had barely ceased to stoop when the full weight of a far more centralised authority than the King had ever dreamed of fell upon their shoulders. Heavy, onerous and efficiently collected taxation poured into Westminster to fund the struggle to achieve or maintain the right to impose such exactions. Parliament had its back to the wall when Civil War broke out, and governed accordingly.

It has been remarked by historians that the Royalists' primary asset was the person of the King, an obvious rallying symbol, and more easily defined than the collective leadership of the Peers and Commons at Westminster. To carry that view a step further, and to suggest that it was the King's evident plight that created a sympathetic response in his favour, would be a natural corollary. It is also arguable that, on the verge of, and in, military defeat, the King commanded quite as much sympathy, tinged now with pity, as an anonymous poet of 1647 made clear. The author of *Upon His Majesties Comming to Holmby* succinctly conveyed both the clear association between the defeated King and the defeated and sequestered Royalists, whilst clearly maintaining the personal nature of their wartime association:

> Thy poor distressed Cavaliers rejoyced,
> To hear thy Royal Resolution voyced,
> And are content, far more poore to bee,
> Then yet they are, so it reflects from Thee:
> Thou art our Soveraigne still, in spite of hate,
> Our zeale is to thy Person, not thy State.

Another anonymous Royalist author published in 1648 classified his party as 'a distressed company of Noble-men, Gentlemen and others, who having Engaged their Estates and Credits to compound with the Parliament, are all retired to private life, to eat the bread of carefulness'. They had been 'beaten out of all their defences, but that of a good Conscience, which remains impregnable'.[35] Their struggle to 'suppresse Rebellion that Child of Hell, that Parent and Nurse of all Mischeife'[36] had come to nothing, but whilst the King lived and was able to negotiate, then the hour of their triumph might yet be at hand, and the suffering vindicated.[37] Charles I's followers, though their condition had undergone change during and in the wake of the Civil War, saw no cause in 1648 to alter their stance, and all that was really missing which had been present in large measure from 1642 until 1646 was the resources in men and money to make good the rising of that year. By identifying their own reduced circumstances with those of the King himself, they maintained, under adverse conditions, the primary bonding of the war years. In their consciences they knew they had acted rightly, whether they subscribed to the ideal of obedience for its own sake or represented themselves as rational champions of the Crown. Their cause had been 'to defend him, whom God hath exalted, to keepe the King in that Throne wherein God hath set him, against those that would remove him from it'.[38] At least by 1644, many Royalists perceived that the removal of the King from the throne must be an inevitable consequence of a lost war, and viewed Parliament's tenacious denials as falsehoods intended to dupe 'many an ignorant subject' into believing 'that a man may become a martyr for his country by being a traitor to his prince'.[39]

For the Royalists it was impossible that the King could be where his authority was not, although there were enough who would accept that view to provide Parliament with its supporters. It was impossible that Peers and Commons, each and every one of them individual subjects of the King, could collectively aspire to equal status in the affairs of government. 'The two Houses of Parliament', ran a clause in a Royalist oath imposed in Herefordshire in 1644, 'without the King's consent hath noe authority to make lawes, or to bind and oblige the subject.'[40] Colonel Sir Charles Dallison chose to entitle the tenth chapter of his vindication 'the Subjects of this Nation . . . are obliged with their lives and fortunes, to assist and preserve the [King's] person, and just rights . . .' (the use of the qualification 'just' is token of Dallison's rational Royalism).[41] As Edward Symmons avowed in the prefatory material of his own work,[42] his task was 'to vindicate my Soveraigns Name and Honour, to which as a subject I am bound by common Allegiance, Oath and Protestation'. Hobbes declared that 'those whom the Parliament called delinquents [were] none but the King's best subjects'.[43] St John tells us, Symmons explained, that 'we should be ready to lay downe our lives for our Brethren . . . much more then to hazard them, for the sake of our Publike Father'.[44] In 1646 eight captured Royalist colours were brought to London from the field of Torrington, 'one of the Lord Hopton's, with this motto "I will strive to serve my sovereign king" '.[45] Hopton, the former MP and committee man at Westminster, was guided by his conscience to fight against the pretensions of his former colleagues tooth and nail, and conscience maintained his commitment to live up to his chosen motto when, as has been said, all was in ruin around him.

II

The vast reservoir of loyalty upon which King Charles I was able to draw in 1642 and afterwards, and which he must have had good cause to believe was there, required organisation and direction. Disciplined obedience, structured loyalty and calculated sacrifices were the essence of successful war. From the King and his advisers and ministers, civilian and military, the direction of the war was passed down for execution in the field by the generals and regimental commanders. A large number of them, the vast majority, took up arms for conscience's sake, some few from coercion or by the example of others. One of the inherent problems for the King in revealing his necessity to his loyal subjects lay in controlling their actions without impairing their 'fidelity and zeale to your Majesties person and cause'.[46] Royal trust led some of them to imagine themselves to be the best arbiters of what was immediately best for the King's interest, the kind of attitude that could lead to both disobedience and inaction. In this they might also have claimed to be guided by their consciences.

Conscience, in that it is an inner prompting or conviction of moral certitude, whether in relation to actions committed or in relation to acts omitted, is the most difficult of the words that may be used to express the nature of Royalist belief. The concept of service is accessible, even if the dignity of servitude is, 350 years on, a forgotten concept. Similarly, loyalty conveys an immediate understanding of commitment come what may, in the case of the Royalists, expressed towards the King both as a man and as a monarch. As for conscience, Sir Henry Slingsby of Moor Monkton in Yorkshire, an unrepentant Royalist if ever there was one, intimated to his sons not long before his death that:

My high obligations confirmed by Oath, and bound in, I must confess, with an inviolable tie of Religious Love, had so inseparably united my thoughts to the devotion of allegiance as the serious and constant Observance of it begun to have that influence over me, as in the end it Resolv'd to a case of Conscience.[47]

For Slingsby the certitude of the morality of his actions as a Royalist came after his resolution to support the King. He accepted the constraints of his role as subject and the imperative of obedience to his King, but it took the bitter experience of prolonged war and defeat, it seems, to give him any degree of moral conviction. How much was this true of other Royalists, who, when they did choose to justify their actions, introduced the promptings of conscience as a prime instigator? Slingsby, melancholic, brooding, contemplative, a long way removed from any image of the swaggering and boisterous Cavalier, was just the type of man of whom martyrs and sacrifices are made. He went to his death in 1658 as he went off to war in 1642, with resignation and stoic fortitude. One is left with the feeling that defeat and the eventual killing of the King were the true begetters of moral conviction, and that adversity was a sign of righteousness.

In his seminal study of Somerset between 1625 and 1640 T. G. Barnes observed that 'the nation was on the threshold of an era when men responded to the dictates of conscience'.[48] It should be no surprise that his conclusion was based upon a consideration of the opposition attitude towards the imposition of Ship Money as an extraordinary fiscal measure of the Crown when men 'had to make the choice between the claims of their neighbours and their King, the choice that was no choice at all. It is easy to underestimate the importance of such consciences.' Barnes requires us to understand that this developing pressure of individual conscience led to the struggle against the Crown waged by Parliament in peace and war from 1640.

The preponderance of scholarly works has for long been in favour of study of Parliament and its supporters in one form or another, with the consequence that the moral high ground has for long been the preserve – unreasonably so – of the King's opponents. Yet it is undeniable that what Barnes saw as the state of affairs up and down England during the Personal Rule of

Charles I could as well be applied to the circumstances of 1642 and, with equal value, to the deliberations and decisions of Royalists as well as rebels. The element of moral certainty has to be restored to the Cavaliers, and emphatically so, if the profundity of the struggle of 1642 to 1646 is ever to be properly construed. Barnes knew that there were gentlemen in England who, from selfish considerations, resented any form of taxation but who also, from considerations of governmental and social stability, did not balk at paying up. It is at least arguable that the moral high ground over Ship Money belonged rather to those who paid, with whatever reluctance, than to those who declined and forced confronation.

By the same token, it is reasonable to suppose that those who remained loyal to King Charles from 1642, and hazarded everything in his cause, should be seen as guardians of a collective conscience that recognised the King's authority as crucial to that of Parliament, if not superior thereto. If there was far more polemic pouring out of London to justify the actions of the Parliament in terms of political and social and religious imperatives, that was because it was Parliament and its supporters who absolutely needed to justify their proceedings. Since they often preached to the converted, and made little discernible headway in swaying Royalists over to their cause, the moral certitude of Royalism was unimpressed by the semantics of rebels scrabbling for the moral justification which was inherently with the Royalists. 'I beleev,' many a Herefordshire civilian was required to swear in 1644, 'that the Earls of Essex and Manchester, Sir Tho: Fairfax, Sir Will: Waller, Coll. Massie . . . pretendinge to fight for King and parliament, doe thereby become actuall rebells . . . to be prosecuted and brought to condigne punishment.'[49] Precisely and succinctly so. Even the military success of the Parliament (impossible without Scottish military aid, which is an important point) failed to persuade many Royalists of any error in their ways. The execution of 1649 merely proved the propriety of Royalist contempt and disgust.

Very few Royalist commanders saw fit to justify their position for the benefit of their opponents or for neuters. Dr Aylmer observed that 'for many people of conservative views, acceptance of the world of order, hierarchy and inequality broadly as they find it . . . is so obviously sensible as to need no intellectual defence or justification'.[50] As he also pointed out, not all Royalists shared the same religious position, or advocated similar constitutional principles. What drew them all together was loyalty to King Charles, to which they necessarily subordinated personal political or religious beliefs. This was true in general terms of the Royalist party, and had to be true specifically for the fighting commanders whose military authority depended largely upon their subordination to centralised direction. The 'obviously sensible' nature of their views, of their loyalty, would have been difficult to articulate, and anyway, as has been pointed out, Parliament and its supporters cornered the market in necessary justificatory prose.

Self-evident rightness must account for the strange lack of explanation in the 'diary' of Colonel Sir Henry Slingsby.[51] Although he used his journal to muse upon the political and religious issues of the period from 1639 to 1642, and came down somewhat equivocally in a moderately Anglican stance, there is not a hint of the motivation which led him into regimental command. He was summoned to York by the King and commissioned 'to command ye Regiment of ye trainbands of ye City' and, a little later, given 'an order . . . to take 20 of a company to do ye duty of a soulgier, & to be a guard to ye King's person'.[52] Slingsby found his soldiers reluctant, and failed to fulfil the commission, 'so this was pass'd over & no more done'. A little later the Earl of Crawford 'had spoken to ye King for me to have a Commission for a Regiment of foot, but . . . unless I would find arms for ym wn they were rais'd, it would not be grant'd'.[53] A further period of inaction followed, until he was advised to put a small garrison into Knaresborough Castle (he had an interest in the town and had sat in the Long Parliament as one of its MPs), but he was pre-empted in this by a neighbour, Sir Richard Hutton of Goldsborough.[54] An attempt by Slingsby to put vigour into his Trained Band troops in York was blocked by the Earl of Cumberland.[55] Finally, on 13 December 1642, the Earl of Newcastle, who had superseded Cumberland, issued a commission to Slingsby to raise a regiment of foot, one of several new regiments to be raised. Thus, after tedious waiting which did not dampen his willingness, Sir Henry became a colonel for the King.[56]

The diary for this period shows, though not in so many words, that Slingsby was keen to secure a command, and it follows from that that he identified closely with the King's cause. During the frustrations of the period from April to December 1642 his diary betrays no hint that he may ever have reconsidered his conviction, nor does it betray any ill-feeling towards either Cumberland or Sir Richard Hutton. That the ultra-Royalist Earl of Crawford chose to speak for Slingsby implies an association between the country gentleman and the Scottish professional soldier, but it may merely have been that Crawford was billeted upon Slingsby at the Red House outside York, just as later Scottish commanders were to be. Crawford's influence was used on Slingsby's behalf, but the conditions were such that Slingsby could not meet them.

During these crucial months there must have been debate and discussion wherever Slingsby went. He betrays no hint of it. He was familiar with Sir Thomas Fairfax, and described a meeting with Fairfax in the city streets, but in his account of the exchange of words that passed between them it would be impossible to detect the attitude of a determined King's man. It must be a not unreasonable conjecture that the way in which Slingsby came into army command was a widespread and common process, a wholly natural consequence of the acceptance of the principle of obedience and service to the King. Only in later life, and on the eve of execution, did Slingsby occupy his pen briefly in vindication of himself, being even then much more concerned to guide his sons in right principles than to justify himself to them or anyone. Thus the Slingsby diary presents a man aware of religious and political discord, conscious of the contemporary debates, but offering no direct link between the conclusions of meditation and the actions of commitment. To quote Dr Aylmer, Slingsby's diary, like many Royalist diaries, is 'not quite what we might expect'.[57] But this is not to dismiss it. On the contrary, Slingsby's diary of events between 1642 and 1646, partly contemporary, partly written up from memory, is one of the most vital Royalist accounts of the war which we possess. Genuinely unconcerned with himself, Slingsby writes as an observer, underplaying his own participation, which was considerable, clearly (though he would have denied it) courageous, and often very close to the centre of the Royalist war effort. There will be much more to be said of him later. The diary is such a document that, since there is nowhere in it any account of the diarist's thought processes in 1642, we are obliged to concur with Dr Aylmer that here was a conservative country gentleman whose position was so eminently sensible that no justification was necessary.

But then again, it is unlikely that Slingsby wrote with an intention that his diary should be read. It is a wholly unself-conscious collation of events and genuine affection for both the King and for some of Slingsby's fellow commanders, particularly the Kentish colonel Sir John Mayney,[58] and if it was intended to be read by anyone, then it was clearly aimed at Sir Henry's children, but even that is not readily apparent. It may be too much to expect that a diary written so exclusively for private purposes should contain a public justification of the diarist. Perhaps this is why many other Royalists' diaries disappoint, on the political level at least. Since we find an almost uniform indifference to vindication and apology, that alone must tell us something about these men and their attitudes.

The search for clear, public expressions of principle by Royalist colonels is unrewarding.[59] Sir Francis Wortley's explanation of himself in 1642 has been considered, and his writing subsequent to 1646 shows a clear continuum. The most expansive and cogently argued of all Royalist self-vindications is, however, that of Colonel Sir Charles Dallison, published in 1648, and entitled *The Royalists Defence; Vindicating the King's Proceedings in the Late Warre made against him.* The title itself is unequivocally combative and defiant, and in this respect compares well with Wortley's lack of repentance.

Dallison was a Lincolnshire man of secure and conventional background, the son of Sir Thomas Dallison, who died in 1626, and connected through his mother with the Lincoln oligarchy. He was Recorder of Lincoln when the Civil War broke out in 1642. A trained and practising lawyer, knighted by King Charles on 14 July 1642, Dallison was appointed to the Commission of Array for his county and, before the year was out, accepted a commission to command a regiment of horse as its colonel. In 1644 he fell into Parliament's hands, but was exchanged quickly, and was a commander in Newark on Trent when the war ended in 1646. Excepted from pardon, he went abroad and was in France when the 1648 rising took place. Upon his return he was fined at a half, £465, which was cut to £351 in 1650. He was accused of tolerating Roman Catholics and favouring a Catholic alliance to secure the restoration of King Charles II, but although he came from a partially recusant background, his writings imply impatience with religion in whatever form.[60] The Dallisons were well represented in the King's army. A cousin, Colonel Robert Dallison, served alongside Sir Henry Slingsby and Sir John Mayney in 1644, in which year he was created a baronet, and, with his father, William, compounded on a fine of £1,300. As late as 1658 Robert Dallison was noted as a reliable King's man in his native county.[61] A third Dallison, Thomas, of another branch of the family in Lincolnshire, commanded as colonel the regiment of horse of Prince Rupert, and was killed in action at Naseby in 1645.[62]

Charles Dallison set down for public consumption 'the motives which induced the Authour to take up Armes for the King' in the preamble to his text, and went on to make it clear that it was the issue of the Militia Ordinance which drove him into arms. His reasoning is worth quoting in full:

Hereupon I seriously bethought my self, whether I was obliged herein to obey the King, or the Members; and resolved the Laws of England ought to be my guide, which I find to be thus: That this Nation is governed by a known Law, that Law expounded by the Judges of the Realme, Those Judges appointed and authorised by the King our only Supreme Governor, unto whom alone all the people of England are obliged (in point of Soveraignty and Government) to submit themselves. Then I considered in whom the power of the Militia was before the making of the Ordinances. Secondly, what alteration those Ordinances made.

For the first, I found that the Militia of the Kingdome by the known law was inherently in the King.

For the latter, that no New Law can be made, or the Old changed but by the King, with the assent of the two Houses of Parliament: And finding the King therein to dis-assent, I did without scruple resolve the law was not altered, therefore the Militia still in the Crown, and consequently, that it was my duty herein to obey the King's Command, not the Members. Then I considered what was the offence of a Subject to joyne with those Forces raised by the Members, which I found, to be the crime of High Treason.

And lastly, it being the duty of every Subject not onely to decline opposing his Soveraigne, but to assist Him against all disloyall actions, I took up Armes for Him, (and in His defence) in this War.[63]

Later in the book, Dallison repeated that he 'was obliged in duty, by the Lawes of this Realm, by the Law of Nature, by the Law of Reason, and by the Law of God' – which for Dallison came a poor fourth – 'to assist Him . . . upon these grounds I took up Armes for Him, in His defence'.[64]

It needs to be remarked that Dallison published anonymously, and at a time when he was both excepted from pardon and exiled in France. That being so, we may accept his argument as a genuine account of his reasoning in 1642, and not merely afterthoughts: for there was nothing exculpatory in the way Dallison wrote, and nothing in what he wrote that would curry favour with the victorious Parliament. He would have agreed entirely with Hobbes that 'to demand of the King the power of pressing and ordering soldiers; which power whosoever has, has also, without doubt, the whole sovereignty'[65] represented the most ambitious assault of all upon the King's prerogative. 'He that hath the power of levying and commanding the soldiers . . . has all other rights of sovereignty which he shall please to claim.'[66] Parliamentarians would certainly have answered that in the affirmative as well, recognising that to leave the King with the power of levying soldiers was to leave him with the crucial weapon that he might yet use both to coerce Parliament and to enforce the political *status quo* of 1640. But, for most Royalists, Dallison's and Hobbes's reasoning would have been wholly credible.

For Dallison and others, if there was a threat of tyranny, it came from Westminster, which is a view that Sir Hugh Cholmeley adduced in 1645 to account for his going over to the King (or back to his allegiance) in 1643.

for my part I cannott imagine a condition soo lowe shall force a new dialect uppon me or anythinge incompatible with the resolution of a gentleman, and the office I bear . . . 'Tis well known I always abhorred whatsoever tended towards tirranie . . . I daily heare of impositions upon men's consciences and personall liberties by your party . . . all acts of Grace being inseperable from the sovereigne power, of which you cannot be ignorante, though perhaps unwillinge to name the Kinge, lest men shoulde make observations upon your ingratitude . . .[67]

Cholmeley was addressing himself to the Scottish soldier Sir John Meldrum in February 1645, the year in which Meldrum was killed besieging Cholmeley in Scarborough Castle. Cholmeley was one of that not inconsiderable group of men who, initially commanders in Parliament's armies, went over to the King, often during the heady days of 1643. On the whole, once they had made the shift they stood by it, and Cholmeley's view of the tyranny of Parliament would have been acceptable to Dallison, who saw the possession of the militia as vital for any body claiming sovereignty. But, as with Slingsby, so with Cholmeley, it is only incidentally that we come across anything in the way of rationalised expressions of principle. Cholmeley's *Memoirs* and his narratives of the siege at Scarborough and of the battle of Marston Moor[68] contain little to illuminate that crucial moment at which the decision was taken, in his case, to support the King and turn away from Westminster. Cholmeley, who sat in the Long Parliament as MP for Scarborough, there revealed himself as no root-and-brancher[69] and his views may have been not dissimilar to those of his friend and fellow Yorkshireman, Slingsby. In fact, where Cholmeley is concerned, it may be easier to surmise why he went over to the King than to begin to understand why he was Parliament's man for six months.

A relative latecomer to colonel's command under the King was Sir Richard Grenvile, 'a good commander but a little too severe'.[70] Born in 1600, the younger brother of Sir Bevil Grenvile (who was killed in action in 1643), Richard was knighted in 1627, created a baronet in 1630, fell foul of the Earl of Suffolk over his marriage to the widow of Sir Charles Howard, and by 1641 was soldiering in Ireland against the Catholic rebels. His military experience went further back than Ireland, and he was reckoned to be 'an old experienced soldier' whose nature was 'tempered with great severity, if not cruelty'.[71] This side of his character endeared him to the members at Westminster, who praised his 'signal acts of cruelty' against the Irish. In 1643 Grenvile returned to London, expecting to secure a command in the Parliament's army under Sir William Waller. That was when his innate sense of loyalty to the King asserted itself, so he later claimed:

it was without the least design of engaging myself, for I knew my allegiance to my sovereign was check to me to lift up my hand against him, and the reverence I bare to the name of a Parliament which I find hath and doth yet deceive many, thwarted my resolutions in offering my service to his Majesty, where I knew it was due . . . to speak plain English to you, I found religion was the cloak for rebellion . . . The privileges of this Parliament were to be bound by none of the former . . . how the King's name was used against himself, was so odious to me as ridiculous . . . I withdrew myself to my becoming and lawful duty to his Majesty at whose feet I have now laid myself from whence no fortune, terror, nor cruelty shall make me swerve.[72]

Historians who have accepted the full measure of Parliament's hate campaign against its former darling would do well to note that, at this juncture in his eventful life, as he said, so he did. 'Sir Richard Greenville was proclaimed traitor by the general, and the proclamation nailed on the gallows.'[73] King Charles himself warned the Earl of Bath (Grenvile's nephew) against meddling with him, excusing the 'roughness of a soldier'.[74] Arrogant, dangerous and spasmodically brutal, Grenvile inspired intense loyalty amongst his men and a commensurate measure of terror in his enemies. Excepted from pardon and driven into exile, his career from 1646 degenerated into vituperation and bitter acrimony with fellow Royalists until his death in 1658.[75] The point, however, is that once he had returned to his allegiance, which he liked to think he had never really abandoned, he remained constant, and the prime target of a sustained campaign of abuse by Parliament's propagandists. The reasoning that he offered for his return to the King echoes that of Cholmeley, and would have been understood and accepted by countless Royalists whose loyalty since 1642 had been unequivocal.

It is a singular fact that men such as Grenvile and other unrelenting killers such as Sir Francis Doddington and Michael Woodhouse, to name but the most notorious, had a necessary place in the Royalist war machine. Edward Symmons, the clergyman who may be considered the authentic voice of Anglican Cavaliers, reminded the Royalist soldiers that 'your imployment [is] to inflict sharpe punishment upon rebellious men'. They must show themselves to be 'inexorable, and not abate one jot of the punishment [they were] commanded to inflict'.[76] The commissions by which Grenvile and others waged war issued from the King, Symmons reminded them, but were granted by God: 'a right Commission makes the warre itself lawful to the Souldier . . . for the Subjects duty is, to minde his owne call rather than the cause'.[77] There is no doubt that Grenvile, Doddington, Woodhouse and many others did not suffer from a 'lukewarm temper, or what the French call entre-deux'.[78]

To return to the notion of Dr Hutton's feral gentry, it is one thing to acknowledge their existence, quite another to deplore (if that is the historian's task) their contribution to the King's war effort. Their role and place within the Royalist cause is altogether more complex. Symmons, writing after the defeat of 1646, deplored what he believed was a widespread lack of zeal on the Royalist side:

The best on our side in generall, being not armed or quickened, with such stings of Hatred, as they on their side are, have been more heavy and dull in their opposite desires, and inferiour to them in their attempts and practises. They by tumbling and tossing like heaps of snow rowled up and down, have grown great and mighty: and we, by our frosty coldness, have given them leave to harden: Whereby they are encreased to that stupendious heap we see; though 'tis possible yet that a thaw may come . . .[79]

Symmons expanded on this argument, claiming that the

chiefest care of too many amongst us hath beene to damp the endevours of good men, in such places where they might have been most serviceable. . . . yea I have heard it said, that the surest and speediest way, for one to bring himselfe to ruine, among many of the King's men, was to be more active and honest than others.[80]

This is not the same accusation as that levelled by Sir Philip Warwick, who claimed that:

there was in the Army a negligent or dissolute Party, those out of it, that followed the King upon conscience of religion and law, were neglected, when there was great opportunity to have own'd them, and thereby to have own'd loyalty . . .[81]

Warwick was singling out the adverse effect on the war effort of drunkards and selfish commanders, amongst whom George Goring may well have figured, restraining those whose sole purpose was to serve their King as effectively as they could with no thought for themselves, Warwick's

very many considerable Gentlemen, nay rich Yeomen, who had never received favour or beneficence from the King [yet who] crowded to share with him in his hazards, and left their estates at home, that they might follow him abroad: (which since hath been too much forgot).[82]

Symmons, however, was arguing that the Royalist cause lacked the necessary fervour because – if he is to be read aright – they lacked what was vital to the rebels if the rebels were to survive, simple hatred (for Symmons would not have attributed to them any finer factor to account for their resilience). Thus in the context of Symmons's view, and given his emphasis on the inexorability which the King's soldiers should show when he spoke in 1644, then men like Grenvile were essential, and probably more effective than, for example, a Slingsby or a Charles Dallison.

Of course, any post-1646 commentator, in seeking to account for defeat, had to recognise perceived weaknesses in the organisation of the King's war, given that the cause itself was both just and approved of by God. That could not be denied, and failure must therefore be due to the shortfall in the commitment of the soldiery. From that vantage point, the way in which men like Grenvile fought may have seemed on balance the more useful.

If the fundamental tenets of service to the King rested upon a belief in the inherent rightness of the King's cause, and an evident commitment to its furtherance, then what the Parliament chose to define as the excesses of its most violent enemies were in fact a pure implementation of the soldier's duty. Certainly, there were some Royalist commanders who regarded Grenvile and his kind as political liabilities and who genuinely abhorred their brutality. Yet who among them (indeed, who among the members at Westminster?) denounced such savagery when used against the Irish rebels? The fact of Grenvile's welcome into the King's army, his commissioning and the power which it gave him to direct war operations, shows that expertise such as his was wanted. Further, Parliament's bitterness towards Grenvile was less because of what he did than that he did it for the King and not for the Parliament.

It will be remembered that Clarendon made very much this point in discussing the exchange of messages between the King and Parliament in 1642 over the Militia Ordinance. He pointed out that Parliament was alarmed by the King's obstinacy over the militia because if the members had not the 'managing of the war in Ireland' – if it should be 'taken out of their hands' – then 'instead of having a nursery for soldiers of their own' they would themselves be at the mercy of such men.[83] To return to Dr Hutton's feral gentry, it may be arguable that, whilst some may have emerged, there were some who were sought out for their particular skills by both sides early in the war. The King's army certainly encouraged the gentry working under moral constraints, but it also encouraged the killers. Terror, after all, has always been a useful weapon of war.

The King's armies existed to protect the person of the King, to maintain his authority, and to bring his enemies either to their knees or to the negotiating table. The purpose of soldiers in war is to kill, and to kill a sufficient number of the enemy as will bring them to defeat or surrender. Whatever the finer feelings of Sir Henry Slingsby, for example, may have been, he would have had to acknowledge that this was what both he and Grenvile had to do, and that Grenvile did it probably with more efficiency and perhaps with relish.

Symmons therefore saw nothing hypocritical in urging the King's men to ever more rigour on the one hand, and on the other praising them as 'Christians chose out of many by Almighty God, to suffer for his sake: to be in your Age the glory of Religion and the honour of your Nation'.[84] They were encountering widepsread rebellion, considered bestial and satanic by loyal men, and a thing to be met with vigour and the certitude of a just cause.

'Those Loyall men,' Symmons characterised the beaten Royalists, 'who for Conscience and duty sake . . . have adhered to their Soveraign . . . what shall I say unto you (most worthy and approved).'[85] It is clear that Symmons's profound affection for the King was matched only by the degree of his affection for some at least of the King's fighting men, amongst whom he spent the war as a regimental chaplain. As will appear, he was not blind to their faults, and could castigate them to their faces whenever he felt it necessary, but, when all was weighed up, he recognised them as men of no little consequence. 'You are no chaffe,' he assured them, 'the wind hath not blown you away, nor can the flaile hurt you.'[86] In Symmons's view, they carried in their bearing and commitment a traditional and dignified virtue, and he conceded that temporal matters were as important to them as spiritual, as he expressed it:

'tis not for Gods truth only, that your engagement is; but for your Countrey too, and dulce est pro patria mori, it hath at least, in old time been so accustomed; nay, what good man can wish life to see his Countrey buried? . . . they are over greedy to live, that think it not an honour to die at the funerall Celebration of Church and Kingdom . . .[87]

What was inexcusable amongst rebels was excusable in Grenvile and in Symmons's own colonel, Michael Woodhouse, because their necessary rigour was sanctioned by the King's commission, which made a right cause and a just war. Neither Symmons nor Warwick blamed defeat on the effects of the excesses of 'feral gentry', but rather, if scapegoats were necessary, on the malevolent influence in royal councils of self-seeking and half-hearted men – Royalist equivalents of the Earl of Manchester – who hampered the conduct of war.

III

The historiography of the Civil Wars has shifted its ground considerably in recent years, though S. R. Gardiner for one heralded the adjustment ninety years ago. The English civil war of 1642–46 is now subsumed within the broader framework of the British civil wars. Scholarship has more than redressed this particular balance, showing both the indirect influence of the Bishops' Wars upon events in England, leading to war in 1642, and the very much more direct impact of the Irish rebellion of 1641. The pivotal struggle between the Crown and the members at Westminster over the Militia and control of the armed forces would probably have come anyway, but the Irish rising forced the issue. Professor Russell has put this British emphasis into sharp perspective by pointing out that the purely English aspect of the war of 1642–46 lasted only sixteen months, from August 1642 until December 1643.[88]

It is to be hoped that Professor Russell was merely carried away by the relative novelty of the British context, for the argument as to the Englishness of the English civil war can be stretched even further. It was, after all, the fright engendered in London by the great Royalist victory at Adwalton Moor in June 1643 that provided the necessity for an alliance between the Parliament and the Scots, and thus the British dimension of the war emerged after twelve months. Further, if the personnel of the rival armies, from first arming in the summer of 1642, are studied, then the opposing army commands were well diluted with Scottish, Irish and European officers. Surely, however, the point about the war of 1642–46, whatever its broader political context, is that it had its first beginnings in England and Wales, and was fought through to its bitter conclusion within the same definable national boundaries. In so far as the King was concerned, the Irish war was something that could be put on hold, so that English forces operating there could be brought back to recruit hs armies. Montrose's campaigns in Scotland were fought independently of events in England, and anyway came too late: the home-grown resistance to the Covenanters should have emerged in 1643 if it was to have any impact upon the crucial role played in England by Scottish troops. Indeed, it could be argued that Parliament's ultimate victory depended upon introducing 'foreign' forces in very large numbers, on terms which stiffened Royalist resistance. The Scottish alliance was forced upon Parliament from dire necessity, and is a true measure of their sense of desperation rather than recognition of a common cause. Unless, of course, if the Scottish invasion was pre-emptive, mutual fear of the King's intentions created a common purpose.

As has been said, there was a Scottish presence on both sides in England from 1642, with a proportionately larger number high in the command structure of the Royalist armies. The Scots' personal motivations were not dissimilar to those of their English Royalist comrades, in so far as their actions can be interpreted or construed. Patrick Ruthven, commander-in-chief under the King from 1642 until 1644, owed his eminence to a lifetime's experience in European wars, which caused some to stigmatise him as a soldier of fortune.[89] Yet Ruthven voluntarily returned to Scotland from Sweden in 1638, and accepted a royal commission to hold Berwick on Tweed against his fellow countrymen in 1640. The earldom of Forth in the Scottish peerage was bestowed upon him in 1642, and in May 1644 he was advanced to the earldom of Brentford in the English peerage, which may be thought considerable attainments for a soldier of fortune. He was recognised as 'a man of naturall courage, and purely a Soldier, and of a most loyall heart, (which he had many occasions to shew, before the war was ended . . .)'.[90] Considering that Ruthven was sixty-nine years of age in 1642, that alone was sufficient cause for him either to retire into private life (abroad if necessary) or accept an advisory role. He had distanced himself from his fellow Scots in 1639, and remained constant to the cause of Charles I and then to that of Charles II, dying in 1651.[91]

'Lodi' Lindsay, Earl of Crawford, likewise recommended himself on the strength of his military service under Philip III of Spain. A Roman Catholic, he had succeeded to the earldom in 1639 on his brother's death, and thus added title and landed estate to the accumulated military experience that had been his lot as a younger brother. Crawford, because of his religion destined anyway to be at odds with the Covenanter temper in Scotland, sided openly with the King in the Bishops' Wars, and was implicated both in the 'Incident' of 1641 and in military gatherings near London in January 1642. He became a colonel that year, and ended his life in exile in 1652.[92]

Sir John Henderson was another Scottish Catholic with a long military pedigree in Europe who served as the King's governor of Dumbarton in 1640. In 1642 he was with the King in York and referred to as a 'confident instrument' of the King, whom he served both as governor of Newark upon Trent until 1644 and as a colonel of horse. Thereafter he was in Denmark in an ambassadorial capacity. He died in 1658, by which date he was suspected of having become an informer to Cromwell's spymaster John Thurloe.[93]

Of James King, created Baron Eythin in the Scottish peerage in 1643, it was reported in 1640 that he was in particular favour with the King. 'General King . . . has just departed after a visit to the court,' it was reported, 'refusing to become a rebel with the rest of his countrymen, to which he had been often invited with offers of great command among them. It is a duty which none of his nation have paid but himself.'[94] On the strength of long experience of command in Europe, James King became a colonel and Lieutenant General of the Foot in the army of the Earl of Newcastle from 1642, under whom he served until in 1644, in the wake of Marston Moor, he returned to Europe. He died in Swedish service in 1652.[95] What King, Henderson, Lord Crawford and Ruthven had in common was early resistance to the Covenanters of a very active type, as well as shared experience of war. Indeed, it could be said of all four that they had been so long away from their native country that they were almost by definition out of step with developments there. Their sense of loyalty and obedience to the King was therefore undiminished, as they clearly demonstrated. They and other senior Scottish officers, few enough in regimental command – Colonels Will Murray, William Stuart (although he was semi-resident in England anyway), Lord John Stuart and Andrew Lynsey, for example – were a permanent feature of the Royalist armies, just as a small number of Scots served the Parliament. What is certainly true is that, given the financial exigencies of both sides, such Scottish professionals surely cannot have taken up arms for the monetary reward. Their service has to be seen as a demonstration of principle.

The Anglo-Irish element in Royalist military command was

also small but invariably, like the Scots, was in evidence as early as 1639/40. One exception, however, was Oliver FitzWilliam, eventually the second Viscount FitzWilliam and, in 1663, Earl of Tyrconnell. FitzWilliam was a Catholic loyalist, serving against the Irish rebels under the Earl of Ormond. In 1645 he found his way to England by way of France, where Queen Henrietta Maria made him a messenger to her husband. Upon his arrival at court he was either given or intended to have a commission to raise a regiment in the King's service, and his sphere of operations was to have been the Midlands. FitzWilliam had landed interests in both Staffordshire and Nottinghamshire. Whether the commission was ever fulfilled, however, is unclear.[96]

Four Irish Royalists who did command in England were Bryan O'Neill, James Ussher, Richard Donnell and Robert Walsh. O'Neill had served as a major against the Scots in 1639/40, and was appointed colonel of a foot regiment in October 1643 shortly before he was advanced to a baronetcy.[97] James Ussher of Donnybrook had also served as a major against the Scots, was in arms at Edgehill, and became colonel of Prince Maurice's regiment of dragoons before he was killed in action at Lichfield in April 1643.[98] Richard Donnell was a captain in 1639, and his Civil War career shows strong Welsh associations. He commanded a Trained Band force in Glamorganshire in 1643 and was appointed governor of Swansea on the nomination of Charles Gerard in 1645. Donnell appears to have belonged to the inner group of Prince Rupert's confidants, and was with the prince in France in 1647, but the following year he returned to Wales for Poyer's rising. As late as 1658 he was still associated by name and rank with Glamorganshire.[99] Robert Walsh came of good family in Waterford, connected through his mother with the Butlers, and in 1642 attached to the household of the Queen. He fought as a captain at Edgehill, was appointed lieutenant-colonel under George Vaughan, and became a full colonel by 1644. He had been knighted in the field at Edgehill, and was associated, like Donnell, with Prince Rupert. Walsh remained in exile in Europe during the 1650s and, as in the case of Henderson the Scot, was reputed to have turned informer. He died in his old age in 1690.[100]

All these men, and others like them, whether Scottish or Anglo-Irish, were subjects of the King and understood that their duty led them into armed support for his cause. Of the handful of Europeans who came into England to fight with the Royalist armies it is difficult to go beyond the conclusion that they were probably adventurers or attached to the person of the Queen, or perhaps Prince Rupert, and were recruited by them. One such man is the mysterious Baron Dhona, Doner or D'Aunneau, who was buried in Newark on Trent on 27 June 1643, having been killed in action.[101] According to the burial entry, the baron was a general of the Queen's forces, indicating that he had preceded or accompanied her to England earlier that year. In 1668 the Swedish ambassador to England was Christof Dohna, Count Dohna, who may have been a relation.[102] On the other hand a careful historian of Newark suggested that the baron was a kinsman of the Prince of Orange, and either a Dutchman or of the German family of Dhona or Dohna.[103] The mere burial entry is insufficient justification to classify the baron by rank, and he is cited here as an example of the difficulty of identifying European soldiers with any certainty. One European officer who was almost certainly a colonel in the royal armies was the Frenchman Nicholas Saint-Pol, who styled himself the Vicomte de Saint-Pol, and who effected a marriage with the widow of a Royalist lieutenant colonel, John St John. The first clear reference to Saint-Pol does not occur until 1644, so that the precise date of his arrival in England may have been later than that of the Queen, whilst his area of operations included Chester, North Wales (where he was general of the horse under Lord Byron) and the West Country. Saint-Pol was still serving the Stuarts in 1650, but by 1653 had gone into service elsewhere in Europe.[104] Little other than national origin distinguishes Saint-Pol from the Scots Henderson and Crawford, Ruthven and King, in the nature of their lives, but there was no obligation of duty upon Saint-Pol.

As for the enigmatic Lord Muller, who commanded a regiment based upon recruits from Cornwall, Devon, Somerset and Berkshire,[105] nothing other than the suggestion that he was a German is known.

IV

Those who accepted the King's commission and prominence in his armies, whoever they were, wherever they came from, whatever their social origin or religious beliefs, in their acceptance of the commission accepted publicity. Not a few of them became known nationwide, and all of them were to become familiar, at least by name, beyond their immediate frequented localities. Not surprisingly, there was widespread reluctance to assume such notoriety, a reluctance not indicative of any unwillingness to serve but born of caution, of waiting upon events. It was very clear that any who took up the King's cause in arms would be traitors in Parliament's eyes. It was equally unclear what would become of such 'malignants' and Cavaliers if the threatened war turned out to be mere sabre-rattling preceding a negotiated settlement. Surely some of those expressing surprise at Sir Francis Wortley's sword-drawing in April 1642 were registering shock that he should have gone so far so soon. Clarendon was particularly critical of the peers who came to the King at York in the summer, accusing them of thinking that they showed 'high merit' in absenting themselves 'from the company and place where all the mischieve was done' but, beyond that gesture of innocence, felt no need to go further, at least (and these are not Clarendon's words) for the time being.[106] At the same time there must have been those who felt the King should resort to arms as soon as Hotham shut Hull against him, although Clarendon implies that this was a view held in hindsight: 'if he had raised forces upon his first repulse at Hull his service would have been very much advanced, and . . . the Parliament would not have been able to have drawn an army together'.[107] Given the nationwide uncertainty, and the apparent unwillingness of most men to go too far too soon – which some historians have quite wilfully interpreted as lack of enthusiasm for the King's cause – the criticism noted by Clarendon should be relegated to the eternal fault-finding of a beaten party. For, as Dr Hutton properly points out in his study of the Royalist war effort in Wales and the Marcher and West Midland counties, 'the most serious of all divisions of the English people had occurred in a mere five months',[108] and when Edgehill was fought in October 1642 the King had an army to match that of the Parliament (far longer in the making) and cavalry that grew accustomed to chasing the dust of fleeing opponents.

Men were held back from showing themselves for the King both by uncertainty as to the precise course events would take, and also by what seems to have been a widespread belief that any hostilities would be soon over, and the work was best left to less circumspect followers of the King. This 'general received opinion', as Clarendon termed it, 'that it would be quickly at an end' in his view 'contributed . . . to the continuance and length of the war'.[109] The caution of men who would very soon show themselves forward and loyal to the King thus deprived Charles of that overwhelming force both of men and of opinion that might have settled Parliament within weeks. Clarendon always professed to believe – and in this he was not alone amongst his Royalist contemporaries – that it was always a few who 'opposed and resisted' the Parliament[110] but those 'few' grew rapidly in numbers in the wake of Edgehill. It might fairly be supposed, though it is not susceptible of proof, that some at least of those who held back did so because they did not think the King stood a chance of military success: they must have been agreeably surprised as the word of Edgehill spread around the country, and gave to them the incentive which they needed to show where their sympathies lay.

Two groups within the Royalist party attracted the particular hostility of Parliament, the King's advisers and counsellors and officers of state who adhered to him and, where they were not one and the same, his army commanders, generals, colonels and other field officers – indeed, anyone who voluntarily sided with Charles Stuart. It is, however, necessary to be careful of the way in which the word volunteer is used, because it presupposes profound freedom of choice. In fact, men like Sir Henry Slingsby, Sir Richard Grenvile, Sir Charles Dallison, and even the Scots and Anglo-Irish commanders already mentioned, had very little intellectual choice open to them. Their status required them to make a decision – few genuinely neuter gentlemen can be said to have saved themselves harmless during the war – and their inclinations, attitudes of mind or rational thought processes had led them into a political position. This is not to deny that their stand was taken upon principle, only to suggest that the mere existence of principle limited the possibilities for them. The mysterious Baron Dohna and the wild Frenchman Nicholas de Saint-Pol had more genuine freedom of choice than most of their fellow British, Royalist commanders.

Nevertheless, there were ways of demonstrating loyalty without running the hazards of army command. The provision of money and plate, weapons and horses, and recourse to a Royalist garrison, were testimonies of support. Parliament treated all those who inhabited Royalist garrisons, whether they were there of their own volition or driven there by the war, as equally culpable, and the Royalists took much the same view, although they were never in a position to exploit it punitively. Army command brought with it the risk of death and mutilation, and whilst the recipient of a royal commission to raise a regiment or to otherwise serve in person in the war might yet fail to fulfil the instruction, there was never any shortage of willing officers. To go further down the hierarchy of soldiering, to the rank and file of the regiments, the regular army of the King was to be based upon the volunteer force rather than the obligatory service of the militia or Trained Bands. In theory volunteer regiments were just that, made up of men who took the wage offered and to whom neither the King nor his commanders looked for any very marked sign of Royalism other than a readiness to fight under discipline. Yet even here the true degree of voluntary involvement must be suspect, for, as Richard Gough showed in his *History of Myddle*, in which he looked back to the Civil War and remembered the Royalist recruitment in his parish, the rank and file were subjected to pressures as well. These could be economic, the army offering a new road to possible fortune and independence, or social, communities forcing out their disruptive elements. As the war progressed, men were simply pressed into regiments to recruit their numbers, but the element of coercion for the rank and file was actually there from the very beginning, if claims made after 1646 are accepted at face value.

The records of the Committee for Compounding are full of the excuse of coercion which rarely if ever found a sympathetic hearing. Thus Robert Brown of Croscomber in Somerset, who had been commissioned as a captain under the Marquess of Hertford, protested that he had been 'overawed by the potency of the enemy', William Forth of Wigan claimed that the Earl of Derby, no less, 'drew his sword against him several times, vowing his death therewith', which seems improbable, and did not save Forth in the event; James Collier of Newton in Lancashire claimed he was obliged to serve the Earl of Derby because he was his tenant, and Jasper Denham and his son John, of Somerset, were 'bound by the terms of their lease, being tenants of Lord

Hertford'. Eliseus Stert of Brixton in Devon clearly had the measure of the Parliament's invective, and cited 'the great cruelty shown by inflicting death with the halter and sword and by starving to death great multitudes by most rigorous imprisonment, with famine and stench' as the cause why he joined the Cavaliers. Ralph Shorrock, a Lancashire man, marched with Sir Gilbert Houghton because he was his servant and 'took up arms . . . at his master's command'. Humphrey Cornwall of Burrington in Herefordshire claimed that he had been in arms in his own defence, but was caught up in the *posse comitatus* and thus inveigled into bearing arms for the King. Robert Proctor of Somerset claimed that he had been threatened with death by Sir Richard Grenvile. An interesting excuse that was no excuse at all was that proffered by Edward Dobson of Hull, who said that he had been 'constrained by the extraordinary strict dealing of Sir John Hotham' to join the King's forces, which may mean that Hotham, having reason not to trust Dobson, expelled him from the port. Edward Lewen of Christchurch in Hampshire, on the other hand, claimed to have been drawn into arms by the 'precedent and example of men famous and eminent for their great parts'. Finally, Thomas Heape, a tenant of the Earl of Derby in Lancashire, claimed he was 'threatened from his dwelling house' by the earl and rode as a common trooper. In 1663, however, Trooper Heape revealed himself to have been a quartermaster in a cavalry regiment.[111]

How far these exculpatory claims may be taken at their face value is a matter of personal judgement. Those historians who have chosen to see them as proof that the Royalists coerced simple men into arms should perhaps remember that Parliament chose not to accept any such excuses, recognising them as a damage limitation exercise by beaten men. After the Restoration, Royalist rank and file inundated the county Quarter Sessions with petitions for pensions and cash hand-outs, citing their wartime service and the wounds they had sustained. These petitions would have been easier to verify than the lies and half-truths they or their comrades indulged in back in 1646. In the first place, most such Restoration petitions were countersigned by the former officers of the claimants, and if a maimed and wounded man appeared at the sessions his disability was plain to see. In fact there were so many thousands of such petitions that Grand Juries in several counties called a halt to the liberality of the justices. Such Quarter Session records are a truer guide to popular Royalism than the excuses of defeated Royalists may be evidence of widespread coercion. Of course, coercion in its many forms may well have driven some men against their inclinations. The claims of the rank and file and of junior officers as to the cause of their being in arms can never be examined in sufficient number to warrant conclusions. For the regimental colonels it is a different matter altogether. Parliament recognised them to be enemies of its proceedings, and dealt with them, if not even-handedly, then according to the degree of their enmity. Few colonels tried to excuse themselves after the war. Many were dead anyway, and those who went into exile without being excepted against adequately demonstrated their continuing enmity. There are, however, cases of Royalist colonels who abandoned the King, claiming to have discovered the error of their ways. Their defection was recognised by Parliament as an indicator of weakening Royalist morale (much as Royalists interpreted defections to them from the Parliament's armies). This was certainly a right judgement in the case of Colonel Sir Edward Duncombe, since he was one of the first Yorkshire gentlemen to align himself openly with the King's proceedings. Parliament's friend Lord Howard of Escrick, who was constantly sending despatches from York to London in the spring of 1642, made sure that Duncombe's name was well known at Westminster, and further stigmatised him as a man of little worth, at least socially. King Charles, who knighted Duncombe on 27 June, officially acknowledged his importance in bringing into the city a Trained Band regiment from the North Riding to act as a guard to the King's person. The regiment's colonel, Robert Strickland, put in an appearance later, but his loyalty proved more lasting than Duncombe's. Commissioned as a colonel to raise a dragoon regiment, Duncombe did so in time for the battle of Edgehill, where he fought. In 1643 he returned to Yorkshire, where his property lay, to recruit a cavalry regiment, which, by the end of that year, had disintegrated from want of pay. In May 1644 Duncombe turned himself in in Yorkshire, and materially assisted the Parliament's forces there during the siege of York. No punitive proceedings whatsoever were taken against him, which suggests that he did not resign his commission with the King's consent, but simply abandoned the cause and went over to the enemy.[112]

His case is comparable with that of another Yorkshireman, Robert Brandling, who came of a strongly Royalist and partially Catholic family in Durham. Robert Brandling acquired Yorkshire property through his opportunist marriage to one of the co-heiresses of the Lindley family at Leathley. Having served in the south with the dragoon regiment of Colonel Edward Grey as a captain, Brandling returned to Yorkshire and, after a period as lieutenant-colonel under Charles Brandling of Alnwick in Northumberland, was given command of the cavalry regiment of Colonel George Heron, who had been killed in action in June 1643. In February 1644 Brandling was taken prisoner in an otherwise successful Royalist engagement with the invading Scots at Corbridge on the Tyne, but he was rapidly exchanged, which argues for his worth to the Royalists. Yet, when York fell, Brandling, who had been in the city and may well have fought on Marston Moor, offered his services to Lord Fairfax and was promptly accepted as a colonel of cavalry in the Parliament's army. He served in that capacity for the rest of the war, during the 1648 rising, and against Charles II in 1651. All proceedings against him were waived when he changed sides, and the sequestration of his property was finally lifted in 1647. To the Royalists, Colonel Brandling remained a 'very knave' to his dying day, in 1669, though he did spend a few weeks in prison during the 1650s for allegedly conspiring against Cromwell.[113]

The treatment of Duncombe and Brandling may be contrasted with that of George Brydges fifth Baron Chandos, who at the age of twenty-two in 1642 had been appointed Lord Lieutenant of Gloucestershire by Parliament's Militia Ordinance. Chandos accepted the legality of the King's Commission of Array, and in November was colonel of a cavalry regiment, with which he gave consistent service until 1644. In April that year, however, he fell out with Prince Rupert over the latter's proposal to make Sir William Vavasour colonel-general in Gloucestershire. Despite attempts to placate him, in a fit of umbrage Chandos resigned his commission, gave out he was intending to go to France, but went to London and surrendered himself there. He was confined and a fine of £4,976 was imposed upon him in 1646. Clearly, his move was not truly a defection, though it was perhaps dereliction of duty, and his subsequent record until his death from smallpox in

1656 indicates his residual loyalty to the Stuarts.[114]

Defections such as these, and those of Piers and Richard Edgecumbe in Cornwall in January 1646, were relatively few. Colonel Piers Edgecumbe's decision to go over to the enemy was taken in the nadir of Royalist fortunes, and though he rode with Fairfax against Colchester in 1648, his heart was never in it. As a former MP, member for Camelford in the Parliament of 1640, he could expect precious little in the way of sympathetic treatment, and his fine totalling £3,788 showed how ineffective Fairfax's intervention on his behalf actually was. Edgecumbe was conspiring in 1650.[115] Neither Edgecumbe nor Chandos really changed his principles, which is probably why they suffered punitive fines when Duncombe and Brandling, in arms for Parliament, escaped similar treatment. Genuine and lasting changes of heart on the part of Royalist colonels were very few, and the defection process was not one-way, either. Grenvile, in theory at least, abandoned Parliament – at least, Parliament considered it so. Sir Hugh Cholmeley did it, and never swerved thereafter. Even Sir John Hotham attempted it, and paid with his life. Sir Faithful Fortescue actually went over to the King in the midst of the battle at Edgehill, and remained constant through all vicissitudes that befell his new cause. Indeed, Faithful Fortescue was probably never attached to the Parliament at all, but, as was said at the time, was with them almost by accident.

Fortescue's change of sides was one of the most spectacular of the Civil War, and is worth considering. He was a sixty-one-year-old professional soldier when Edgehill was fought, the son of a Devonshire gentleman who had sought his fortune in Ireland. He married a daughter of Viscount Drogheda, was knighted in 1606, and secured grants of land in County Antrim. On the very eve of civil war he was dismissed from his governorship of Carrick-fergus by the Parliament to make way for a Scottish garrison and governor, leaving him in extreme arrears of pay and with his property overrun by Irish rebels. He was, as was said of him, a man in need of employment, and he travelled to England, where he was given command of a body of horse for Ireland, only to find himself drafted into Parliament's army under the Earl of Essex with the rank of major under Sir William Waller. Clarendon graphically describes how Fortescue's men advanced from their lines, discharged their pistols into the ground, and offered their services to Prince Rupert. It was a blow to Parliamentary morale, a fillip for that of the Royalists, and the action of a man unhappy with the company he found himself keeping. The Parliamentarian pamphleteers had a field day with 'Faithless Fortescue', but he, having shown his allegiance, did not subsequently abandon it and was in arms as late as 1651 at Worcester.[116]

References to Fortescue after Edgehill indicate that he was a full colonel in the Royalist army, a rank which he retained in 1651. Presumably the King commissioned him, welcoming yet another experienced soldier into his service. All commissions, as has been said, derived from the King, whether the King bestowed them personally, signed by his own hand, or whether they were issued using the sign manual, which any authorised official could do. Likewise, the King could issue commissions authorising his generals to issue them in his name, so that Prince Rupert, Prince Maurice, the Earl of Newcastle and other Grandees could formally create regiments and choose colonels in their own areas. In their turn, the selected colonels would commission their inferior officers, although, where a newly commissioned colonel might be relatively inexperienced, it was not unusual for him to borrow a professional soldier more or less permanently to act as sergeant-major (or major) of the new regiment. Any colonel, whether commissioned to raise a regiment or promoted to regimental command, required a formal commission of his appointment. Trained Band colonels who found themselves translated to command of volunteer regiments had also to be thus confirmed. There are, however, as in all systems, anomalies. Clearly, some Royalist commanders actually commissioned themselves, and received informal recognition of the fact.

Thomas Bulkeley of Anglesey may be an example of this small group. On the strength of his local influence and power he assumed military rank to himself and on behalf of his son, Colonel Richard Bulkeley, who was also occasionally styled 'general'. There is no doubt that Richard was a Colonel of the Trained Bands before 1642, though here again his rank must have been nominal, since he was born in 1626, and when he surrendered Beaumaris Castle at the end of the Civil War was barely twenty years of age. Nevertheless, other, formally commissioned Royalist colonels recognised the authority of the Bulkeleys in their island, even if they did not like it, and Parliament's commanders too had to negotiate with Thomas Bulkeley on equal terms for the island's surrender in 1646.[117]

It is quite likely also that James Stanley seventh Earl of Derby assumed rank to himself relative to his position as the leading figure in Lancashire. Then again, as Lord Lieutenant of Lancashire, in this respect one of Parliament's unavoidable mistakes, Derby (or Lord Strange, as he was before his father's imminent death) had control over the militia regiments, and was able, enacting the Commission of Array, to call them to their colours. However, this authority throughout the period of his military activity in Lancashire, from 1642 until the spring of 1643, derived solely from his lieutenancy. This may explain why the volunteer regiments in the county, among others those of Thomas Tyldesley, Viscount Molyneux, Thomas Dalton and the Gerards, were constantly drawn away for service elsewhere in England at times when they were crucially needed by the earl. It may have been because his authority over them was non-existent, whereas his control of the less effective Trained Bands was the surer. Derby, like the Earl of Cumberland, whom the King left behind in control in Yorkshire in the summer of 1642, had no duly constituted military authority other than that of Lord Lieutenant. Military reality in the Civil War was such that whereas the structure of peacetime military authority was utilised wherever possible in implementing the Commission of Array, the formalisation of regular forces on a full-time basis for the duration of the war bypassed the system. This explains why, for example, Commissioners of Array in many counties found themselves more concerned with raising money than with raising men as the war dragged on. Their military function was limited and initial.

The Earls of Derby and Cumberland are both excluded from this study on the basis of their identifiable military status, and so, too, are the Bulkeleys, on the strength of their perceived assumption of rank that does not appear to have been formalised, although it seems probable that Richard Bulkeley was a full colonel when he fought at Y Dalar Hir in 1648.

Although the formal structure of armies existed in embryo in England in 1642, it needs to be remembered that in that year two quite enormous and unprecedented military machines emerged to confront each other. Paper schemes of regimental strengths and the hierarchy of command were there to provide uniformity of purpose and discipline, but within the evolving military system were vagaries and anomalies. Derby's authority was inferior to that of the Earl of Newcastle, who was a fully constituted general, but Newcastle did not push his authority in Lancashire until after the departure of the Earl of Derby for the Isle of Man. There were sensitive areas touching upon personal honour and dignity which had to be observed even as professional armies were developing, and Newcastle, whose authority did extend to Lancashire, was inhibited from using it until the county was lost through the inadequate resources available to Derby as Lord Lieutenant. Lancashire volunteer regiments drifted into Newcastle's army from the spring of 1643 onwards, just as others had earlier gravitated or were commanded towards the King's Oxford-based army. When it is considered that both inferior officers and men tended to swap regiments upon whim or fancy, or exchanged a sedentary commander for a more dashing figure, then the relative flexibility of the evolving discipline of war was everywhere. In such circumstances, individuals could appropriate ranks to themselves which were not formally given them, even if in practice they were likely to be recognised. It is the clear and precise evolution of rank distinctions which marks the development of truly professional forces, with gradations of seniority by commission inherent in that development. In England in 1642 all this came together in a rush, on both sides, and that some anachronisms remained is wholly understandable.

It has been shown with what difficulty Sir Henry Slingsby got himself a regimental command, and it will have been inferred that his Trained Band colonelcy was not in his view a true military command, nor best suited to do his king service as he wished to do. Given the lack of money and arms in 1642, they were most likely to secure regiments of their own who had the means to equip them and make at least a stab at drawing near respectable numbers (prescribed at 500 cavalry for a horse regiment, 1,200 or so infantry for a foot regiment). Thereafter these regiments came, in theory at least, within the responsibility of the King and his war chest and arsenals, and although Slingsby did not say as much, it is likely he secured his regimental command from Newcastle because the means were available to the earl to equip new regiments. Nevertheless, men of affluence who achieved regimental command expected, or were required, to draw upon their own resources to supplement or make good shortfalls in centralised pay and equipment. Such a system could function only whilst income from land and other ventures was flowing smoothly, and once a colonel's estates were spoiled by war or overrun by the enemy the income dried up, diverted to Parliament's uses. This single exigency of war wrecked many regiments which were not worsted in the field. All the courage and commitment in the world could not remedy that. A consequence was the emergence, as the war went on, of entire troops of officers who lacked men to command.

Such officers were ordinarily termed Reformadoes, 'men of undoubted courage' according to a Parliamentarian writer.[118] In October 1645 there were brought into York 'near 500 prisoners, most of whom were formerly commanders in the King's army, who marched Northwards as common troopers'.[119] The same writer ventured upon a categorisation of the prisoners:

Some of the private soldiers I have taken into service, others that were pressed men I have discharged, and there remains about one hundred and fifty that I believe will never change their partie so long as they live. They are most of them troopers that have beene in the same service formerly with the gentlemen that are prisoners . . . whensoever they are sett at libertie it will be an addicion of so many stout desperate men to the enemies strength.[120]

Since these were men with 'no estates', they would be 'sodainly ready in every parte of the kingdome to rise upp in armes', the writer concluded. If what he was describing was not a deep commitment to the Royalist cause, what else can it have been? For, in 1645 and 1646 at least, the Parliament's armies in the provinces would have welcomed the accession of veteran troops that might have come from soldiers defeated, seeking continued employment. But these reformadoes and troopers 'will never change their partie so long as they live'. This was the face of armed Royalism which had made the King's armies almost masters of the kingdom in 1643, had retained the capacity to shake the Parliament in 1644, and came within a whisker of defeating the New Model at Naseby in 1645. The cause for which they continued to demonstrate such profound attachment was the old cause of

1642, that of the King, commanding their obedience, loyalty and vigour against rebellion made manifest. The quality of these men is the best measure of Parliament's triumph.

Notes

1 This chapter amplifies but does not rehearse the material and argument employed in P. R. Newman, 'The King's servants: conscience, principle and sacrifice in armed Royalism', in J. Morrill, P. Slack and D. Woolf (eds.), *Public Duty and Private Conscience: Essays presented to G. E. Aylmer*, Oxford, 1993.
2 Conrad Russell, *The Causes of the English Civil War*, Oxford, 1990, p. 22.
3 A. Pritchard (ed.), Abraham Cowley, *The Civil Warre*, Toronto, 1973, p. 115.
4 John Rushworth, *Historical Collections, 1659–1701*, V, p. 360.
5 Sir Edward Walker, *Historical Discourses upon Several Occasions*, 1705, p. 50.
6 Henry Ferne, *A Reply to Several Treatises*, 1643, p. 72.
7 John Kenyon, *The Civil Wars of England*, 1988, p. 39.
8 P. R. Newman, *Royalist Officers in England and Wales, 1642–60: a Biographical Dictionary*, New York, 1981, p. 422. The impact of Wortley's action is discussed fully in Newman, 'King's servants'.
9 Anon., *A Loyal Song of the Royall Feast, kept by the Prisoners in the Tower*, 1647.
10 Newman, *Royalist Officers*, p. 423.
11 Historical Manuscripts Commission, Thirteenth Report, Appendix, I, Manuscripts of the Duke of Portland, I, 1891, pp. 15–18.
12 W. H. Coates, A. S. Young and V. F. Snow (eds.), *The Private Journals of the Long Parliament, 3 January to 5 March 1642*, New Haven, 1982, p. 40.
13 Newman, *Royalist Officers*, p. 242.
14 *Ibid.*, p. 248.
15 Coates, Young and Snow, *Private Journals*, pp. 91–2.
16 *Ibid.*, p. 97.
17 Newman, *Royalist Officers*, p. 290
18 W. H. Coates (ed.), *The Journal of Sir Simond D'Ewes*, Archon edition, 1970, p. 88.
19 Newman, *Royalist Officers*, p. 233.
20 Coates, *Journal of Simond D'Ewes*, p. 110.
21 Newman, *Royalist Officers*, p. 205.
22 *Ibid.*, p. 201.
23 F. T. R. Edgar, *Sir Ralph Hopton: the King's Man in the West, 1642–1652*, Oxford, 1968, p. 184.
24 Ferne, *A Reply*, p. 87.
25 F. Tönnies (ed.), *Thomas Hobbes' Behemoth, or, the Long Parliament*, with an introduction by Stephen Holmes, Chicago, 1990, p. 45.
26 Charles Dallison, *The Royalists Defence: Vindicating the King's Proceedings in the Late Warre made against him*, 1648, p. 112.
27 Tönnies, *Hobbes' Behemoth*, p. 44.
28 *Ibid.*, p. 51.
29 *A Fuller Answer to the Treatise Written by Dr. Ferne.*
30 For example, by Gerald Aylmer in 'Collective mentalities in mid-seventeenth-century England', II, 'Royalist attitudes', *Transactions of the Royal Historical Society*, fifth series, 37, 1987; and by John Sanderson, *'But the People's Creatures'*:

the *Philosophical Basis of the English Civil War*, Manchester, 1989, chapter 3.

31 Sir Francis Wortley, *Characters and Elegies*, 1646, pp. 11–12.

32 Sir Robert Filmer, *Patriarcha*, in J. P. Somerville (ed.), *Patriarcha, and other Writings*, Cambridge, 1991, pp. 43–4.

33 *Ibid.*

34 Tönnies, *Hobbes' Behemoth*, p. 4.

35 Anon., *Certaine Considerations Touching the Present Factions in the Kings Dominions*, 1648, p. 3.

36 Edward Symmons, *A Military Sermon*, Oxford, 1644, p. 23.

37 *Certaine Considerations*, p. 3.

38 Symmons, *Military Sermon*, p. 25.

39 Filmer, *Patriarcha*, p. 5.

40 T. T. Lewis (ed.), Letters of Lady Brilliana Harley, *Camden Society*, 1853, pp. 255–6.

41 Dallison, *Royalists Defence*.

42 Edward Symmons, *A Vindication of King Charles: or, A Loyal Subjects Duty*, 1648, preface, unpaginated.

43 Tönnies, *Hobbes' Behemoth*, p. 115.

44 Symmons, *Vindication of King Charles*, preface.

45 Bulstrode Whitelock, *Memorials of the English Affairs*, Oxford, 1853, I, p. 576.

46 C. E. Long (ed.), Diary of the Marches of the Royal Army during the Civil War; kept by Richard Symonds, *Camden Society*, LXXIV, 1859, p. 271.

47 'A Father's Legacy: Sir Henry Slingesby's Instructions to his Sons', York, 1706, in Daniel Parsons (ed.), *The Diary of Sir Henry Slingsby*,1836, p. 207.

48 T. G. Barnes, *Somerset, 1625–1640: a County's Government during the Personal Rule*, Cambridge, Mass., 1961, p. 242.

49 Lewis, Letters of Brilliana Harley.

50 Aylmer, 'Royalist attitudes', p. 1.

51 Parson, *Slingsby Diary*.

52 *Ibid.*, p. 76.

53 *Ibid.*, p. 77.

54 *Ibid.*, p. 81. For Hutton see Newman, *Royalist Officers*, p. 207.

55 Parsons, *Slingsby Diary*, p. 82.

56 *Ibid.*, p. 87.

57 Aylmer, 'Royalist attitudes', p. 2.

58 Newman, *Royalist Officers*, p. 250. Mayney left a somewhat unimaginative account of his services, entitled 'Services Performed by Sir John Mayne of Linton', in manuscript form which is preserved in the Alnwick Castle archives of the Duke of Northumberland. Mayney's account tallies with that of Slingsby and is independently verifiable.

59 Newman, 'King's servants'.

60 Newman, *Royalist Officers*, p. 99.

61 *Ibid.* M. A. E. Green (ed.), *Calendar of the Proceedings of the Committee for Compounding* (henceforth CCC), 1889–92, p. 1340.

62 Newman, *Royalist Officers*, p. 100.

63 Dallison, *Royalists Defence*, p. 2.

64 *Ibid.*, p. 113.

65 Tönnies, *Hobbes' Behemoth*, p. 79.

66 *Ibid.*, p. 80.

67 HMC, *Tenth Report*, Appendix, VI, Braye Mss, 1887.

68 *The Memoirs of Sir Hugh Cholmeley*, 1787. C. H. Firth (ed.), 'Sir Hugh

Cholmeley's Narrative of the Siege of Scarborough' *English Historical Review*, 32, 1917, and C. H. Firth (ed.), 'Sir Hugh Cholmeley's Memorials Touching the Battle of York', *English Historical Review*, 5, 1890.

69 Coates, *Journal of Simond D'Ewes*, p. 152.

70 J. Loftis (ed.), *The Memoirs of Anne Lady Halkett and Ann Lady Fanshaw*, Oxford, 1979, p. 117.

71 Sir Philip Warwick, *Memoires of the Reigne of King Charles I*, 1701, p. 431.

72 HMC *Fifteenth Report*, Appendix, VII, Somerset Mss., 1898, p. 70.

73 Whitelock, *Memorials*, I, p. 245.

74 HMC *Fourth Report*, I, De La Warr Mss, 1874, p. 308.

75 Newman, *Royalist Officers*, p. 165.

76 Symmons, *Military Sermon*, p. 26.

77 *Ibid.*, p. 23.

78 Warwick, *Memoires*, p. 233.

79 Symmons, *Vindication of King Charles*, p. 163.

80 *Ibid.*, pp. 163–4.

81 Warwick, *Memoires*, p. 219.

82 *Ibid.*

83 W. D. Macray, (ed.) *The History of the Rebellion and Civil Wars in England . . . by Edward Earl of Clarendon*, Oxford, 1888, II, p. 35.

84 Symmons, *Vindication of King Charles*, p. 296.

85 *Ibid.*, p. 296.

86 *Ibid.*, p. 296.

87 *Ibid.*, p. 297.

88 Russell, *Causes of the Civil War*, p. 218.

89 Loftis, *Halkett and Fanshaw Memoirs*, p. 119.

90 Warwick, *Memoires*, p. 229.

91 Newman, *Royalist Officers*, p. 322.

92 *Ibid.*, p. 233.

93 *Ibid.*, p. 186.

94 HMC, *Third Report*, Northumberland Mss 1872, p. 82.

95 Newman, *Royalist Officers*, p. 215.

96 *Ibid.*, p. 123.

97 *Ibid.*, p. 278.

98 *Ibid.*, p. 384. W. Bell Wright, *The Ussher Memoirs*, 1889, pp. 141, 290.

99 Newman, *Royalist Officers*, p. 113.

100 *Ibid.*, p. 396. *Lords Journals*, V, p. 30. HMC, *Fifth Report*, I, Report and Appendix, House of Lords Mss, 1876, p. 19.

101 HMC, *Twelfth Report*, Appendix, IX, Beaufort Mss, 1891, p. 538.

102 W. E. Knowles Middleton (ed.), *Lorenzo Magalotti at the Court of Charles II: his 'Relazione d'Inghilterra' of 1668*, Ontario, 1980, p. 63.

103 Cornelius Brown, *The Annals of Newark upon Trent*, 1879, p. 167.

104 Newman, *Royalist Officers*, p. 324. M. A. E. Green (ed.), *Calendar of the Proceedings of the Committee for Advance of Money* (henceforth CAM), 1888, pp. 1010–11. HMC, *Thirteenth Report*, Portland Mss, I, 1891, pp. 344–5.

105 *A List of Officers Claiming to the Sixty Thousand Pounds Granted by his Sacred Majesty for the Relief of his Truly Loyal and Indigent Party*, 1663, cols 97–8.

106 Macray, *Clarendon's Rebellion*, II, p. 182.

107 *Ibid.*, pp. 211–12.

108 Ronald Hutton, *The Royalist War Effort*, 1982, p. 3.

109 Macray, *Clarendon's Rebellion*, II, p. 461.

110 *Ibid.*, I, p. 2.
111 CCC, pp. 972, 1089, 1092, 1278, 1289, 1470, 1493, 1544–5, 1607, 1640, 1810. *List of Officers*, cols 109, 152.
112 Newman, *Royalist Officers*, p. 116.
113 Ibid., p. 140.
114 *Ibid.*, p. 46.
115 *Ibid.*, p. 119.
116 *Ibid.*, p. 142. W. B. Bannerman (ed.), The Visitation of the County of Sussex . . . 1633–1634, *Harleian Society*, LIII, 1905, p. 35. Coates, *Simond D'Ewes Journal*, p. 182. HMC, *Fifth Report*, I, House of Lords Mss, 1876, p. 41. HMC, *Fourth Report*, I, House of Lords Mss 1874, p. 50. Macray, *Clarendon's Rebellion*, II, p. 360.
117 Newman, *Royalist Officers*, pp. 47–8.
118 T. W. Webb (ed.), Military Memoir of Colonel John Birch . . . written by his Secretary, *Camden Society*, new series 7, 1873, p. 34.
119 HMC, *Thirteenth Report*, Portland Mss, I, 1891, p. 294.
120 *Ibid.*, pp. 476–7.

CHAPTER TWO[1]

'Bullets of gold'
The social origins of armed Royalism

I

'In our unnatural wars,' wrote the Royalist Sir John Oglander, 'the true grounds of which' few understood, the King's side were 'almost all gentlemen and, of the Parliament's, few. As one said, "The King shot bullets of gold for lead".'[2] In May 1663 another Royalist was assured by no less a Cavalier than Charles Lord Gerard of Brandon (who kept a full-time hangman in his employ when he commanded in South Wales for the King) that 'there were very few lawyers that adhered to the King, and spoke ill as to the same thing of the nobility in general that were made before the war'. Gerard, who had himself been ennobled by King Charles in recognition of his military service, concluded that 'the King's cause was truly and constantly maintained by the English gentry'.[3] Edward Walsingham, in his biography of the Catholic Royalist Sir John Digby, made the same point in tandem with a sneer at the Parliament's supporters. The contribution to the King's cause by the gentry, at all levels of rank and authority in the army, was plain: 'divers of them being gentlemen of good quality and breeding, who in former tyme had kept better men for their servants than many of the [Parliament's] commaunders'.[4]

A Parliamentarian general of some skill and resource, Sir William Waller, in his memoir, indirectly made the same point as that made by Oglander, Gerard and Walsingham:

I confess, upon the breaking out of the war (which I look'd upon as pro aris, et facis) my passion to the Parliament imbolden'd me to offer my service, as farr as to the raising of, first a troop (when there were but six appointed in all, and it was something to find gentlemen that would engage).[5]

Clarendon likewise made the same point about the relative

gentility of the two sides. Always, he wrote, in the 'dismal inequality of this contention . . . some earl, or person of great honour or fortune, fell, when, after the most signal victory over the other side, there was seldom lost a man of any known family or of other reputation'[6] fighting on Parliament's part. For the Royalists this was a matter of both pride and sadness. The number of gentlemen, whether *nobiles minores* or *nobiles majores*, who espoused the cause of the King emphasised the rightness of that cause. They were ranged against rebels, and those rebels, led (in Royalist eyes) by a few rebellious and seditious men of standing, threatened not only the Crown but the social order of which monarchy was the keystone. Inevitably, armies commanded and officered by gentlemen in large part motivated by a sense of personal loyalty to the King would be inclined to measure their losses as much by the quality of slain gentry as by the number of common soldiers killed or disabled. It is almost as if the armed involvement of plebeians and others was incidental to the necessary commitment of gentlemen to the same cause. As the war progressed, and Royalist regiments became so depleted that often only the officers remained, it was not uncommon to find whole troops composed of captains, majors and other senior field officers who, bereft of troops, disdained for that reason to lay down their arms or their commissions. Such men, as will be shown, saw themselves as carrying on the spirit of the cause of 1642 to the bitter end in 1646, nurturing it as their cause, product of the fusion of the King's necessity and the gentry's sense of obligation and honourable service.

Clarendon recognised the Achilles heel of gentry activism, what he referred to as an 'immoderate disdain of danger and appetite of glory'[7] which manifested itself, for example, at the storm of Bristol in 1643. There Colonels Slanning, Buck and William Villiers second Viscount Grandison were killed outright leading their men into the breached walls, and John Trevanion sustained his mortal wound. Four regimental colonels with other officers wiped out in, as Clarendon may have believed, the precursor of many pyrrhic victories to come. Of Slanning and Trevanion Clarendon wrote that they were 'led by no impulsion but of conscience' to serve their King. Having been MPs at Westminster, they had seen at first hand the 'ill practices and designs of the great conductors' at Westminster.[8] Clarendon's use of the word 'conductor' was significant, for it conveyed to his contemporaries the notion of the rebellious MPs and Peers at Westminster as organisers of war, towards which they were moving long before they showed their hand. Slanning and Trevanion, therefore, had seen through the mask, and acted accordingly. They and Brutus Buck were two types of Royalist, Viscount Grandison a not untypical example of an Irish peer of limited income who had long pursued an expressly military career.

There is every reason why these men should serve as a prelude to the survey of the King's regimental colonels with which this chapter is concerned, for they were wholly representative of hundreds of others. Sir Nicholas Slanning, of Maristow in Devonshire, knighted in 1632 when Vice-Admiral of his county, was thirty-three when he was killed, a married man with family responsibilities and social and political status in his county. Having served as a soldier in European wars as a younger man, he had returned to Devonshire and had sat in the Short Parliament for Plympton Earl, and in the Long Parliament as one of the two members for Penryn. A contemporary noted his 'discerning wit' his 'staid and solid judgement', and, when he died, he 'left an excellent name behind him'.[9] There was nothing of the 'merry lad' about Slanning, any more than there was about John Trevanion, who, in certain respects not unlike Slanning, and only three years the other's junior, had no military experience to draw upon. His father, Charles, was or became shortly after John's death in action a colonel as well. Through his marriage John Trevanion was son-in-law to 'Jack for the King' Arundel of Trerice in Cornwall and had represented Lostwithiel in the Long Parliament alongside his brother-in-law Richard Arundel, also a serving colonel by 1643. Trevanion, then, was part of a family commitment to the King as Slanning, whose son was born post-humously, was not.[10] Nothing in Trevanion's ascertainable career would qualify him for the role of the typical Cavalier, other than the manner in which he, like Slanning, courted death in action, giving rise to Clarendon's remark about an appetite for glory. But any colonel worth his salt led from the front, setting an example to his rank and file.

The involvement of Charles and John Trevanion in regimental command was somewhat unusual. The heirs of families account for only a small number of commissioned colonels, some eighty-eight out of a total of 505 whose familial status is clearly evidenced. The father was part of the substantial activism shown by family heads, some 277 of whom from all over England and Wales commanded regiments between 1642 and 1646. They were twice as numerous as those officers who can be shown to have been either the younger sons or the younger brothers of family heads, 140 in all. These figures demonstrate something far more than token support for the King from men obligated but lacking enthusiasm. The direction of the King's regiments was very much in the hands of solid and respectable gentry and peers, knights and baronets. The younger sons and brothers were often the military arm of a family loyalism that was expressed in other ways, as will be shown. If Gerard had stated that the Royalist armies were the respectable gentlemen of England in arms, he would not have been wide of the truth, for the armies were made up of those regiments which essentially conservative men raised and presented for the King's service in defiance of perceived rebellion. If as Mark Fissel[11] has shown, the King and his advisers in 1639 seriously contemplated importing mercenaries to deal with the Scots, they had no need to worry about that in 1642. There was a vast reservoir of willing support which Slanning and the Trevanions exemplified.

Colonel Brutus Buck, who was also killed at Bristol, represents a second but minor element in Royalist regimental command, the career soldier of respectable gentry origins who had lived most of his adult life in the service of foreign powers. By 1642 Buck was in England, officially as Captain of Sandown Fort on the Isle of Wight, but also named for service in Ireland against the Catholic Confederacy, where he was intended to serve as a lieutenant-colonel under the President of Munster. Such 'a modest stout commander . . . of good experience in war' would have been sought after by both King and Parliament. Buck accepted appointment to the King's Commission of Array in Hampshire, was given a regiment shortly thereafter and was killed at its head.[12]

In the fourth of the colonels killed at Bristol, William Villiers second Viscount Grandison, were combined the career soldier (in his case perhaps a reflection of insufficient income); a peer (albeit of the Irish peerage) and so one whom Gerard affected to criticise; and, perhaps incidentally relevant, a representative of the Villiers family, William being nephew to George Duke of Buckingham. Grandison fought against the Scots in 1639 and 1640, first as a captain and then as a commissioned colonel, and in 1642 was named to go into Ireland for service, like Buck, against the rebels. Parliament, suspecting him, dismissed him from his command and, out of employment, he accepted a commission under the King and was recruiting in Somerset in the summer. At the time of his death he was both regimental colonel and Colonel General of Foot under Patrick Ruthven.[13]

By the time Slanning, Trevanion, Buck and Grandison met their deaths the peculiar hazards of regimental command were already exacting sacrifices. Royalist colonels of 1642–46 stood a one-in-five chance of being killed outright, mortally wounded or succumbing to disease and privation. During those years 125 of them perished and, of the remaining number, between 1646 and 1660 a further 142 met their deaths, from natural causes, subsequent fighting, murder or execution. This meant that 44 per cent of those who took upon themselves regimental command for the King did not survive to see the full restoration of monarchy in 1660. What we might call the 'turnover' in regimental commanders was high, and accounts for the relatively high number of identifiable colonels of the first Civil War, for each had to be replaced by a new appointment or promotion from the ranks below, provided there was still a regiment left to command.

Sir John Oglander's 'bullets of gold' were the gentry and, like Gerard, he was well aware that without their support there would have been no Royalist cause. In the broadest sense the gentry (those untitled gentlemen excluding the male members of peerage families but including knights) accounted for 67.5 per cent of the King's colonels, and they sustained commensurately the greatest losses in action amongst that rank. The deaths of Slanning, Trevanion and Buck, and of the minor peer Grandison, in one action, convey that. Since the conventional image of the Cavalier is well ingrained both in the popular imagination and, not surprisingly, in the minds of many historians, it is worth positing what research indicates may have been the 'typical' Cavalier commander, the norm, as it were, against which men like George Goring and other 'merry lads' may be contrasted.

The average Royalist colonel would have been of untitled

gentry status when commissioned, drawing his income from land and rents with which he was directly associated, rather than an absentee Grandee reliant upon his steward or bailiffs. There was a one-in-three chance that his father would have been a knight. Married, and head of his family, he might be anywhere between thirty five and forty five years of age, and invariably a regular communicant of the Anglican church. The precise nature of his religious belief might best be expressed in the conservative preamble to the will of Colonel Sir Patricius Curwen, who died in 1664:

I utterly abhor and renounce all Idolatry and Superstition, all Heresy and Schism, and whatever is contrary to sound religion and the word of God, professing myself with my whole heart to believe all the Articles of the Christian and the whole doctrine of the Protestant Religion taught and maintained in the Church of England.[14]

At the time of commission the gentleman colonel would find himself related to at least one other family in which Royalist activism was to be pronounced. Jordan Crossland of Newby in Yorkshire, for example, commissioned in 1642 (in which year he was also knighted), was brother-in-law of Colonel William Prideaux, killed in 1644, and of Major William Flemming of Rydale in Westmorland. Crossland was also uncle to Major Richard Tancred of Whixley in Yorkshire. Just as it was by no means unusual for the average gentleman colonel to have sons and brothers committed in some way to the King, we find that Crossland's son Jordan served as a captain under his father.[15] Crossland, as a Yorkshireman, came from a populous and large county which contributed a far greater number of colonels to the Royalist army than any other. But the average gentleman commander might come also from Somerset, Lancashire, Devon or Cornwall and, perhaps surprisingly, from Kent or Lincolnshire.

As well as familial and estate responsibilities, such a man would have official duties as well, perhaps as a JP, invariably as a Grand Juryman. But the degree to which minor gentry figured in the regimental command may be evidenced by the fact that of the total number of colonels only 235 (or 39 per cent) can be shown to have exercised any form of office in their locality or county, although this is a figure which could be revised upwards. Trevanion and Slanning died as MPs when they fell at Bristol, and in this they were somewhat exceptional. Some 119 of the King's colonels had experience of the Commons as MPs, of whom seventy were members of the Long Parliament until they were expelled from the House or abandoned it for the King's service. The average gentleman colonel, however, would more likely have been an elector rather than a candidate at an election.

Possessed of estate and property, often within one county and rarely dispersed far from the family seat, the average colonel would have compounded for his possessions. There is positive evidence to show that 356 colonels' estates were compounded for either by the delinquent himself or by his heir or family or trustees. The legal process for the recovery of such estates was laborious and labyrinthine, local committees and the central committee at London often being at variance. The financial burden imposed by armed service, and by punitive fines afterwards, deprived the average ex-colonel of the means to resume his activism in the cause. So most ate of the bread of carefulness, waiting upon events, if not actually reconciled to the change in government. Flirtation with conspiracy in the 1650s might be through a junior family member, but the impetus to action came from those in exile, unable or unwilling to compromise: former Royalist activists who had run the hazard for the King, whether colonels or otherwise engaged, were regarded with constant suspicion, at least by local Parliamentarian neighbours and officials. Of such men in Devonshire the County Committee reported to London that leniency towards them was a waste of time: 'their Satanical spirits are still in enmity'.[16] It would have taken a lot longer than ten years of republicanism to reconcile convinced Royalists to the overthrow of the monarchy. Yet the average gentleman commander sat quietly until the Restoration, doing nothing very much to hasten it, but certainly doing even less to make the task of the republican government any easier.

The Royalist gentry had proved their worth in battle, and the gentleman colonel, for all his staid and respectable demeanour, was a dangerous enemy, not to be overcome by threats and terror, but only to be rendered quiescent by seizure of property, legalised plundering and punitive fines. The composition procedure was so tediously involved that it seems almost to have been devised as a means of occupying the minds and time of delinquents as much as to provide the state with funds: as a punishment it failed to persuade them of the error of their former ways, though it did succeed in materially weakening them. The gentleman colonel, if he survived 1646 and lived to 1660, was monarchy's guarantee, along with other activists, that the Republic could not last. Given the reality behind the Cavalier myth, the degree of commitment shown to the old service by such men indicates that conservatism in mid-seventeenth-century England was a force to be reckoned with, and that the intimate links between Crown and commonalty were a deal tighter than the King's enemies probably perceived. The capacity of the 'reformer' to be surprised by the dogged resistance of others may have been as salutary then, and in the strict sense of the word, as now.

The gentry comprised 54·7 per cent of the King's regimental colonels, or 67 per cent if the knights, the leading element of the *nobiles minores*, are included amongst them. The remaining colonels were drawn from the baronets (fifty-nine indivduals) and from the peerage (seventy-nine peers or other family members). Ninety per cent of the colonels belonged to the gentry in the very broadest sense of the word, the remaining 10 per cent being comprised of some thirty-two whose precise social standing remains unknown, and a mere handful of professional lawyers (not representative of their calling, if Gerard is to be believed), plebeians, merchants (who might also aspire to gentility and probably came from a gentry background) and the odd 'musician' or two.

Gerard's comments on the relative merits of gentry, peers and lawyers as Royalist activities applied, of course to the Royalist cause in its widest sense. He was not singling out regimental commanders, and contrasting the contribution of specific groups to that specific role. Yet his criticism can be effectively applied in that way and tested, since it is eminently worthy of consideration and was clearly not his own particular and peculiar view of the 1640s and 1650s. When he spoke in 1663 Gerard was as formidable a figure then as he had been when he was let loose on South Wales in 1644. In his mid-forties, 'his whole body, covered with scars' from his wartime service, a man who 'always looks to his own interest, and his soldiers know yt'; a man who 'abhors wine' but was 'loved by the women',[17] he had been created Lord Gerard of Brandon in 1645. From 1649 he had served in the important office of Gentleman of the Bedchamber to King Charles II, and would be raised to the earldom of Macclesfield in 1679. His opinion, coming from a man of unswerving loyalty to the Stuarts, though perhaps coloured by years of exile and intrigue, and the experience of plots that fell short when they were translated from the court in exile to the land of England, requires attention. His own familial commitment to the Crown was extensive and not untypical of many other gentry families, and, if he applied his family's loyalty as a marker whereby to assess the performance of others, he would have found many who passed such a stringent test. Not only amongst the gentry, where the Stradlings of St Donats, the Arundels of Trerice (and other branches of the family) and the Byrons of Nottinghamshire figure highly, but also amongst the peerage families which he professed on the whole to have found wanting. Enumeration of the social status of the King's colonels when in receipt of their commissions shows very clearly that, where the gentry were concerned, Gerard's estimation was not merely flattery for his own social class. How far did his comment upon the lawyers, therefore, reflect reality?

II

Gerard's contention would probably have been that, since the King's proceedings were both self-evidently proper and legally sanctioned, lawyers, better qualified than most to judge of that, would have done better to have demonstrated their approval rather than hold aloof. Lawyer detachment, rather than lawyer enmity, was what Gerard criticised. The difficulty in subjecting Gerard's view to analysis is in determining how far the 'lawyer' may be distinguished from the 'gentleman' which, then at least, he invariably was by background. To identify those of the King's colonels whose primary source of income, or primary interest, lay in the law provides only ten examples, one of whom, the most eminent, could better be categorised as a peer and great official of state. He, Edward Lord Littleton, had only a very nominal connection with armed support for the King, being commissioned in March 1645 to command a regiment in the city of Oxford which was to be called upon in time of emergency but which would otherwise be exempt from routine duties. Within five months Colonel the Lord Littleton was dead anyway. Yet his part in the

King's war is of interest. His background was that of a country gentleman in Shropshire, where he was born in 1589. Like many other men of similar origins, he passed through university and the Inner Temple (an educational process which gave many landed gentlemen a knowledge of the complexities of law) and became a barrister in 1617. He rose steadily in the law, becoming Chief Justice of North Wales in 1621, Solicitor General in 1634 and a Privy Councillor and Chief Justice of the Common Pleas in 1640. Knighted in 1635, he was elevated to the peerage as Baron Littleton in 1641. He had been an MP in 1614, 1625 and 1628 and was associated with the Petition of Right. Then, in 1641, Lord Keeper Finch lost office, and Littleton was chosen to replace him. Upon Littleton therefore fell the vital task of sending the Great Seal to the King at York in May 1642, which he himself followed north in equal secrecy to associate himself and his office with the King's proceedings.

Littleton's behaviour as Lord Keeper prior to his abandonment of London for the King's court had, however, alienated many of the King's committed supporters and, to a degree, the King himself. He had shown himself 'most confident for the legality' of the Militia Ordinance,[18] the very issue which had convinced the less eminent lawyer-cum-country gentleman Sir Charles Dallison of the illegality of Parliament's proceedings. 'Hee begun to be the darling of the lords' house and much confided in, hee had the casting voice for [the Militia] and argued itt often and stronglie as very necessary and lawfull.'[19] So, when Littleton finally slipped away from London, it 'struck some with amazement, in some rais'd coller, in others joye . . .'[20] but though 'a man of courage, and of excellent parts and learning' he found himself 'not much respected by [the King] or his courtiers'[21] because of his abysmal record in the Lords. There were plenty of other Royalists who, until the spring or summer of 1642, appeared to be hostile to the King, but who in the event proved otherwise. Ralph Hopton was a case in point. Little was held in the way of grudge against them. Littleton, so eminent a lawyer and officer of state, however, could hardly be excused. Clarendon was far more sympathetic to the Lord Keeper, dwelling upon his gentle birth, his courage as a swordsman when young, his learning and repute in the law, stating that 'he had raised himself into the first rank of the practisers in the common law courts' solely by virtue of his 'own abilities' which in turn had attracted the notice and favour of both Strafford and Laud. Yet, observed Clarendon, once the Great Seal was given into his charge 'he seemed to be out of his element, and in some perplexity and irresolution' appearing 'so totally dispirited that few men shewed any respect to him but they who most opposed the King'.[22] Once Littleton had made the move to York, he could go nowhere other than with the King, and so came to Oxford and ultimately to a colonelcy which nodded towards the physical courage of the man rather than to anything else.

Lesser men and lesser lawyers who achieved regimental command under the King were John Farmery of Heapham in Lincolnshire, Chancellor of the Diocese of Lincoln and MP for the city in the Short Parliament;[23] Dr John Godolphin of Dartmouth in Devon and London, a younger brother of Colonel 'Black William' Godolphin of Spargor in Cornwall;[24] William Moreton of Winchcomb in Gloucestershire, who was knighted in 1643;[25] Richard Palmer, also a Gloucestershire man, who served as Provost Marshal in the Royal army as well as a colonel until disowned by the King for his plundering regiment, indicative of poor discipline:[26] Robert Phelips of Montacute in Somerset, the second Royalist son of the court's vigorous critic Sir Robert Phelips, who died in 1638;[27] Edmond Pierce from Kent, knighted in 1645 and Advocate General of the Oxford Royalist army;[28] William Smith of Buckingham, called to the bar in 1641 and MP for Winchelsea in the court interest after the expulsion from the Commons of another future colonel, Nicholas Crispe;[29] Edward Chisenall of Chisenall in Lancashire, who apparently had not time to take his oath at Grays Inn before he became involved in Royalist activism;[30] and William Mason, a Norfolk gentleman, who raised a force in the Inns of Court in January 1642 to guard the King's person, and through whom Chisenall may have been drawn into arms.[31] None of these men appears to have recorded the grounds of his decision to take up arms for the King, though William Moreton, actually a Worcestershire man who had married and settled in Gloucestershire, appears to have been drawn into arms by his client George Brydges Lord Chandos, but proved himself to be 'better grounded in his loyalty' than the baron whose 'creature' he was reckoned.

William Smith of Buckingham was part of a complex familial Royalism which probably induced him to accept regimental command. His father-in-law, Sir Alexander Denton of Hillesden House in Buckinghamshire, materially assisted the recruitment and offered Hillesden as the regiment's base. Sir Alexander's son, John, was also recruiting a regiment at the same time, late in 1643. Needless to say, perhaps, William's father was also a known Royalist to his death in 1645. Smith's army career was short-lived. Hillesden was raided in March 1645, Colonel Smith taken prisoner, and his regiment broken up.

Two of these lawyers fulfilled legal functions in the army, Palmer as Provost Marshal and Pierce as Advocate General, in conjunction with their colonelcies. Most such legal posts tended to be filled by more junior officers, so that below the level of regimental command there was a sprinkling of other trained lawyers. But in all other respects the war service of these men differed in no particular from that of their fellow commanders who were not lawyers. Of them all, Mason was militarily the most precocious and eminent, from January 1642 until as late as 1663 serving the Stuarts either in arms (for which he was knighted in 1645) or in secret service. Like Pierce, he had a small estate, valued at £229 2s in 1648 for personal effects, and real property of £59 value. He never compounded. When Pierce settled his fine, it was at a tenth, and amounted to only £82.

The lawyers as colonels were subsumed within a war machine in which their professional expertise was of less importance (unless they fulfilled specific additional roles in the army) than their military competence and their loyalty. This is a point which needs to be kept in mind when the social or other status of a regimental commander is considered. Although social status was ordinarily the criterion which would determine whether a man should receive a commission in the first place, military necessity dispensed with the niceties of peacetime notions of precedence. It might not be unusual, for example, as will be shown, for a younger son or brother to hold higher rank than father or elder brother. By the same token, noblemen not infrequently found themselves subordinate in rank to mere gentry, whilst the elevation of successful soldiers to titles of honour was never commensurate with promotion to military rank of higher standing. In these respects the armies of the Civil War period were far less socially exclusive in their rank structure than armies of the eighteenth and nineteenth centuries were to be. That is probably a reflection of the imperative which obliged the King, and Parliament, to draw together and arm forces in the space of a very few months indeed, and the structure created under those circumstances held good for the duration. The Royalist armies did not undergo any formal reorganisation of command such as that which Parliament forced through with its Self-denying Ordinance but the mere fact of the Oxford parliament requiring attendance of peers and MPs necessarily created a change in the personnel of army and regimental command: but that did not mean, at least at regimental command level, any marked downward social shift in appointments and promotions.

These points are well illustrated when the role of the peerage in regimental command is examined.

III

Gerard regarded the contribution of the nobility to the King's cause in general as particularly wanting. Yet the proper assessment of that contribution, particularly where army command is concerned, should take account not only of the contribution of individual titled noblemen but also, and necessarily, of familial involvement in a wider sense. Moreover it is arguable that commitment in arms should not necessarily be expected of the peerage: their role as military magnates was archaic, and military affairs had effectively passed into the hands of the gentry in their capacity as deputy lieutenants, the very active arms of the often nominal peer as Lord Lieutenant. That the King should turn to the peerage for support in 1642 was unavoidable, whenever he could find peers as Lord Lieutenants who were prepared to ignore the Parliament's conflicting commands to them. In the period of transition between peace and open war, men such as the Earl of Cumberland in Yorkshire and Lord Strange (subsequently Earl of Derby) in Lancashire, provided willing focal points around which Royalists could gather, but the departure of both peers from active service before the spring of 1643 in no way undermined the contribution of their respective counties to the overall war effort. They had set a process going which then possessed its own momentum, and no loss to the King was involved in either Cumberland's or Derby's virtual abandonment of a military role (even though Derby's withdrawal was largely forced upon him by enemy military activity). Thus, when the peerage is shown to have been actively involved in routine regimental command and duty, its presence can as readily be explained as a sign of profound personal commitment, since the latter can be seen as enforced or imposed by considerations of Grandee obligation.

The most successful – for a time – of Grandee commanders, both as a regimental colonel (in which capacity he turned the tide of battle at Adwalton Moor in June 1643) and, commensurately, as a general, was William Cavendish Earl of Newcastle. Part of the reason lay in the confidence placed in him early in 1642 by the King, and his integral role in a strategic plan which developed in advance of the move towards armed conflict. The earl was high in royal favour: if the King, shaken by the attitude of many peers during the Bishops' Wars, needed a reliable magnate, Newcastle was wholly loyal. Although the attempt to impose the earl as governor upon Hull – which, if successful in January 1642 would have been a major strategic gain for the King – failed in the event, nevertheless, Newcastle had demonstrated his indifference to censure or pressure from Westminster. In June, the King established at York and the port of Hull firmly in potentially enemy hands, Newcastle was commissioned to take control of the four northernmost counties, Durham, Northumberland, Cumberland and Westmorland. The strategic objective, at least initially, was to provide him with the territorial means with which to raise any army in anticipation of the Queen's arrival from Europe, and an army, furthermore, which was for that reason not immediately to be included in whatever other military preparations the King might be constrained to make during the summer. In effect, Newcastle was given an independent command before war even began, and his army, known also as the Queen's army, operated within a narrow and clearly defined strategic plan. The King's trust in the earl was fully justified, for Newcastle had not only created a well trained and substantial force of almost 8,000 by June 1643, but he made sure that he found commanders of real military ability, recognising that his own military rank rested upon his perceived reliability and the prestige of his earldom and territorial influence. The earl invested all his familial dignity and pride in the service, proving at times a general of perception and capacity. But to what extent the reality of the northern army lived up to Parliament's fear of its potential may be in question. Parliament did view its employment farther south as a real threat. It took Newcastle's storming victory on Adwalton Moor in June 1643 as a sign to proceed rapidly into alliance with the Scots. The earl's achievements, however, possessed precious little substance. He effectively brought about his own ruin by winning a victory he entirely failed to capitalise upon. It was not what he did next so much as Parliament's anticipation of what he might do that mattered.

Other Grandees performed with a resolution equal to that of the earl, but none of them with the degree of autonomy that he enjoyed: none of them, it might be argued, held for a crucial moment the outcome of the Civil War in their hands as Newcastle seems to have done. None of them has been so consistently denigrated by historians as he. But all criticism of Newcastle has tended to turn upon irrelevancies: fashionable Grandee with a well developed sense of dignity he may have been, but he was also physically tough and, in some things, very shrewd. The problem with him was that, in terms of the overall war effort, he achieved virtually nothing.

The support of peers for the King gave added *gravitas* to the propriety of his proceedings: so long as they aligned themselves it did not matter in what form, additional to financial help, their loyalty might be displayed. But the King and his advisers showed no indication of tying themselves to the military functions of peers. The Commission of Array bypassed them, appealing direct to the broader gentry, from which group substantial commitment was to be expected. It must have been recognised by the King and his advisers that, with certain evident exceptions, a number of peers could not be relied upon. Not merely those like Saye and Sele, Stamford and Bedford whose inclinations were known, but men such as Lord Paget, who delayed their decision as long as they could and, when they did opt for one side or the other, surprised themselves and many onlookers.

If the peerage commitment in regimental command (at time of commission) is assessed solely in terms of titled nobles, then the figure of thirty-eight or 6·3 per cent of all colonels is unimpressive, and more so is the fact that nine of these held Scottish (three) or Irish titles (six). But family commitment, both of commissioned peers and of others who supported the King, shows no fewer than seventy-nine colonels. Some of these were also the loyal members of families otherwise ranged against the King, for example Henry Percy (himself enobled in 1643) was brother to the tenth Earl of Northumberland, and Colonel Sir Robert Howard of Clun in Shropshire was the uncle of James third Earl of Suffolk. The Earl of Bedfordshire's brother commanded Prince Rupert's Lifeguards.

One of the six Irish peers, William Villiers second Viscount Grandison, has already been noted as a victim of the fighting for Bristol in 1643. Without exception, the other five were English landed gentry enjoying Irish titles and possessing landed interests in Ireland. Foremost of them, in military terms, was Richard second Viscount Molyneux of Maryborough. The othes were William second Baron Brereton of Leighlin: Robert Viscount Cholmondeley of Kells: Thomas Pope second Earl of Downe; and Richard Vaughan second Earl of Carbery, a powerful Welsh gentleman whose military role in south-west Wales compares unfavourably with that of the Earl of Newcastle in northern England. Viscount Molyneux, seated at Sefton in Lancashire, adhered to the King in the summer of 1642 and was present in arms, bereft of any command, at the bitter end in 1646. At Marston Moor, commanding the second line of the Royalist right wing, he had briefly but tenaciously held up Cromwell's headlong charge which was to win the battle for the Parliament and its allies. Familial involvement was represented also by the viscount's younger brother and heir, Caryll, twenty when war broke out, an open Catholic and, before the war was ended, the butt of enemy hatred as a bloodthirsty killer. Charles Gerard, who was a neighbour of the Molyneux brothers and soldiered for a time alongside them, knew their quality and, if he had considered them as included amongst the 'nobility in general', must also have excluded them from his observation: he would almost certainly have approved of Caryll, who succeeded to the title on his brother's childless death in 1654 but who, unlike Gerard, remained constantly loyal to the House of Stuart, attempting to oppose the foregone conclusion of the 1688 *coup* against James II.[32]

Viscount Cholmondeley's contribution to the King's war was initially considerable. Seated in Cheshire, like Brereton, in which county he had served as sheriff and for the city of which he had sat as MP at Westminster, Cholmondeley was almost sixty in 1642.

A baronet since 1611, he had secured his Irish title in 1628. By the time the King entered Cheshire in September 1642 the viscount had two full regiments raised and armed for the service, a gesture which neither the King nor Parliament forgot. In 1645 Cholmondeley was elevated to the English peerage as Baron Cholmondeley of Wyche Malbrank, and after the war was almost ruined financially by a fine of £7,742. He died in 1659.[33]

Regimental command was soon dispensed with by Richard Vaughan Earl of Carbery, Parliament's chosen Lord Lieutenant of Cardiganshire and Carmarthenshire. Like Cholmondeley in Cheshire and North Wales, Carbery rapidly raised and equipped regiments for the King's service, but sent them away under the command of his brother, Colonel Henry Vaughan, who, in the event, proved himself far more committed to the service than did the earl. Carbery's part in the war effort has been examined by Dr Hutton,[34] who has shown that the earl's early successes in southwest Wales ran aground on a policy which, for example, the Earl of Newcastle never made the same mistake of following: the creation of small garrisons which necessarily depleted the field army. A determined and experienced enemy commander, Rowland Laugharne (who went over to the King in 1648), operating out of Pembroke, took these garrisons one by one, until he had overrun Carbery's command, which in turn led to the earl's disgrace. In short, whatever his affections for the King's cause may have been, the earl's period of command was a disaster waiting to happen, and Charles Gerard, who later commanded with real effect in South Wales, can have had nothing but contempt for his Grandee predecessor. Carbery himself used the good offices of Laugharne to evade compounding for his estates.[35]

Of the Scottish peers two, who were actually Scots by birth, have already been noted: Patrick Ruthven Lord Forth and Ludovick Lindsay sixteenth Earl of Crawford. The third was Walter second Lord Aston of Forfar, a Catholic rescusant seated at Tixall in Staffordshire. A reference to him in 1643 commanding a force of 'two flying colours', suggestive of a much under-strength regiment, shows an attempt to fulfil a commission. He served in Ashby de la Zouch and Lichfield garrisons, in the latter of which he was at the surrender in July 1646. Late in 1645 Lord Aston endeavoured to use the good offices of the Parliamentarian Earl of Denbigh to get permission to retire quietly to his house, but his delinquency and recusancy were against him. He went into exile.[36]

The English peers who in person exercised regimental and sometimes army command divide more or less evenly between those who were the first possessors of their titles (though not necessarily first-generation peers) and those whose titles went back a generation further or more. Of the first group, two were nominal commanders: Edward Lord Littleton and Henry Carey first Earl of Dover. Like Littleton, Dover was appointed to command a regiment of Oxford gentlemen, scholars and their servants to do duty in the event of siege but otherwise exempted from routine discipline. Unlike Littleton, however, the earl had fought as a gentleman volunteer at Edgehill in the Lifeguard, perhaps intent upon proving himself, for as late as May 1642 he had been in London and named to the Committee for the Defence of the Realm.[37]

These two aside, the other first-generation holders consisted of Robert Berty first Earl of Lindsey; Arthur first Baron Capel of Hadham; William Cavendish first Earl of Newcastle; George first Baron Digby of Sherborne (heir to the earldom of Bristol); Robert Dormer first Earl of Caernarvon; Charles Howard Viscount Andover (heir to the earldom of Berkshire); Francis Leigh first Baron Dunsmore; John Lord Paulet of Hinton St George; Robert Pierrepoint first Earl of Kingston; Thomas Wentworth first Earl of Cleveland (whose father had been a peer) and his son Thomas Baron Wentworth (summoned to the Lords in 1641); and Philip Stanhope first Earl of Chesterfield. The second group comprised George Brydges sixth Baron Chandos; Spencer Compton second Earl of Northampton; James Compton third Earl of Northampton: James Hay second Earl of Carlisle; James Ley third Earl of Marlborough; Warwick second Lord Mohun; Henry Mordaunt third Earl of Peterborough (who abandoned Parliament when his father fell mortally ill); Baptist Noel third Viscount Campden; William sixth Lord Paget of Beaudesert; Henry Parker thirteenth Lord Morley and Mounteagle; John Paulet fifth Marquess of Winchester; John Savage second Earl Rivers; William Seymour first Marquess of Hertford (who succeeded to the earldom in 1621); the self-confessedly reluctant Royalist Henry Lord Spencer of Wormleighton, the third

Baron;[38] and Montagu Berty second Earl of Lindsey, who may already have been commissioned before he succeeded to the earldom.

With certain evident exceptions, Charles Gerard would probably have excluded most of these peers from his general criticism of the nobility. Certainly, there were some deeply committed Royalists amongst them as well as some commanders of note. The Lord General of the King's army in August 1642, the first Earl of Lindsey, has been cited by some historians as a typical Grandee commander preferred to high command by the King because of his social status. That argument was always untenable. Lindsey's suitability for command rested upon a long military record, and that such an experienced general should also have been a peer of the realm was a bonus for the King. Also important was the fact that Lindsey and his opposite number, Parliament's general, the Earl of Essex, had soldiered together in Europe in other days. That Lindsey might therefore have had insights into Essex's capacity as a commander was probable.

The Earl of Lindsey's period of command, however, from August until October 1642, was cut short dramatically by his own stepping down and his immediate death from wounds at Edgehill. The circumstances by which Lindsey ended his life fighting as a colonel alongside his heir, Montagu Berty, in hand-to-hand combat will be familiar: the slight, all the worse for being unintended, put upon him by the King when the latter's nephew, Prince Rupert, whose military reputation was less solidly based than the earl's, was given independent command. Perhaps it was Rupert that Lindsey had in mind when, lying fatally wounded, he reportedly complained 'that if it pleased God to spare his life, he would never goe into the field with boys againe'.[39] The earl's son, Montagu, second Earl of Lindsey, maintained the family commitment to the King, as did a younger son, Sir Peregrine Berty, who commanded a regiment of cavalry from 1642 and who, when the time came to compound with Parliament for his sequestered property, repeatedly temporised over the National Covenant, to which he was required to subscribe.[40]

Lindsey's sons were old enough to make their own choice when war broke out, at least in theory. Certainly neither of them showed any reluctance to fight, and both remained constant to the very end. In the case of the sons of the Earl of Newcastle, however, the alternatives may have been severely limited. Newcastle, whose loyalty was unquestionable, expected a similar resolve from his heir, Charles, and the younger son, Henry. Precisely how old the brothers were in 1642 has yet to be established: Charles may have been born in 1625; he most certainly sat in the Long Parliament as MP for Retford in Nottinghamshire, which meant election at the age of fifteen or sixteen. Henry, clearly, was even younger than that, yet both were regimental commanders in their father's northern army, presumably delegating active command to others, but technically commissioned colonels. In 1644, on the very eve of the battle of Marston Moor, Newcastle (since 1643 a marquess) refused to allow his sons to be taken away to safety, requiring them to do as he intended to do, and to prove their loyalty with the hazard of their lives. The two brothers claimed in 1647 that they were in the care of their tutors during the time that their father was commanding in the North[41] but the evidence is entirely the other way – though, doubtless, Newcastle kept them at their studies whenever time allowed. Charles Viscount Mansfield, by family agreement, eventually made his peace with the Republic and was living quietly in England from 1652 until his death in the Little Castle at Bolsover in 1659. Newcastle himself and the younger son appear to have remained in exile together until 1660.[42]

This family involvement, which mere recitation of titled nobles tends to conceal, was evidenced by, among others, the Comptons, Wentworths, Somersets and the prolific house of Howard in its various branches. Sir Philip Warwick, who was in a position to know, ascribed the commitment of Spencer Compton second Earl of Northampton to a deep personal attachment to the King: 'his person was very valuable, and he had bin bred with the King . . . and he had as much love to his Master, as loyalty'.[43] The earl's war was short. In March 1643, in the midst of a victory over the enemy at Hopton Heath in Staffordshire, Northampton was unhorsed and, when offered quarter, refused it. His head was shattered by a halberd blow.[44] Clarendon had this death in mind, among many others, when he bemoaned the way in which victories were so often bought at the expense of the loss of good men of quality and example. Spencer Crompton's son and heir, James, twenty-one years of age and MP for Warwickshire in the Long Parliament, succeded to his father's military ranks – as a colonel and as Colonel General of Warwickshire and Northamptonshire – and to the favour of the King. Two other sons of the second Earl were also in arms for the King. Charles Compton acted as lieutenant-colonel under the third Earl and was knighted in 1643, and Colonel William Compton proved himself a resilient and gifted governor of Banbury, though his youthfulness (he was only a little over eighteen years of age) was often held up as a wonder. 'He shewed much of an old solider, (though a young man never engaged before) in fortifying [Banbury], cheering his men, and so ordering his provisions, that they served him to extremity.'[45] When the war was over, James, the third Earl, found himself nearly crippled with a colossal £30,000 debt partially inherited from his father, considerably augmented by expenses arising from the war. His final fine was fixed at £20,820 10s, and the family property in Somerset was claimed by one creditor owed a substantial £5,000. The financial wrecking of the Comptons was not peculiarly their experience: countless families found themselves in seriously straitened circumstances as a result of largely wartime credit. Financial outlay is as good a guide to commitment as is the presence in arms of the able male members of a family. Concepts of honour that required Comptons, Bertys and Cavendishes to appear also required them to dip deep into their coffers and to borrow where they could, even to pawning goods, as the Earl of Cleveland evidently did. The Comptons' experience of loyalty and its consequences was commonplace.[46].

The Earl of Cleveland had served alongside Lindsey at La Rochelle, but other than that was essentially a landed Grandee. As Captain of the Gentlemen Pensioners when war broke out he exercised an honorary command, and he was wounded in action at the first battle of Newbury in September 1643. Regimental command did not come his way until the spring of 1644, when he took over an existing regiment which he led with devastating panache at the battle of Cropredy Bridge in June. It was said of the Parliamentarians that they 'thought the devil had come upon them', but whether the earl had found a true flair for field command or not was never seriously put to the test, for he was unhorsed and taken at Second Newbury in October 1644 and thereafter remained a prisoner in London, his exchange not being consented to by the Parliament. His debts, quite apart from the goods which he had pawned in the King's interest,[47] amounted to £100,000.[48] His son and heir, Thomas Lord Wentworth, called to the House of Lords in 1641, became a regimental colonel before February 1643, a year before his father's appointment, and in 1644 succeeded to the prestigious command of the Prince of Wales's Horse, vacated by the death of its original colonel, Sir Thomas Bryon. Lord Wentworth rose higher in army command, serving as Field Marshal General to George Goring in the West Country, and replacing him when Goring resigned. Some thought him a 'lazy and inactive man' and his promotions may have had more to do with his being on the spot than with his apparent suitability. By the end of the war he was subordinated to Ralph Hopton, whom he served as General of the Horse. An accomplished field officer, Wentworth need not have been fitted for an organisational and co-ordinating command level. His service until then was exemplary: rather like Lord Littleton in other circumstances, he clearly found himself out of his depth, which need not detract from his qualities as a battlefield leader.[49]

Baptist Noel third Viscount Campden entered the King's service in 1642 alongside his father, the second Viscount, both of them as troop commanders. The father died in March 1643 at Oxford, and Baptist succeeded to the title whilst commanding his cavalry at Belvoir Castle in Leicestershire. He was commissioned as a colonel to raise both horse and foot regiments, but it is unclear how successful he was. He was certainly one of those peers who took the opportunity of attendance at the Oxford parliament to lay down his field command, and by October 1645 had made his way to London to compound and excuse his delinquency. A massive fine of £19,558 (subsequently cut to £9,000) reflected the fact that when war broke out he was a member of the House of Commons as an MP for Rutland.[50]

James Hay second Earl of Carlisle, who had soldiered in Germany as a young man, followed much the same course of action as Lord Campden when summoned to the Oxford parliament. Whether he actually fulfilled his commission as a colonel is similarly unclear, though he was actively in arms. At his composition he protested that he had but sixty followers, which figure equates well with a cavalry troop at full strength, and his regiment may not have reached anywhere near full complement. Carlisle was son-in-law of Francis Russell, the fourth Earl of Bedford, whose political role before his death in 1641 has provided historians with ample grounds for speculation as to his influence over events at Westminster had he lived. If the actions of Bedford's children may be any guide to the father, it is worth noting that his daughter Margaret, married to Lord Carlisle, proved overtly more committed to the Stuarts than her husband. She was imprisoned in 1650 for 'disservice' to the Commonwealth.[51] Her brother, William fifth Earl of Bedford, though General of the Horse for Parliament at Edgehill, wavered, went over temporarily to the King in 1643 (as, permanently, did the Earl of Peterborough) and fought at First Newbury in September. A younger brother, John Russell of Shingay in Cambridgeshire, became colonel of Prince Rupert's own regiment of foot, the Bluecoats, in succession to Harry Lunsford. John Russell, as MP for Tavistock in the Long Parliament, had openly opposed the publication of the Grand Remonstrance, and when he came to compound faced a fine at a half, £7,000, cut through the influence of Sir Thomas Fairfax to £2,204 3s, at a tenth.[52] The Earl of Carlisle can be seen as part of the Russell connection: certainly he came well below the Earls of Bedford in precedence, but how much his political attitude was imbibed from the Russells and how much was his own considered judgement it does not seem possible to say.

A Warwickshire neighbour of the Comptons who had represented the county as an MP in 1625, Francis Leigh, first Baron Dunsmore from 1628, was early active on the King's part. In August 1642 he led forces against Warwick Castle not in any formal military capacity but as a Commissioner of Array appointed by the King to levy troops. The function and intent of the Commission of Array have been widely discussed by historians, not least the question of whether, in its archaic nature and wording, it was counterproductive. The Commission of Array, which bypassed untrustworthy Lords Lieutenant who in 1642 had all been recently appointed by Parliament, and resurrected the military duties of the sheriffs, was aimed directly at the county gentry: its use was a recognition of where the King's potential support lay. It is an arid form of historical debate to ponder the effectiveness of the Commission of Array when the very fact of the existence of Royalist regiments in considerable number demonstrates its efficacy. What is perhaps little appreciated is the extent to which the Commissioners of Array and the regimental commanders were not infrequently one and the same, as Dunsmore was. At least 150 of the regimental colonels were names as Commissioners of Array, and the implications of this figure (which can only be revised upwards) are important. It means that military control in the counties tended to be delegated to, and to remain with, those selected for already apparent trustworthiness and known loyalty in the otherwise formative period of the early summer of 1642. Those Commissioners of Array who accepted regimental command in person, and by virtue of having done so not infrequently marched away from their counties, left vacancies which had to be filled by renewals of the original commission. As Dr Hutton has shown,[53] such renewals enabled the unwilling and downright hostile to be removed from the lists, and to be replaced by loyal gentry. But he has also shown how well advised the King was as to which members of county society could be relied upon to execute his commands, and the emergence of a Royalist army in the summer and autumn of 1642, and its subsequent increase in number of regiments and size, demonstrates pretty effectively the King's awareness of where his support lay: his certainty that the support was there to be drawn upon. From the arrival of the King at York in March 1642, though no evident record of it survives, a more or less informal campaign of canvassing support must have been going on throughout England and Wales, the canvassers being the primary movers in the creation of a Royalist army. Lord Dunsmore was probably one such. The effectiveness of this organisation of support may be felt to parallel, but upon a far wider scale, the Parliament's orchestration of 'popular' support through the petitions of 1641. Further, the organisation of loyalists and development of forces demonstrate, if such demonstration were necessary, that inter-county and inter-regional communications were efficient. Historians have tended to concentrate upon the phenomena of neutrality movements to be found in some counties to the extent of excluding the serious and widespread preparation of others for war. The presence of known activists in some neutrality discussions may imply that neuters were backed for expedience's sake and to make time for partisans to organise. It is tedious to affirm that nobody wanted a war: some did, and there were enough men willing to accept it as necessary to render the impact of neuters minimal.

Lord Dunsmore as a Commissioner of Array, and as many others did, took upon himself the immediate formation of armed units and showed no hesitation in using them. Clarendon said he was 'of a rough and tempestuous nature, violent in pursuing what he wished' and that he 'had some kind of power with forward and discontented men'. This could be taken to mean that Dunsmore was well able to organise and bring together men willing to fight, and he had his counterparts nationwide. Such men were necessary to the King in the preparation for war. Lord Dunsmore, advanced to the earldom of Chichester in 1644 when he was appointed Captain of the Band of Gentlemen Pensioners, as many peers did gave up his regimental command to sit in the Lords at Oxford. Unlike both Campden and Carlisle, however, he did not use that opportunity as a half-way point towards submission in London. He remained in Oxford to the very end in 1646, and eventually compounded at a tenth £3,694.[54]

From the foregoing it is clear that the involvement in regimental command of a peer often involved members of his immediate family at a similar or lower military rank. So, too, there were instances of commissions going to the heirs and other sons (or brothers) of peers even though the peer in question remained aloof, hostile, or served the King in other ways. John Russell, for example, like his brother-in-law Carlisle, opposed the Earl of Bedford until the earl came over to the King. It has also been shown that peer commitment might be at a subordinate rank to that of a son or younger brother. For example, Sir Francis Fane, KB, a younger brother of Mildmay Fane second Earl of Westmorland, enjoyed a colonel's commission under the Earl of Newcastle, whilst the earl himself was taken prisoner in 1642 as a cavalry captain serving in the Prince of Wales's regiment of horse under the command of Colonel Thomas Byron, a Nottinghamshire gentleman knighted only in September 1642. Fane, governor first in Doncaster and then in Lincoln, fell into enemy hands in May 1644: Parliament was not prepared to agree either to his exchange or to that of his brother, the earl, and their continuing imprisonment at London removed the Fanes as a family from the King's war effort.[55]

Three peerage families were represented in regimental command by illegitimate offspring. The brothers (by the same mother) Dudley and Gamaliel Dudley (alias Sutton) were two of the many bastard children of Edward fourth Lord Dudley, who died in 1643 at the age of seventy-two. Dud Dudley joined the notorious Sir Francis Wortley's regiment as a major before achieving full colonel's status. His brother Gamaliel, recently returned to England from Leyden University, took a colonel's commission under Newcastle, rose to the rank of brigadier (which at that date was somewhat ill defined) and acquitted himself with distinction, to be knighted in 1646 by the King.[56] Colonel John Scrope (alias James) was the eldest illegitimate son of the long-dead Emmanuel Scrope Earl of Sunderland, and, in concert with his mother, Martha James, garrisoned his house at Bolton in Wensleydale for the King. Parliament had a particular animus against Colonel Scrope, for no readily apparent reason. It endeavoured, by the severity of the fine imposed upon him, to effect his financial ruin, forcing him to sell off all his property (of which he was tenant for life, with reversion to three sisters) to meet the £7,000 demanded. His death in London in 1646 of plague deprived Parliament of a very substantial sum. Parliament's vindictiveness was out of all proportion to what appears to have been his delinquency: garrisoning his house, and permitting Prince Rupert to appoint a professional soldier, Colonel Henry Chaytor of Croft in Yorkshire, to govern it during the siege of 1644–45. Other than the fact that Scrope was a Catholic, nothing in his wartime record (so far as can be discerned), and certainly nothing in the proceedings against him, can account for Parliament's severity.[57]

Henry Clifford fifth Earl of Cumberland, as has been said, exercised military control in Yorkshire for the King in his capacity as Lord Lieutenant and designated Lieutenant General. He appears neither to have raised nor to have commanded a regiment in his own right, and when in December 1642 he handed authority in the county over to the Earl of Newcastle he retired into the administrative committees in York. Regimental command, however, was represented by George Clifford, the illegitimate son of the third Earl of Cumberland and a cousin of the fifth. Colonel Clifford, whose identity has been established by Dr Spence,[58] was 'experienced in the wars' and it is remotely possible that he commanded a Trained Band regiment led prior to the outbreak of war by the earl. Colonel Clifford was mortally wounded in action in early 1643 (in which year the earl also died) and buried in York.

The family of Howard, through three of its branches, made the largest contribution of any single family to the regimental command of the King's army, but only one Howard peer was directly so involved. Charles Howard Viscount Andover was the twenty-seven-year-old heir of the first Earl of Berkshire, who was himself an active Royalist without holding military command. Viscount Andover was commissioned on 11 October 1642, and his regiment fought at Bristol, where Slanning, Trevanion, Buck and Grandison were killed. Had the war broken out much later, the viscount would have been *en route* to Venice on an embassy from the King. (The King's representative there, Gilbert Talbot of Lacock in Wiltshire, was recalled in 1644 and upon return to England was commissioned to raise and command a regiment.) Four other sons of the Earl of Berkshire appeared in arms, two of them as full colonels. His second, Thomas (who ultimately succeeded as third Earl), had been accused in 1642 of involvement with the muster at Kingston on Thames after the attempt upon the Five Members. The accusation was serious, for Thomas Howard at that date was MP for Wallingford, and he must have been absent from the House for the crucial period, although he himself denied any involvement. Thomas was commissioned twice as a colonel, in December 1642 and in November 1643, and opted for exile rather than make any attempt to compound for his delinquency. The third son, Henry, of Revesby in Lincolnshire, served as governor of Malmesbury and as early as March 1645 was present in London seeking to compound for his property. Henry Howard admitted to his rank, claiming that he had accepted it in good faith, believing the King's army had been raised 'for defence of the Protestant religion and the liberties of the subject'. Disillusion set in with the collapse of the Uxbridge Treaty negotiations. Unlike the rest of his family, Henry appears not to have been suspected of, or accused of, popery, but his reported explanation of himself sounds very much like special pleading. Two other sons, Robert and William, served as lieutenant-colonels under, respectively, Viscount Andover and Henry Howard, their elder brothers.[59] These and other cases also illustrate the way in which regiments could have very strong family control.

The Berkshire Howards were descended from the second son

of Thomas Duke of Norfolk, who had been executed in 1572 for plotting against Queen Elizabeth. Another significant contribution to the King's cause came from the descendants of a younger son of the duke, Lord William Howard of Naworth, who died in 1640. Three of Lord William's five sons survived him, and all three held colonels' commissions under the King. Charles Howard of Croglin in Cumberland, referred to as 'the Duke of Norfolk's grandchild' when his presence in Skipton Castle in 1645 was reported, was, like all the family, a Catholic. He died in 1652.[60] His brother, Sir Francis, of Corby in Cumberland, knighted in 1617, had actively collected Catholic money towards the King's war against the Scots in 1639, and was a Deputy Lieutenant of his county when the Earl of Newcastle commissioned him 1642. Sir Francis Howard's war service is no better detailed than that of his brother Charles, but he was certainly in the garrison of Hereford when it surrendered in 1646. He died in 1659. The youngest of Lord William's surviving sons, Colonel Thomas Howard, served against the Scots in 1640 as a lieutenant-colonel, and was killed outright on 1 December 1642 at the head of his regiment when Newcastle stormed the defended bridge across the Tees at Piercebridge. Through marriage, Colonel Thomas was connected with the Catholic Eures of Bradley in Durham, whilst Sir Francis Howard's first wife had come of the Catholic and, in 1642, Royalist family of the Prestons of Furness in Lancashire: Colonel Sir John Preston died of wounds in 1645. The son of the marriage of Sir Francis and Ann Preston, also called Thomas, was killed as a colonel at the battle of Adwalton Moor on 30 June 1643. Sir Philip Howard, the nephew of Charles, Francis and Thomas, was killed in action as a cavalry colonel at Rowton Heath near Chester in 1645.[61]

Perhaps as an antidote to the impression of Howard solidarity that the foregoing conveys, the abandonment of both Royalism and Catholicism by Charles Howard of Naworth, great-nephew of Colonels Sir Francis, Charles and Thomas Howard, may be mentioned. Perhaps twelve years old when his great uncles took up arms for the King, Charles Howard can only have learned the bitter lessons of the failure of the royal cause without ever being involved in its comradeship. His marriage to the daughter of another Howard, the Parliamentarian Edward Lord Howard of Escrick (who was also a grandson of the executed Duke of

Norfolk) drew him firmly away from the family's commitment. He served as commander of Cromwell's Lifeguard and as a colonel in the Protectorate army; as an indication of his trustworthiness, he came to share control of northern England with Robert Lilburn, acting as deputies for John Lambert, the Major General assigned to the north.

Colonel Sir Robert Howard of Clun has already been mentioned as uncle of the Parliamentarian peer the Earl of Suffolk. He was also the natural father of Colonel Robert Villiers (alias Howard) by Frances the wife of John Villiers Viscount Purbeck. Robert Villiers was barely eighteen when he became a colonel on 15 June 1643, and not yet twenty-one when he surrendered to the Parliament. To excuse his delinquency, he claimed that his mother (whose death at Oxford in 1645 may have set him free) and, probably, his natural father, with whom his mother had lived openly until 1642, pressured him into accepting a commission. That may well have been true. Colonel Sir Robert Howard, a Long Parliament MP who had abandoned the House in early summer 1642, resisted to the bitter end as governor of Bridgnorth. Yet reaction against his mother's alleged coercion can hardly in itself explain the total switch in allegiances which ensued. Colonel Villiers eventually married the daughter of Sir John Danvers, a regicide, and assumed his father-in-law's surname, identifying himself wholly with the course of action taken against King Charles. When, in 1658, Viscount Purbeck died, Robert Danvers renounced the title and, at the Restoration, was heard to say that the execution of Charles I had been a lawful thing and that he would have done it himself if no one else had been willing. How much of Colonel Robert's desperate need to identify himself had to do with his childhood experience of a cuckolded father, a whore for a mother, and a domineering natural father, is impossible to say, but so thorough a shift in loyalties is almost unique in the period, far more than mere coat-turning, which was often entirely a matter of expedience. It is ironical that, when Danvers died, his widow assùmed the dignity of Viscountess Purbeck.[62]

The commitment of other peerage families in regimental and field command may be more briefly rehearsed. Three sons of Conyers Lord Darcy and Conyers (who died in 1654), including his heir, Conyers Darcy, commanded for the King. Conyers

Darcy was crippled in the fighting at Burton on Trent in 1643, and command of his regiment devolved upon a younger son, Marmaduke 'Duke' Darcy, who was twenty-eight when he assumed command. A third son, Henry, was lieutenant-colonel in the foot regiment of John Belasyse, his nephew. John Belasyse himself was the second of the sons of Thomas Belasyse first Viscount Fauconberg, and proved to be one of the most diligent of the King's regimental and garrison commanders. He was advanced to a peerage in 1645 as Baron Belasyse of Worlaby in Lincolnshire. Lord Darcy's contribution to his sons' service is not known, but Belasyse's first regiment was equipped and paid for by his father, the viscount.[63]

One-eyed Colonel Henry Hastings, Colonel General of Leicestershire, Derbyshire, Nottinghamshire and Rutland, was the twenty-two-year-old second son of Henry Hastings fifth Earl of Huntingdon and through his mother was related to James Stanley Earl of Derby, the King's leading supporter in Lancashire. Henry's elder brother Ferdinando (who became sixth Earl in 1643) was named in honour of their maternal grandfather. Whilst his brother, both before and after his accession to the earldom, played a wholly equivocal role in the war, Henry's 'loyal and faithfull endeavours' earned him the favour of the King, and of Prince Rupert,[64] and he was advanced to the peerage as Lord Loughborough in October 1643. Nominally under the command of the Earl of Newcastle, Hastings appears to have flouted the earl's authority, and there is no doubt that his disobedience led materially to the destruction of the Yorkshire Royalist army at Selby on 11 April 1644: this in turn hastened the siege of York and Newcastle's abandonment of his campaign against the invading Scottish army. Hastings the soldier was at the receiving end of much Parliamentarian hate propaganda. His nickname 'Rob-carrier' was coined by Parliament's pamphleteers, and criticism of the indiscipline of Hastings's soldiers was rife at Oxford as well: 'you are not without enemies here', he was warned immediately following his peerage.[65] He came very close to a localised war with the Royalist garrison in Lichfield, and from 1644 was virtually a raiding commander from his garrisoned family seat at Ashby de la Zouch, which he surrendered in 1646.

Colonel John Coventry of Barton in Somerset was the second son of Thomas first Lord Coventry of Aylesborough, Lord

Keeper of the Great Seal from 1625 until his death in 1640. The second Lord Coventry, although loyal to the King, played no active part in the prosecution of the war. Colonel Coventry, MP for Evesham in the Long Parliament, was particularly active in Somerset in 1645 raising fresh recruits for the King,[66] and remained in arms until the rendition of Exeter in 1646. From his point of view, though he need not necessarily have foreseen it, this was a shrewd piece of judgement, for he was comprised within the terms for the surrender of the city. Thus he avoided a heavy fine as an MP, and compounded at a tenth. Richard Weston first Earl of Portland, Lord High Treasurer to Charles I from 1628 to his death in 1635, was, like Lord Coventry, closely associated with royal policy during the Personal Rule, with the further problem of his Catholic wife, a Waldegrave. The eldest surviving son of that marriage, Jerome, became second Earl, and was confined in London from the summer of 1642 until permitted to join the King at Oxford in August 1643. He played no effective military role, but his younger brother Thomas was in arms and in action as early as September 1642 at Powick Bridge. A year later, Thomas Weston was appointed colonel of the regiment that had been George Lord Digby's. Digby, summoned to the Lords in 1641 as Baron Digby of Sherborne, was the heir to John Digby first Earl of Bristol (whom he succeeded in 1653 whilst in exile), a peer whose hesitation in the critical months of 1642 has led to him being classified as a Parliamentarian who went over to the King prior to Edgehill. Bristol's hesitancy was no more pronounced – indeed, somewhat less prolonged – than that of the Earl of Kingston, whose sympathies were always with the King. The contrast is drawn between the apparent Parliamentarianism of the father and the strong court associations of the son. Yet George Digby's desertion of the Commons for court favour, ostensibly over the trial of Strafford, was much more of an about-face than the father's. Both men were excepted from pardon in 1648, by which time the notoriety of George Digby had quite eclipsed the delinquency of the Earl of Bristol.[67] The second son of the earl was Colonel John Digby, who served as Quartermaster General, Major General and then General of the Horse under the Marquess of Hertford. Like George, he was a member of the Commons, having been returned for Milborne Port in Dorset. His colonelcy came in succession to the Viscount Grandison killed at Bristol, and John Digby was severely wounded at Torrington in February 1646. Unlike his brother and father, he was even then cited as a 'rank noted and most active papist' and he died as a seminary priest in Pontoise in 1664.

The extended family relationships of Royalist commanders have been touched upon in the case of the Earl of Carlisle and the Russells, George Digby's wife Ann was another daughter of the fourth Earl of Bedford, and he was thus related by marriage both to Colonel John Russell, of Rupert's Bluecoats, and to Carlisle, who it has been suggested may perhaps best be seen as part of the Russell connection in the late 1630s. The Countess of Bristol was the widow of Sir John Dyve, whose son Lewis, thirteen years George Digby's senior, was step-brother to the Digby brothers. Lewis Dyve was raising a regiment for the King in August 1642, having come over from Rotterdam ahead of his mentor, Prince Rupert, and distinguished himself both as a regimental and as a garrison commander, and in his stubborn contempt for the House of Commons.[68] The Digby–Russell–Hay–Dyve connection, exemplified by the pattern of armed service to the King, illustrates the extent to which inter-familial commitment was as marked as involvement within the immediate family group, and demonstrates that overt Royalism was rarely an isolated phenomenon.

Colonel William Eure of Old Malton in Yorkshire, killed in action at the head of his regiment on Marston Moor in July 1644, was the second son of William fourth Lord Eure, who, though he did not die until 1646, played no discernible part in the war. The family was Catholic, and Colonel Eure's elder brother Ralph (who died in 1640) was married to a daughter of Thomas first Lord Arundell of Wardour. The pattern of marriages amongst Catholic families is familiar enough ground. In the context of the Civil War, it meant that whilst the Eures in Yorkshire, in the person of William Eure, organised and recruited for the King, his brother-in-law Thomas second Lord Arundell (killed in 1643 at Stratton) was undertaking identical service in Wiltshire and Somerset. Although Lord Arundell himself did not command at the regimental level, his son and heir Henry, the third Lord Arundell, was both a colonel and a commander of the Lifeguard of Horse to the Marquess of Hertford. Henry Arundell's mother, Blanche, was a daughter of Edward Somerset fourth Earl of Worcester, and thus the third Lord Arundell was nephew to the single most powerful Catholic Royalist of them all, Henry Somerset fifth Earl of Worcester and from 1643 first Marquess. The financial contribution of the Somersets to the King's war chest is widely known, the Earl of Worcester exercising his considerable influence in South Wales on behalf of the King, and materially contributing to the creation of the first armed forces that attended upon the King when he was at York. Although not himself a military commander, Worcester's sons were well to the fore: Edward the eldest, who in 1646 became sixth Earl and second Marquess of Worcester, styled Lord Herbert of Raglan during his father's lifetime; Lord Charles Somerset, who was a commissioned colonel and who drowned in 1647; and Lord John Somerset of Pantley in Gloucestershire, who served as a lieutenant-colonel in the foot regiment of Edmund Fortescue and who, by marriage to a daughter of the first Lord Arundell of Wardour, was brother-in-law to Colonel William Eure of Old Malton, as well as cousin to Colonel the third Lord Arundell.

The Eure–Arundell–Somerset connection is extended through the marriage of Edward Somerset to the sister of Robert Dormer first Earl of Carnarvon,[69] creating a link of interrelated active Royalist families from Yorkshire to South Wales and via Wiltshire to Buckinghamshire. The only point of contrast between this grouping and that of Hay–Russell–Digby lies in the Catholicism of the former. Such a pattern was clearly not exclusively a peerage phenomenon: the Crossland–Prideaux–Flemming–Tancred connection has already been mentioned, and there will be occasion to note other alliances subsequently. Such commitment on the part of related but distinctive families, frequently manifesting itself in regimental and other command levels of the royal armies, is evidence of the way in which distant parts of the kingdom were actually more closely knit, through county society, than the prevailing road systems might suggest. This, and the all too obvious process of organising support in the spring and summer of 1642, meant a wide catchment area for the King's generals, and a very rapid expansion of mobilisation from the central direction imposed by the King's Council of War. Gentry connections, coupled with willingness and facilitated by opportunity, made the creation of a Royalist fighting force relatively smooth.

Charles Gerard's criticism of the pre-war peerage, whether it is taken as applying to the first-generation peers who owed their advancement to Charles I, or as having a wider application, was ungenerous. Perhaps he meant it to be understood that he regarded the peerage as natural supporters of the Crown and was disappointed in his expectations of them, as he had been in the resolution of the lawyers. From the foregoing it will be apparent that peerage commitment in command level, quite apart from support in other ways, was not inconsiderable; indeed, the noble families of the kingdom contributed in personnel on a scale which paralleled that of the untitled gentry.

IV

Nevertheless, it remains the case that the clear majority of Royalist regimental colonels came from the ranks of the untitled gentry and the knights, 67 per cent of the total. This was Gerard's background, and his own familial involvement was by no means untypical. When war broke out Gerard was twenty-four, the eldest of the sons of Sir Charles Gerard of Halsall, Lancashire, and through his mother he was related to the Royalist Fittons of Gawsworth. He showed an aptitude for war, though he had no direct experience of it, and won the favour of Rupert, Ralph Hopton and Edward Nicholas, the King's secretary, who described Gerard as the 'galantest honestest person' about the King. This was a polite way of appreciating Gerard's bluntness. Gerard's assiduous service led to his advancement to the peerage in 1645 as the first Lord Gerard of Brandon, and he showed nothing but resolution during the 1650s. His younger brother, Edward Gerard, began his war service as a captain under Viscount Grandison, but achieved colonel's rank when his brother moved into South Wales as commander-in-chief in 1644. In that same year another brother, Gilbert, commanded Charles Gerard's Lifeguard. Two uncles were also actively in arms: Gilbert Gerard, who was mortally wounded near Ludlow in 1645 as a colonel, and his younger brother Ratcliffe, who served as his lieutenant-colonel. Of the Gerards of Halsall a Welsh enemy, many of whom had cause to hate Charles, observed that they were 'the most rude, ravenous and ill-governed house that I believe ever trod upon the earth'.[70] Another branch of this 'ill-governed' house, the Gerards of the Bryn, was represented in arms by

Richard Gerard of Garwood in Lancashire, who was successively lieutenant-colonel and then colonel of the prestigious (and Catholic) Queen's regiment of horse, replacing Henry Jermyn in command. Richard Gerard had soldiered in Europe in the armies of Spain and, in 1634, had spent some time in America. His prolonged absence from England made it impossible for the authorities to prove, from recusancy proceedings, the undoubted Catholicism that he professed, and when he came to compound he was admitted at a tenth on a fine of £100. The Gerards, in common with many Lancashire Royalist families, had strong Catholic associations. Charles Gerard, however, seems to have had no particular religion at all, even though his Parliamentarian enemies conceived of him as the grand papist. If anything, he was a practising pragmatist.

Gerard's elevation to a peerage, well merited in Royalist eyes, makes him something of an exception amongst the untitled gentry colonels of 1642–46. Indeed, social advancement commensurate with military achievement was no more evident than military advancement ensuant upon social elevation. A total of 128 elevations came the way of colonels in the period between 22 August 1642 – the official commencement of hostilities – and April 1646, when the King made his way secretly to surrender to the Scots: if the figure represented 128 individuals, this would amount to just over 21 per cent of all colonels, but clearly it is more complex than that. There were, for example, certain colonels who may be said to have accumulated honours, and the best example of this is also the most singular. Colonel Henry Bard's family background was that of a younger son of a Middlesex clergyman. It is possible that he had experience of soldiering in Europe, and he certainly acquired his colonel's rank by taking over regimental command from the undoubtedly professional Colonel Thomas Pinchbeck. Bard was knighted in November 1643 and twelve months later was advanced to the dignity of baronet. On 18 July 1645 he was created Baron Bard of Drumboy and Viscount Bellamont in the Irish peerage. Such details as there are of his military service do not explain his rise.[71] No other serving colonel of untitled gentry status when commissioned, achieved such honours, albeit the Irish peerage was a lesser honour than the English peerage Bard would certainly have had from Charles II had he lived. On the other hand, it can be said that, whereas Bard advanced by stages, Charles Gerard moved from untitled gentility to an English peerage in one step. Of course, Gerard's father had been a knight. Charles Gerard's uncle Gilbert, killed in 1645, was knighted in 1643. He was one of only eighty-five gentlemen colonels (25 per cent of the total number of mere gentry; 14 per cent of all serving colonels) to be so honoured after commission and before the war's end. Knighthood went most often during the war to serving soldiers and was not infrequently bestowed on the field of battle, with the necessary precedence which that gave to the recipient over the hereditary baronetage. A good example of such a battlefield accolade is John Cansfield of Robert Hall in Lancashire, who was knighted on 4 November 1643 for outstanding bravery. When knighted he was serving as major of the Queen's regiment of horse but no immediate promotion followed. However, in the autumn of 1644 Cansfield was made third colonel of the regiment in succession to Richard Gerard, and was promoted over the head of the lieutenant-colonel, William Crofts of Saxham in Suffolk.[72] It appears to have been only Cansfield's Catholicism (a brother and a son became Jesuits) which debarred him from the governorship of Oxford in August 1645, the appointment going instead to the Protestant Sir Thomas Glemham. Religious sensitivities must have been more pronounced at that date, since Oxford had already had a Catholic governor in 1643, Sir Arthur Aston.[73]

Apart from Bard, two of the knighted colonels also acquired baronetcies. Francis Gamul of Chester, MP for the city in the Long Parliament, was advanced to a knighthood and baronetcy at Oxford in April 1644. Thomas Prestwich of Holme in Lancashire was made a baronet at the same time and in September knighted for his courage at the battle of Ormskirk on 30 August. This suggests that Prestwich (whose son and heir served as major in the regiment) led his troops at Marston Moor.

Eighteen hereditary baronetcies were created for Royalist colonels in the war years, three of which – those for Bard, Gamul and Prestwich – followed upon wartime knighthoods. This may also have been the case with the baronetcy conferred upon Colonel Sir Richard Crane of Woodrising in Norfolk, who commanded Prince Rupert's Lifeguard of Horse. His knighthood dated to September 1642, and it is by no means certain that he was at that time a commissioned colonel. On Crane's death from wounds in 1645 his honours were extinguished: there was no issue of his brief marriage to the daughter of Colonel Sir William Widdrington of Northumberland, a baronet who was to be the recipient of one of the eighteen new peerages (Scottish and Irish creations excluded) which came the way of regimental colonels during the course of the war.[74]

The number of wholly new hereditary honours created for these men numbered forty-one in all, less than half the number of knighthoods bestowed amongst them. The point has earlier been made that a knighthood, matters of precedence arising from accolade on the field of battle notwithstanding, was not an hereditary honour. No amount of knighthoods could inflate the exclusive membership of the *nobiles majores*. They could pose no threat as James I's new order of baronets had done. It was in the King's interest, if he were to honour his commanders, to adopt a policy based upon social expedience. He could show liberality in granting non-hereditary honours and be parsimonious when it came to baronetcies and peerages. The King, fighting among other things to defend a social order that appeared to be under threat from a rebellious Parliament, and of which he was the sole guarantor, could not himself contemplate the expansion of the *nobiles majores* beyond what was reasonable and might be done in normal, peacetime conditions. Although King Charles relied heavily upon the mere gentry for the creation of his armies and the prosecution of the war, he was not obliged to countenance a revolution in county and national affairs by excessive generosity in rewards.

Firstly, the concept of service to the King in the crisis of rebellion did not involve the creation of a contract between monarch and loyal subjects: it was not a matter of the one undertaking to improve the status of the other in return for military effort. Secondly, whatever chance there may have been of a negotiated settlement, which must entail compromise with peers and baronets who had adhered to the Parliament, could easily falter if the King's party displayed a substantial cluster of newly ennobled men seeking office and favour commensurate with their new status. Knighthoods allowed the King to reward clear merit in individuals without increasing the membership of the exclusive *nobiles majores*: expansion of the knightly group within the mere gentry meant nothing, for the honour died with the recipient. If the King and his advisers did not take such a pragmatic view of the reward system available to them during the war, nevertheless, the pattern of accolade and creation must have been consciously determined. Parliament, of course, refused to recognise any honours conferred by the King after his arrival at York in 1642, and denied any man's right to composition as a delinquent if the petition to compound was expressed as coming from a recipient of wartime honour.[75] The petition would have to be redrawn and delivered to be accepted.

Of the new baronets one, Francis Hawley, of Buckland Sororum in Somerset, went on from the baronetcy conferred in March 1644 to an Irish peerage created in July 1645. He became Lord Hawley of Donamore, County Meath. Unlike Bard, however, Hawley was given no knighthood, although some allusions to him seem to imply it. His father, however, had been a knight, his maternal grandfather was a knight, and he himself was married to the daughter of a knight, Sir Ralph Gibbs of Honington in Warwickshire. This kind of background status made Hawley, who was also a very good soldier of some experience, a suitable candidate for advancement.[76]

Two of the new baronets had been knighted well before Civil War began, Sir Richard Vivian of Trelowarren in Cornwall and Sir Edward Waldegrave, a Norfolk gentleman with an estate at Hever in Kent. Vivian, knighted in 1636, was MP for Tregony in the Long Parliament, and a Commissioner of Array as well as a colonel of foot. Waldegrave was under investigation by Parliament in February 1642 because, although a 'notorious' Catholic, he had been appointed a JP.[77] His knighthood had been conferred in 1607, and when war came in 1642 and he travelled west to join the King he was seventy-four years old. This 'vigilant old Collonel' was nevertheless an active cavalry commander, and the baronetcy of August 1643 acknowledged this. He died in 1650.[78]

The remaining baronetcies went predominantly to gentleman of very localised significance. John Acland of Columb John in Devonshire (June 1644); Edward Acton of Aldenham Hall in Shropshire (January 1644); John Croke of Chilton in Buckinghamshire (1645); Robert Dallison of Greetwell in Lincolnshire (1644); Wolstan Dixie of Market Bosworth, Leicestershire (given a warrant in 1645, the baronetcy confirmed in 1660); John

Knightley of Offchurch in Warwickshire (warrant 1645, confirmation 1660); Gervase Lucas,[79] of Fenton in Lincolnshire (May 1644); Bryan O'Neill of Dublin (November 1643); John Pate of Sysonby in Leicestershire (October 1643); John Preston of Dalton in Furness in Lancashire (1644); and William Vavasour, a professional soldier originally from Yorkshire but essentially peripatetic (July 1643). Vavasour and O'Neill aside, the recipients were all very much respectable country gentlemen who, but for the opportunity afforded by war to serve the King personally, may well not have improved their social status, bequeathing hereditary rank to their descendants. Acland, Croke and Dixie were the eldest sons of knights, and the maternal grandfathers of both Croke and Dixie had been knights as well, whilst Acland's father-in-law was a baronet. Dallison, Knightley, Pate and Preston had no immediate titled ancestors, but Knightley, like Acland, had a titled father-in-law, Sir Lewis Lewkenor, a family well represented in armed service to the King. Two were colonels, Anthony Lewkenor of Sussex and Christopher Lewkenor, MP for Chichester in the Long Parliament, who was knighted as a colonel in 1644. Acland's brother-in-law Lewis Lewkenor was a lieutenant-colonel and was knighted in the winter of 1644/45.

Wolstan Dixie came over from Ireland perhaps as late as 1645 to take regimental command under the King. He and Pate were similar to Vavasour and O'Neill in that they had experience in war, although Pate's apparently was little more than as a captain against the Scots in 1640. In the other cases there is no evidence of military involvement before 1642. Dixie came to England too late to make much of a personal impact upon the course of the war, whilst O'Neill, who had served against the Scots in 1639, though noted at Skipton Castle in 1645,[80] evades investigation of his wartime service. William Vavasour, however, played a long and significant part in the interests of the King. He and his brother, Charles (who had been made a baronet in 1631), both went into the wars of Europe as young men. The elder brother was serving in Ireland in 1641 and was recalled to England with his regiment in the autumn of 1643, but Charles Vavasour did not command in England: his regiment mutinied, he resigned his commission, and his pacified troops passed to Colonel Matthew Appleyard. Sir Charles Vavasour died in Oxford in March 1644. William, the younger brother, came back from Europe in 1639 to take a command against the Scots, and was involved in the Army Plots of 1641. Taken at Edgehill in 1642, he escaped from custody and as well as being given a regimental command was made Colonel General in Herefordshire, Monmouthshire, Glamorganshire, Brecon and Radnor. Rupert, in August 1644, appointed him Field Marshal General, and Vavasour was closely connected with the Prince, sharing his disgrace after the fall of Bristol in 1645. Colonel Sir William Vavasour fought his last action at Copenhagen in 1659 in the Swedish armies: ('the King of Sweden . . . sent to have [his body], they found him strip[p]ed and some ouglie bodie had cutt of his eares'.[81] The case of the Vavasour brothers neatly illustrates the way in which men of gentry background (their father had been a knight) could pursue a military career as an adjunct to, and not instead of, the maintenance of status and gentility at home: Charles Vavasour's baronetcy in 1631 affirmed that. Matthew Appleyard, the Lincolnshire country gentleman who assumed command of Vavasour's regiment in 1643/44, having been its lieutenant-colonel on service in Ireland, had passed through university and taken his BA before embarking upon a soldier's life. After 1660, in his adopted county of Yorkshire, Appleyard became a JP and MP for Hedon. These three men exemplify the way in which we should perceive the role of the professional soldier. Appleyard and William Vavasour were not alien intrusions into the royal army; rather, they were men of some status but more military experience.[82]

Colonel John Preston of Dalton in Furness, a Catholic, was mortally wounded in 1644 and died the following year. He is present as a comrade in arms in Sir Henry Slingsby's diary,[83] which shows that he fought at Marston Moor before becoming a part of Sir John Mayney's efficient brigade of broken regiments that had escaped that battle. Preston's wife was a daughter of Colonel Thomas Morgan, a Monmouthshire gentleman established at Heyford in Northamptonshire, and like Preston, a Catholic. Colonel Morgan, after distinguishing himself at Roundway Down in July 1643, was killed outright a few months later at First Newbury. His son Anthony, Preston's brother-in-law, had been knighted on the eve of Edgehill, where he fought, and became a colonel by commission on 29 June 1643. The Catholic, Royalist and familial links between Preston and the Morgans were recognised by Parliament, which in 1646 set aside the property of both families to clear the debts of John Pym.[84] Further, the Commissioners of the Great Seal appointed as guardian to the Preston children a Parliamentarian officer, Colonel Edward Cooke, a distant relation, with the usual instructions in such cases, to rear them as Protestants.

More peerages were distributed among serving colonels than were baronetcies, but marginally so if those of Scotland and Ireland are distinguished. Three new Irish peerages were created: for Henry Bard, already mentioned; for Robert Cholmondeley, who, as has been said, was made Earl of Leinster in 1646 (and who had received an English peerage in 1645); and Colonel Sir William Ogle, the governor of Winchester. Ogle was a Northumbrian by birth, but marriage took him to Hampshire and specifically to Winchester, where he settled. Knighted in 1628, he represented the city as MP in the Short and Long Parliaments. Like the Vavasour brothers, Ogle had a military career long before 1639, when he served as a colonel against the Scots. Like the Vavasours, he was serving in Ireland when, in 1643, he was recalled by the King, seized Winchester, and held it until October 1645. His Irish peerage as Viscount Ogle of Catherlough was granted to him after he had survived a court martial over his surrender of Winchester.[85] Two new Scottish peerages were also created, and notice has been taken of that awarded to Patrick Ruthven Lord Ettrick, who also advanced to an English peerage as Earl of Brentford. The recipient of the other was James King, created Baron Eythin in late 1643 at the same time that the Earl of Newcastle was advanced to a marquessate, and for the same military service. King had openly sided with the Crown against the Covenanters back in 1639, but in 1642 he was in Holland, where the Queen herself recruited him to serve under Lord Newcastle (commanding general of 'her' army) as Lieutenant General of Foot as well as a colonel in his own right.

Three of these lesser peerages, therefore, went to men of long-standing military experience, whilst a fourth – Bard's – recognised recent military achievement. Qualification for one of the eighteen English peerages created for serving or formerly active colonels was somewhat more stringent. Omitting the titles created for Ruthven and Cholmondeley, the other new peerages were those of Jacob first Baron Astley of Reading (1644); John first Baron Belasyse of Worlaby (1645); John first Baron Byron of

Rochdale (1643); John first Lord Frescheville of Staveley (a war-
rant was issued in 1645 but the patent came in 1665); Charles first
Lord Gerard of Brandon (1645); Henry first Lord Hastings of
Loughborough (1643); Ralph first Baron Hopton of Stratton
(1643); Henry first Baron Jermyn of St Edmundsbury (1643);
Francis Leigh first Earl of Chichester (created in 1644, when
Leigh was already Baron Dunsmore); John first Baron Lucas of
Shenfield (1643); Henry first Baron Percy of Alnwick (1643)
Edward Somerset first Earl of Glamorgan (1645, but styled Lord
Herbert of Raglan as heir to his father, the Earl of Worcester);
Henry Spencer first Earl of Sunderland (1643, but already Baron
Spencer of Wormleighton): Richard first Baron Vaughan of
Emlyn (1643 but since 1634 second Earl of Carbery in the Irish
peerage); William first Baron Widdrington of Blankney (1643);
and Henry first Baron Wilmot of Adderbury.

Francis Leigh and Henry Spencer were already peers of
England in their own right; Vaughan, the unsuccessful commander in south-west Wales, had an Irish peerage. Edward Somerset
would, in 1646, succeed to the marquessate of Worcester as heir.
Thus, including Ruthven and Cholmondeley, six of the eighteen
new peers were either already ennobled or, in Somerset's case,
likely to succeed to an existing title. There may have been three
successions by serving colonels to extant peerages: Henry
Arundell as third Baron Arundell of Wardour; Henry Wilmot as
second Viscount Wilmot of Athlone in the Irish peerage;[86] and
probably a serving colonel at his succession, Montagu Berty, as
second Earl of Lindsey.

Of the remaining twelve (including Wilmot) Belasyse, Hastings
and Percy were the sons of English peers and as such comprised
within the *nobiles majores*. The only new peers whose fathers had
been of mere gentry status were Astley, Hopton and
Widdrington, yet they themselves when ennobled were, respectively, a knight, a Knight of the Bath, and a knight and
baronet. Only three untitled gentlemen were advanced to
peerages, Jermyn, Lucas and Wilmot; two had fathers who were
knights, the other's father was an Irish peer. The same was true of
John Frescheville, but although his ennoblement was intended in
1645 he had to wait twenty years for it to become actual. Three of
the eighteen peers were Catholics: Belasyse, Somerset and
Widdrington. Accusations were laid against Charles Gerard cer-

tainly, and John Lucas possibly, wrongly.

Clearly, if the gentry commanding regiments for the King saw the opportunity of acquiring higher social status, they were to be disappointed. It is unlikely that they saw the war in this purely selfish light. Nor had they benefited particularly in the distribution of honours that preceded the outbreak of war, when the King, not unreasonably, sought to encourage potential supporters with marks of his favour. Of the knights who enjoyed that honour at the time of commission, only twenty-three had been knighted either in 1642 or in 1643: 31 per cent of all knights commissioned as colonels owed their knighthoods to the anticipation of war. Similarly, of the fifty-nine baronets who took commissions, only nine, or 15·25 per cent of them, received their hereditary titles in the same period. This tends to add a further dimension to Gerard's remark about the gentry maintaining the King's cause with constancy: the majority of them left off fighting as the gentlemen they had been before they assumed command functions, but poorer in pocket and ousted nationwide from whatever pre-war official posts they had filled. The mutuality of experience in defeat which Royalists liked to suppose mirrored and was mirrored by the King's personal condition was very real, and significant.

Consideration of the way in which single families contributed several members both to regimental command and to other forms of activism should not conceal the fact that army command was very widely distributed indeed. Of the 603 identified colonels, not omitting the handful of Europeans, Scots and Irish officers, it can be shown that they came from 529 distinctive families, however those families may have been related one to another. But of those families fifty-five contributed two or more regimental commanders, although rarely as many as the Howards in three branches of their family. One gentry family in particular, that of the Byrons of Newstead in Nottinghamshire, encapsulates the Civil War experience of many, largely because no fewer than eight male members of the family (an uncle and seven brothers) were directly involved in regimental or field command in general. The progenitor of this prolific family was Sir John Byron, knight, who died in 1625. His younger brother, Nicholas, a colonel from January 1644, was seated at Gaines Park in Essex, where in theory a secondary branch of the Byrons should have been established. Nicholas was, however, mortally wounded in 1645 and his widow, a Dutch woman, took their son Ernestus Byron back to Holland, though he was in England in 1657, 'now of age' to compound.[87]

The head of the family in 1642 was Sir John Byron, Knight of the Bath. His career before the war, as a soldier in Europe but as, among other things, MP for Nottingham in the 1620s, illustrates the difficulty of isolating the experienced or professional soldier from the gentleman of status in domestic terms. For Byron, as for the Earl of Lindsey and many others, military experience provided a further dimension to his life but only rarely subordinated all else.

In 1641 the King appointed Byron to the Lieutenancy of the Tower of London to replace Thomas Lunsford, against whom the Commons were prejudiced. The Commons were no more satisfied with Byron than they were with Lunsford and secured his removal as well in February 1642.[88] Sir Edward Deering, MP from Kent and later a colonel under the King, thought him 'a gentleman of moderation and especiall worth',[89] and there was technically nothing against Byron holding so sensitive a post other than his clear association with the King and court. Byron's elevation to the peerage in 1643 as first Baron Byron of Rochdale gave lustre to his new appointment as Field Marshal General in North Wales, where he replaced the luckless Arthur Lord Capel of Hadham. When Byron died in exile in 1652 the peerage passed to his brother Richard, his heir.[90] Sir Richard Byron, knighted in September 1642, became govenor of Newark on Trent, though a local Royalist colonel, Gervase Holles, thought him 'a person of a narrow soule and every way unequall to the charge'.[91] Thomas Byron, also knighted in September 1642 when he was colonel of the Prince of Wales's Regiment of Horse, was murdered at Oxford on 9 December 1643. His assailant, Hurst, was executed after a court martial.[92] Robert Byron resigned his commission in Ireland in 1642 to serve the King as a colonel, and was knighted at Oxford in 1644. He was arrested in Ireland after 1645, and spent the ensuing fifteen years in prison. Even the Cromwellian Major General Goffe, who thought him no longer a threat, could not secure his release.[93] That, above all else, tells much about Robert Byron. Gilbert Byron was first commissioned as a major in Sir John's regiment, but was a colonel in his own right by 1644. He had been one of the followers of the King when the attempt was made upon the Five Members in January 1642, a fact which cannot have escaped the Commons any more than his kinship to the erstwhile Lieutenant of the Tower. Gilbert died in 1654. Of the two other Byron brothers, Philip (probably knighted in 1643 or 1644 by Lord Newcastle, whose autonomous command included that privilege) was killed defending York as a colonel in 1644. William, the only brother not to achieve regimental command, was knighted in 1646 and thereafter seems to disappear from history.

Allowing for the size of the Byron family, and acknowledging that, with the possible exceptions of Philip and William, all the brothers had some form of pre-war military experience, the family's history during the war may be said to be fairly representative of many such gentry families. John Byron's peerage was exceptional; his death in exile was not. Two, perhaps three, brothers perished between 1642 and 1646. Four of them were made knights, but none of them other than John himself secured any hereditary title, though clearly from 1643 Richard Byron had expectations, provided he survived and his elder brother had no heirs by his second marriage to a daughter of Robert Needham Viscount Kilmorrey. Nevertheless, as the younger brothers of a peer of the realm, all six of John's siblings theoretically entered the *nobiles majores*, each of them (as the patent of the barony made clear) capable of becoming heir to John Byron. Richard and Gilbert were admitted to compound for their estates; John was denied pardon by Parliament, and Robert seems to have been considered a fit person to set at liberty. As for Major William Byron, he is representative of those Royalist officers, some of them colonels, who, by virtue of gaps in the historical record, to all intents and purposes seem to have, and actually may have, ceased to exist in or after 1646.

The involvement of all surviving adult male members of a single family in the King's cause is made impressive by the number of Byrons there were, but the same thing would apply if only father and son, or two brothers, were engaged in the same service and were the only male representatives of their families. This situation was widespread, and the notion of token activists cannot really be sustained any longer. There are traceable instances of divided families and of related families at odds during the war, but the concept of the token younger son or brother as a familiar figure in Royalist armies is merely a tendentious ploy of those who would deny the King any meaningful support at all. Merely selecting at random from amongst the regimental colonels yields concrete evidence of considerable, unhesitating and more important, long-term active support for the King amongst the gentry in its widest sense.

The Gerards have been noticed. In Glamorganshire the Stradlings, headed by Sir Edward Stradling, second Baronet from 1637, had four adult male activists: Sir Edward's brothers Henry, knighted in 1642; John, who assumed command of Sir Edward's regiment when he was taken at Edgehill; and Thomas, who served as lieutenant-colonel under his brother John. All, except Thomas, died before 1649, and Colonel John Stradling perished in prison at Windsor.[94] Sir Henry Slingsby of Moor Monkton in Yorkshire served alongside his younger brother Thomas, who was a colonel of horse in the army of the Earl of Newcastle. The Kent branch of the family, the sons of Sir Guilford Slingsby, Comptroller of the Navy, were all in the service at one time or another between 1642 and 1646. The head of the family was Colonel Guilford Slingsby, killed in early 1643 serving under Newcastle; two of his brothers, Arthur and Walter Slingsby, achieved regimental commands and a third brother, although not a colonel, fought in the defence of Bristol in 1645. A son of the Rector of Rothbury in Northumberland, Charles Slingsby, was knighted by Newcastle and killed in action as an infantry colonel at Marston Moor.[95] In Herefordshire Colonel FitzWilliam Conyngsby, expelled from the Commons as a monopolist in 1641, had three of his sons engaged in the war, one, Humphrey, as his own lieutenant-colonel, the other two serving in other regiments.[96] John Arundell of Trerice in Cornwall, known as 'Jack for the King', 'an old gentleman of near four score years of age', was a colonel of foot. His eldest son, Richard, MP for Lostwithiel, was also a colonel, and in 1665 was created first Baron Arundell of Trerice in 'memory of his father's service, and his own eminent behaviour'. The father had died in 1654. Of the other sons, John, MP for Bodmin in the Long Parliament, was killed in arms as a colonel in November 1644; Francis also became a colonel, and William Arundell was a commissioned officer, perhaps under his brother-in-law, Colonel John Trevanion.[97]

The Stradlings and the Arundells were Catholics, the Slingsbys and Conyngsbys Anglican: in this as in many other aspects of the service, a difference in faith drew no serious distinction between the involvement of one family and another.

Sir Harvey Bagot of Blithfield, Staffordshire, was committed to the King.[98] A knight and an MP, Sir Harvey was a Commissioner of Array and his eldest son Richard, intended for service in Ireland, accepted a commission as colonel and was killed at Naseby in 1645. Richard's younger brother, Harvey, took over the regiment as its colonel by promotion.[99] Their brother-in-law, Robert Arden of Parkhall, Warwickshire, was commissioned as a colonel on 20 February 1643.[100] The Covert brothers, sons of Sir Walter Covert of Maidstone in Kent, who died in 1632, were the brother-in-law of George Goring. Colonel Thomas Covert was commisioned in August 1643 to raise both horse and foot. Upon his death soon afterwards his brother and subordinate, John, became colonel on Goring's recommendation to Prince Rupert.[101] Gervase and Anthony Eyre, of Yorkshire and Essex respectively, were half-brothers, the sons of Anthony Eyre of Laughton en le Morthen in Yorkshire, who was not himself active. Gervase, knighted in 1639 when in arms against the Scots, died of sickness induced by wounds when a serving colonel in May 1644. Anthony, who had also served against the Scots, succeeded Gervase as colonel and is referred to as a Major General in Newark garrison.[102] Rowland Eyre of Bradway in Derbyshire, a Catholic recusant, commanded a cavalry regiment in which his younger brother William was lieutenant-colonel.[103] Such cases could be rehearsed time and again from every county of England and most of Wales.

Notice has been taken of the fact that 529 families provided the 603 colonels identified as serving between 1642 and 1646, of which fifty-five families provided two or more such officers. Analysis of composition proceedings and other material serves to show that, of the remaining 474 families, at least 139 had members other than the colonel whose activism brought them to the notice of the Parliament. This figure, which again refers only to the activism of 1642–46, ignores second-generation activism, which was a widespread phenomenon. It would indeed have been remarkable if some at least of these 529 families had not experienced some internal divisions in the matter of allegiance. It is worthy of note that not all the sons of Jack-for-the-King Arundell of Trerice were Royalists. One son commanded in the armies of the Parliament, presumably abjuring the Catholic faith in which he had been brought up.

V

Yet the number of divided families for which the evidence is very reliable is small, no more than thirty-four in all. Perhaps the most serious of differences would be those between father and son, of which there are eight clear cases. That of Colonel Francis Cooke is the most bitter, since the evidence shows no reconciliation and the Parliamentarian father, Thomas Cooke, an Essex gentleman, transferred his vindictiveness to his son's widow and children. Francis Cooke fought against the Scots in 1640, presumably with no parental approval: he was twenty-seven when in 1642 he joined the royal armies and was commissioned as a colonel of foot. His father disinherited him, and became himself a colonel in the armies of the Parliament. Francis was eventually killed defending Colchester Castle in 1648, where a good many diehard Royalists found themselves beleaguered. At the Restoration his widow, Priscilla, petitioned that Charles I had extended his protection to the family because of the father's enmity, and that he continued to do nothing for the welfare of his grandchildren.[104] Perhaps a more famous case of father–son enmity is that of the Mauleverers of Allerton in Yorkshire, Sir Thomas Mauleverer first Baronet, who died in 1655, being one of the King's judges in 1649. His eldest son and heir, Richard, broke with his father in 1642 when he was nineteen, made his way to Oxford, where he may have secured his colonel's commission, and subsequently fought with the Northern Horse in 1644/45, Newcastle's old cavalry regiments, brigaded under Sir Marmaduke Langdale and Gamaliel Dudley. Colonel Mauleverer was knighted on 28 March 1645, which suggests that he had distinguished himself in the relief of Pontefract. He, too, fought at Colchester in 1648: indeed, it is possible that for both Mauleverer and Cooke the implacable hostility of their fathers kept them actively in arms. But this may devalue their commitment, and it is not proven. Sir Richard compounded on a personal estate left to him by his uncle, William Mauleverer, and succeeded his father in the baronetcy.[105]

Other sons with rebel fathers were Colonel John Corbet of

Stoke in Shropshire, whose father, Sir John Corbet Baronet, may well have tried to help his son avoid the financial penalties of his Royalism. Colonel Corbet was one of those who subscribed to the Oath of Allegiance to the Commonwealth, so the familial division may have been less fraught than Cooke's, for example.[106] Colonel Edward Hopton of Canon Frome in Herefordshire succeeded to the regimental command of Allen Apsley, and was knighted in June 1645 for his courage when Leicester was stormed. The degree of his father's opposition may have been slender, and some reckoned him only a neuter. There is no evidence of extended enmity.[107] Colonel Thomas Sandford of Howgill in Westmorland, heir to Sir Richard Sandford, knight, 'was chosen colonel of a regiment of his countreymen and accepted a commission from the Earl of Newcastle', though he possessed no estate of his own, despite marriage, and lived in his father's house. His wife, a daughter of the Royalist delinquent Sir George Dalston, of Dalston Hall in Cumberland, was sister to Colonel Sir William Dalston, MP for Carlisle (despite his Catholicism), of which city he was constable when war broke out. Sandford's relations may have drawn him towards Royalism, though that he was chosen as a commander by others indicates either a well known political stance or recognised military competence. In 1644 Colonel Sir Thomas Sandford (he had been created a baronet in 1641) took the Covenant, perhaps administered to him by his father, serving as a JP in their county and Parliament's nominee.[108]

Three colonels found their sons in arms against them. Sir Henry Bellingham of Helsington in Westmorland, knight and baronet since 1620 and member for Westmorland in the Long Parliament, was opposed by his son James, who became recruiter MP for the county in 1646. The uprising of 1648, however, brought them together in arms for the King, James serving under his father, whose colonelcy was revived. Both men died in 1650, and Sir Henry's grandson not long before that, so the family in the male line was extinguished.[109] Conyers Darcy, heir to the barony of Darcy and Conyers, has already been noticed in the context of familial involvement, the Darcys providing two colonels and a lieutenant-colonel for the King. Colonel Darcy's eldest son, Conyers Darcy, was a colonel in Parliament's northern army. Sir Gilbert Houghton, second Baronet, of Houghton Tower in Lancashire, and his brother Ratcliffe Houghton were both in arms for the King and both were dead by 1648. Sir Gilbert's younger son, Gilbert Houghton of Wheelton, served as a major in the regiment of Sir Gilbert Gerard of Halsall, but the son and heir, Richard, was an active committee man in Lancashire in 1644 and was returned as recruiter MP for the county in 1646.[110] The younger son, Gilbert, was son-in-law of Colonel Sir Francis Gamul of Chester.

Ten of the colonels had brothers on Parliament's side: George Brydges Lord Chandos, Fulk and Henry Hunks from Warwickshire, Thomas Monck of Potheridge in Devon, Henry Percy (whose brother was the tenth Earl of Northumberland), William Ratcliffe of Foxdenton in Lancashire, Edward Rostern, also from Lancashire, Edmund and Henry Verney of Claydon, Buckinghamshire, and Richard Cholmeley of Whitby, whose half-brother was Sir Hugh Cholmeley. Richard's not inconspicuous war service has been over shadowed by that of his more famous half-brother, who returned to his allegiance in February 1643. Richard, the son of their father's second marriage, soldiered in the West Country, where he met and married the daughter of Colonel the Lord Paulet of Hinton St George and was knighted at Exeter in July 1644. Lord Paulet resigned his own colonelcy in favour of his son-in-law, who was shot dead near Lyme Regis in October the same year.[111] (The colonelcy thereupon passed to a complete unknown, Thomas Walker, who defies identification.)

The rarest division to be met with within a family is that between husband and wife, but this was a problem for Colonel John Frescheville of Staveley in Derbyshire. His second wife, Sarah, the daughter of Sir John Harrington of Bagworth, had developed anti-court animosities resulting from a property dispute with the Earl of Strafford.[112] The gossip in 1645, when Colonel Frescheville surrendered Welbeck House to the Parliamentarians, was that he had remained loyal only until he had secured a barony, fulfilling his wife's ambition for him.[113] Yet Frescheville's war service, his wife's Parliamentarian sympathies notwithstanding, had been exemplary: he raised a troop of horse which he took to Edgehill, was wounded severely at First Newbury in September 1643, and served as governor of Welbeck when the Royalists recaptured the house in July 1645 until its surrender. Prior to the war, and when the war began, he was a Gentleman of the Privy Chamber to the King, and had served against the Scots in 1639/40. His wife proceeded with composition for her husband's estates whilst he kept out of the way in Europe, and he remained suspect throughout the 1650s. Ironically, Sarah Frescheville enjoyed the dignity of a baron's wife for only a month or so, for she died in 1665: Frescheville's warrant had been made in 1645, but the patent did not pass for twenty years. His third wife, Anna Charlotte de Vic, was the true beneficiary of what many regarded as Sarah's scheming.[114]

Wife trouble may also have been a problem – if anything was, which is doubtful – for Robert Dormer first Earl of Carnarvon[115] and for Colonel Shallcross, like Frescheville a Derbyshire gentleman. Shallcross had married Elizabeth, the daughter of Thomas Bagshaw of The Ridge in Derbyshire,[116] of whom it was said, in 1644 'Mrs. Elizabeth Shallcrosse . . . is accompted to be a well wisher to the proceedings of Parliament and hath suffered much by her husband's delinquency . . .'[117] Although this was said of her by those who were in a position to know, some caution must be exercised. When the remark was made, the Shallcross property in Derbyshire and Staffordshire had been overrun and sequestered. Colonel Shallcross was still in arms, riding with the Northern Horse. It may be that Mrs Shallcross was doing the best she could to soften the Stafford committee's treatment of her husband's estate, although, if that were so, then someone acquainted with her must have drawn attention to any hint of duplicity. The evidence is inconclusive. Colonel Shallcross certainly abandoned the King's service in mid-1645 and was pursuing his composition vigorously by November, perhaps building upon the goodwill created, or fostered, by his wife. Shallcross remained a suspect throughout the 1650s, reckoned 'the forwardest man to appear' in 1651 and undoubtedly restive in 1659. There is nothing further concerning his wife.[118]

Some Royalist colonels found themselves at political odds with relatives who were (or who have since become) significant figures in Parliament's camp. Indeed, some were so significant that the Royalism of their relatives has been almost wholly obscured. Colonel Allen Apsley's brother-in-law, for example, was John Hutchinson, the governor of Nottingham and one of the King's judges in 1649. Hutchinson's fame rests largely upon the priggish biography of him written by his wife.[119] In 1660 Colonel Apsley endeavoured to intercede on Hutchinson's behalf, but the regicide was gaoled until his death in 1664. By his second marriage Colonel Sir Thomas Aston, baronet, of Aston in Cheshire was brother-in-law to the moderate Parliamentarian Simond D'Ewes: Simond D'Ewes's brother, Lieutenant Colonel Richard D'Ewes, was killed in action in 1643 in the Royalist regiment of Colonel Richard Bolles, which had previously been that of William Lord Pagett. Colonel the Lord Chandos's brother-in-law was Edward Montagu, Earl of Manchester, the somewhat reluctant commander-in-chief of Parliament's efficient army of the Eastern Associated Counties. Chandos's wife died in 1652, and his second wife, Jane, was the daughter of the impeccably Royalist John Savage second Earl Rivers, who had served as a colonel between 1642 and 1646, abjuring his Catholicism in the latter year in order to compound.

Colonel Richard Egerton, seated at Pickering Lyth in Yorkshire, was originally a Cheshire man: his father-in-law was Sir William Brereton, Parliament's able commander-in-chief in that county.[120] Colonel James Hamilton, a Scot who had served against the Covenanters in 1639/40 and became Major General of the Horse to Prince Maurice, was uncle to the Covenanter General the third Earl of Haddington. Colonel Roger Mostyn, a Flintshire gentleman, was married to the daughter of Sir Martin Lumley, who represented Essex in the Commons throughout the war but was to be excluded at Pride's Purge in 1648. The daughter of Colonel John Redman of Wrayton in Lancashire, who died in 1644 as governor of Pontefract, was married to the Parliamentarian Colonel William Forbes; her brother William was killed in arms as a Royalist captain in the year of their father's death.[121] William Seymour first Marquess of Hertford, colonel and Lieutenant General for the King in the west was the brother-in-law of Parliament's general and, to the Royalists, the heir of treason as personified by his father, Robert Devereux Earl of Essex.

The divisions within families can, however, be too heavily stressed, even if the juxtapositions may afford interest. Clearly, divisions within the immediate family were significant. They indicate to us the existence of familial tensions which may have had their origins long before the war itself, and they also show that profound political differences could put at variance those whose other mutual interests proved not strong enough to withstand political enmity. To itemise the cases in which Royalist colonels found themselves opposed by, or opposed to, relatives by marriage cannot carry with it any real significance unless we are to suppose that the bonding in the form of wife and sister should have precluded disparate interests. Marriage, being a fusion not of families but only of the two individual members concerned, whatever the rationale behind the alliance might be, cannot be seen as the creation of an identity of purpose for two previously unconnected families. The pattern of family relationships evidenced by a consideration of Royalist colonels, whilst it suggests something more far-reaching, surely indicates a random consensus in attitude, and the same is true of the findings concerning division. The extent to which division could ever be shown to have been a substantial factor of the Civil War would be determined by the evidence; and we will always lack of the means of knowing to what extent family members may have disapproved of the activism of one or more of their number, without themselves adopting active opposition. If the accusations against Mrs Shallcross and Mrs Frescheville were justified, nevertheless the disapproval of their husbands' Royalism did not drive them away, and it is conceivable that only in the event or likelihood of defeat did they find their alternative principles. Yet the briefly fashionable adoption of Sir William Waller's notion of 'this war without an enemy' (which only ever found favour amongst those who knew nothing of the causes of the war) falls flat in the face of the reality of familial division. For the enemy within the family is more immediate and disruptive than those far-off personages with whom its members may feel themselves aligned. We ought to be aware – though we can never know how often it was true – that families tense with disputation and argument over matters political and religious may have found the war itself a profound relief. Physical division then took the place of attitudinal division, war coming as a breath of fresh air that, inevitably, turned into a storm.

VI

Since the evidence is far from clear-cut, the alleged division in the Grenvile family between the brothers Bevil and Richard (to which allusion has been made) is omitted from the foregoing. Parliament certainly felt that Grenvile had betrayed them, but Sir

Richard felt otherwise and, further, there is no evidence that he actually took up arms for the Parliament in the first place. What Parliament expected of him and what he intended is another matter. Yet this introduces the perhaps more productive area of investigation, the role of the coat-turners and side-changers. Some twenty-four of the King's colonels changed sides between 1642 and 1646, fifteen going over to the Parliament, the rest abandoning Parliament to serve the King. Over a further five Royalists entertained some suspicions which were for the most part unfounded. The general pattern of side-changing, as would be expected, reflected the way that the war seemed to be going. Of those who abandoned Parliament for the King, all did so either in 1642 or in 1643. If Sir Richard Grenvile were not omitted as a side-changer, then his shift of allegiance in 1644 would be very late indeed. In that year, desertions to the Parliament began. With the exception of two North Welsh commanders, John Aldersey and Thomas Ravenscroft, who changed sides in 1643 under peculiar local circumstances, the rest of the desertions to the Parliament began in July 1644.

The nine colonels who began the war in the armies of the Parliament all, clearly, assumed active military roles in the King's service. This was not always true of those who, abandoning command in the royal armies, went over to the Parliament. Contemporaries did regard, for example, Lord Chandos as having turned his coat, but Chandos did not fight for Parliament against his former comrades any more than did Colonel William Coryton of Newton Ferrars in Cornwall. Coryton's is, anyway, a curious case. Professor Russell[122] has identified him as a part of the 'Godly reformation' group in the Commons, where he sat as MP for Launceston until expelled in 1641 for corruption. It may be that William Coryton found himself at home in Cornwall at the wrong time, when the Commission of Array arrived to which he was appointed, and his Trained Board command as colonel may have been an unavoidable necessity. How active he was, also, is debatable. His son John was a lieutenant-colonel under Sir John Berkeley, and seems never to have served with his father. Coryton's wife, Philippa, was said to have acted as a spy for Fairfax in 1645/46. The son's resolution contrasts strongly with his mother's duplicity and his father's lack of enthusiasm, and the true Royalism of the family may have been vested in a younger son. William Coryton certainly assisted Parliament in the reduction of Cornwall, not that that in itself enabled him to avoid composition. This suggests he changed sides quite late, and that he had given up military involvement earlier still.[123]

The most startling change of sides was that of Colonel Faithful Fortescue, who chose the moment battle began at Edgehill to go over to the King with his troops.[124] Other important defections followed, including Sir Hugh Cholmeley, Parliament's governor of Scarborough, and Henry Mordaunt Earl of Peterborough.[125] A soldier of exceptional ability, James Chudleigh, the younger son of the Parliamentarian Sir George Chudleigh, baronet, went over to the King after his capture in 1643, and took the family with him. His father went to Oxford and as late as 1651 declined to take the Engagement. Another brother, Thomas, served in arms for the King as well. James Chudleigh's case is no record of a wholesale change of heart. He had, for example, been involved in the Army Plots in 1641, a breeding ground for future Royalist colonels and commanders (twenty-three of the colonels of 1642–46 were involved in conspiracy between 1641 and February 1642), but had been unable to secure a command in the King's army in 1642. Hence his appearance in his native West Country as a Parliamentarian Major General with a startlingly good record of innovatory tactical manoeuvres before his capture on 16 May 1643 at Stratton. He thenceforth commanded a regiment for the King, until his death in action on 6 October 1643.[126]

In that same year, and again in the West Country, Colonels Pretty and Wagstaffe abandoned Parliament's service. Pretty, a Monmouthshire gentleman who had soldiered in Europe before joining the King against the Scots in 1639, fell into Royalist hands when Bristol was taken, and was offered a commission. He ended the war in Raglan Castle, where the Somersets had maintained a strong garrision since 1642. Joseph Wagstaffe, the youngest son of a Warwickshire gentleman was, like Pretty, a professional soldier who, somewhat unusually, had served in French armies until 1642, when he returned to London and was commissioned as a lieutenant-colonel. He was captured in January 1643 and offered a regiment, which he accepted. A man of 'jollity and mirth' and 'generally beloved', he rose to the rank of Major General and was knighted in 1644. Captured in 1646, he escaped prison in London and went back into French service, but was heavily involved in the planned rising of 1655 in the West Country, where he fought and was defeated in March.[127] In June 1643 Major Horatio Cary abandoned Sir William Waller and went over to the King. He, too, was a professional soldier and had served in Ireland under the Royalist Colonel Joseph Bampfield, reputedly an 'Irishman' but more than likely a planter. Cary, who was knighted at some stage in the war, became a brigade commander and fought as such at Naseby, did not compound, and was in arms again in 1648.[128] Colonel George Barnes, according to Edmund Ludlow,

was brother to an honest gentleman who was chaplain to my father . . . for whose sake and because he had the reputation of being an old soldier, a thing much valued by Parliament at that time, my father had procured him a considerable employment in their service, in which he continued as long as their constant pay lasted, but that failing, he ran away to the King.[129]

Were it not for Ludlow's memory of Colonel Barnes we should have known very little indeed beyond the bare facts (such as they are) of his military service. Like Pretty, Wagstaffe, Cary and other side-changers, Barnes was a professional soldier, and Ludlow's attitude to him shows what Ludlow himself thought of such men. But the King's service can have been no more, and was inevitably in the long run a good deal less, lucrative than the Parliament's. Barnes's constancy, however, was unflagging, and his son and heir was killed serving with him in 1644 near Lyme Regis. Whilst, therefore, it can be argued that those who went over to the King (excepting Cholmeley, Peterborough and men of lesser military rank) were predominantly career soldiers who may have supposed they could foretell the war's inevitable end in 1643 and acted from self-interest, what is quite baffling is their constancy thereafter. If they were not motivated at first by conscience or principle, did they become part of a Royalist spirit that overcame their more mercenary inclinations? For those who went from the King to Parliament were, without exception amongst the colonels, gentlemen of standing who may well, in 1644, 1645 and 1646, have acted from self and family interest. Few of those took up arms against their former colleagues.

Duncombe's and Brandling's desertion of the King has already been mentioned.[130] Brandling, who went over to Parliament's northern army in July 1644, actively commanded troops against his former comrades in arms, earning general and widespread opprobrium in the process. Others who turned their sword against the Royalists were Colonel Robert Keys, who was plotting to go over with his regiment early in 1644, and ended up with a commission to raise a new regiment for Parliament,[131] Colonel Roger Lort of Stackpoole Court in Pembrokeshire, who went to London in 1644 after the disgrace of Lord Carbery, and returned to South Wales armed with a new commission,[132] and Colonel Anthony Ashley-Cooper of Dorset, who abandoned the King's cause in January 1644 and became Field Marshal General in his county for the Parliament thereafter. Yet, of these three, Keys was goaled in 1647 for plotting against Parliament, and Lort was accused by Rowland Laugharne of bestowing 'himself in disgorging private rancker and malice', serving the interests of his former Royalist neighbours, and having become 'a subtle ambo-dexter'.[133]

Of all those who abandoned the King, the clearest apparent motivation can be ascribed to Colonel Sir Edward Deering of Surrinden in Kent, whose complex shifts in association whilst an MP for his county in the Long Parliament have been noted by historians. A contemporary view of his parliamentary behaviour must have prepared one observer, at least, for his about-face:

I must confesse itt did ever runne in my head that Sir Edward Deereing has so used to turne round in his Studie that hee would doe the like in the Parliament House. Pray god his much turning hath not made his head dazie, and that hee doth not turne out of his right witts.[134]

Deering was not commissioned as a colonel until 2 July 1643, but he made every effort to recruit a regiment, until a summons to the Oxford parliament put an end to field command. It was whilst he was at Oxford, he was to tell the Commons in 1644, that he became disillusioned with the King: 'since the cessation in Ireland, and seeing so many papists and Irish rebels in the king's army and the anti-parliament set up at Oxford, and the King's councils wholly governed by the popish party' he found that his 'conscience would not permit him to stay longer'.[135] A Royalist, however, reckoned Deering went over to the enemy because his request to be made sheriff of Kent was spurned.[136] This is not to deny Deering a genuine change of heart, but it will not escape notice that the motives which he presented to the Commons for having abandoned the King were, if correctly reported, a mere recapitulation of Parliament's own propaganda, telling them what they were telling the country at large. Nothing in what Deering said evidences any personal crisis of conscience, unless he were taken in by Parliament's own propaganda. The cynical Royalist view of the 'knave' may have been nearer to the truth at least in spirit. He certainly had no chance to prove his change of heart, dying in July 1644 of 'an apostume'.[137]

Others who chose to go over to the Parliament and in so doing materially assisted in its victory without actually fighting for it (and to be distinguished from those who merely surrendered) included Colonel Piers Edgecumbe of Cornwall, cited earlier, who was in arms against the Royalists in 1648; Colonel Sir Thomas Hanmer, baronet, of Hanmer in Flintshire and with property at Isleworth in Middlesex; and Sir Trevor Williams, baronet, of Llangibby in Monmouthshire. Hanmer, whose wife was maid-of-honour to the Queen, appears to have been motivated by the way the war was going and disappointment, like Deering, in personal ambition. In November 1645 he petitioned that he had been forced into arms in 1642, at Shrewsbury, presumably the last place to be if a gentleman wished to avoid involvement in the King's cause. He was also, at that date, Cup-bearer to the King and so either in favour or kept close for other reasons. Hanmer's change of heart was, however, complete, and he used his power in North Wales against the Royalists in 1648, though he did not take up arms for the Parliament before then.[138] Sir Trevor Williams's behaviour is altogether more complex. He was commissioned in March 1643 as a colonel and involved in the defeat sustained by the Raglan forces at Highnam Bridge in Gloucestershire that month, but was released and commissioned anew in July. There was yet a third commission in January 1644. In July 1645 he was noted as commanding sixty men at his house, but by September the King had ordered his arrest. Williams appears to have been saved by the Somersets of Raglan, and in October, 'not at all the honester', had raised forces in what appears to have been a neutralist movement with 'shewes of being for the parliament'. A 'dangerous' man full 'of craft and subtlety, very bold and resolute', it may be that Colonel Williams, seeing the way the war was going, looked to his own interest; he may also, like many Welsh Royalists, have been offended by the command Charles Gerard exercised in South Wales. The sincerity of Williams's change of coat, however, may be gauged by his involvement in the 1648 rising against the government.[139]

The other side-changers who opted for Parliament were Colonels Thomas Glynne of Glynliffon, Caernarvonshire, in 1643; Colonel Howell Gwinne of Llanbrayn, Carmarthenshire, in 1646; and William Williams of Vaynol, Caernarvonshire, in 1645. None of them fought against the Royalists, and as for Howell Gwinne, he was accused of declaring in 1646, 'Heigh God, heigh Devil, I will be for the stronger side.'[140] Included amongst the side-changers must probably be Richard Vaughan Earl of Carbery, whose disgrace in 1644 led to his search for accommodation with Parliament through the good offices of their then champion, Rowland Laugharne. The leniency of his treatment recognised both his influence and his change of heart, and Vaughan's assistance to the Parliament thenceforth did not even waver in 1648, when his debt to Laugharne was not enough to bring him back into the field for the King.

Suspicions as to the loyalty of five other colonels were at some point in the war widely entertained. Colonel Thomas Blague, a Suffolk gentleman who was governor of Wallingford, was rumoured in 1644 to be contemplating going over to the enemy with his troops.[141] Colonel Sir Thomas Gower of Stittenham in Yorkshire, whose first wife had been a Howard of Naworth, was sheriff of his county in 1642. It was alleged then that he 'first invited Hotham to sally out of Hull', and rumour had it that this caused his dismissal as sheriff and replacement by Colonel Sir Richard Hutton of Goldsborough. Hutton and Gower were soldiering together in 1645, in which year Gower was captured at Rowton Heath and Hutton killed at Sherburn in Elmet.[142] The attitude to him in 1642 appears to have been based upon his political attitudes of 1640/41 and nothing more substantial than that. Colonel Henry Hunks of Warwickshire (but resident in Devonshire), who had both a Royalist brother (Colonel Fulk Hunks) and a Parliamentarian brother (Colonel Hercules Hunks), was accused of conniving with the enemy in 1643 to surrender Banbury to them, only a few months after being knighted by the King. Discharged from his commands, he sat through a court of inquiry which exonerated him, and he was reinstated in November.[143] Much the same thing befell Colonel Richard Feilding, who was accused of betraying Reading to the enemy in 1643 but who was likewise exonerated.[144] His case was not comparable with that of Lieutenant Colonel Francis Windebank, who was shot by firing squad in 1645 for dereliction of duty in the face of the enemy besieging Bletchingdon House. Windebank was accused not of treachery but of cowardice. The fifth suspect, Henry Wilmot, is discussed elsewhere.[145]

Abandonment of the King's cause in the closing months of the war by army colonels was not commonplace, and such cases must be distinguished from the surrenders of beaten men. In only a few instances can it be shown that the side-change was anything other than temporary, convenient expedience. This contrasts with the resolution shown for the King's proceedings by those, largely professional, colonels who came over from the Parliament in 1643.

VII

This chapter has subjected to scrutiny Lord Gerard's remarks of 1663 about the social status of those who maintained the cause of King Charles I. Applying his observations to the King's regimental colonels, it has been shown that Gerard underestimated the contribution of the peerage to that specific level of command, whilst conceding the justice of his praise of the 'gentry'. It has been argued that it is not merely to the individual's commitment that attention should be paid, but to the individual as part of a familial involvement and often as but one of a number of representatives from related and like-minded families. It has shown that there was very little difference between the degree of familial commitment amongst the *nobiles minores* and amongst their social superiors, just as numerous of them experienced the chronic financial crises involved in defeat, sequestration and the compounding procedures. The experience of civil war for holders of hereditary titles and their families was no different, unless occasionally in degree, from that of untitled and mere gentlemen. Nor, it has been shown, did military service seriously break down the distinction between the *minores* and *majores* by permitting uncontrolled movement by the former into the world of the latter: that knighthoods were the preferred means of rewarding distinguished conduct in the field or for the cause in general is clear, whereas elevations to newly created peerages were exceptional and very rarely came the way of gentlemen. Gerard was one of a handful of exceptions to the general rule.

Oglander's view of the King's supporters as 'bullets of gold' expended in a war against their social inferiors has been shown, in his terms, to have been accurate. The *nobiles minores* and *nobiles majores* accounted for 90 per cent of the regimental commanders: the *minores* for 67 per cent, the *majores* for 23 per cent, showing that a clear majority of them were untitled gentlemen or knights at the time they were commissioned into the King's armies. To test Oglander's view more fully, it would be necessary to possess evidence for the Parliament's regimental commanders similar to that which has been sought for their Royalist counterparts. Such a comparative study, beyond the scope of the present work, would be a test of Waller's belief that, when the war began, very few gentlemen (in the broadest sense of the word, perhaps) felt able or inclined to adopt the Parliament's cause as their own. The point has been made earlier, that it was easier for a man to identify with the King than with the many-headed Parliament, and that it was precisely that ability to identify with the King and the King's readiness to confide in his subjects which was the fundamental strength of Royalism and of the Royalists. It was not an ideological matter but a common interest, perceived by the King and his supporters to be so. The point has already been stressed[146] that the presence in the King's armies of colonels and other officers of wide military experience does not invalidate the view of those armies as gentry-led and gentry-raised. It is now obvious that military accomplishments were as much a part of many gentlemen's 'education' as the conventional progress through university and the Inns of Court or the Temple: some gentlemen pursued a military life in much the same way as others pursued the law, without ever losing their gentility or the fact of their background and status in their localities. That is why any analysis of the King's officer corps, whether it be at regimental or other command level, would be wrong to include a category of 'professional soldiers' which might be taken to imply that those comprised within it would be soldiers of fortune. It is surely one of the most startling truths about the English civil war that there were enough committed Englishmen and Welshmen on either side to maintain the war for the length of time it lasted.

Ten per cent of the colonels cannot readily be classified as belonging to the untitled gentry, and this includes a figure of thirty-two whose precise social status remains elusive, though some of them may well have been mere or parochial gentlemen. This group includes the Irishman (a vague term in the 1640s) Joseph Bampfield, whose precise surname even is in doubt: it was said of him, by those who mistrusted him, that he changed his name from Bamford to Bampfield to imply a connection with the Devonshire Parliamentarian Sir John Bampfield, baronet, of Poltimore,[147] though why he should have done so escapes reason. Other colonels of uncertain social status include John Barnard, killed at Canon Frome in Herefordshire in 1645,[148] Henry Crow, possibly a Carmarthensire man who, it would appear in 1660, had no form of income whatsoever,[149] Robert Harris of Devonshire, for whom the evidence seems to imply minor parochial status, nothing more,[150] Thomas Pert, who was knighted in 1643 when already a colonel, and who was killed near Bodmin in March 1646,[151] and Henry Tillier, Major General of Foot under Prince Rupert in 1644, who appears to have come from nowhere and to have disappeared into France in 1648.[152]

Given the social structure of regimental command, it might be a fruitless search to try to identify plebeian colonels, but they do appear to have been there, though it is necessary to define the word 'plebeian'. The term is taken here to apply to all those below the status of gentleman, whether defined by that inferiority – for example, in the use of the word 'ignobilis' – or described in terms of a trade or other means of livelihood. Technically speaking, this would necessarily include any colonel described as a merchant. However, as with the case of Colonel Marmaduke Rawdon, such a classification is misleading. Rawdon was the son of a Yorkshire gentleman who, by common usage, was styled 'esquire': his mother was the daughter of a merchant trading to Bordeaux. Rawdon was apprenticed in London to the clothworking trade, and met and married the daughter of a Hertfordshire gentleman, Thomas Thorogood, through which marriage he came to be seated at Hoddesdon. Rawdon was sixty in 1642, an alderman of London, and had been MP for Aldburgh in Suffolk in 1628. He may be seen as a not untypical example of a country gentleman by birth who, through trade, restored himself to his original gentility, in which case he may be more properly designated as a gentleman when commissioned. From 1643, when he was knighted by the King, it mattered little, anyway.[153] In the case of Thomas Colston of Bristol, however, there is every reason to suppose that when he was commissioned he was still engaged in trade: moreover, nothing appears to be known of his social origins. That he was sheriff of the city in 1629/30 is evidenced, and as a JP he was demoted in 1645 by Parliament.[154] A more curious case is that of Colonel Thomas Sandys.

There is a possibility that Sandys was admitted to Grays Inn in 1639, when he was styled as of Northborne in Kent.[155] He may also have been the son of Robert Sandys of Baynard Castle Ward in London but, if so, then the great-grandson of Edwin Sandys Archbishop of York.[156] It is almost certain that at some time between 1642 and 1646 Sandys was knighted (he was granted a baronetcy as well in 1662/63), whilst references to him indicate that he was a London merchant. The clue may lie in a duel fought in France in 1647 between Sandys and another former Royalist officer, a French adventurer called Saint-Michel. Sandys and Saint-Michel were both wounded, but their seconds shot each other to death, and Sandys's second was Colonel Ambrose Jennings, a Birmingham-born London innkeeper described as 'ignobilis'.[157] The association of Sandys and Jennings may reasonably be supposed to have reached back prior to the war, and Jennings's social status, or lack of it, seems clearly established. The duel was fought over Sandys's refusal to sign an IOU for gambling debts due to Saint-Michel, or, rather, Sandys's refusal to sign on the grounds that he could not write. He may have been avoiding his obligation, or it may have been true: if so, he can hardly have been the Grays Inn student of 1639 or, it may be supposed, the great-grandson of an archbishop. Sandys remains, therefore, unclassifiable.[158]

Ambrose Jennings is readily identified as plebian, as is Colonel Sigismund Beeton, described by one who knew him as a 'shoemaker's son'.[159] Beeton was promoted by the Earl of Newcastle and was for a time governor of Newcastle's principal residence, Welbeck in Nottinghamshire, but was killed in action in Lincolnshire in July 1643. Colonel Thomas Hooper, knighted in 1644, was a man of 'mean Education and small Extraction' but that may mean merely parochial gentry.[160] Hooper's knighthood was due to the Earl of Cleveland, who regarded him as a protégé, and Sir Thomas became in due course colonel of Prince Rupert's Dragoons. In 1648 he disappears from the record, imprisoned as a Royalist insurrectionary.

Plebeian origins may also be attributed to Colonel Richard Page, who rose through the ranks in the prestigious regiment of Colonel Sir William Pennyman of Marske in Yorkshire. Pennyman was an early associate of the court, and when sitting as MP for Richmond in the Commons not only opposed Strafford's trial but openly visited Sir John Byron when he was a prisoner under Parliament's disfavour.[161] Pennyman appointed Page as his major; where Page came from is entirely unknown, though the rank of major was not unusually assocated with soldiers of experience. When Pennyman died in Oxford in August 1643 the regiment passed to a cousin, James Pennyman of Ormesby, who had previously been its lieutenant-colonel, and Page stepped up a rank under him. Colonel Sir James Pennyman (knighted in 1642) resigned his command in 1644 and went into Europe, whereupon Page assumed regimental command and was knighted the following year for his part in the storm of Leicester. A grant of arms ensued. Page remained active for the cause well into the 1650s, but died in a debtors' prison in Paris before 1659. Page's obscurity, the lack of ascertainable evidence about his background, suggests low social status, though the grant of arms could equally well have been made to a mere parochial gentleman as to a plebeian. The mystery surrounding Page will probably never be resolved: he is best classified as of unknown status, but plebeian origins are not out of the question.

The brothers George and Sebastian Boncle (the name is also rendered as Bunkly) were sons of an 'official' at the court of King James I, and came from Greenwich in Kent. George, the elder brother, was described as a professional musician, whilst his father's precise standing is unclear. However, in 1640 he was a Groom of the Bedchamber to the Prince of Wales, implying gentility, which gentility was confirmed by his knighthood in 1645. He died of wounds, imprisoned in London after Naseby, and his younger brother (who escaped Naseby and became colonel in the other's place) died in European service some time after 1651.[162] The assumption of mere gentry status in both instances seems valid, but George Boncle's musicianship suggests that he taught or played (or both) for fees: he may, therefore, if such a categorisation means anything at all, be assigned to that of 'entertainer'. He was certainly no mean soldier, fighting at Edgehill, in the storm of Bristol where Slanning, Buck, Trevanion and Grandison fell, and commanding cavalry which relieved Basing House in September 1644. His brother served with him as his subordinate.

It would therefore seem, to follow Oglander's turn of expression, that, amongst the 'bullets of gold' in regimental command, the King was also firing 'bullets of lead'. Yet their contribution at that level of command was minimal. Had the King's cause been insufficiently supported by the gentry matters might have been otherwise. As it was, Gerard was right: the King's cause was constantly maintained by the *nobiles,* whether *minores* or *majores.* The rest were mere auxiliaries.

Notes

1 This chapter represents findings based upon the 603 colonels identified for the period 1642–46. The great majority of those mentioned in what follows are in my *Royalist Officers.* I have cited the references therein, and additional references, where the treatment of a specific officer requires it, but have not cited a reference for straightforward allusion to an individual.

2 F. Bamford (ed.), *A Royalist's Notebook: the Commonplace Book of Sir John Oglander,* New York, 1971, p. 109.

3 T. Ellison Gibson (ed.), *Crosby Records: a Cavalier's Notebook,* 1880, p. 264

4 G. Bernard (ed.), Walsingham's Life of Sir John Digby, 1605–1645, *Camden Society,* XII, 1910, p. 98.

5 Sir William Waller, *Vindication of the Character and Conduct of Sir William Waller Kt,* 1793, pp. 108–9.

6 Macray, *Clarendon's Rebellion,* III, pp. 20–1.

7 *Ibid.,* p. 110.

8 *Ibid.,* p. 113.

9 Loftis, *Halkett and Fanshaw Memoirs,* p. 117. Newman, *Royalist Officers,* p. 343.

10 Newman, *Royalist Officers,* p. 378.

11 I am grateful to Professor Mark Fissel for allowing me to read the typescript of his forthcoming *The Bishops' Wars: Charles I's Campaigns against Scotland, 1638–1640,* Cambridge, 1993.

12 Newman, *Royalist Officers,* p. 47. J. and G. F. Matthews (eds.), *Abstract of Probate Acts in the Prerogative Court of Canterbury, 1645–1649,* 1906, p. 88. Coates, Young and Snow, *Private Journals,* pp. 244, 413.

13 Newman, *Royalist Officers,* p. 393.

14 J. F. Curwen, *A History of the Ancient House of Curwen,* Kendal, 1928, p. 148.

15 Newman, *Royalist Officers,* p. 96.

16 CCC, p. 549.

17 Knowles Middleton, *Relazione d'Inghilterra,* pp. 83–4.

18 Whitelock, *Memorials,* I, p. 171.

19 D Gardiner (ed.), *The Oxinden Letters, 1607–42,* 1933, p. 301.

20 *Ibid.*
21 Whitelock, *Memorials*, I, p. 174.
22. Macray, *Clarendon's Rebellion*, II, pp. 109–11.
23 Newman, *Royalist Officers*, p.128, CCC, p. 1371.
24 CAM, p. 1423. F. G. Marsh, *The Godolphins*, private press, 1930, pp. 20–5, corrects the identification of William Godolphin given in Newman, *Royalist Officers*, p. 159. John Godolphin does not appear in *Royalist Officers*. CCC, pp. 336, 1587.
25 Newman, *Royalist Officers*, p. 265. CAM, p. 483.
26 Newman, *Royalist Officers*, p. 285.
27 Newman, *Royalist Officers*, p. 295. CAM, p. 1159. HMC, Bath Mss, II, 1907, p. 121.
28 Newman, *Royalist Officers*, p. 296. CCC, p. 1358.
29 Newman, *Royalist Officers*, p. 349. CAM, pp. 42, 436, 1233. Whitelock, *Memorials*, I, p. 311. CCC, p. 1035.
30 Newman, *Royalist Officers*, pp. 69–70. CCC, p. 21. S. R. Gardiner (ed.), The Hamilton Papers, *Camden Society*, new series, 27, 1880, p. 167.
31 Newman, *Royalist Officers*, p. 248. R. Hovenden (ed.), Visitation of the County of Kent, 1619–1621, *Harleian Society*, XLII, 1898, p. 191.
32 Newman, *Royalist Officers*, pp. 258–9. CCC, pp. 21, 46, 85, 120, 739, 1140.
33 Newman, *Royalist Officers*, p. 71. CCC, pp. 60, 100, 103, 112, 120. CAM, p. 1422.
34 Hutton, *Royalist War Effort*, pp. 68–75.
35 Newman, *Royalist Officers*, p. 306. HMC, *Thirteenth Report*, I, Portland Mss, I, 1891, p. 353. Coates, Young and Snow, *Private Journals*, p. 351.
36 Newman, *Royalist Officers*, p. 11. CCC, pp. 89, 1876–7. CAM, pp. 1021–2. HMC, *Fourth Report*, I Denbigh Mss, 1874, p. 273.
37 Newman, *Royalist Officers*, p. 243. CCC, pp. 1716–7. *Lords Journals*, V, p. 48.
38 Newman, 'King's servants', pp. 230, 232.
39 C. Severn (ed.), *The Diary of the Reverend John Ward*, 1839, pp. 91–2.
40 Newman, *Royalist Officers*, pp. 26, 27. Warwick, *Memoires*, pp. 228–9. HMC, *Report on the Mss of Reginald Rawdon Hastings*, II, 1930, p. 135. CAM, p. 518.
41 CCC, p. 1799.
42 Newman, *Royalist Officers*, pp. 65–6. G. Isham (ed.), The Correspondence of Bishop Brian Duppa and Sir Justinian Isham, 1650–1660, *Northamptonshire Record Society*, XVII, 1951, p. 170.
43 Warwick, *Memoires*, p. 255.
44 Newman, *Royalist Officers*, p. 80.
45 Warwick, *Memoires*, p. 256.
46 Newman, *Royalist Officers*, pp. 80, 321–2. CCC, pp. 261, 3272.
47 CAM, p. 153.
48 Newman, *Royalist Officers*, pp. 403–4. Long, Diary, p. 102. HMC, *Fifteenth Report*, Appendix, II, Hodgkin Mss, 1897, p. 113. CAM, p. 153
49 Newman, *Royalist Officers*, p. 404.
50 Newman, *Royalist Officers*, p. 274. HMC, Eighth *Report*, Appendix, II, Manchester Mss, 1881, p. 59.
51 Newman, *Royalist Officers*, p. 183. CCC, pp. 312, 376.
52 Newman, *Royalist Officers*, p. 320. CCC, p. 93.
53 Hutton, *War Effort, passim.*
54 Newman, *Royalist Officers*, pp. 228–9. HMC, *Second Report*, Lyttleton Mss,

1871, p. 36.

55 Newman, *Royalist Officers*, p. 126. G. W. Marshall (ed.), Le Neve's Pedigrees of the Knights, *Harleian Society*, VIII, 1873, p. 7. CCC, pp. 92, 239, 443, 494.
56 Newman, *Royalist Officers*, p. 115. CCC, p. 2804.
57 Newman, *Royalist Officers*, p. 336. CCC, pp. 67, 108, 159, 205, 207, 472, 608.
58 R. T. Spence, *Skipton Castle in the Great Civil War*, Otley, 1991.
59 Newman, *Royalist Officers*, pp. 199–202. CCC, pp. 879–80, 1967–71. *Calendar of State Papers, Domestic*, 1663–64, p. 93. Coates, Young and Snow, *Private Journals*, p. 66. CAM, p. 436.
60 CCC, pp. 2671–4. CAM, p. 1237. Spence, *Skipton Castle*, p. 7. R. N. Dore (ed.), The Letter Books of Sir William Brereton, I, *Record Society of Lancashire and Cheshire*, 123, 1984, p. 164.
61 Newman, *Royalist Officers*, pp. 199–201. CCC, pp. 99. 124, 232, 431, 585, 696.
62 For Villiers see Newman, *Royalist Officers*, p. 392. HMC, Bath Mss, II, 1907, p. 165. HMC, *Fifth Report*, I, Report and Appendix, Sutherland Mss, 1876, p. 154. For Howard, Newman, *Royalist Officers*, p. 200. Warwick, *Memoires*, p. 166. CCC, p. 1573.
63 Newman, *Royalist Officers*, p. 21. J. Moone, 'A Brief Relation of the Life and Memoirs of John Lord Belasyse', in HMC, *Ormonde Mss*, new series, II, 1903, pp. 379–81.
64 HMC, *Rawdon Hastings Mss*, p. 107.
65 *Ibid.*, p. 121.
66 CCC, p. 1678. CAM, pp. 1398–9.
67 George Lord Digby is considered at greater length in Chapter Three, below.
68 Newman, *Royalist Officers*, p. 111. CCC, pp. 67, 91, 98, 523, 588, 1303–8. CAM, p. 1451. Coates, Young and Snow, *Private Journals*, p. 367.
69 Lord Caernarvon is discussed in Chapter Three below, Somerset in Chapter Four.
70 Dore, Brereton Letter Books, II, 1990, p. 424.
71 Newman, *Royalist Officers*, p. 16. A. R. Maddison (ed.), Lincolnshire Pedigrees, I, *Harleian Society*, L, 1902, p. 79.
72 Newman, *Royalist Officers*, p. 57. CCC, p. 21. Crofts is in Newman, *Royalist Officers*, p. 93. *Commons Journals*, V, p. 169. CCC, p. 616. Coates, *Journal of Simond D'Ewes*, p. 149. Coates, Young and Snow, *Private Journals*, p. 391.
73 For Aston see Chapter Four, below.
74 For Crane see Newman, *Royalist Officers*, p. 91. Widdrington is discussed in Chapter Four, below.
75 CCC, p. 49.
76 Newman, *Royalist Officers*, p. 182.
77 Coates, *Journal of Simond D'Ewes*, p. 263.
78 HMC, *Fifteenth Report*, Appendix, VII, Somerset Mss, 1898, p. 79. *Ibid.*, Hodgkin Mss, 1898, p. 99. CCC, p. 114. Newman, *Royalist Officers*, p. 395.
79 See Chapter Three, below.
80 Dore, Brereton Letter Books, I, p. 164.
81 L. M. Baker (ed.), *The Letters of Elizabeth Queen of Bohemia*, 1953, pp. 280–1. Newman, *Royalist Officers*, pp. 388–9. Coates, *Journal of Simond D'Ewes*, p. 110. Coates, Young and Snow, *Private Journals*, p. 181. Whitelock, *Memorials*, I, p. 530. HMC, *Thirteenth Report*, Appendix, I, Portland Mss, I, 1891, p. 296. HMC, *Fifteenth Report*, Hodgkin Mss, 1897, p. 113. CAM, p. 1361.
82 Dr Hutton covers Vavasour's war service in *War Effort*, pp. 112–19 and *passim*.

83 Parsons, *Slingsby Diary*, p. 123 *et seq.*
84 CCC, pp. 214, 1898–1904. CAM, p. 305. Newman, *Royalist Officers*, pp. 304, 262–3.
85 Newman, *Royalist Officers*, pp. 277–8. CCC, pp. 93, 105, 1059. HMC, *Mss in Various Collections*, I, Records of Quarter Sessions in Wiltshire, 1901, p. 106.
86 Wilmot is discussed in Chapter Three, below.
87 Newman, *Royalist Officers*, p. 55. CCC, pp. 1205, 3245. CAM, p. 1343. D. A. Pennington, and I. A. Roots (eds.), *The Committee of Stafford, 1643–1645*, Manchester, 1957, p. 34. Dore, Brereton Letter Books, I, p. 84. HMC, *Fourteenth Report*, Appendix, VII, Ormonde Mss, I, 1895, p. 186.
88 Coates, Young and Snow, *Private Journals*, pp. 37, 353.
89 L. B. Larking (ed.), Proceedings [in] the County of Kent, *Camden Society*, 1861, p. 68.
90 Newman, *Royalist Officers*, p. 54. CCC, pp. 138, 633, 3258.
91 A. C. Wood (ed.), Gervase Holles' Memorials of the Holles Family, 1641–52, *Camden Society*, second series, LV, 1937, p. 188.
92 HMC, *Rawdon Hastings Mss*, p. 111. Newman, *Royalist Officers*, p. 56. See also Chapter Three, below. Oddly, in 1660 his widow stated that her husband had 'fallen at Hopton Heath', where he was most certainly wounded but not killed, see CSPD 1660–61, pp. 256–8.
93 Newman, *Royalist Officers*, p. 56. HMC, *Thirteenth Report*, Portland Mss, 1891, I, p. 487.
94 Newman, *Royalist Officers*, p. 359–61. HMC, *Thirteenth Report*, Portland Mss, 1891, p. 322. CAM, p. 1202.
95 Newman, *Royalist Officers*, pp. 345–7.
96 Newman, *Royalist Officers*, p. 83. CCC, pp. 247, 280, 351, 426, 430, 534, 1689. M. A. Faraday (ed.), Herefordshire Militia Assessments of 1663, *Camden Society*, fourth series, 10, 1972, p. 60.
97 Newman, *Royalist Officers*, pp. 5–7. CCC, pp. 117, 335, 382, 387, 487, 515–6, 522, 2020. Mary Coate, *Cornwall in the Great Civil War*, 1933, p. 106, reckoned William to have been a full colonel by 4 June 1643. William Arundell is in CCC, pp. 91, 254, 269.
98 CCC, pp. 89, 1814. CAM, p. 420.
99 Newman, *Royalist Officers*, pp. 13–14. HMC, *Fourteenth Report*, Ormode Mss, I, 1895, p. 122. R. Josten (ed.), *Elias Ashmole*, 5 vols, consecutively paginated, p. 349. HMC, *Rawdon Hastings Mss*, p. 109, CSPD 1660–61, p. 296.
100 J. Fetherston (ed.), The Visitation of the County of Warwickshire . . . 1619, *Harleian Society*, XII, 1877, p. 74. Newman, *Royalist Officers*, p. 4.
101 Newman, *Royalist Officers*, p. 90. CCC, p. 787. CAM, p. 467.
102 Newman, *Royalist Officers*, pp. 124–5. HMC, *Twelth Report*, Appendix, IV, Rutland Mss, I, 1888, pp. 516–7. CCC, pp. 107, 2744. CAM, p. 656, 1320.
103 Newman, *Royalist Officers*, p. 125. G. D. Squibb (ed.), Visitation of Derbyshire, 1662–1664, *Harleian Society*, new series, 8, 1989, p. 121. CAM, p. 1436.
104 Newman, *Royalist Officers*, p. 84. W. C. Metcalfe (ed.), The Visitation of the County of Essex 1634, *Harleian Society*, XIII, XIV, 1878, p. 381. HMC, *Tenth Report*, Appendix, IV, Stewart Mss, 1885, p. 92.
105 Newman, *Royalist Officers*, p. 249.
106 Newman, *Royalist Officers*, p. 85. CCC, pp. 205, 325, 623, 735.
107 Newman, *Royalist Officers*, p. 196. CCC, p. 1478. Long, Symonds' Diary, p. 196.

108 Newman, *Royalist Officers*, p. 327. CCC, pp. 203, 2457. HMC, *Thirteenth Report*, Portland Mss, I, 1891, p. 33.
109 Newman, *Royalist Officers*, p. 23. CCC, pp. 46, 62, 137–8, 510, 520–1, 1867. CAM, p. 1380.
110 Newman, *Royalist Officers*, p. 198. CCC, p. 2724.
111 Newman, *Royalist Officers*, p. 71. CAM, p. 1342. HMC, *Fifteenth Report*, Hodgkin Mss, 1897, p. 103. HMC, *Fourth Report*, I, De La Warr Mss, 1874, p. 296.
112 HMC, *Fourth Report*, I, House of Lords Mss, 1874, p. 53.
113 *Ibid.*, De La Warr Mss, 1874, p. 296.
114 Newman, *Royalist Officers*, p. 145. CAM, p. 962.
115 See Chapter Three, below.
116 Squibb, Derbyshire Visitation, pp. 117–8.
117 Pennington and Roots, *Stafford Committee*, p. 225.
118 Newman, *Royalist Officers*, p. 340. CCC, pp. 122, 750.
119 James Sutherland (ed.), *Lucy Hutchinson's Memoirs of the Life of Colonel Hutchinson*, Oxford, 1973, is the best edition.
120 Norman Dore's edition of the Brereton Letter Books, *op. cit.*, is one of the most consummate works of scholarship in local and national studies in the last fifty years.
121 Newman, *Royalist Officers*, p. 312. W. Greenwood, *The Redmans of Levens and Harewood*, Kendal, 1905, p. 167.
122 Russell, *Causes of the Civil War*, p. 20.
123 Newman, *Royalist Officers*, p. 87. CCC, pp. 398, 1945.
124 See above, Chapter One.
125 For Cholmeley see above, Chapter One. For Mordaunt see Chapter Three below.
126 Newman, *Royalist Officers*, p. 71. CCC, pp. 1879, 2691.
127 Newman, *Royalist Officers*, pp. 305, 394. For Wagstaffe also, Fetherston, Visitation of Warwickshire, p. 289. A. Clark (ed.), *The Life and Times of Anthony Wood*, Oxford, 1891, p. 195. Whitelock, *Memorials*, I, p. 201. HMC, *Fourteenth Report*, Ormonde Mss, I, 1895, p. 122.
128 Newman, *Royalist Officers*, p. 64. HMC, *Fourteenth Report*, Ormonde Mss, I, 1895, p. 123.
129 C. H. Firth (ed.), *The Memoirs of Edmund Ludlow, 1625–1672*, I, Oxford, 1894, p. 62.
130 See above, Chapter One.
131 Newman, *Royalist Officers*, pp. 214–5.
132 Newman, *Royalist Officers*, p. 237.
133 HMC, *Thirteenth Report*, Portland Mss, I, 1891, pp. 270, 338. CAM. p. 1019.
134 Gardiner, *Oxinden Letters*, p. 296.
135 Whitelock, *Memorials*, I, p. 238. Firth, *Ludlow Memoirs*, pp. 85–6.
136 HMC, *Rawdon Hastings Mss*, p. 118.
137 Sir H. Ellis (ed.), The Obituary of Richard Smith, *Camden Society*, 1848, p. 21.
138 Newman, *Royalist Officers*, p. 175. Marshall, Le Neve's Pedigrees, p. 104. CCC, p. 943. CAM, p. 271.
139 Newman, *Royalist Officers*, p. 414. CCC, p. 2947.
140 Newman, *Royalist Officers*, p. 171. CAM, pp. 730–1.
141 For Blague see below, Chapter Three.
142 Newman, *Royalist Officers*, p. 163. HMC, *Fifth Report*, Sutherland Mss, 1876,

p. 142. CCC, p. 1043.
143 Newman, *Royalist Officers*, p. 205.
144 Newman, *Royalist Officers*, p. 130. Coates, Young and Snow, *Private Journals*, p. 181. HMC, *Tenth Report*, Stewart Mss, 1895, p. 69.
145 See Chapter Three, below.
146 See the discussion in the Introduction, above.
147 Newman, *Royalist Officers*, pp. 15–16. HMC, *Thirteenth Report*, Portland Mss, I, 1891, p. 65.
148 Newman, *Royalist Officers*, p. 17. HMC, *Rawdon Hastings Mss*, pp. 111, 135–6. This may also be CCC, p. 501.
149 Newman, *Royalist Officers*, p. 96.
150 *Ibid.*, p. 177. CCC, p. 153.
151 Newman, *Royalist Officers*, p. 293.
152 *Ibid.*, p. 373. Whitelock, *Memorials*, I, p. 433. CCC, p. 2862.
153 Newman, *Royalist Officers*, p. 311.
154 *Ibid.*, p. 78.
155 J. Foster (ed.), *The Register of Admissions to Grays Inn*, 1889, p. 221.
156 J. J. Howard (ed.), The Visitation of London, II, 1633/35, *Harleian Society*, XVII, 1883, p. 228.
157 Newman, *Royalist Officers*, p. 210. Howard, Visitation of London, p. 9, may refer.
158 Newman, *Royalist Officers*, p. 329. Knowles Middleton, *Relazione d'Inghilterra*, p. 84. CCC, p. 190. CAM, p. 1096.
159 Newman, *Royalist Officers*, p. 21. The late Peter Young suggested in conversation with me in 1979 that Beeton may have been a German, but there is apparently nothing to substantiate that. Nor, for that matter, is there proof that he was English.
160 Newman, *Royalist Officers*, pp. 195–6.
161 Newman, *Royalist Officers*, p. 292. Coates, Young and Snow, *Private Journals*, p. 54. HMC, *Tenth Report*, Appendix, IV, Corporation of Bridgnorth Mss, 1885, p. 434. Long, Symonds' Diary, p. 160.
162 Newman, *Royalist Officers*, p. 49.

CHAPTER THREE

'That nice and jealous profession'
Character and personality in regimental command

I

It is in the nature of the historical record that we are able to determine a man's social status, familial position and, often, his religion when we do not know, for example, what manner of man he may have been. This is more than true of the King's colonels, who, for the most part, reveal themselves to us as names to which may be appended circumstances of their lives. As for hair colour, height, fashion of speaking, hesitancy or spontaneity, and all the other factors which determine how we think of living men, the record is most often non-existent. Such pen portraits as have survived are so often the perceptions and opinions of those who, knowing the living man, took much for granted: their illustrations are necessarily limited if not one-sided. Moreover, when it comes to dealing with the personalities and characters of Royalist commanders, we are very much at the mercy of their enemies, whose propaganda machine has often proved so effective that, 350 years on from the events, we tend still to subscribe to unfair and unjust caricatures. The task is to understand the context of characterisation, and to seek to discern whatever rudimentary or substantial truths may be revealed in the tendentious and avowedly or covertly hostile. For example, Clarendon's description of Lord Dunsmore,[1] an early activist against whom he entertained some disliking, can be interpreted in quite another way than that which Clarendon intended.

It is clearly not only in Parliamentarian writings that hostility to certain commanders can be found. Clarendon again, writing of the court of inquiry which exonerated Colonel Richard Feilding from charges of treachery over the surrender of Reading, indicated that even so Feilding's reputation remained sullied: 'So fatal are all misfortunes, and so difficult a thing it is to play an after-game of reputation, in that nice and jealous profession',[2] of arms. Ill feeling between comrades in arms, rivalries and jealousies plagued army command on both sides, and any man's judgement may be distorted by real or imagined affronts. There was also the problem of court gossip. A typical victim of this was the Earl of Newcastle. It was reported to him in April 1643 that a Lady Cornwallis in Oxford had said of him that

you were a sweet general, lay in bed until eleven o'clock and combed till 12, then came to the Queen, and so the work was done and that General King did all the business.[3]

Other critics, less vindictive than Lady Cornwallis, but court-based (such as Sir Philip Warwick), have contributed to what remains a common view of Lord Newcastle amongst historians whose credulity, clearly, cannot always be suspended. The context of Lady Cornwallis's reported remark is relevant: that the earl in April 1643 had the person of the Queen in his care, for whom he had raised an army in the first place. Secondly, one of the functions of a subordinate officer such as James King was that he should undertake routine army business. Newcastle, both general and courtier, under the constraints of two such disparate roles, must meticulously observe the requirements of both. If he was most naturally a court Grandee, nevertheless, two months later he charged on foot with pike in hand at Adwalton Moor and won a sweeping victory. There was more to the earl than mere Grandee, but because he was a Grandee his every action was scrutinised. That was true of all Royalist commanders who made any name for themselves, and some of whom found that their reputations, however well founded, went before them.

The typical Cavalier was a country gentleman approaching or in early middle age, married, with a family and the commensurate burden of responsibilities such a stage in life brings. The 'merry lads' who became the Cavaliers as they have been popularly discerned were atypical: but the nature of their lives and actions laid them open to enemy propaganda, and the efficient machine which served Parliament developed and promoted the myth of the King's supporters as it was for long received: 'The maine Argument which the Enemies have to keepe the people in Rebellion, is, their Declarations to them of the wicked and deboish'd lives of the Cavaleers,' observed Symmons.[4] Men such as George Goring were so much easier to caricature than men such as Sir Henry Slingsby or Sir Nicholas Slanning, representative of so many Royalists the Parliament would have been glad to have had on its side if it could have won them to its cause. It is widely known that the term 'Cavalier' was intended as one of abuse. As Symmons reminded his listeners, 'your enemies call you Cavaliers, a name as they take it of great reproach else you may be sure they would not call you by it'.[5] The word meant the very antithesis of what was respectable: it symbolised irresponsibility and recklessness, with connotations of the outlaw, although not until the eighteenth century did the word enter the language as representative of what was high-handed or contemptuous. In such a sense it remains in use, carrying with it the kernel of Roundhead scorn. Since the Royalists nevertheless assumed the label, it was necessary to redefine the word, to make it, as it were, their own, and to deprive it of its scurrilous overtones. Symmons made the most effective attempt at such a new definition, which cannot be quoted other than in *extenso*:

A Compleat Cavalier is a Child of Honour, a Gentleman well borne and bred, that loves his King for conscience sake, of a clearer countenance, and bolder looke then other men, because of a more Loyall Heart: He dares neither oppose his Princes will, nor yet disgrace his righteous cause, by his carriage or expressions: He is furnished with the qualities, of Piety, Prudence, Justice, Liberality, goodnesse, Honesty; He is amiable in his behaviour, couragious in his undertakings, discreet and gallant in all his executions: he is thoroughly sensible of the least wrong that is offered to his Soveraigne, and is a professed enemy to all Rebells: the aymes of his sword are not only to dissever the malignity of those forces, that have conspired the ruine of Monarchy and Innocency: He fears no evill thing to come upon himselfe, but contemnes all dangers, that looke towards him: He dares accept of deaths challenge to meet it in the field, and yet can embrace it as a speciall freind when it comes into his chamber, where he is allwayes making provision for its better entertainment: in a word, He is the only reserve of English Gentility and ancient valour, and hath rather chose to bury himselfe in the Tombe of Honour, then to see the Nobility of his Nation vassalaged, the Dignity of his Country captivated, or obscured by any base Domestick enemy . . . This is a compleat Cavalier, and if any of you be not according to this Character, beleive mee you are not right, nor the men you ought to be.[6]

The qualities which Symmons defined were those of a Christian and a gentleman: his Cavalier was 'well borne and bred' and was driven by conscience in the defence of his King. He was striving to present a model against which the King's followers might measure themselves, and he was not ignorant of the fact that there were those who fell far short of the ideal, men who were not 'the men you ought to be'. Elsewhere in the sermon he admonished 'Gentlemen and Souldiers' that their 'practice of vice and sinne will both dishonour God, and your selves in that service wherein you are imployed'. Since these Cavaliers were 'better borne and bred than those are, who doe accuse you' they should, naturally, 'walke worthy your imployment'. As for the commanders of soldiers, their task was to punish sin in those under them, since 'in these sad and dismall dayes' there was no more gallant a sight 'then a valiant and religious Souldier'.[7] They were, after all, said Symmons, under an employment put upon them by God: 'you are his Messengers to execute his will'.[8]

Symmons's failure to promote his definition of a Cavalier beyond the exclusive circles of Royalist commanders and soldiery was due both to Royalist defeat and, in Symmons's own view, to those who fell dramatically short of the ideal. In his *Vindication* he emphasised the 'prophaneness and high impiety in some others of our side' which obstructed God's blessing upon their wholly righteous cause: 'never any good undertaking had so many unworthy attendants; such horrid blasphemers and wicked wretches as ours hath had'.[9] Royalist and Parliamentarian divines alike were inclined to explain failures as consequent upon the faults of their own side which deprived them of God's good will. Symmons's bitter denunciation of the extent to which Royalists fell short of the measure of an idealised Christian gentleman (which is what he wished the word Cavalier to represent) became more angry in the wake of defeat. He claimed to have endured threats from those who had attended his sermons, 'the prophaner sort of our Cavaleers', to beat and pistol him for his denunciations of their 'blasphemy and dissoluteness, their self-seeking, lust-pleasing, and King-neglecting baseness'.[10] Yet, he concluded,

a day may come, when the world may see, that we who adhere to the King for Conscience sake, (for what ever is said of us to the contrary) have as truly hated the prophaneness and vilenesse of our own men, as we have done the disloyalty and Rebellion of the Enemy: For indeed, the truth is, betwixt them both (as betwixt two mil-stones) the King, his Cause, and our selves too, are ground in pieces . . . without all question, neglect of Religion, and want of Discipline, hath weakened and undone the Kings Armies . . .[11]

The King's armies were beaten in a war of attrition: Symmons's explanation of defeat would have encompassed the military reality but would have attributed the fact of it to the withdrawal of divine approval and intercession. The good Cavaliers, he would have argued, sacrificed by the bad. The Parliamentarians certainly seized upon what they thought were good examples of licentiousness on the King's side, and pushed them for all they were worth. If Symmons's writings had any general impact after 1646, he could fairly be accused of furthering the Parliament's war of insinuation, and the self-righteous anger of a disillusioned Royalist clergyman should not be allowed to conceal the fact that very few identifiable Royalists could be shown to have brought profound disrepute upon their own side. A thorough reading of the pamphlets issuing from London during the 1640s shows that, specific targets aside, the hate propaganda was concerned either with the behaviour of anonymous rank and file or with creation of the mythical, typical Royalist. The extent to which Parliament's propaganda entered the awareness of Royalists is clear:

Truly all, or the greatest part, of the King's commanders were so debased by drinking, whoring and swearing, that no man could expect God's blessing on their actions – witness Goring, Ogle, Prince Rupert, Bellamont &c. They were so confident of their cause and that God would give success and a blessing to it, although they were never so bad, which made them little to use their own care or endeavours or manage their affairs with any discretion or judgement. They imputed their failures to want of money, for they would idly spend it as fast as they had it, not caring how they burdened the country, thereby making of their friends their enemies.[12]

Sir John Oglander's assertions contain a mixture of truth and falsehood digested in the wake of defeat, by a man who clearly felt the cause was let down by its superior officers. His charge against Goring will be considered, but it is nowhere shown that Rupert, or Bard (Viscount Bellamont) were drunkards: if, by Ogle, Blundell meant Colonel William Ogle, the governor of Winchester, who apparently surrendered the city when in adrunken state, he forebore to mention (perhaps did not know) that others attributed Ogle's state to his wife's sudden and recent death. A court martial discharged Ogle from accusations of dereliction of duty, but, as Oglander proves, how 'difficult a thing it is to play an after-game of reputation', as Clarendon said.

Sir John Oglander probably subscribed (though, he may have had some personal doubts) to the widely held view that the King's cause was so self-evidently just that it could not fail either in obtaining God's blessing or in achieving vindication in the field. Defeat, then, was a shock to a man's scale of values and beliefs, and required to be explained. Oglander's emphasis upon others' views that want of money lay at the root of failure was as close to the truth as it was possible to get if the withdrawal of God's blessing be discounted. Moreover, in drawing attention to the iniquities of free quarter and excessive foraging, which were forced upon the King's commanders, by lack of sufficient money, Oglander echoed the criticism of Edward Somerset Lord Herbert of Raglan, whose criticism of Patrick Ruthven turned largely upon that issue. Somerset's view was that Ruthven, who had criticised him for paying upon the nail for whatever his soldiers required, which put others' reliance upon free quarter in a bad light, was that Ruthven did not take a rounded view of his responsibility as a general for the King. Ruthven, the career soldier and a Scot, 'here today and God knows where tomorrow . . . needed not care for the love of the people'. Somerset, on the other hand, 'though I were killed myselfe I should leave my posteritie behind me, towards whom I would not leave a grudge in the people',[13] had to be motivated by a sense of social and political responsibility if he was properly to serve the King. Symmons would have found in the attitude of this Catholic commander a fit candidate for inclusion in the order of Compleat Cavaliers, Ruthven clearly not (though he was no drunk, nor noticeably godless). Yet it would have been impossible for the war to be prosecuted at all, if the Compleat Cavalier had been a stickler for the niceties of peacetime propriety. The clash between Somerset and Ruthven was a matter of mutual jealousy, inspired by Ruthven's half-jesting complaint to the King which drew the other's rebuke.

Oglander's swipe at specific Royalist commanders, in perhaps three of four cases unjust, brings back to consideration the primary matter of this chapter: the characters and personalities of those of the King's colonels concerning whom any evidence remains to us. George Goring, one of Oglander's four named scapegoats, and the less easily defended, may be presented as well suited to the Parliamentarian definition of a Cavalier, and at odds with that which Symmons wished to propagate. 'Goring, who had turned wantonness into riot, turn'd riot into madness'; he 'favoured too much his own riot',[14] observed Sir Philip Warwick, who presents a court view of the man. Ann Lady Fanshawe went into more detail:

He was generally esteemed a good and great commander . . . of vast naturall parts, for I have heard your father say he hath dictated to severall persons at once that were upon severall dispaches, and all so admirably well that no one of them could be mended. He was exceedingly facetious and pleasant company, and in converse, where good manners were due, the civilest person imaginable, so that he would blush like a girle, which was naturall to him. He was very tall and very handsom. He had been married to a daughter of the Earl of Cork, but never had a child by her. His expences were what he could gett, and his debauchery beyond all presedents, which at last lost him that love the Spaniards had for him, and that country not admitting his constant drinking, he fell sick of a hectick fever, in which he turned his religion; and with that artifice could scarce get to keep him whilst he lived in that sickness, or to bury him when he was dead.[15]

Goring was born in 1608, the eldest son of George Goring of Hurstpierpoint in Sussex, who was created first Baron Goring in 1628 and first Earl of Norwich in 1644: there was a second son, Charles, seven years Goring's junior, who served his brother as lieutenant-colonel during the wars. The father was a general in the 1648 uprising.[16] Goring soldiered in Europe between 1633 (at the latest) and 1639, when he returned home to take up the governorship of Portsmouth. In that year he and a group of his friends were at Newport, Isle of Wight, where they:

got a ladder and drank healths at the top of the [gallows] and there Goring made a recantation for his former disorders and wished the people, of which they had store about them, to take example by him how they came to that place.[17]

His command at Portsmouth drew him to John Pym's attention, who cannot have expected much of Goring, knowing the latter as

MP for the port and aware also of his inauspicious and self-seeking involvement in the Army Plot. Pym informed the Commons in November 1641 that 'Colonel Goring had verie wicked men under him. That there was a chirurgeon of the garrison was a papist.'[18] The King looked to Goring, but he, in 1642, abandoned Portsmouth to the Parliament and went into Europe, returning later in the year in the Queen's service, to be Lieutenant General and Colonel of Horse under Lord Newcastle. At this juncture his equivocation of the preceding year, and more, seems to have vanished. The 'merry lad' who had been reckoned a follower of the Earl of Holland and an enemy of Strafford[19] committed himself to the King's cause and fought with distinction. Lady Ann Fanshaw's informant was right in that particular. In 1645, with an independent command in the West country, Goring's performance began to falter: he was frequently drunk and his troops, who appear to have been loyal to him, undisciplined, guilty of the very fault that Oglander had recorded. Throwing down his commissions, Goring (Lord Goring since his father's earldom) went into France and, although in theory planning to return to England,[20] remained in exile and took service in Spain, where as Lady Fanshaw noted, his drinking and the heat weakened him. He died, poor and virtually forgotten, in 1657.[21] Another tale of him, recounted by Blundell, seems typical:

The merry tale told by Jo. Molyneux of the drunken frolics betwixt the Lord Goring and Admiral Opdam. Opdam having been pressed to sacrifice some garments of better value than the rest of the drinkers had, to the health of the King, took the like advantage of Goring, and caused him to burn a cloth of gold doublet on the like occasion. Which affront was retorted on Opdam, when Goring caused a foetid tooth to be plucked out of his own head, to the honour of the party they drank to, and Opdam (for shame) was constrained to second the frolic with a sound tooth.[22]

Goring's weakness was a commonplace weakness, and he was, on the other hand, physically brave, an efficient administrator and gifted commander though, ultimately, unreliable. Over him Symmons, Oglander and Warwick could well shake their heads despairingly.

Another merry lad who drew down upon himself early notoriety and the enmity of the Commons, and whose reputation has been hounded over the intervening centuries by his bad press in

1641/42, was Colonel Sir Thomas Lunsford. Clarendon, who certainly must have known him personally, described him as of an ancient Sussex family 'of a very small and decayed fortune, and of no good education'.[23] The poor education Clarendon attributed to his having had to flee the country in 1637 'to avoid the hand of justice for some riotous misdemeanours',[24] involving attempted murder. The Royalist Edward Sackville fourth Earl of Dorset summed up Lunsford's reputation: 'A young outlaw who neither fears God nor man, and who, having given himself over to all lewdness and dissoluteness, only studies to affront justice'. He would, said Dorset, rather be taken for a 'swaggering ruffian than the issue of that ancient and honest family'.[25] The King pardoned Lunsford in 1639, in time for him to recruit a Somerset regiment with which he served against the Scots. Sir John Coke, suffering from the depredations of royal troops in June 1640, solicited Lunsford's help, and found him to be 'a brave gentleman and discreet'.[26] This is important, for the fact is that everything said against Lunsford thereafter was based upon the alleged incidents of his earlier life. Not until January 1642, when he attended the King in the Five Members affair, had he put a foot wrong since his return to England in 1639. Clarendon, noting that Lunsford had 'the reputation of a man of courage and a good officer of foot' whilst serving in France, also said that at the time of his appointment to the Tower he was 'little known' and 'utterly a stranger' to the King. Further, that his appointment was pitched upon by George Digby, who would have preferred his own half-brother, Lewis Dyve, in the post.[27] Shortly after Lunsford's acceptance, William Tompkins, MP for Weobley, rose in the Commons with a motion 'that hee understood that a verie dangerous person was to be made Leiftenant of the Tower'.[28] Lawrence Chambers gave evidence against Lunsford's character, none of which was verifiable, all of which was ammunition for the MPs opposed to the appointment of a man very clearly connected with the court through Digby:

Lawrence Chambers . . . shrewed that hee knew him . . . in the Low cuntries wheere hee was soe given to drinking and quarrelling that all sober and civill men avoided his company, that hee was much indebted and afterwards rann out of the Low cuntries in to France . . . a debauched quarrelsome man, verie desperate, and fitt to execute any dangerous designe . . . [In France] when hee received monie to pay his souldiers, hee rann away from thence with the said monie.[29]

'Soe dangerous a person and unworthie of the place' as Lunsford was, it was clear to some in the Commons that a 'designe of the papists to ruine the true religion' was afoot and Lunsford's appointment demonstrated that it was 'now growing to a maturitie'.[30] Lunsford, Coke's discreet gentleman, was a mere pawn in the Commons' attack upon the King and his advisers, and his rapid withdrawal from the post encouraged Parliament to target his successor, Byron. The King's knighting of Lunsford was not an accolade for a ruffian but a reward for service willingly given. Nor was it misplaced. In October 1642 Lunsford commanded a foot regiment in which his brothers Henry (killed as the regiment's colonel at Bristol in 1643) and Herbert also fought, and was taken, lamed, at Edgehill. Imprisoned, but not otherwise proceeded against, not even for debts allegedly contracted whilst Lieutenant of the Tower,[31] Lunsford was released in 1644 and returned to the King's service. He had no difficulty in compounding at a sixth in 1649 and went quietly off to America, where he died in 1653.[32] He has for long been accounted a Cavalier in Parliament's terms, his characterisation based upon innuendo and hearsay and the traces of a wild youth, nothing more. That Lunsford may have undergone a personal reformation during his enforced military service in Europe is plausible: nothing in his war-time career suggests excesses. The beneficial effects of a military life were recognised by Sir Henry Slingsby, a man so far removed from Parliament's projection of the 'Cavalier' that he might well be cited as an exemplar of Symmons's definition. Of the soldier's life, Slingsby observed that:

I like it as a commendable way of breeding for a young Gentleman, if they consort ymselves with such as are civil, & ye quarrel lawfull: for as idleness is ye nurse of all evil, infeebling ye parts both of mind & body. This employment of a soulgiers is contrary unto it: for it greatly improves ym, by enabling his body to labour, his mind to watchfulness, & so, by a contempt of all things but yt employment he is in, he shall not much care how hard he lyeth, nor how meanly he fareth; – whereas ye independence of a private life, makes one insolent, & not easily brought under subjection. The business of a soulgier will learn him to be dutifull and obedient to his commanders without reply: how equal & just it is: it makes one not over fond of this life, but willing to resign it, whether of both shall happen, death or life, being exercis'd in ye continuall peril of life.[33]

Such a transformation was remarked upon by contemporaries of Robert Dormer first Earl of Carnarvon, who was killed commanding his regiment at First Newbury in September 1643. Sir Philip Warwick, who justifiably reckoned the Earl to be 'a Gentleman of an excellent spirit', noted the change that came over him with the advent of civil war: 'formerly he had made use of his wit somewhat prophanely, which humour he now shook off; and turned into seriousness and extraordinary diligence'.[34] The earl's wife, a daughter of Philip Herbert fourth Earl of Pembroke (who was dismissed by King Charles as Lord Chamberlain in 1641 and was a prominent Parliamentarian), may have been a strange mate for the pre-war Carnarvon. Among other things, it was noted of her in 1639, when they were both at court, that:

Lady Carnarvon conditioned, before she would promise to be of the [masque], that it should not be danced upon a Sunday, for she is grown so devout by conversing with Lord Powis[35] and the doctor that now she will neither dance nor see a play upon the Sabbath.[36]

The attribution of strict religious observation to Lord Powis, which demonstrates that Puritan leanings were no bar to loyalism during the Civil War, calls to mind, incidentally, what was said of Edward first Lord Montagu of Boughton, who died in prison in London in 1644:

a man of a plain downright English spirit, viz. of a steddy courage, of a devout heart, and a true son of the Church of England; yet so severe and regular in his life, that he was by the most reckoned amongst the Puritans.[37]

Symmons would have accounted Montagu and, probably, Powis as Cavaliers within his terms.

Carnarvon's dissoluteness before 1642 nevertheless went hand in hand with a high disdain of danger. For Clarendon he was 'the Earl of Carnarvon (who always charged home)'[38] and, fighting against the Scots in 1640, he:

fought madly like himself, for being forsaken by his countrymen, he made good the place whilst he had any powder and shot, and after threw his pistols at them, then drawing his sword fought manfully till he was relieved and brought off.[39]

Three years earlier, when he was with the fleet, the story was told of the earl:

comming from supper where meate and drinke was noething scarce, as sayth the songe, goeing into the cabbin whitch was as good a roome and wherein was as good a bed in whitch he was to lye as any he could have on shoare, from thence into the gallery where he had the prospect of a greate fleete a cleere sky and a calme sea, he swore there was noe soe happy life as to live in sutch a ship and reade roamances, but by God's blood he would have three whores.[40]

In war 'an excellent discerner and pursuer of advantage upon his enemy', Carnarvon met his death through the precipitate pursuit of the enemy that characterised him as fighting man. He was wounded in action at Lansdown in July 1643, where Bevil Grenvile was killed, and met his death wound at Newbury when carelessly in pursuit of fleeing Parliamentarian troops. His death occasioned the King great personal grief, and at a time when death in battle was still frightening and exemplary he became the subject of eulogy.[41]

The 'merry lads' of the Bishops' Wars and Army Plots were the originals of the Cavalier image as Parliament chose to promote it. In an age when most people had ceased to believe in ghouls and monsters it was necessary to reinvent them as a means of undermining civilian support for the King's war effort. The Cavalier debauchee with his 'shag hair [worn] down to his heels' whose task was to ravish virgins and plunder poor men[42] was a skilful propaganda construct, against which even Royalists such as Symmons and Oglander measured their comrades and commanders. What it meant was that a man such as Goring, whose single weakness was drink, in the popular mind took on all the attributes of the archetype. Symmons, ill prepared and unaccustomed to war and the life of the camp, conscious of the effectiveness of Parliament's hate campaign, unaware of being influenced by it, inflated the realities of military life out of all reasonable proportion. If he was, as he later claimed, threatened by those of his own side because of his sermons, he probably deserved it. On the one hand he was trying to create an ideal Royal soldier who could never have existed (though some men came close, but not because of effort to do so), imbued with the qualities of birth and breeding: and, on the other, denouncing the common run of rank and file who ran the same risks but were regarded as expendable. A well-meaning

but sanctimonious army chaplain, half doing the enemy's propaganda work for them, stood a pretty fair chance of being threatened with a pistolling. It was easier for him and other, civilian or
semi-civilian, supporters of the King to concern themselves with
the way in which the war must be won. For most soldiers, the
winning was the primary concern, their lives, gentle or plebeian,
being on the line.

England was militarised in a few months in the middle of 1642,
bringing on domestic war fought by hastily raised but conven-
tionally structured armies. These, on the King's side at least,
mirrored in their leadership the distinctions of normal peacetime
society. In the midst of these cataclysmic events, seen by many as a
struggle for the *status quo* against the unpredictable social and
political consequences of the King's defeat, men like Symmons
panicked. He conveys the impression that at times he felt more
threatened by those armed for the King's defence than by the
forces of the Parliament. Symmons wanted discipline for the
'mean bred Persons' who could 'shoot off Pistols or Carbines' and
kill with 'a bullet . . . Valiant Gentlemen',[43] and if those same
gentlemen were not models of peacetime propriety, then the
cause, in its widest sense, was endangered.

The widespread propaganda image of the Cavalier was that of
the drunken, debauched in the widest sense, blaspheming (and
therefore godless), lustful young blade – though age itself was no
determinant of membership of that miserable body. The war
itself extended the image to gather up along the way viciousness
and cold-blooded barbarity, creating Cavaliers out of men such as
Michael Woodhouse and Francis Doddington who in other respects were unsuited to the label. The merry lads, to misquote Dr
Hutton,[44] turned feral, the inevitable further downward spiral
from excessive social drinking and low company. Thus the term
Cavalier could embrace such disparate characters as Goring,
Caernarvon, Will Ashburnham, Henry Percy, Henry Jermyn (the
Queen's favourite) and perhaps even Colonel Gervase Holles. It
also certainly embraced the least likely candidate-of all, super-
ficialities aside: Henry Wilmot.

II

The Cavaliers, the swordsmen, if Parliament was to be believed,
were the true face of what had emerged as a Royalist party. They

were irrevocably linked with the King's success or failure, loyal often to the death but from no finer motives than lack of choice and a desire for indulging their predatory tendencies. It is therefore significant to find amongst them both a Goring, who threw up his commissions in a fit of drunken pique, and Wilmot, who came close to betraying the King in the interests of peace. Of him Sir Philip Warwick observed that:

he that marks Wilmotts whole progress thro' this warr, shall find him much affected to be an umpire of peace; which had bin well done, if he had quitted the King's army, and gone into his Council, than a decider of the contest by the sword; though the Gentleman wanted no courage nor experience, nor, I hope, loyalty.[45]

The combination in Wilmot of the commanding officer and the seeker for peace, to which Warwick took exception as incompatible roles, would also have puzzled Hobbes. He reckoned to distinguish between the soldiers and the restraints imposed upon them by those in royal councils who wished to effect a compromise settlement. Hobbes supposed that there was a strong and wide tendency to conceive of England as governed by 'not an absolute, but a mixed monarchy': because of that, he wrote, 'if the King should clearly subdue . . . Parliament [then] his power would be what he pleased, and theirs as little as he pleased'. To Hobbes the seeds of the King's military defeat were in this attitude, for:

though it did not lessen their endeavour to gain the victory for the King in a battle, when a battle could not be avoided, yet it weakened their endeavour to procure him an absolute victory in the war. And for this cause, notwithstanding that they saw that the Parliament was firmly resolved to take all kingly power whatsoever, out of his hands, yet their counsel to the King was all occasions, to offer propositions to them of treaty and accommodation and to make and publish declarations; which any man might easily have foreseen would be fruitless; and not only so, but also of great disadvantage to those actions by which the King was to recover his crown and preserve his life. For it took away the courage of the best and forwardest of his soldiers, that looked for great benefit by their service out of the estates of the rebels in case they could subdue them; but none at all, if the business should be ended by a treaty . . .[46]

Setting aside Hobbes's attribution of baser motives for loyalty than others suggested, his observation reflected the truth that war is only ever in the hands of soldiers when fighting is immediate and necessary. Otherwise, the direction of strategy and objectives lies with politicians. In the same section of his *Behemoth*, however, Hobbes also gave it as his view that the King's soldiers 'though they were men as stout as theirs' nevertheless 'because their valour was not so sharpened with malice as theirs were of the other side, they fought not so keenly as their enemies did'.[47] The whole point about the Cavalier, if he ever existed as Parliament depicted him, was his extreme and wanton maliciousness. If there was, as Hobbes insisted, a lack of hatred on the part of the King's soldiers, then the influence of the true Cavalier can have been minimal, and confined to the immediate area of operations where such a man might find himself by accident of war. If, further, as Hobbes indicates, the lack of hatred and malice reflected equivocation towards ultimate victory and the nature of it, then the Cavalier had no direction of the war effort, merely an element within it. If the King's war was waged with the restraint, which Hobbes implies, and with the consequences that came of that, then we can posit the coexistence of two fairly distinctive Royalist parties: the wagers of all-out war, invariably the commanders and their soldiers, and including amongst them the Cavalier archetypes, and, on the other hand (one might almost say, against them) the King's civilian advisers and certain of his councillors. 'For though he had as good officers at least as any that then served the Parliament, yet I doubt he had not so useful counsel as was necessary,' Hobbes declared.[48] In this context the attributes of the merry lad and the compromiser exemplified by Wilmot seem distinctly odd: a fighting commander who appears to have taken upon himself the role of negotiator.

Wilmot's credentials for army command were as good as any. He was the son and heir of Charles first Viscount Wilmot of Athlone, whom he succeeded in the title probably in 1644. Service in Europe preceded command during the Bishops' Wars, and he was returned to the Commons as MP for Tamworth in 1640. Like Goring (with whom Clarendon was at some pains to compare him) he was implicated in the Army Plots (though unlike Goring he did not seek to betray them) and was expelled from the House of Commons. In August 1642 he was recruiting a cavalry regiment for the King. Sir Bevil Grenvile noted him in October as 'my noble friend, the brave Wilmot'. On 6 April 1643 he was appointed Lieutenant General of Horse and Dragoons under Prince Rupert,[49] and was advanced to the peerage as first Baron Wilmot of Adderbury in June. On 13 July he scored a stunning victory over the insouciant Sir William Waller at Roundway Down to relieve Devizes. A little over a year later he was arrested.

'He was a man proud and ambitious and incapable of being contented', a hard drinker whose reputation gave him considerable influence over others of that kind. He was 'much beloved in all the good fellowship of the army', said Clarendon, 'which was too great a body', he added, complementing Symmons.[50] Unlike Goring, however, Wilmot's debauchery did not lose him the respect of his officers, for he could, according to Clarendon, 'shut it out from his business; never neglected that, and rarely miscarried in it'. He never drank when the enemy was in sight, unlike Goring, who couldn't resist a tipple in the midst of an engagement if he felt so inclined. Both men valued their friendships slightly, but Wilmot 'violated them the less willingly' and was possessed, moreover, 'of more scruples from religion to startle him, and would not have attained his end by any gross or foul act of wickedness'.

Clarendon's only too obvious dislike of Goring allowed him to indulge Wilmot somewhat, though elsewhere he acknowledged that Wilmot's time as Lieutenant General of the Horse was not 'employed to the King's advantage', though Charles himself could not readily perceive it. His importance in military affairs Clarendon attributed to Patrick Ruthven's old age, deafness and incoherence, which, with injury, would soon drive him from command altogether, though without a stain upon his character for loyalty. As for Wilmot, Clarendon thought him too well aware of his own military limitations, and from that awareness arose a desire to prove himself instrumental in bringing peace whilst he was still in a position of authority and in the King's regard, to benefit from it. In other words, selfish interests led Wilmot to appear to flirt with treachery, whereas, for Clarendon, George Goring, who would 'without hesitation, have broken any trust, or done any act of treachery, to have satisfied an ordinary passion or appetite',[51] was indisputably the lesser man. Yet, whatever was urged against Goring's character, he never really found himself needing to win at the 'after-game of reputation' as Wilmot demonstrably did.

Wilmot's arrest in August 1644 nearly precipitated a mutiny amongst his officers, who pressed the King for an explanation.[52] The officers, styling themselves the Old Horse, pretended to excuse their temerity on the grounds that they 'may not have reason to suspect themselves partakers of [Wilmot's] crymes, having ben ... executors of his commands'. The King's reply indicated that he took exception to their petition, since it obliged him to 'publishe more then perhaps we ever intended to the unfaithfulnes and ingratitude of a person whome we had ... trusted [and] so many severall wayes obliged'.[53] The charges against Wilmot were then itemised and, perhaps because of this openness, found to be a deal more profoundly serious than they might otherwise have been. He was accused of endeavouring to 'possesse the officers ... with a disvalew and contempte of his Majesties person' (which was as good as saying that the petitioners were being watched as well), and that he intended actively to 'draw men to revolt from their allegiance'. In specifics, the King made it clear that Wilmot's motivation was selfish, instancing his dislike of the influence of Princes Rupert and Maurice in the King's affairs, and an alleged plot to conspire with Parliament to dethrone Charles in favour of his eldest son, 'who had no share in the causes of these troubles'. To this end, Wilmot had entered into a correspondence with the arch-rebel the Earl of Essex and had informed him that there was a party of 'many good freinds' to the earl in the King's army.[54]

Wilmot's public rebuttal of the charges against him was far from persuasive. His offences 'reacheth noe farther then words, though of such nature as are as disagreeable to my loyalty and duty, as they were alwayes distant either from my intentions or expressions'. Yet it turned ultimately upon an appeal to consideration of his previous, substantial, service to the Crown (though doubtless King Charles had revived for him by Wilmot's accusers the remembrance of the man's bitterness towards Strafford in 1641)[55]

Wilmot's plot, whatever it was, however representative it was, did not come to anything: Clarendon, acknowledging the man's faults of character, nevertheless seems to have imputed no other motives to him than those which proceeded from those defects he chose to itemise. Wilmot's war was over, however, and his future lay in attendance upon and courageous association with the

Prince of Wales. The case is, however, important not for Wilmot's failure in his scheme (and the opportunity which it afforded Clarendon to reveal his extreme bias against Goring), but for the way in which it so amply demonstrates that the Cavalier of Parliament's creation need not have been as committedly loyal as other, less extravagant gentlemen were. The problem with Wilmot was that he conceived of himself as far more significant a political figure than he was a soldier: he did not understand himself, and laid himself open to the scrutiny of far cleverer men than he. If he was not trepanned into potential treason, he was the kind of man who very well could have been. An anecdote from 1649 may be felt to illustrate this, again collected by Captain William Blundell.[56] George Lord Digby, upon his arrival in France in that year, was met by Wilmot, who tried to provoke a duel over the machinations against him in 1644. Digby, whom Clarendon thought 'a man of the greatest presentness of mind, and the least unappalled upon danger, that I have known',[57] declined to fight, on the grounds that too much loyal blood had already been shed, but Wilmot pushed the matter, accusing Digby of cowardice. At the end of his tether, Wilmot told Digby that Prince Rupert himself had vowed to shoot Digby dead when next he saw him.

But here the Lord Digby changeth his copy, and that which he would not before accept in defence of his own honour, he offers now to his enemy in defence of another. For charging the Lord Wilmot grievously for having aspersed . . . a person of so great worth and a Prince of the Royal blood of England, he requireth satisfaction with his sword for the Prince's honour.

In the ensuing duel, Wilmot was disabled. Blundell relished the way in which Digby had turned the situation in his own favour and, by so doing, presented himself as the champion of a prince whom he knew to be animated against him but whom he thus effectively neutralised. Wilmot in all this was the dupe of George Digby, whose 'presentness of mind' Clarendon so admired.

At the same time that Wilmot fell from favour and command in 1644 another of the merry lads of 1640/41 was dismissed as well, Henry first Baron Percy of Alnwick. Clarendon didn't like him much, either: 'as much inclined to mutiny as the lord Wilmot . . . much a bolder speaker, and had none of those faculties, which the other had, of reconciling men to him'. Percy's advance to a peerage, and to generalship of the Ordnance from having been a regimental colonel, was attributed to the Queen's favour, as was his barony, which, Clarendon remarked bitterly, 'obliged the king to bestow the same honour on more men'.[58] Percy was far more unpopular a man than either Wilmot or Goring, and his friendship could bring, in some eyes at least, censorous judgements with it: 'Prince Rupert is not that gallant man we tooke him for you may judge it by Percys being his cheef favorite in the world,' it was said in July 1643.[59]

Lord Percy (advanced to his peerage in 1643) was the fourth of the sons of the ninth Earl of Northumberland and, as has been noticed, his brother the tenth Earl was a prominent Parliamentarian. He was also related through his mother to the Earl of Essex. In 1640 he sat in the Short Parliament as MP for Portsmouth, the seat to be occupied by Goring in the Long Parliament. He served as a colonel of horse against the Scots from 1639, but, implicated in the Army Plots of 1641, he was obliged to flee to France, only returning to England in 1642 in time to secure a command for the King's service. In 1643 he led a regiment of infantry south to Oxford from Lord Newcastle, and in May was appointed General of the Ordnance (in which rank he was replaced, when dismissed in 1644, by Ralph Hopton).[60] Ian Roy has suggested that Percy's generalship was largely nominal, and that the real work of the office continued to be done by subordinates.[61] Thus Henry Percy accumulated honours in 1643 through the Queen's intercession, and this may well have gone to his head in much the same way as Wilmot supposed himself to be an arbiter for peace. Both men suffered disgrace, neither repaired his reputation, and Percy went into France in 1645 never to return. He died in 1659, a year after Wilmot.

The Percy–Rupert friendship did not outlast the disgrace of 1644. The attribute of a direct manner of speech led Percy into a confrontation with Rupert in exile. Out hunting together with the Prince of Wales, Rupert rode up to Percy and seized his bridle, telling him 'he should presently give him satisfaction'. They dismounted and drew their swords; 'it is reported the Prince had advantage in the lenth of his sword, which in France is conceaved no advantage'. Within a short space, 'after the second passe' Percy was cut in his right side and, when they closed, he fell and injured his hand. Rupert's wartime friend Colonel Will Murray then separated them. 'The wound is voyde of danger, and they both haveing foughten [and] valiantly, the Prince, being as skilfull in his weapon as valiant, had only the advantage of the successe'.[62]

III

A propensity to duel has also been reckoned, then and since, as a part of the Cavalier image: it is redolent of prickly character and an over-developed sense of personal honour. Attention has already been paid to that duel between Sandys and Saint Michel in which the seconds killed each other whilst the main protagonists walked wounded away.[63] Digby outwitted and outfought Wilmot, and Rupert proved his superior swordsmanship over a courageous Percy. Of Colonel Gervase Holles of Grimsby in Lincolnshire it was remarked in 1636 that he was a 'forward young fellow' when it came to undertakings of this nature, and that he intended to act as a second in a duel between unknown antagonists. The Earl of Clare, John Holles, who died in 1637, wished Gervase to pursue a legal career and to give up the exercise of arms.[64] Holles chose otherwise, became a colonel and fought with some distinction at Adwalton Moor in 1643. In 1645 he was proposing to go into Venetian service against the Turks, and in 1646 was commissioned by the French to command a regiment in their armies, to which Parliament assented, glad to see him and a small number of ex-Royalist soldiers so employed.[65] Colonel Sir Nicholas Crispe, an alderman of London expelled from the Commons as a monopolist in 1641, fought and killed in a duel a brother officer, Lieutenant Colonel Sir James Enyon in 1643: Crispe was forty-five, his victim fifty-six years of age, a country gentleman from Flore in Northamptonshire. It was said that Crispe repented the deed and wore tokens of mourning the rest of his life.[66]

The resort to the sword evidenced by duels and by occasional challenges issued across the no-man's-land of a battlefield, was symptomatic of the tensions of a 'nice and jealous profession'. Bulstrode Whitelocke encountered extreme hostility when he was in Oxford under a safe conduct as part of a delegation from Parliament to the King which included the Earl of Northumberland. He recalled that, 'having occasion to walke in Oxford streets towards his lodging, and having sent his man about business', he ran into some gentlemen and former MPs who recognised him.

They saluted him 'with scorne & anger . . . they with rudenes said they wondred that the King would graunt his safe Conduct for Rebells to come to his presence'. They wondered also that Whitelocke dared to walk about Oxford 'in the face of so many of the Kings servants, without expecting to be cutt in pieces'. According to Whitelocke he took issue with them about calling the commissioners from Parliament rebels, and 'they replyed with many Oaths Dam me, sinke me, & the like' in proper Cavalier fashion. Hands then went to swords, but Whitelocke was saved by the arrival of Colonel Sir Humphrey Bennet, his brother-in-law, who, 'being a tried valiant man, whom the King had knighted' intervened. 'He with a fierce countenance, & laying his hand uppon his sword, did sweare that if any of them spake one word more of such language . . . he would thrust his sword into that parties gutts.'[67] Bennet had reasons of kinship for saving Whitelocke from the consequences of his own rebellion, but also was sensitive to the best interests of the King, whose honour was involved in the safe conduct. The matter passed over, the Royalists dispersed. This was the same Bennet of whom a 'true character' was drawn in November 1645 attesting to his period as Royalist sheriff of his native Hampshire, 'in which office he was both very active and very cruel, and also as he was a commander in the King's army even to the undoing of many a godly an honest man . . . so dangerous a person'.[68] Clearly, his comrades in arms thought him so, too, if Whitelocke's story is accurate.

Accusations of cruelty against Royalist colonels were common, predictable, necessary from Parliament's point of view, and are impossible to refute. Most such allegations, even that against Viscount Molyneux's brother Caryll,[69] were so vague that the basis for them may be considered tendentious. But in some cases the charges were very specific indeed. One colonel whose name was continually cropping up was Sir Francis Doddington of Barrow in Somerset,[70] an 'intransigent and bullying Royalist' but one whose political antecedents were somewhat equivocal. He refused to contribute money to the war against the Scots in 1639, but in June 1642 set his hand to the county petition in favour of the maintenance of episcopacy.[71] Captured in October 1642, he was released in 1643, when he was commissioned. In July the following year he commanded forces to reduce Woodhouse garrison near Frome, and it was what happened then that marked him down thenceforth. 'That bloody tyrant Sir Francis Dorington' (sic)[72] took the house and hanged fourteen of its defenders out of hand, as subsequent petitions confirmed.[73] Edmund Ludlow recorded that Doddington exacted retribution for six Irish soldiers who had been hanged by Parliament's commanders. The prisoners 'being most of them clothiers, were hanged upon the same tree; but one of them breaking his halter, desired that what he had suffered might be accepted . . . notwithstanding which, they caused him to be hanged up again.'[74] 'They' were Doddington and Lieutenant Colonel William St Leger, whose soldiers had been hanged as Irish rebels. Ralph Hopton put a stop to the hangings. Thereafter, Doddington's name attracted stories of atrocity. 'It was certified by letters, that [Doddington] meeting an honest minister upon the way near Taunton, asked him "Who art thou for, priest?" Who answered "For God and his gospel",' whereupon Doddington, understandably and predictably, shot the man to death.[75] Such stories are impossible either to prove or to disprove, and what matters, after all, is not so much the veracity as what others chose to believe possible of the man. Parliament excepted him from pardon, denied him composition, and drove him into exile.

The story was told of Thomas Leveson of Wolverhampton in Staffordshire, the King's governor of Dudley Castle and a colonel of horse and foot, that in April 1642 he assaulted John Tanner, an armourer. Tanner had at his workshop in Wolverhampton some armour of Leveson's which Leveson went to collect but which Tanner declined to hand over on the instructions of the Deputy Lieutenants. Leveson was a known Catholic. Tanner was denounced as a 'fool and a knave' and 'a stinking rogue' and 'with a cane which he had in his hand' Leveson struck him about the head 'two or three blows'.[76] This incident followed upon a bitter dispute between Leveson and the Deupties. His period as a commander for the King was to be marked by an intensive feud with his nominal commander-in-chief, Henry Hastings Lord Loughborough, and an independence of mind which caused him to stand fast to his command at Dudley until May 1646. Parliament excepted him from pardon, denied him composition (despite the terms upon which he surrendered Dudley Castle) and drove him, like Doddington, into exile. Leveson died in the household of the Prince of Condé in France in 1652, his belongings sold to defray the cost of his burial.[77]

In view of Edward Symmons's strictures as to the proper behaviour to be expected of a Compleat Cavalier, it is curious to note that his *Military Sermon* was dedicated to Colonel Michael Woodhouse, commander of the Prince of Wales's Regiment of Foot and Major General of Infantry under Arthur first Lord Capel. Having served in Ireland[78] and probably in Europe before that, Woodhouse joined the Royalists in 1643. In March 1644 he stormed and took Hopton Castle in Shropshire, a small fortalice not capable of sustained defence. By the rules of war, not ordinarily enforced, the defenders of an untenable garrison could expect no quarter if the besiegers were put to the trouble and ensuant loss of blood in storming it. Woodhouse, however, captured most of the garrison alive, lined them up by the dry ditch, had them shot, and the throats of the still living summarily cut. He may even have done this himself. The unenviable reputation which he thus earned proved useful when he came to take Brampton Bryan Castle, the home of the Parliamentarian Harleys in Herefordshire.[79] Dr Hutton saw the incident at Hopton as a sign that the war was changing, that the brutalisation of it had begun. If it were possible to show that, thenceforth, atrocities and atrocity stories multiplied, there would be some justice in that judgement, but as then, so later, such incidents were few and far between. Many callous acts, moreover, derived directly from Parliament's decision to hang Irish prisoners out of hand, and the largest single atrocity of the war, the murder and mutilation of women after Naseby, was down to God's army, the New Model. It is easy to take incidents such as those at Hopton and Woodhouse out of context and to infer from them a deterioration in the courtesies of war. Those courtesies were largely mythical, anyway, even where the gentry was concerned: in the cases of Woodhouse and Doddington, and atrocities attributed to Colonel Sir Lewis Kirk, the evidence concerns individual acts, not any coherent policy centrally resolved upon. Parliament's rule as to the fate of Irish prisoners (which some of its commanders deplored) is the single example of authorised wholesale atrocity for the entire period of the war. What Doddington, Woodhouse, Kirk and others did should not be taken as a sign of increasing Royalist desperation. Indeed, it is arguable that impending success and actual success inclined soldiers to brutality, and provides a context for the savage treatment meted out to Royalists in 1648. No one was killed out of hand, so far as is known, after Marston Moor in 1644 or Adwalton Moor in 1643, but at Naseby in 1645 victorious troops indulged their taste for slaughter with no restraint. Some of them, subsequently, indulged it a little further in Ireland in 1649/51.

Incidents of torture recorded during the wars are few. Colonel Sir Lewis Kirk, a career soldier and vigorous in his tasks, was accused of 'exquisite and unutterable' torments inflicted on the wife of John Cresswell of Bridgnorth, of which town Kirk was for a time governor. Mrs Cresswell was gaoled, her husband said for twenty-five weeks and underwent torments with 'twisted cords, screws, and fire, until her nail and flesh was bored through and the marrow fired out of the bones'. She was a spy for the Parliament – her husband did not deny that – and repeatedly refused to denounce her employers.[80] Here again there is no corroborative evidence, but Kirk's peacetime record was none too respectable. In 1641 he had been an accomplice of Henry Parker Lord Morley and Mounteagle in the murder of a Captain Peter Clarke. It was alleged that Lord Morley did the killing, but Kirk was found guilty of the actual deed, and further proceedings were held up by the outbreak of war. Morley, like Kirk, became a colonel for the King, though less actively so.[81]

For every allegation made against a Royalist between 1642 and 1646 could be found something similar alleged against a Parliamentarian. 'An horrid outrage was committed' in 1642, before war began in earnest, 'by Coll. Edwin Sandis, and others, sent by the Close Committee, at ye house of Sir William Butler, in Teston [Kent], his servant tortured by fyer, hymself, then at ye wells nigh Tunbridge, on the news, flying to ye King'.[82] Butler took up arms under the King, commanded a regiment, and was killed in action at Cropredy Bridge in 1644. It was alleged at the time that he was killed by one of his own men, deliberately, 'whom, his comrades requited'.[83] No other source suggests this.[84] It should be pointed out in Butler's case, but not as an extenuation of Sandys' actions, that he was already an outspoken Royalist who had sworn to 'justify every word' in a pro-episcopacy petition sent up to London from Herefordshire.[85]

IV

Just as there were colonels who drew attention to themselves by excesses of one kind or another, so there were many whose primary and sometimes sole claim to fame derived from their diligence and resolution in the service, going so far (as in the cases of Dives and Stawell) to defy the Parliament at the very bar of the Commons' house. Colonel Charles Lloyd of Moel y Garth in Montgomeryshire applied himself diligently to the study of military engineering, though 'but a young man and, some thought, much too greene for such an employment, beeing only studious in the mathematicks'.[86] Colonel Thomas Tyldesley of Myerscough in Lancashire, whose loyalty was unflinching from 1642 until his death in action in 1651, aroused nothing but respect. Parliament noted him early in his native county; 'Tilsley ... doth more harme than any man I know,' they were informed.[87] This 'noble and generous-minded gentleman' earned the King's particular favour:

The greatest of my misfortunes is that I cannot reward so gallant and loyal a subject as you are as I ought and would [Charles wrote to him in 1646]. I . . . desire you to hold out [in Lichfield] until Oxford be rendered which will be ranked amongst the rest of the good services done by you to your most assured friend.

Yet Tyldesley was no paragon of the virtues of the Compleat Cavalier: it was simply that he addressed himself diligently to the task in hand. 'It was a saying of Sir Thomas Tildesley (as his lady told me), that he would follow his business close, to the end that he might the more enjoy his pleasures.'[88] He may have had much in common with the first Earl of Lindsey, whose death at Edgehill in 1642 meant that he died with his reputation intact. Clarendon acknowledged Lindsey's considerable military skills, and noted that he was 'thought very equal' to the demands upon a commander-in-chief. 'Albeit he indulged to himself great liberties of life, yet he still preserved a very good reputation with all men . . . of a generous nature, punctual in what he undertook and in exacting what was due to him'.[89] Clarendon also thought highly of Sir Jacob Astley, a sixty-three-year-old Norfolk career soldier who brought his son Bernard into the war with him (and lost him in action, mortally wounded at Bristol in 1645):

An honest, brave, plain man . . . as fit for the office of Major General of the foot, as Christendom yielded. Discerning and prompt in giving orders, as the occasion required, and most cheerful and present in any action. In council he used few, but very pertinent words.[90]

Astley took over the regiment of the disgraced Colonel Feilding, eventually replacing Charles Gerard in South Wales as Major General and then as Field Marshal General.[91] He had been ennobled in 1644.

To underline his approval of Colonel Henry Gage, Clarendon did as he was to do in showing sympathy for Wilmot: contrasting him with someone he clearly disliked – in Gage's case, Colonel Sir Arthur Aston. Gage came of a Surrey family whose line boasted, in the person of Gage's grandfather, a Knight of the Garter. 'He was in truth a very extraordinary man, of a large and very graceful person . . . besides his great experience and abilities as a soldier, which were very eminent . . . a very good scholar,' Clarendon observed and, moreover and significantly, accomplished in the nuances of court life. Aston, whom the writer disliked, 'crossed [Gage] in any thing he proposed, and hated him perfectly; as they were of natures, and manners, as different as men can be'. Aston's 'rough nature' and 'immoderate love of money' were the chief drawbacks of a man who, in Clarendon's opinion, 'had the fortune to be very much esteemed, where he was not known; and very much detested, where he was'.[92] Both men were Catholics, and Aston the first and last Catholic governor of Oxford, which appointment, it was implied, reflected the Queen's choice and favour. Gage succeeded him in the post, and was mortally wounded in January 1645. Sir Henry Slingsby, who knew him, noted, 'A man much lament'd, being a compleat Soulgier & a wise man.'[93] Sir Edward Walker further corroborated Clarendon's opinion: 'The loss of this Man was generally lamented, and with much reason: for if you consider his Birth, Learning, Courage, and great Experience in War, with his singular Humanity and Temper, scarce any Prince had a worthier servant'.[94] Aston, the sufferer by this comparison, who wanted to evacuate the entire civilian population from Oxford, was 'hack'd and chop'd to pieces' in 1649 when Cromwell stormed Drogheda in Ireland.[95]

Eulogies which followed upon the deaths, ordinarily in action, of Royalist colonels clearly laid stress upon the positive merits of their subjects. That would hardly be otherwise. Two such cases are worthy of consideration, however, in that the nature of the deaths of Richard Bolles and Sir Charles Cavendish bring to mind Clarendon's observation on the excessive disdain of danger which many commanders demonstrated.[96] Carnarvon was not unique in a careless disregard for death, and in this respect he and many others lived up to Symmons's recommended Cavalier attribute: 'he dares accept of deaths challenge to meet it in the field'. Charles Cavendish was the second son of William second Earl of Devonshire, who died in 1628. The third Earl adhered to the King but spent the years from 1642 until 1645 in Europe. Charles, twenty-two when war began, had spent much of his younger manhood travelling; 'he went into Greece, all over; and that would not serve his turne but he would goe to Babylon . . . but to see Babylon he was to march in the Turk's armie'. He was given, in 1642, the task of recruiting the Duke of York's Regiment of Horse, at Prince Rupert's instigation. The recruitment took place largely in the area that lay in the south of Newcastle's territory, in southern Yorkshire and in Lincolnshire, where Cavendish had his principal residence.

It is a measure of Clarendon's Oxford-based view of the war that he barely notices Cavendish, and even confuses him with another of the same name. Aubrey, however, who noted his subject's tours in Europe and the Near East, recorded also the funeral sermon preached in 1674, when Cavendish's body was translated to his mother's grave at Derby, by William Naylor. Naylor praised Cavendish exuberantly as 'the soldier's mignion, and his majesties darling' and, continuing in the same vein, affirmed that 'the King's cause lived with him, the King's cause died with him – When Cromwell heard that he was slaine he cried upon it We have donne our businesse'. Maybe. Certainly Cavendish animated the cause in his native country, and he was killed in action there at Gainsborough on 27 July 1643. The sermon, however, drew nearer to a certainty when Naylor spoke of 'two things . . . this commander knew not, pardon his ignorance, – he knew not how to flie away – he knew not how to aske quarter'. The first of these, though not a truly soldierly attribute, naturally followed from the second, contempt for the rebels who surrounded him. His horse 'mired in a bog . . . the rebels surround him, and take him prisoner: and after he was soe, a base rascall comes behind him, and runs him through.'[97] Another source states that he was killed by a thrust under the short ribs.[98] Surrounded and disarmed, Cavendish probably refused to ask for quarter and so was despatched. Spencer Compton Earl of Northampton died in a similar way at Hopton Heath.

Richard Bolles of Theddlethorp in Lincolnshire was a fifty-year-old veteran of Europe and the Scots wars when he assumed command of the infantry regiment raised by Lord Pagett, late in 1642. He fought at the storm of Bristol, where so many officers fell, but survived to end his days in a sacrificial gesture of defiance to the rebels. A memorial to the 'renowned Martialist Richard Bowles' was later set up in Winchester Cathedral to record his death at Alton Church in Hampshire on 13 December 1643. According to the memorial he and a force of 500 men (from Wallingford, Clarendon noted) found themselves surprised by 5,000 rebel troops. Bolles and about eighty of his men fled into the church, which they held for several hours before the enemy broke in and killed him and sixty of his men, taking the rest. 'His gracious Soveraign hearing of his high commendations, in this patriotic expression said "Bring me a Mourning Scarffe, I have lost one of my best Commanders in this kingdom." '[99] From an enemy source the intensity of the church fighting is confirmed:

Nay, at the entring of that church, dreadful to see the enemy opening the doore when ready to receve you with their pikes and muskets, the horses slaine in the allies of which the enimy made brestworks, the churchyard as well as the church being covered with dead and wounded, amongst whom you long strugled . . . from which dayes service you escaped with a few dry blowes with the musket stocks of those who afterwardes, soe many as were liveing and able, were caried prisoners to Farnham; the choicest men, for soe many, that were taken since the beginning of theis warrs.[100]

The writer of this account, intent upon boosting the image of his master, the Parliamentarian Colonel John Birch, saw the fight at Alton from the attackers' viewpoint. Clarendon, explaining the context of the fighting there, confirmed the nature of the fight. He stated that Bolles withdrew to the church for cover, hoping to hold out there until relieved, but the enemy attacked even before the doors could be barricaded. After a 'short resistance, in which many were killed' the survivors threw down their weapons on offer of their lives. Bolles, however, kept his sword in his hand and refused quarter: 'with the death of two or three of [his] assailants, he was killed in the place; his enemies giving him a testimony of great courage and resolution'.[101]

Whatever the precise sequence of events may have been, the fierceness of the fighting is clear, and Bolles's contemptuous dismissal of surrender remarkable. Clearly, sacrificial gestures such as this could be made by a veteran soldier as well as by a reckless young man such as Cavendish, or the Earl of Caernarvon. His action is comparable with the collective self-sacrifice of the Whitecoats on Marston Moor, for which the only explanation must be, in their case and in that of Bolles (and some of his men) a scorn both of death itself and of the enemy capable of inflicting it. These men did not lack the 'edge' which Hobbes felt was missing in general from the King's soldiers.

The death of Bolles at Alton in December 1643 may have been the last of the deaths in action which had the power to stop men in their tracks. The widespread slaughters that lay ahead, the commonplace loss of regimental commanders and others, became all too familiar. The death in action of an eminent commander or Grandee which hitherto could be held up as a measure of the commitment that should be shown to the King's cause, emphasising the *jus ad bellum*, and simultaneously illustrate the bitter sadness of civil war, thenceforth sank into the general pit of bloodletting. The will to eulogise such as Sir Bevil Grenvile, Colonels Thomas Morgan, Sir John Smith and Sir John Digby[102] began to falter. Nor, anyway, were the deaths of commanders always noble, or able to be perceived as such by omnivorous poetasters and professional hacks, on either side. Colonel Sir Charles Blount, an Oxfordshire gentleman, was shot dead by a Royalist sentry at Oxford in May 1644, unrecognised.[103] Colonel Sir Thomas Byron was shot down (apparently deliberately) in December 1643, also at Oxford. Bulstrode Whitelocke had occasion to remember Byron with kindness, his recollection betraying also what he, Whitelocke, should expect of a gentleman of birth such as himself, though ranged against him in war. Whitelocke's house at Fawley Court had been occupied by Royalist troops who, despite orders to the contrary from Sir John Byron, plundered extensively and at will. They were but 'brutish common soldiers'. Whitelocke's children were there in the care of William Cooke and had 'better usage' for Sir Thomas Byron quartered in that house:

and asking whose children they were was answeared that they were the children of a young woman there, Wm Cookes daughter butt he replyed that they did not looke like her children, and wished them not to be afrayde to tell him whose children they were, for they should have no harme. they then confest they were Wh[itelocke's] children, and prayed they might have no hurt done them, Sr Thomas sayd it were a barbarous thing to hurt those pretty innocent children, and kissed and made much of them, and shewed great generosity . . .[104]

Other colonels perished from illness and disease contracted as a result of their service. Colonel Sir William Pennyman died of consumption at Oxford, where he was governor, in August 1643. Sir William Saville, governor of York, died suddenly in January 1644 from an unspecified disease. He had not been ill for long.[105] Pontefract Castle in Yorkshire, a major Royalist garrison both in 1642–45 and again in 1648, must have been an unhealthy place. Colonel Sir John Redman, its governor, resigned in late 1644 and died shortly afterwards of TB. His successor, Colonel Richard Lowther, died at Newark in August 1645 of a consumption contracted whilst in Pontefract. Colonel Gervase Cutler, a divisional commander at Pontefract under Lowther, succumbed to consumption and died on duty on 25 June 1645.[106] Nathan Drake, the painstaking diarist of the siege of Pontefract, noted:

This day morning, that worthy knight Sir Gervis Cuttler departed this life, the enemy not suffring any fresh meate ever to be brought to him since he fell sick, onely one chickin and one poore joynt of meate his lady brought with hur 2 daies before he departed, neither will the enemy suffer him to be buryed in the Church, nor conveyed to his owne habitation to take place with his auncestors.[107]

Cutler was buried in the castle 'first cophined and then the cophin and all wraped up in lead, and after a funerall sarmond he was buryed in the Chapeel . . . with 3 gallont vollyes of shott according to the honour of such a brave souldyer as he was'.[108] Wherever possible, honourable interment followed upon the death of a commander but, as the war dragged on and death became more frequent and widespread, it was not always possible. Sir Henry Slingsby lost a cousin and a nephew at Marston Moor in July 1644: 'both of ym slain in ye field; ye former [his nephew Colonel

John Fenwick] could not be found to have his body brought off, ye latter [his cousin, Sir Charles Slingsby] was found and buri'd in York minster'.[109]

V

Now and again a Royalist commander met a fate which must have struck all who heard of it as ironical. The best-known case is that of Robert Pierrepoint first Earl of Kingston, whose nature inclined him to avoid involvement in the King's cause until he was satisfied of its prospects. (A younger son, Francis, was a rebel colonel before his father showed his hand, but none too committed.) Clarendon recounted at length the story of Kingston's equivocation in 1642 and that of his neighbour, Francis Leake first Baron Deincourt. The story is often cited as an example of the unwillingness of neuters to commit themselves, but that is misleading: Deincourt and his sons turned out for the King in person, and two of the family were killed in arms. As for Kingston, when invited by Lord Capel to contribute ready money in 1642, he denied that he had any to hand, but said his neighbour Deincourt had a good store of it: he was 'good for nothing, and lived like a hog, not allowing himself necessaries' and should have had about £20,000 in the 'scurvy house in which he lived'. At the same time, Lord Deincourt was visited by John Ashburnham on the same errand bearing a letter from the King with his sign manual, which Deincourt allegedly pretended not to recognise: but he told Ashburnham that though he, Deincourt, had no ready money to advance, he had a neighbour, Lord Kingston, 'that never did good to any body, and loved nobody but himself, who had a world of money', which Deincourt promised to prove.[110] The story, rooted in local rivalry between two peers, undoubtedly received embellishment at the court, where it was current gossip in the summer of 1642. Kingston's affections were entirely with the King. In May 1642 he declined to attend Parliament, excusing himself by a lameness in his leg,[111] and he had a tendency to represent himself as aged (he was fifty-eight in 1642) and not up to much.[112] Nevertheless, he took an informed interest in matters military, as he demonstrated in March 1639, when the preparations for the Bishops' Wars were under way:

I pray you forgett not that I told you my servant Bowskill assured mee from the armorer of Nott[ingham] that two of myne armors with a little cost may be made good cuirashiers a la moderne, and that I besought you to commaund my said servant att my charge to have them made fitt for your service immediately and to accept also a black armor of myne for your own body, being of a singular proof and though not in full fashion yet of more use for you when you shall have occasion to putt on armor then any of these new, which bee unable to resist a paper bullett, and bee pleased to remember I told you when service happeneth the fashion of armes will not be observed.[113]

Kingston stood 'a few months neuter . . . and being a man of great wealth and dependencies, many people hung in suspense', it was said. It might also be said that, far from being neutral, Kingston was one of those who waited to see the success or otherwise of the King's more forward adherents before committing himself, and that is not neutrality. On 25 March 1643 he accepted a commission as a colonel, and in May was made Lieutenant General over Lincolnshire, Rutland, Huntingdonshire, Cambridgeshire and Norfolk. His period of service was short: captured in July, he was being transferred by boat to Hull when Royalist gunners opened fire on the vessel to intimidate the guards. The earl was killed outright by his own side.[114]

His hesitation before actively committing himself to the war is not comparable with that of William sixth Baron Paget of Beaudesert. Paget's political record and familial associations marked him down as a Parliamentarian. He supported the proceedings against Strafford and Archbishop Laud, and had been one of the twelve peers who petitioned the King to summon a Parliament in 1640.[115] His father-in-law was Henry Rich first Earl of Holland. Clarendon marked Paget down as one 'who had contributed all his faculties to [Parliament's] service, and to the prejudice of the King's, from before the beginning of the parliament'. He had been 'one of their teasers to broach those bold high overtures soberer men were not willing at first to be seen in'. Apparently committed to the Militia Ordinance, Paget was appointed Lord Lieutenant of Buckinghamshire ('one of the most confiding counties') but then, noted Clarendon, 'convinced in his conscience [he] fled from them'.[116] The Lord Paget:

not long after this began to boggle, and was unfixed in his resolutions: and upon the king's publishing of his commission of array, and declaration against the ordinance of parliament for the militia, (his lordship's heart failing him, and being unsatisfied in his judgement,) he revolted from the Parliament and went to the King.[117]

'Tuesday last arrived . . . Lord Paget . . . having submitted to the King, and acknowledged the error of meddling with the Militia of Buckinghamshire.'[118] As well as divulging whatever he could about Parliament's proceedings, Paget undertook to raise troops as a colonel, the quality of which may be assessed from the fact that the regiment which Bolles led at Alton was first recruited by Paget. In 1644 he surrendered himself to the protection of the Earl of Essex, and went to Parliament 'expressing much sorrow for his deserting the parliament and adhering to the enemy, whose counsel and designs he now seeth to tend to the destruction of the kingdom'.[119] His composition was moderate in view of his record, his defection (one among several late in 1644) serving the Parliament's interest very well indeed. When his father-in-law Holland becaome a Royalist general in 1648 Paget kept aloof and, though later accused of conveying money, was not proceeded against. Holland was beheaded in 1649. Paget officiated at the coronation of Charles II in 1660.

Paget, like Littleton, the Lord Keeper, surprised most observers by going over to the King, the residual pull of loyalty to the Crown playing upon what may have been personal rather than political uncertainties. The year 1644 was one of several defections from the King, Paget was not alone in it, and the Wilmot 'plot' occurred a month before Paget's surrender to the Earl of Essex. His own future well-being may have directed his political decisions, and he was no more a principled Parliamentarian than he was a principled Royalist. Both changes in his allegiance occurred when the going was becoming perceptibly tough.

Henry Lord Mordaunt, heir to John Mordaunt first Earl of Peterborough, went over to the King in April 1643. His father at that date lay dying of the consumption that killed him the following June, whereupon the earldom descended to his Royalist son. The father's association with Parliament, in whose interest he commanded troops and was General of the Ordnance, is hard to explain. He was by no means trusted. In the Commons his papist upbringing was held against him, and when his friends protested that he had converted and conformed to the Protestant religion and 'had duly observed prayers in his family and duly frequented the church' Sir Philip Stapleton 'said that he was very doubtful of such converts'.[120] He was, further, 'a keeper of ill company', to which the rejoinder of his friends was less than satisfying: 'He is a very noble lord when he is himself, but there are a great company of debauche[d] men which comes to his house and therefore' he was not to be confided in.[121] Nevertheless, Parliament confirmed him as Lord Lieutenant of Northamptonshire under the Militia Ordinance, and he was commissioned in its army – that may reflect the relative dearth of men of standing available in 1642. His son, the second Earl, commanded under his father, but once his father's illness had taken hold he went over to the King, whom he served with far more diligence than Paget. It is possible, from his later career, that he had no sympathy with his father's new religion, any more than he evidently had with the cause of Parliament. As a cavalry colonel Peterborough fought and was wounded at First Newbury in September and, though summoned to the Oxford parliament, continued to exercise field command at Cropredy Bridge and Lostwithiel in 1644. In July that year he fought a duel with a Captain Willoughby 'whose father is steward to the Earl of Northampton; Willoughby wounded in the shoulder and thigh, the Earl safe without hurt. Willoughby challenged.'[122] Though he surrendered in 1645, and proceeded to compound, he was involved in the Earl of Holland's uprising in 1648 and obliged to compound a second time for his property. Clarendon did not affect to notice Peterborough except in the context of the 1648 rising, and then in passing as one of any number of loyal officers ready to rise that year.

Mordaunt's restraint before he went over to the King reflected either filial duty or paternal control. Both Paget and Littleton clearly experienced crises of conscience of some degree of other. A case that may fall between the two is that of Warwick second Lord Mohun, who succeeded to the title in 1640 though the second son of the first Lord. He was one of the earliest to attend upon the King at York and had left there with his loyalty clearly shown. However, once back in Devon he equivocated: so soon as any Royalist musterings occurred in Cornwall, Mohun forebore 'to join himself to the King's party, staying at home at his own house and imparting himself equally to all men of several constitutions'. What happened next is open to interpretation.

According to Clarendon, when news came of the battle at Edgehill and the King's march on London 'he took a journey towards London . . . and presented himself to his Majesty at Brainford as sent from Sir Ralph Hopton and the . . . gentlemen engaged in Cornwall'. It is possible that Mohun was attempting to get through to London, but finding the King between him and the city, presented himself as a messenger from the West Country. Clarendon, however, may well have divined the real reason for his journey, which was to have himself commissioned to a command in his locality. If that was so, then Mohun, like others, waited upon the events of the war before choosing to commit himself openly to the cause he had already indicated that he supported. Upon his return to the West Country 'he immediately raised a regiment of foot, behaving him[self] as actively, and being every way as forward in the advancing the great business, as any man; so that men imputed his former reservedness only to his not being satisfied in a condition of command' to which his status entitled him.[123] Yet 'he had not the good fortune to be very gracious in his own country' and his command status apparently annoyed other Royalists.[124] Even so, he fought hard, and in 1643 became Colonel General of Wiltshire, Hampshire, Devonshire, Somerset and Cornwall, with Exeter and Bristol. Prince Maurice favoured him, but upon his summons to the Oxford parliament in 1644, as with so many peers, his activism fell away and he was replaced in the generalship by Sir John Berkeley. A committee of the Commons was subsequently set up to hear charges of brutality against Mohun, but he proceeded to his composition unchallenged. His overt Royalism faded after 1649, he took the Engagement of Loyalty to the Commonwealth and renounced his loyalty to Charles II.[125]

When Mohun achieved his appointment in 1642, overall command in the west lay with William Seymour Marquess of Hertford, one of those Grandees whose initial support for the King led to his employment in high military command. Hertford's early career and political involvements are widely known. His royal descent and his association with the opposition to the King – he, like Paget, had petitioned for a parliament in 1640 – required the King at the very least to neutralise him, which he did by appointing him Governor of the Prince of Wales in succession to the Earl of Newcastle. Hertford's brother-in-law was the Earl of

Essex, but 'nothwithstanding all his allies, and those with whom he had the greatest familiarity and friendship, were of the opposite party' Hertford himself (created marquess in 1641) showed no further tendency towards opposition. Clarendon did not think Hertford fit for the office of governor of the heir to the thorne: 'He was of an age not fit for much activity and fatigue, and loved, and was even wedded so much to his ease, that he loved his book above all exercises.' He took no delight in conversation or in argument, but then, as Clarendon recognised, tutors could do all that. The important thing was that Hertford, 'of an universal esteem over the kingdom', should be seen as associated with royal proceedings, and since his loyalty to the established church was also well known, he was an essential adjunct to those proceedings in the months leading up to open war.[126]

Hertford's military role, as colonel and Lieutenant General in the south-west and South Wales, followed naturally upon his proven loyalty, though the vastness of his command reflected preliminary organisation rather than the practical division of the country that would follow upon the first few months of warfare. Whitelocke noted that Hertford was the first general appointed by the King,[127] and Lindsey was the second. Leaving aside Newcastle, who was clearly the first, the difference between Hertford and Lindsey was primarily that Lindsey had wide military experience and was recognised as a military figure. His appointment indicates that the King was only too well aware that social prestige and territorial influence were not in themselves to be the sole criteria for army command.

Hertford may be compared with the Earls of Cumberland and Derby, transitional figures in the emergence of Royalist armies. Hertford's military achievements, setbacks aside, culminated in the storm of Bristol in July 1643, costly though it was. These achievements are best seen as the work of his subordinates, Hopton and Maurice, and his coadjutor Rupert. Thereafter, Hertford retired to court life at Oxford, with a better record of achievement than either Derby or Cumberland – or, come to that, Carbery and Arthur Lord Capel, whose abilities were not suited to a war with its own momentum. Age – Hertford was fifty-six in 1643 – had little to do with the marquess's retirement. He had roused himself from the natural lethargy which Clarendon perceived to be his primary characteristic, and had acquitted himself well enough, not least in his reliance upon professional sub-ordinates.[128]

VI

Defiance of the Parliament in the wake of defeat in 1646 was widespread amongst all ranks of the Royalist armies, and could take many forms: in voluntary exile, in resistance at the local level to sequestrators, in the undervaluing of estates for the purposes of composition, and in readiness to take up arms again should the opportunity arise. The son of Colonel Sir Thomas Eyton of Shropshire, 'a very wild young man', became a highwayman and was arrested for shooting down a Parliamentarian officer near St Albans in 1657.[129] The survival of the spirit of Royalism after 1646, and particularly after 1649, so frequently encountered in contemporary sources, evidences the profundity of commitment to the cause of the Crown. As has been said, it would have taken the Republic far longer than the time allotted to it to reconcile these men and others, too young to have fought in 1642, who nevertheless imbibed loyalism from activist fathers and brothers. If Royalism in its original form perished in the wake of defeat, to reappear in a transmuted form in 1648 and afterwards, the spirit of the First Civil War Cavaliers did survive.

Historians have chosen to make the point that the 'Royalist' rising of 1648, and the attempt by Charles II to regain his throne, would have been impossible without Presbyterian and other, formerly enemy, help. It might also be argued that the Presbyterian reaction of 1647/48 and subsequently would only have been dangerous to the New Model and its political collaborators given the residual activist commitment of a large number of experienced Royalist commanders of 1642–46. Wherever the former interpretation arises there is an implicit assumption that material defeat in 1646 deprived Royalism of the unity of purpose necessary to resurrect the cause. Further, that the King's necessary political machinations of 1646–48 effectively removed the original basis upon which his supporters had fought for so long, so hard. The financial consequences of defeat for countless Royalist soldiers and commanders were almost insupportable. The whole process of sequestration – punitive fines, land and property sales and composition – did deprive many of them of the resources with which to make good a continuing commitment.

The King's move towards Presbyterianism and the Scottish alliance did appear to set at nothing the Anglicanism of Royalists. Against this must be set two factors to which historians need to pay more attention: the development of a widespread comradeship amongst Royalists that emerged from the war years, which could very well have been intensified by defeat – such is human nature, after all – and the legacy of hatred towards Parliament which the punitive processes can only have intensified. Many Royalists may have been overawed by the machinery of state-directed persecution, but they were a sullen, uncooperative, irreconcilable body. It was, after all, the tenacious defenders of Colchester in 1648 who proved harder to subdue than the largely Scottish invasion force which entered England that same year with its small contingent of Old Cavaliers in its command structure. It is irrelevant that the Royalists failed after 1646 and before 1660 to bring to fruition any of their proposed risings, conspiracies and plots: what is relevant is that time and time again there were men ready to commit, with a pedigree of resistance to Parliament that had its roots in the old service.

Some Royalists took their defiance of Parliament to the very bar of the House of Commons itself. Two colonels did so, Sir John Stawell and Sir Lewis Dyve. Professor Russell has explained Stawell's Royalism pejoratively: he has described him as an obsessive anti-Puritan and equally obsessive in his 'fear of the lower orders'.[130] Presumably Stawell's obsessive anti-Puritanism was more striking in degree and intensity than the obsessiveness of Puritan writers and preachers with the abolition of the church structure to which Stawell subscribed. Clarendon thought him 'a gentleman . . . who had from the beginning of the parliament' (Stawell represented Somerset in the Commons) 'shewed very great affection to the person of the king, and to the government that was settled, both in church and state', which was plainly no more and no less than many men of his standing, such as Sir Henry Slingsby, had done or would do. 'From the beginning of the war [he] had engaged both his own person and his two sons, in the most active part of it, with singular courage; and had rendered himself as odious to the parliament, as any man of that condition had done.'[131] Stawell's 'fear' of the lower orders was no greater than that of many Royalist gentlemen who saw the structure of their society seemingly threatened by rebellion and the stirring of the people by preachers and pamphleteers. Nor was his fear motivated by his personal safety – quite the contrary, for he risked everything not only before 1646 but afterwards. A Grand Jury in Somerset found him guilty of high treason[132] in September 1646. Brought to the bar of the Commons, 'Sir John Stowell . . . refused to kneel and behaved himself with very much boldness and obstinacy.'[133] He refused to take the National Covenant and was committed to the Tower to await his trial on the charge of treason. On 14 March 1649 – he had been all this time in prison – Parliament ordered that he be proceeded against for his life, and in June 1650 his name was added to those to be considered by the High Court of Justice. Stawell had made the journey to London voluntarily in 1646 to proceed to his composition, but his absolute refusal – which he reiterated in 1653 – to take the necessary oath (pleading the terms for the rendition of Exeter) had brought him to the dangerous pass in which he found himself. Though he did not in the end come to trial, and was admitted to compound in 1653, he was not to be released until the Restoration was imminent. Nothing in the record shows that he flinched from the fate that had befallen him and would befall other Royalists who similarly refused to compromise with, or were excepted from pardon by, the Republic.[134] Stawell's second son, Edward, was wounded in 1644 as a regimental colonel, and the third son, George, held a troop command during the war.[135]

Sir Lewis Dyve, George Digby's half-brother whom Digby would have preferred to Lunsford in the Lieutenancy of the Tower, was as obdurate as Stawell. He had been taken notice of by the Commons as a suspect papist in February 1642 and was to be sent for as a delinquent.[136] His father-in-law, Sir John Strangeways, MP for Weymouth and Melcombe Regis (a Straffordian who served in the Commons until expelled at Pride's Purge[137]) stood surety for him and his continued liberty.[138] An associate of the Stradlings[139] and, from the summer of 1642, when he was in Rotterdam, of Prince Rupert, Dyve exercised regimental command until his capture at Sherborne in 1645. Taken to the bar of the Commons, he, like Stawell, 'demeaned himself very superciliously and proudly, seeming to refuse to kneel'. Unlike Stawell, Dyve was not himself an MP, though he had sat in the Commons in the 1620s in the seat held from 1641 by Strangeways. After a period in the Tower and other prisons,

Dyve escaped, made his way to the Isle of Man (assisted *en route* by his mother's tenantry) and there joined the diehard Sir Marmaduke Langdale. He eventually got away to Europe.[140]

VII

Insights into the characters and personalities of other Royalist colonels are not infrequently met with, though often they are but vignettes which others, who knew them, for reasons of curiosity noted down. Countless colonels and other officers appear in the proceedings of the committees for Advance of Money and for Compounding, as well as in other official documents, as 'notorious' or 'hearty for the king', and these almost obligatory denunciations by Parliamentarian committee men and others serve only to show the residual loyalism of otherwise defeated men. Occasionally something more may be said, as in the case of Colonel Nicholas Borlace of Newlyn in Cornwall, who had been MP for Tregony in the Short Parliament. In October 1650 the county committee reported on him as the 'most eminent commander here of that party for the late King'[141] and they were having no end of trouble from him. It arose from the committee's objection to Borlace's composition, fixed upon a fine of £320 in June 1649, he being comprised within the articles for the surrender of Truro in 1646. The committee represented that Borlace, as a Catholic delinquent, could not be admitted to compound, and the legal wrangles that arose from that dragged on without resolution until 1655. During this time Borlace, the committee alleged, presumed 'by his wit, boldness, and false information' (he 'being of an importunate and clamorous spirit') to make the Truro articles mean more than it had ever been intended they should mean – that is, that they extended no further than to protect those comprised within them from plunder by the Parliament's soldiers. If Borlace had his way, they argued, 'all the delinquents in this county . . . will crave the same'. He was merely, they thought, protracting the whole business in the hope of political change, though he was well known in Cornwall as:

the most cruel oppressor of any . . . in this county or elsewhere; and his wife, children, and family, as they are of the same religion, so run hand in hand with him in the same acts of cruelty . . . they have always desperate persons at hand to swear to their proposals.

In this vein, and with further allusion to Borlace's 'notorious wickedness', the Cornish committee men desperately fought back against him.[142] Borlace had the patience and subtlety to play the system for all it was worth against his enemies, going so far as to appeal to Cromwell himself. The local committee were clearly unnerved and quite unable to cope with him: he derided their authority by appealing over their heads, appearing to enlist Parliament's leading generals of the war years, Fairfax and Cromwell, on his behalf. Borlace was not alone in his use of time-wasting and obstructive tactics, whether these proceeded from pure self-interest, which would be readily understandable, or wartime animosity, or a fusion of the two. The composition process is full of Royalist colonels and others who persistently undervalued their property, lied openly and quite brazenly about their wartime activities – Sir Edward Rodney of Somerset, the author of the monarchist tract *Of Divine Providence* (1626) is a fine example of that[143] – challenged and resisted their local committees and in all other ways sought to protect themselves and their estates as much as the laws would allow them, and then some. Borlace, his extreme resolution and his reputed Catholicism notwithstanding, may reasonably represent them all. Even those who rushed to compound, pleading their case and showing all signs of contrition, such as Rodney, never shook off the suspicion of their neighbours.[144]

Rodney claimed that he had been a most moderate enemy, that he had never fined, imprisoned or sequestered any man for adhering to the Parliament. The same was said of (not by) Sir Thomas Gower of Stittenham in Yorkshire: 'one whose moderation towards the Parliament and their friends begat him long imprisonment by the King, and as one who was also plundered by the Earl of Newcastle'.[145] Gower's advocate, recommending leniency for him, was Sir Thomas Fairfax. It will be recalled that Gower had been under suspicion in the summer of 1642 for 'encouraging' the Hothams, and he was dismissed as sheriff of Yorkshire in favour of the more resolute Sir Richard Hutton of Goldsborough (who was to be killed in action in 1645). Gower had been active in the Militia Ordinance as late as May, when the King was already at York – but then, so had Lord Paget in Buckinghamshire and other future Royalist commanders in their counties. If Gower was confined, perhaps under house arrest – and there is no reason to doubt it – his imprisonment must have occurred between August 1642 and June 1643, for in the latter month he accompanied the Queen's forces south to Oxford. However loosely the term 'plundered' may be used, for his estate to have been so used by Newcastle, Gower must have been under restraint after December 1642. Following his journey to Oxford, little if anything is known of him until September 1645, when he fought and was captured at Rowton Heath, near Chester. More significantly, he consented to his own exchange, which must also have been initiated from the Royalist camp, and continued in arms to the surrender of Oxford.

The two obvious questions that arise are: why was he singled out for punishment in 1642 when he apparently did no more than Paget, and less conspicuously than that peer, and others; and what happened to him after June 1643 to make him so resolute where previously he had been at best equivocal? Nothing appears to offer a resolution of this mysterious Civil War career. He had no apparent links with Parliamentarian families – indeed, his wife was a Howard of Naworth, a family in which Royalism was deeply ingrained. Further, his son Edward served as a major under James King, which means activism before July 1644, and ended the war (with his Royalist grandfather) in Newark garrison. When Anne Lady Halkett came to mention Gower in her memoir, the only aspect of the man which seemed worthy of her comment was his interest in medicine! She must have been aware of his odd career when war began, but passed over it. She recorded that he 'studied phisicke more for devertisement then gaine' and was at pains to describe how he cured a three-year-old boy of smallpox:

by the advise of Sir Thomas Gore . . . hee tooke a purge which carried away a great part of the humour so that nature, as hee said, would bee able to master the rest, and itt had so good successe that hee recovered perfectly well withoutt the least prejudice . . . I cannott butt mention this from the extreordinarynese of the cure.[146]

Given the way in which what we would most want to know about Gower was passed over in favour of an illuminating anecdote, the hit-and-miss nature of surviving contemporary allusions is amply demonstrated. Nevertheless, what was said of men can be either, or both, illuminating and suggestive. Sometimes, there are sufficient views of a man to permit an assessment apart from that enforced upon us by enemy propaganda. Henry Jermyn is a case in point. He was a younger son of Sir Thomas Jermyn, Comptroller of the Household, had political experience as an MP in the 1620s, and entered the Queen's service as her Vice-chamberlain and Master of the Horse in 1639. His well known closeness to the Queen aroused the suspicion and hostility of the Commons, and he was compelled to flee to Europe in 1641 after involvement in the Army Plots. When the Queen herself arrived in France in 1642, Jermyn was made her secretary: the two preceding holders of that post, Guilford Slingsby and Sir John Winter, both served as colonels during the war, and in 1643 Jermyn himself became colonel of the Queen's regiment of horse, her Lifeguard. His military role was brief but not without incident, and he performed well enough in battle, sustaining a bullet wound at Albourne Chase. Command of the Queen's regiment devolved upon Richard Gerard, the Lancashire Catholic.[147] Jermyn's performance in the field drew Cowley's attention:

> The valiant Jermyn stops their hasty course
> Jermin in whom united does remaine
> All that kind Mothers wishes can containe;
> In whom Wit, Judgment, Valour, Goodnesse joyne,
> And all theise through a comely Body shine,
> A Soule compos'd of th' Eagle and the Dove;
> Which all men must admire and all men love.[148]

Not all men. 'Butcherly Jermyn' Parliament stigmatised him, for no readily apparent reason, 'contemptible Harry', whose influence on the Queen, and hers upon the King, were seen as a great malignancy. Yet he was 'an extremely handsome young man, and for that reason was always pleasing to the ladies . . . He is a splendid, fortunate and liberal man, a gambler; all in all, a man who has the favour of the courtiers but is not esteemed by the soldiers'.[149] Clarendon said of him that he 'valued himself upon the impossible faculty to please all, and displease none' and 'in his own judgement, was very indifferent in all matters relating to religion [though he] was always of some faction that regarded it'.[150] In fact, Clarendon's treatment of Jermyn was moderate compared with the way he damned others, such as Goring, and there is some similarity between Jermyn's character, in so far as it is revealed, and that of Harry Wilmot: both men saw themselves as arbiters of the political future after the Civil War, though it is arguable that Jermyn's influence, whatever it may have been before 1646, needed the intricacies of the court in exile to flourish. He was, after all, a consummate courtier, the failing attributed to him by Clarendon being demonstrably a valuable court virtue. Jermyn's intransigent Royalism, as historians have tended to see it, was somewhat at odds with his aspirant diplomacy: but he had little choice other than to except against Parliament, when the Parliament had overtly excepted against him, denying him a place in any post-war England that might emerge from negotiated peace or from Parliament's military victory.

The limits of Jermyn's influence as an arbiter are seen most clearly in the failure of his attempt to bring the Earl of Holland back into royal favour in 1643 – in which year both Jermyn and Wilmot were advanced to the peerage with concomitant increases in their self-esteem. Lord Paget's father-in-law was but one of Parliament's more eminent erstwhile supporters who endeavoured to return to his allegiance, though his pride could not be satisfied even with the help of Jermyn and the Queen, whose confidant and follower the earl had been. According to Clarendon, Holland's overtures to the Royalists followed upon the Queen's return from Europe in February 1643, and Jermyn was his intermediary. Hostility to Holland was rife at Oxford; he was left to cool his heels for two days at Wallingford before being admitted to the city, by which time he realised that he had placed too much confidence in Jermyn and the Queen. A show of commitment in the royal army before Gloucester earned Holland no further respect, though the King had received him cordially enough. Jermyn was prepared to take his cause as far as to side with him in a matter of court preferment against the unimpeachably loyal and well-deserving Marquess of Hertford, but the King's resentment towards Holland was not to be overcome.

Treachery, like rebellion, was for Charles a personal matter: he and his crown were indivisible except by death, and Holland's failure to excuse his earlier defection probably played more upon the King's mind than any other factor. Holland's miscalculation was twofold. He had assumed the Queen's influence over her husband as he had assumed that of Jermyn with the Queen. And he had supposed his 'transgressions' less serious than the King appeared to regard them. Had Holland stood by the King in 1642 it is possible that he might have secured the command that went to Lindsey: he certainly considered himself fitted to such a role, another aspiration in which he was balked at Oxford. Jermyn's part in the Holland affair, considerable as it was, demonstrated most satisfactorily that he could not 'please all, and displease none'.

Jermyn's military participation in the war was short, honourable and of light consequence. It was a necessary deviation from his primary role as court intriguer and manipulator, in which he was less adept than another who also ventured into military command, George Lord Digby. Professor Russell has shown that Digby, like Jermyn, to rehearse Clarendon's judgement, was indifferent in matters of religion. Digby's Erastianism, observed Russell, both divided him from the King, whom he nevertheless served unflinchingly, and made him a resolute enemy of Parliament's religious crusade, upon which its war effort turned.[151] The man himself was:

a well accomplished Gentleman, and of great parts, naturall and acquired, and was now Secretary of State, and was as gallant with his sword, as eminent with his tongue or pen; but he had likewise so much of a Romantick spirit, and of such super-refined policies, that . . . there are some things, which have more wonder in them, than worth . . .[152]

Sir Philip Warwick added later that Digby 'affected Astrology, which I take to be fatall to most, that do so; for it too often draws them off from duty, by supposing their destiny inevitable'.[153] Lorenzo Magalotti, meeting Digby after 1660, did not note any affinity with astrology, but pinpointed his weaknesses then as 'prodigality and licentiousness', though he conceded his strong points were, as Warwick said, 'the sword and the pen; his ornament is poetry'.[154] Clarendon thought Digby 'a graceful and beautiful person' in 1642, 'of great eloquence and becomingness in his discourse' but, like Wilmot, he had a fatal flaw: 'having an ambition and vanity superior to all his other parts, and a confidence peculiar to himself, which sometimes intoxicated, and transported and exposed him'.[155]

It has been shown that Digby lacked neither personal courage nor the wit to turn a dangerous situation to his advantage. His military role, if it is distinct from his political involvements, may have begun in January 1642. He was accused of being present with Lunsford and others at Kingston on Thames[156] and that when his personal carriage was stopped and searched at Mere in Wiltshire it contained thirty-eight cases (pairs) of pistols, five muskets, five war saddles, together with powder – but no bullets.[157] This, and his leading part in the attempt upon the Five Members, forced him into temporary exile abroad whilst Parliament accused him of high treason. He had quickly replaced Lunsford as the 'most universally odious man' in the kingdom. A colonel of horse and dragoons when war broke out, he was wounded at Lichfield early in 1643. Thereafter his military involvement was primarily as adviser to the King, in which capacity he alienated Prince Rupert and others whilst, in 1644, cultivating the friendship of George Goring. Clarendon observed of this alliance that each thought the other his dupe, and so each earnestly embraced the other's friendship. His last military function was in 1645, when he endeavoured to resurrect the north as a source of men and arms for the King, a belated attempt to recover what Newcastle and Prince Rupert had abandoned in 1644. Commissioned as Lieutenant General, Digby took over the depleted but still effective Northern Horse brigades commanded by Langdale, Gamaliel Dudley, Sir William Blakiston and Sir William Mason, the Norfolk lawyer. The resultant expedition was a disaster for the Royalists, whether of the Northern Horse, or those who showed willingness to appear in arms upon the approach of fellow north country men. In the fight at Sherburn in Elmet in October 1645 poor dispositions, usually attributed to Digby's judgement, led to a sweeping victory by Copley's Parliamentarian forces and Digby's flight, with the remnants of the expeditionary force, to the stronghold of Skipton, held for the King by Sir John Mallory of Studley. Mallory, as MP for Ripon, had been one of those who had formed the slowly emerging Royalist party in the Commons, though, unlike most of them, he had refused to sign the Protestation of 1641 (which attracted speculation as to his religious principles). Mallory and Digby, therefore, must have known one another, though their paths in the war had not previously crossed. From Skipton, Digby headed for Scotland, but what was left of his force was scattered in a running fight on Carlisle Sands, Digby, Langdale and other commanders escaping to the Isle of Man. 'Thus those fifteen hundred horse which marched northward . . . within very few days were brought to nothing; and the generalship of Lord Digby to an end,' observed Clarendon.[158] Yet he believed that had the misfortune at Sherburn, which he imperfectly understood, not befallen Digby's men, the Lieutenant General would 'without doubt [have] been master of York, and of the whole north', and as for Digby, he, said Clarendon, attributed his failure less to his own capacities than to 'second causes, for which he could not be accountable'.[159] Clearly, Digby's astrological chart had prepared him for something other than defeat, which he could not 'impute . . . to his own conduct'.[160] Yet what Digby had done had been to destroy the King's finest cavalry brigades through negligent generalship in the face of an inferior enemy.

The remarkable achievements of Langdale's Northern Horse have been traced elsewhere.[161] It was upon the success of their relief ride to Pontefract in February 1645 that Digby's perception of the vulnerability of the north was based, and the successes of Montrose in Scotland had induced the expedition of autumn 1645. That expedition met with success initially: at Cusworth on 14 October and at Sherburn on the 15th, but laxity in the wake of that second engagement led to Colonel Copley's hard-fought victory in the second action at Sherburn. That fight cost the northern Royalists almost as many officers as had the brutal hand-to-hand fighting at Marston Moor in July 1644, and it utterly wrecked the Northern Horse. Digby was unsuited to generalship, though he did not lack courage. As was not unusual, such unsuitability was demonstrated only in shattering defeat.[162]

The more eminent the man, the more likely it is that views and opinions concerning him will have circulated, and some have been recorded. For most of the King's regimental colonels, however, there are only occasional snippets of information that rose above the mundane record of their actions and successes or failures. Sir Samuel Luke, the Parliamentarian governor of Newport Pagnell, picked up a piece of gossip concerning Colonel George Lisle, who had succeeded to the command of the regiment which Richard Bolles had led to Alton in December 1643. Lisle's performance at Edgehill, Chalgrove and First Newbury had led to a commission as a regimental colonel in November that year, but the vacancy for the command of what had been Lord Paget's Foot came up almost immediately. Luke had heard, in October 1644, that the King had proposed to knight Lisle for his services at Second Newbury, but that Lisle had said 'he would not be knighted or receive any honour till he was sure to keep it and then doubted not but he should as well deserve to be a lord as many that were near his Majesty'.[163] Lisle's remark has never been set in context. He was one of the officers who, in August 1644, had signed the letter to the King asking for reasons to justify Wilmot's disgrace; he was therefore one of the officers whose loyalty Wilmot was accused of attempting to undermine. If his words were reported accurately, then he was clearly comparing himself and his deserts with the less than honourable Lords Percy and Wilmot, who had been ennobled in 1643 and had shown their true colours a year later. Not only that, but Lisle's reluctance to accept knighthood until he could be sure to keep it may not unreasonably be taken as a reference to the King's suspicions concerning Wilmot's former subordinates. After distinguishing himself at the storm of Leicester and at Naseby in May and June 1645, Lisle accepted a knighthood from the King at Oxford in December, and became Master of the Household. His indefatigable loyalty led him to Colchester in 1648, and to death by firing squad at the hands of Sir Thomas Fairfax.[164] In that same exemplary bloodletting Sir Charles Lucas was despatched, the Earl of Newcastle's brother-in-law, of whom the Parliamentarian Joshua Sprigge had written well.[165] Clarendon, who regarded the killing of Lucas and Lisle as murder – a judgement in which J. H. Round concurred in 1894[166] – presented a picture of Lucas as very much a bred soldier, lacking in the niceties and courtesies of his background even though he was heir to Colonel the Lord Lucas of Shenfield.

He was very brave in his person, and in a day of battle a gallant man to look upon, and follow; but at all other times and places, of a nature not to be lived with, of an ill understanding, of a rough and proud nature, which made him during the time of their being in Colchester more intolerable than the siege . . . yet they all desired to accompany him in his death.

Lucas was the first to be shot, then Lisle's turn came. There were plenty of witnesses of the scene for Clarendon to have first-hand reports of the exchange of words which passed between Lisle and the officer of the firing squad. Lisle suggested they should step nearer to be sure of killing him. 'I'll warrant you, sir, we'll hit you,' was the reply. 'Friends, I have been nearer you when you have missed me,' he is reported to have said. Clarendon approved of Lisle: he:

> had all the courage of [Lucas], and led his men to a battle with such an alacrity, that no man was ever better followed; his soldiers never forsaking him; and the party which he commanded, never left anything undone which he had led them upon. But then to his fierceness of courage he had the softest and most gentle nature imaginable; loved all and beloved of all, and without a capacity to have an enemy.[167]

Occasionally Clarendon came close to panegyric, as in the case of Henry Gage and even the Earl of Carnarvon. With Lisle he achieved it succinctly.

Also amongst the dead at Colchester, but killed in the heat of action, was Colonel Sir William Campion, the former sheriff of Kent, who had raised infantry and cavalry in the first war. On the very eve of the 1648 rising he had sold his Kent estate to his mother to raise the money with which to pay his composition, and had mortgaged other property at Barn Marsh in Essex. A second fine of £2,114 was levied upon what was left of his estate, including property in Norfolk, following his delinquency at Colchester. Of Campion the contemporary historian of the siege of Colchester wrote that his 'conduct was equal to his courage, and that was only exceeded by his reasone, for nothing was above his daring that was level with his discretion'.[168] The only distinction between Campion and the victims of Fairfax's firing squad was that, unlike them, he had no upbringing in the art of war.

VIII

Not all records descriptive of such men necessarily praise their achievements and their qualities. Colonel Jerome Brett, who served as Major General to Edward Somerset in March 1643, and who was killed either that year or in 1644, came to Sir John Oglander's attention through his marriage to the widow of Sir Richard Worsley, baronet. Brett, noted Oglander, was 'a lubberly captain . . . a heavy, dull, drunken fellow, slovenly and nasty, a man in wants, scarce having linen to keep him sweet'. His bride, on the other hand, was 'fair, handsome and neat, loved clean-liness and a witty, nimble gentle fellow'.[169] They married in 1636, when Brett, a career soldier, was Captain of Southsea Castle and a familiar figure in Hampshire. He did not come of poor back-ground but was the younger brother of a knighted gentleman. Oglander was either taken in by appearances or, as likely, beguiled by the Lady Worsley.

Early in September 1646 a letter arrived in the hands of John Manners eighth Earl of Rutland, the cousin of the dead Earl of Kingston and son-in-law of the Puritan Royalist Lord Montagu of Boughton. The letter contained certain news as to the where-abouts of Colonel Sir Gervase Lucas – 'Judas' – who was then at Newcastle upon Tyne with his wife seeking a ship to take them to France. 'One which came from Newcastle saw and spake with the Beast,' Rutland's informant affirmed. As for the colonel's lady, she was 'the mistery of iniquitye', using 'scandelous and sawcy language' of the earl and his countess.[170] Rutland's Civil War career, though disrupted by repeated bouts of ill health, was nevertheless resolvedly Parliamentarian. Lucas had been his Gentleman of the Horse until 1642, the son of a minor (what Lucy Hutchinson would have called an 'underling') gentleman, of Fenton in Lincolnshire.[171] Lucas's wife had been a waiting lady to the countess. When war broke out, on the strength of a warrant from the King, Lucas had seized Belvoir Castle in Leicestershire, Rutland's principal residence, and had garrisoned it for the King.

The earl's hatred of Lucas probably followed the Royalist to his grave in 1668, for at the Restoration (when Lucas was released from prison, where he had been confined at the earl's instigation) Rutland claimed that Lucas had tried 'incessantly' to persuade him to 'ingage . . . against his Majesty'.[172] Rutland tried all he could to blacken Lucas's reputation as a loyal King's man, and implied that everything he had done had been done out of malice towards the earl and his lady. There may also be a hint that Lucas's wife, for some unknown reason, urged him on in it. Perhaps what really angered Rutland, however, was the loss of three whole years' rents whilst Lucas was in Belvoir, totalling, it was claimed, some £10,000. Lucas may have made something out of it himself, but such income seized from the estate of a proven rebel (as Rutland was from 1642) could lawfully (to the Royalists) be converted to the King's use. Perhaps he had employed some of the money to pay for the baronetcy which was conferred upon him by the King in 1644.

Quite apart from the run-of-the-mill insults hurled at Lucas as a resolute garrison commander by Parliament's pamphleteers, little else surfaces to show that Rutland's 'Beast' was, indeed, bestial. He was personally brave, 'run into the face and shrewdly cutt' in action in 1643[173] and defiant of the 'rebels' in extremity.[174] Symonds, however, who noted Lucas as governor of Belvoir – 'sometime horsekeeper to the Earle of Roteland' – observed that Belvoir was surrendered by him on terms 'for his owne security'[175] when it passed into Parliament's hands in 1646. The truth was that by then the castle was incapable of holding out and could hope for no relief.

Clarendon, who wrote nothing good or bad about Lucas, nevertheless recorded a signal and important service which he did the King in 1645. In the wake of the disaster which befell Digby's Northern Horse in October, the King, then at Newark, abandoned plans for a northward march and determined to return to Oxford, sending word before him. Early on the morning of 3 November:

he sent a gentleman to Belvoir-castle, to be informed of the true state of the rebels' quarters, and to advertise sir Gervas Lucas . . . of his majesty's design to march thither that night, with order that his troops and guides should be ready at such an hour.

With barely 400–500 men as his escort the King set off for Belvoir and there:

sir Gervas Lucas and his troop, with good guides were ready; and attended his majesty till the break of day; by which time he was past those quarters which he most apprehended.[176]

The King's march to Oxford through hostile countryside, in which Lucas and his men played a brief but vital part, followed upon the confrontation at Newark between the King and Prince Rupert and his associates. The 'unheard of insolence' shown to the King, particularly by Sir Richard Willys, over the King's decision to remove Willys as governor of Newark in favour of John Lord Belasyse created a profound rift between Charles and his nephew. Rupert, according to Clarendon, had told the King to his face that the only reason for relieving Willys of his command was his friendship with the Prince. Rupert himself had been disgraced following his surrender of Bristol in September. The confrontation with Willys, Rupert and their associates incensed Charles so much that 'with greater indignation than he was ever seen possessed with' he commanded them from his presence. Perhaps the shadow of Wilmot fell across the King's awareness, perhaps something more sinister, for he confirmed Belasyse as governor, who at once posted guards, as Clarendon implies, for the King's protection. Prince Rupert and the other malcontents, whose offensive behaviour may have been nothing more than injured pride, were permitted to quit Newark, and made their way to Belvoir, where Lucas was the governor. They were still there when the King notified Lucas of his intention to move towards Oxford, for Lucas was instructed on no account to confide in his illustrious visitors. Colonel Lucas performed his duty punctiliously. At a time when the King's personal security seemed to be under threat from some of his own commanders, Lucas – Rutland's 'Judas' – acted in an exemplary manner.[177]

IX

Lucas survived the war years, exile and the hatred of the Earl of Rutland to die in his bed in 1668. Of his fellow colonels of 1642–46, 267 died in one way or another before the Restoration. Eight of them died by execution, of whom three were killed by firing squad, and Lucas and Lisle have already been mentioned. The third to die in such a way was Colonel Sir Nicholas Kemys, knight and baronet, of Cefn Mably in Glamorganshire. Having commanded in the first war, he slipped away from Bath in 1648, where he was taking the waters for his health, and joined the uprising of that year, going to Chepstow Castle, where he commanded. When the castle fell, he was shot dead in the courtyard.[178] The other five were beheaded: Arthur Lord Capel of Hadham in 1649; Eusebius Andrews, a Northamptonshire gentleman, in August 1650; Sir John Urry, beheaded in Scotland the same year; Sir Timothy Featherstonhaugh of Kirkoswald in Cumberland, beheaded at Chester in 1651 (the year in which his son Henry was killed in action at Worcester); and Sir Henry Slingsby of Moor Monkton in Yorkshire, decapitated on Tower Hill in 1658. Clarendon, who knew Slingsby in the Commons in 1640–42, had this notice of him:

Sir Harry Slingsby . . . was in the first rank of the gentlemen of
Yorkshire; and was returned to serve as a member in the parliament that
continued so many years; where he sat till the troubles begun; and having
no relation to or dependence upon the court, he was swayed only by his
conscience to detest the violent and undutiful behaviour of that parliament. He was a gentleman of a good understanding, but of a very
melancholic nature, and of very few words: and when he could stay no
longer with a good conscience in their counsels, in which he never
concurred, he went into his country, and joined with the first who took
up arms for the king. And when the war was ended, he remained still in
his own house, prepared and disposed to run the fortune of the crown in
any other attempt: and having a good fortune and a general reputation,
had a greater influence upon the people, than they who talked more and
louder; and was known to be irreconcilable to the new government; and
therefore was cut off, notwithstanding very great intercession to preserve him . . . When he was brought to die, he spent very little time in
discourse; but told them, 'he was to die for being an honest man, of which
he was very glad'.[179]

Earlier it had been suggested that if anyone came closest to
Symmons's definition of the true or Compleat Cavalier it was
Slingsby. Clarendon's assessment of him is wholly borne out by
Slingsby's own writings, to which attention has been frequently
drawn: his determination to secure a regimental command in the
King's interest, his approval of the beneficial aspects of a soldier's
life, and, most important, his largely objective and often self-
effacing account of the events in which he was personally
involved. This does not mean that Slingsby was a paragon of
Cavalier virtues, or that his life was seen by all as exemplary.
Indeed, it may be merely a reflection of the fact that, of all the
King's colonels, he is the most accessible through his diary and
letters to his sons. To conclude this survey of men who served the
King, by going further into Slingsby's personality, is to return to
the subject of conscience and its workings.

Like many a country gentleman and many fellow MPs who
would be Royalist in 1642, Slingsby had welcomed the coming of
the Long Parliament: 'Great expectance their is of a happy Parliament where ye subject may have a total redress of all his grievances.' This great expectation of the end of what Slingsby
admitted were grievances requiring remedy turned sour for him
when Parliament's attention turned from 'Projectors, & Mono-
polizers, such as levi'd ship mony' to 'All innovators either in

church or state: & as cheif actors therein, they fell upon my Ld of Canterbury & Strafford & accus'd ym of high treason'. Slingsby sided with Strafford, as did some but by no means all of those of the King's future colonels who were then in the Commons. Only thirteen others besides Slingsby, of more than sixty who would secure regimental command between 1642 and 1646, took the bold step of voting for Strafford. Slingsby and his nephew, John Fenwick, aside, they were: James Lord Compton, John Coventry, George and John Digby, Patricius Curwen, Baptist Noel, William Pennyman, Hugh Pollard, Nicholas Slanning, John Trevanion, George Wentworth and William Widdrington.

Slingsby himself did not record his vote in his diary, nor did he choose to dwell upon the proceedings against the earl. His chief sticking point where Parliament was concerned was in religion. He would come in time to regard Puritans and Presbyterians as 'Schismaticks . . . departed from yt faith wherein you were baptized, we make not ye Quarrel, it is you' he would subsequently affirm. He himself was prepared to go along with legislation for depriving the bishops of their votes in the House of Lords and to prevent their 'medling with temporal affairs' but:

I was against ye Bill for taking away ye function & calling of Bishops; this is a business chiefly aim'd at by ye Parliament & solicit'd by our countrimen yt live beyond ye seas in Holland hoping yt if episcopy were abolish'd they might peaceably live at home & enjoy their consciences.

Since, by 1646, they had clearly got their way, Slingsby demanded rhetorically, and knowing it was a waste of time, why he and others like him might not 'expect ye having of yt wch you call'd a Liberty for tender conscience: & not condemn us for yt wch you once approv'd in yr selves'. He remembered how 'in former times' conformity imposed by bishops created scruples over the use of 'a Cap or Sirples . . . the out branches only' and now that Slingsby and others scrupled 'to have root and branch pluck'd up' the reformers should 'judg of our scruple by yr own'.

As far as Slingsby was concerned, and has been shown earlier, it was sufficient reason to maintain episcopacy, since the system was of long duration and an hierarchical structure was necessary. Yet in all other ways he was a true subscriber to the articles of the established church as regards matters of belief, and was possessed of a thorough Protestant approach to those beliefs. For example, of churches and of chapels he could write:

> It is not amiss to have a place consecrat'd for Devotion, as our Churches are, therby to seperate ym for yt use: but we cannot stay our self here, but must attribute a sanctity to ye very walls and stones of ye Church; & herein we do of late draw near to ye superstition of ye Church of Rome . . .

Moreover, he debated such matters with clerics whom he knew in Yorkshire. In York Minster library he became acquainted with Timothy Thurscross, a prebend of York, at a time when Thurscross was underoing some personal crisis of conscience in his own religious belief. Slingsby evidently admired the other's conviction and self-induced poverty, whilst noting that he was 'conformable to ye church discipline yt now is used & to those late impos'd ceremonies of bowing & adoring towards ye altar'. Of such things Sir Henry evidently, if he did not flatly disapprove, entertained serious doubts as to the meaning they might have. 'Wn I ask'd him his opinion concerning this or yt, I thought it came too near idolatry to adore a place wth rich cloths & other furniture & to command to use towards it bodily worship' Thurscross told him 'yt his bowing was not to ye altar but to God especially in yt place'. It was not, let it be added, to the altar itself at the east end of the church, railed off in the chancel, that Slingsby objected: indeed, he maintained such an arrangement in his private chapel at Moor Monkton, which still stands and is much as it was when Slingsby knew it. Slingsby took issue with the nuances in worship that seemed to accompany the sanctity of the altar in its particular place. He did not seem to find the word 'table' a suitable alternative to that of 'altar'.

Slingsby was a man of peaceful inclination, conservative enough to be inherently suspicious of reformers. Had he lived a hundred years earlier, he was the kind of man to have clung to the Old Religion in the face of Henrician change, but, having been raised in the Protestantism of the established church, he looked upon the threat posed by sectaries and Puritans with genuine horror and concern: 'I like their opinion who would not have violence offer'd to ye quiet repose of a country, no not to reform and cure ye same, nor allow of yt reformation wch is purchased wth ye blood & ruine of the citizens.' In his own terms, he was driven into arms to defend King and church against an unavoidable bloodletting reformation of spiritual and temporal life and values. He readily acknowledged to himself that 'he yt will be a right cristian must suffer martyrdom, if not by loss of life, yet by the loss of credit & honour, wch is as dear to many as life, seeing we have experience yt they will venture life in defence of honour'.

He was also able to accept with equanimity defeat and loss in his principles and in his life: 'contrary to ye custom of some in these days yt would ground and establish our religion upon ye prosperity of our enterprises as if our belief had no other foundation yn wt is ground'd by events', Slingsby considered that 'all things come from God' and because of that must be taken in good part. Men were not, ultimately, meant to be 'interpreters and controulers of God's secret designes, presuming to find out ye incomprehensible motives of his works'. His recognition that failure and defeat, disaster and loss, may be the end-product of man's free will rather than signs of divine withdrawal of favour must have led him, had he concerned himself to try to explain Royalist defeat, to be at odds with those who, upon either side, regarded it as a judgement of God. Like countless others, he could not therefore accept that there was anything ordained or perpetual in the temporary overthrow of the King and the creation of a republic. He and countless others could wait upon events and, if opportunity offered and conditions were favourable, seek to bring about a further confrontation with what he and they regarded as an illegal regime. In Slingsby's case it led him to death as a traitor in London, but he found thereafter honourable interment amongst his ancestors when Cromwell's corpse was strung up in chains as a humiliation of the 'good old cause' which Slingsby, to his last breath, had defied unceasingly.

His diary is not solely concerned with matters of public debate and the war through which he passed. He recorded also domestic matters, and (though sparingly if often affectingly) familial as well. If his preoccupation with religion demonstrates the distance between his seventeenth-century outlook and the attitudes of mind of his readers 300 years on, his diary also reveals how little in some respects human nature has changed. He wrote, for example, about some new farming techniques which he had introduced on to his demesne land before the Civil War, 'new grown in fashion, of burning ye swarth they mean to plough, ye ashes whereof by experience they find to yeild a greater increase of corn yn any other manure', and this was 'never herebefore us'd in this latter age'. It had become so widespread in the 1630s that he idly speculated 'this world must be consum'd wth burning'. Less idly, and more than half seriously, he confided to himself:

but sure it may be ye cause of so great winds as we have had this whole year yt hath done so much harm, both by sea and land . . . we heard of ye blowing down of Chimneys, of Wind Mills, and lead of Churches; & likewise of great thunders and lightning ye last Winter.

What he did not do was look back from 1646 to see in such wonders portents of the greater storm to come. Many, then and since, might have done so.

After the battle of Marston Moor on 2 July 1644 Slingsby made good his escape back to York. The city surrendered on terms on 16 July, and he was amongst those who chose to make their way to another garrison to continue to fight for the King. One small incident on that journey illustrates Slingsby's attitude to the 'rebels', as he considered them, and forms a lasting image of the man himself. On the prescribed road to Knaresborough, Slingsby and his fellow commanders were joined by 'Whaley, Cromwell's Leivet: Coll:' who 'goes along with us, discoursing of ye fight on Marston Moor' and who showed himself 'desirous to see Sr. Richard Hutton at whose house he quarter'd'. Whalley endeavoured to persuade Hutton to return home, 'but he would not'. The rebel 'would have persuad'd me to abide at home, shewing how much he desir'd to shake hands with me'. Clearly, Slingsby declined to shake hands. He, at Tower Hill in 1658, Hutton at Sherburn in 1645, reached the respective ends of that journey without ever having compromised their loyalty.

Notes

1 See above, Chapter Two.
2 Macray, *Clarendon's Rebellion*, III, p. 30.
3 HMC *Thirteenth Report*, Portland Mss, 1891, p. 701.
4 Symmons, *Military Sermon*, p. 20.
5 *Ibid.*, p. 22.
6 *Ibid.*, pp. 22–3.
7 *Ibid.*, pp. 20–1.
8 *Ibid.*, p. 19.
9 Symmons, *Vindication of King Charles*, pp. 164–5.
10 *Ibid.*, A5.

11 *Ibid.*, p. 165.
12 Bamford, *Oglander's Notebook*, pp. 117–18.
13 HMC, *Twelfth Report*, Beaufort Mss, 1891, p. 60.
14 Warwick, Memoires, pp. 273–4.
15 Loftis, *Halkett and Fanshaw Memoirs*, p. 130.
16 George Earl of Norwich and Charles Goring are in Newman, *Royalist Officers*, p. 161.
17 Bamford, *Oglander's Notebook*, p. 98.
18 Coates, *Journal of Simond D'Ewes*, p. 169.
19 Warwick, Memoires, p. 45.
20 HMC, *Thirteenth Report*, Portland Mss, 1891, p. 328.
21 Newman, *Royalist Officers*, p. 162.
22 Ellison Gibson, *Cavalier's Notebook*, pp. 260–1.
23 Macray, *Clarendon's Rebellion*, I, p. 478.
24 *Ibid.*
25 Newman, *Royalist Officers*, p. 242.
26 HMC, *Twelfth Report*, Appendix, II, Cowper Mss, 1888, p. 257.
27 Macray, *Clarendon's Rebellion*, I, p. 478.
28 Coates, *Journal of Simond D'Ewes*, p. 336.
29 *Ibid.*, p. 345.
30 *Ibid.*, pp. 346–7.
31 Coates, Young and Snow, *Private Journals*, p. 158.
32 Newman, *Royalist Officers*, p. 242.
33 Parsons, *Slingsby Diary*, pp. 38–9.
34 Warwick, Memoires, p. 260.
35 William Herbert first Baron Powis (1629) was captured in 1644 when Powis Castle, which he had garrisoned, fell to the Parliament.
36 HMC, *Third Report*, Northumberland Mss, 1872, p. 79.
37 Warwick, Memoires, pp. 221–2.
38 Macray, *Clarendon's Rebellion*, III, p. 86.
39 HMC, *Twelfth Report*, Cowper Mss, 1888, p. 260.
40 Newman, *Royalist Officers*, p. 113, and for what immediately follows.
41 For example, Cowley, *The Civil Warre*, pp. 115–6.
42 *Nocturnall Occurrences, or, Deeds of Darknesse Committed by the Cavaleers in their Rendevous*, 1642. *A Barbarous and Inhumane Speech spoken by the Lord Wentworth*, quoted in T. N. Corns, *Uncloistered Virtue*, Oxford, 1992, p. 4.
43 *Ibid.*, p. 73.
44 Hutton, *War Effort*, p. 104.
45 Warwick, Memoires, p. 230.
46 Tonnies, *Hobbes' Behemoth*, pp. 114–5.
47 *Ibid.*
48 *Ibid.*
49 HMC, *Fifteenth Report*, Hodgkin Mss, 1897, p. 98. Newman, *Royalist Officers*, p. 416, unless otherwise referenced.
50 Macray, *Clarendon's Rebellion*, III, p. 102.
51 *Ibid.*, pp. 389–90, 444–5.
52 Long, Symonds Diary, pp. 106–7.
53 *Ibid.*, pp. 107–8.
54 *Ibid.*, pp. 108–9.
55 *Ibid.*, pp. 109–10. Warwick, Memoires, p. 145.

56 Ellison Gibson, *Cavalier's Notebook*, pp. 154–5.
57 Macray, *Clarendon's Rebellion*, II, p. 257.
58 *Ibid.*, III, p. 392.
59 HMC, *Thirteenth Report*, Portland Mss, 1891, p. 124.
60 Newman, *Royalist Officers*, p. 293. CCC, p. 1703.
61 Ian Roy (ed.), The Royalist Ordnance Papers, 1642–1646, Part 1, *Oxfordshire Record Society*, 1964, pp. 20–1.
62 Gardiner, Hamilton Papers, p. 178.
63 See above, Chapter Two.
64 HMC, *Fourth Report*, I, De La Warr Mss, 1874, p. 304.
65 Newman, *Royalist Officers*, pp. 163–4.
66 *Ibid.*, pp. 92, 122.
67 R. Spalding (ed.), The Diary of Bulstrode Whitelocke, 1605–1675, *British Academy Records of Social and Economic History*, new series, XIII, Oxford, 1990, pp. 144–5.
68 HMC, *Thirteenth Report*, Portland Mss, 1891, p. 316.
69 See above, Chapter Two.
70 Newman, *Royalist Officers*, p. 112, unless otherwise referenced.
71 *Lords Journals*, V, p. 134.
72 HMC, *Tenth Report*, Stewart Mss, 1885, p. 122.
73 HMC, *Manuscripts in Various Collections*, I, Wiltshire Quarter Sessions Records, 1901, p. 122. CCC, p. 2172.
74 Firth, *Ludlow Memoirs*, I, pp. 95–6.
75 Whitelocke, *Memorials*, I, p. 295.
76 HMC, *Thirteenth Report*, Portland Mss, 1891, p. 700.
77 Newman, *Royalist Officers*, p. 231.
78 HMC, *Fourteenth Report*, Appendix VII, Ormonde Mss, I, 1895, p. 123.
79 HMC, Bath Mss, II, 1907, pp. 28–38. Newman, *Royalist Officers*, p. 421.
80 CCC, p. 1641.
81 HMC, *Fourth Report*, I, House of Lords Mss, 1874, p. 51. *Lords Journals*, IV, p. 60. Newman, *Royalist Officers*, pp. 216, 286.
82 L.B.L. (ed.), Sir Roger Twysden's Journal, *Archaeologia Cantiana*, I–IV, 1858–61, p. 190.
83 Long, Symonds Diary, p. 22.
84 See, for example, Loftis, *Halkett and Fanshaw Memoirs*, p. 120, and Newman, *Royalist Officers*, p. 52.
85 *Commons Journals*, II, p. 661.
86 J. C. Hodgson (ed.), The Journal of John Aston, 1639, *Surtees Society*, CXVIII, 1910, p. 21.
87 Newman, *Royalist Officers*, p. 381, unless otherwise referenced.
88 Ellison Gibson, *Cavalier's Notebooks*, p. 121.
89 Macray, *Clarendon's Rebellion*, II, pp. 350, 367.
90 *Ibid.*, III, pp. 346–7.
91 Newman, *Royalist Officers*, pp. 9–10 and references therein.
92 Macray, *Clarendon's Rebellion*, III, pp. 407, 441–2.
93 Parsons, *Slingsby Diary*, p. 139.
94 Walker, *Discourses*, pp. 90–5. Newman, *Royalist Officers*, p. 147.
95 Newman, *Royalist Officers*, p. 10. M. G. Hobson and H. E. Salter (eds.), Oxford Council Acts, 1626–1665, *Oxford Historical Society*, XCV, 1933, p. 115. CSPD 1660–1, p. 302. HMC, *Fifteenth Report*, Hodgkin Mss, 1897, p. 98.

96 See above, Chapter Two.
97 A. Clark (ed.), *Aubrey's Brief Lives*, I, Oxford, 1898, pp. 154–7.
98 Newman, *Royalist Officers*, p. 65.
99 J. J. Howard (ed.), *Miscellanea Genealogica et Heraldica*, new series II, 1877, p. 82.
100 Webb, Birch Memoir, p. 45.
101 Macray, *Clarendon's Rebellion*, III, p. 334.
102 For Morgan, Smith and Digby see below, Chapter Four.
103 Newman, *Royalist Officers*, p. 33 and references therein.
104 Spalding, Whitelocke's Diary, pp. 138–9.
105 Newman, *Royalist Officers*, p. 332.
106 *Ibid.*, pp. 97, 240, 312.
107 W. H. D. Longstaffe, A Journal of the First and Second Sieges of Pontefract Castle, 1644–45, by Nathan Drake, *Surtees Society*, XXXVII, 1860, Part 1, p. 65.
108 *Ibid.*, p. 66.
109 Parsons, *Slingsby Diary*, p. 114.
110 Macray, *Clarendon's Rebellion*, II, pp. 332–4.
111 HMC, *Fifth Report*, I, Report and Appendix, House of Lords Mss, 1876, p. 23.
112 HMC, *Mss in Various Collections*, VII, Staunton Mss, 1914, p. 421.
113 *Ibid.*
114 Newman, *Royalist Officers*, p. 297. J. Sutherland, *Memoirs of the Life of Colonel Hutchinson*, Oxford, 1973, pp. 80, 82.
115 Warwick, Memoires, p. 151.
116 Macray, *Clarendon's Rebellion*, II, pp. 181–2.
117 Whitelocke, *Memorials*, I, pp. 170–1.
118 HMC, *Fifth Report*, I, Report and Appendix, Sutherland Mss, 1876, p. 141.
119 Whitelocke, *Memorials*, I, p. 324.
120 Coates, Young and Snow, *Private Journals*, p. 345.
121 *Ibid.*, p. 350.
122 Long, Symonds Diary, p. 36.
123 Macray, *Clarendon's Rebellion*, II, pp. 452–3.
124 *Ibid.*, p. 454.
125 Newman, *Royalist Officers*, p. 257. Whitelocke, *Memorials*, II, p. 114. CCC, pp. 116, 119, 276, 290, 336.
126 Macray, *Clarendon's Rebellion*, II, pp. 527–9.
127 Whitelocke, *Memorials*, I, p. 181.
128 Newman, *Royalist Officers*, p. 339.
129 HMC, *Fifth Report*, Sutherland Mss, 1876, p. 165.
130 Conrad Russell, *The Fall of the British Monarchies, 1637–42*, Oxford 1991, p. 223.
131 Macray, *Clarendon's Rebellion*, III, p. 505.
132 Whitelocke, *Memorials*, II, p. 67.
133 *Ibid.*, p. 61.
134 Newman, *Royalist Officers*, p. 358. CCC, pp., 43, 118, 150, 517, 657, 1176, 1964. Aubrey spoke of him as his friend, *vide* Clark, *Aubrey's Brief Lives*, I, p. 44.
135 Newman, *Royalist Officers*, p. 357. Firth, *Ludlow Memoirs*, I, p. 89. F. T. Colby (ed.), The Visitation of the County of Somerset . . . 1628, *Harleian Society*, XI,

1876, p. 107.

136 Coates, Young and Snow, *Private Journals*, pp. 367–79.

137 D. Brunton and D. H. Pennington, *Members of the Long Parliament*, 1954, p. 242.

138 Coates, Young and Snow, *Private Journals*, p. 404.

139 HMC, *Fourth Report*, House of Lords Mss, 1874, p. 62.

140 Newman, *Royalist Officers*, p. 111. CCC, pp. 1303–8.

141 CCC, p. 335.

142 CCC, pp. 241–2, 2001–6. Newman, *Royalist Officers*, p. 37.

143 Newman, *Royalist Officers*, pp. 316–7. CCC, p. 916.

144 HMC, *Thirteenth Report*, Portland Mss, 1891, p. 588.

145 CCC, p. 1043.

146 Loftis, *Halkett and Fanshaw Memoirs*, p. 32.

147 See above, Chapter Two.

148 Cowley, *The Civil Warre*, p. 113.

149 Knowles Middleton, *Relazione d'Inghilterra*, p. 59.

150 Macray, *Clarendon's Rebellion*, III, p. 156; V, pp. 233–4. Russell, *Causes*, pp. 197–8.

151 *Ibid.*, p. 62.

152 Warwick, Memoires, p. 279.

153 *Ibid.*, p. 290.

154 Knowles Middleton, *Relazione d'Inghilterra*, p. 46.

155 Macray, *Clarendon's Rebellion*, I, pp. 462–3, 506.

156 Coates, Young and Snow, *Private Journals*, p. 58.

157 *Ibid.*, p. 172.

158 Macray, *Clarendon's Rebellion*, IV, pp. 120–2.

159 *Ibid.*

160 *Ibid.*

161 P. R. Newman, *The Battle of Marston Moor, 1644*, Chichester, 1981, p. 140.

162 *Ibid.*, pp. 142–3.

163 H. G. Tibbutt (ed.), *The Letter Books, 1644–1645, of Sir Samuel Luke*, 1963, p. 71.

164 Newman, *Royalist Officers*, p. 235.

165 Joshua Sprigge, *Anglia Rediviva*, 1840 edition, pp. 71, 136–7.

166 J. H. Round, The case of Lucas and Lisle, *Transactions of the Royal Historical Society*, new series, VIII, 1894, pp. 157–80.

167 Macray, *Clarendon's Rebellion*, IV, pp. 387–9.

168 HMC, *Twelfth Report*, Beaufort Mss, 1891, p. 24.

169 Bamford, *Oglander's Notebook*, pp. 69–70. Newman, *Royalist Officers*, p. 42.

170 HMC, *Twelfth Report*, Appendix, IV, Rutland Mss, I, 1888, p. 2.

171 Sutherland, *Hutchinson Life*, p. 69.

172 HMC, *Twelfth Report*, Rutland Mss, 1888, p. 2.

173 HMC, *Thirteenth Report*, Portland Mss, 1891, p. 165.

174 Whitelocke, *Memorials*, p. 539.

175 Long, Symonds Diary, pp. 228, 278. Newman, *Royalist Officers*, p. 241.

176 Macray, *Clarendon's Rebellion*, IV, p. 127.

177 *Ibid.*, pp. 124–6.

178 Newman, *Royalist Officers*, pp. 213–4.

179 Macray, *Clarendon's Rebellion*, VI, pp. 64–5.

180 All the extracts are from Parsons, *Slingsby Diary*, pp. 8, 9, 13, 20, 27–9, 64–5, 67, 121–2.

CHAPTER FOUR

'The Great Loyalty of the Papists . . . Discovered'[1]

The Roman Catholic presence in regimental command

I

It is now a well established fact that Roman Catholic commitment to King Charles I was widespread and as determined as that of Protestant Royalists. For a time, scholarship questioned that which was seemingly self-evident to contemporaries: 'The Papists all over England were all high partakers with [the King] and promoters of his designes, and all the debosht Nobility and gentry and their dependents, and the lewder sort of people.'[2] Given the now general acceptance of a profound Catholic Royalism, though divested of its seventeenth-century conspiratorial implication, the task of scholarship is to explain that commitment. It would seem to fly in the face of logic that a persecuted religious minority should fight for the head of the Protestant state and run the considerable risk of facing perhaps more systematic persecution should the Parliament overcome the King.

Paul Hardacre, one of the first to break with academic preoccupation with Parliament and its supporters, thought that Roman Catholic involvement could be very readily explained: 'The Catholics who endorsed the King must have been motivated largely by their conviction that between the two parties in the civil war their only *chance of toleration* lay with him.'[3] Such an assessment presupposes that Catholic Royalists differed from their Protestant comrades in a very specific way: that they took up arms for the King as a means to the end of securing for themselves religious toleration, the end of secretive rites and punitive recusancy fines. It requires to be shown that Protestant Royalists would have emerged from a successful war feeling themselves under an obligation towards Catholics in general. It ignores the probability that a war won by the King using force of arms would have led to a tightening up of the law against dissent in whatever form. No contractual agreement existed between King and subjects: loyalty was an obligation. Similarly, no agreement under which the King undertook to satisfy certain Catholic demands can be shown to have existed. What individuals may have hoped for and the reality of politics did not coincide. Outright victory for the King would have meant outright victory for the Laudian church, and no need for either to compromise with any form of dissent. The case for toleration would have had to depend upon a negotiated peace involving political dealing, in which the Catholics as an interest group would have enjoyed representation. It is hard to imagine how perilous Parliament's military position would have had to have been for it to countenance such a peace. There are surely no circumstances under which Catholic toleration could have been envisaged. Any Catholic Royalist who supposed, as Hardacre implied, that religious freedom would follow from military commitment to the King would have been deluded by an overestimation of the importance of his coreligionists.

Catholics anyway did enjoy toleration before 1642: there was no serious attempt to eradicate them from the nation. Symmons, who detested Catholicism and was Anglican to his very core, confirmed that:

we do not thinke it lawfull to enter into a Combination, to root them out of the Earth by shedding of their Bloud . . . for we have no warrant in the Gospell to do so. Tis the word of God that is ordained to suppresse false Religions, and not the sword of Man; Fire, Sword and Pistolls are the weapons of Antichrist, and not of Christ.[4]

Symmons regretted that the King's cause made use of Catholics, but he nowhere suggests that as a result there was any obligation to make life easier for them in reward for their loyalty. Loyalty, a subject's duty, would not be loyalty if it were bought by concessions.

The laws against Catholics as recusants were unevenly and only spasmodically enforced to the letter. Often, in the case of Grandees and courtiers and great officials, they were hardly applied at all. The Catholic community, or the recusant part thereof, was tolerated by government as a source of regular income – a traditional policy which Parliament itself chose to follow rather than seek to eliminate Catholics as landowners and people of status. Toleration also underlay the way in which in all other respects, religious differences aside, Catholic and Protestant intermingled and partook of normal social and economic intercourse. The attitude of the average Protestant was precisely that of the Gentleman in conversation with the Lawyer and the Scholar in *Leicester's Commonwealth*: 'And for myself I may protest that I bear the honest Papist (if there be any) no malice for his deceived conscience.'[5] Whatever the predicament of the Catholic clergy (and measures against them were fitful), whatever the content of extremist Protestant literature and sermons, there was no malicious intent on the part of government towards the Catholic laity: the survival of Catholicism as a minority religion was in such circumstances certain. Nor was there a truly identifiable enemy for the Catholics as a community to resist. No matter how far some Englishmen genuinely believed in a popish conspiracy aimed at subverting the state, as John Pym probably believed, it was not a widespread essential in the Protestant psyche. Had it been so, then the incidence of violent anti-Catholic behaviour would have left a deep scar across the history of that century. There is no such scar.

Professor Russell has drawn attention to this amongst Parliament's own active supporters: 'The other group,' he wrote, 'by which Pym was always particularly bewildered, were those who, though not papists themselves, did not particularly mind popery, and in Laodicean style, were willing to work with it when occasion demanded.'[6] If this was true of Parliament, it was equally true of the King's supporters and, taken to its widest sense, of society in general. This is why outbreaks of anti-Catholic violence which accompanied, here and there, the drift into war in 1642 were sufficiently rare to be noted, and, when they involved the destruction or plundering of gentlemen's property, to create alarm amongst Protestant observers. 'The rabble,' wrote Clarendon (Lucy Hutchinson's 'lewder sort of people'), 'entered the house of the Countess of Rivers, near Colchester; on no other ground, than that she was a papist . . . the Countess herself hardly escaping after great insolence had been used to her person.'[7] The coming of war may have put Catholics in fear of similar treatment, the threat of unrestrained plunder rather than government-directed and legalised, and therefore regulated, distraint. On these grounds alone those Catholics who were able to might resort to arms in self-defence, and equate their survival with that of the King's hitherto lenient rule: to extrapolate from that a communal belief in complete toleration is too much.

It is also unwise to think of Catholic response to the war as communal and uniform, quite apart from the fact that some remained neuter whilst others became actively involved. The Catholics were a small minority in 1642: if they were 2 per cent of the total population of England and Wales, that was about it, and they were scattered nationwide. This in itself contributed to the general aura of toleration with which the laity were regarded. There were localised pockets of Catholicism, sometimes dependent upon and taking example from Grandee Catholics (as with the Somersets in South Wales) but more often regional networks of gentry families, their tenants and dependants (as in the north). There was no Catholic political position, as such, on anything. The inheritance of the archpriest controversy and the divisions within the Catholic clergy (who were primarily the target of government) had created a Catholic laity that thought and acted for itself in its own disparate and narrowly perceived interests. There was no movement within lay Catholicism informed by Carerius or Bellarmine which gave a political dimension to the observance of familiar and ancient rites. If the Anglican church with its clearly structured hierarchy and enjoyment of power could be divided within itself as clearly as it was in 1642, to expect any coherent 'Catholic' position in that year is to misread the case.

The part played by Catholic Royalists in the Civil War can only be seen in the same light in which the role of the Protestant Royalist is assessed. Hitherto in this study, beyond allusion to differences in faith, the King's regimental commanders have been considered as a whole, irrespective of those implied divisions amongst them that anti-Royalist writers, sectaries and some Royalists in their apologies tried to insinuate. This is not to say that the Catholic issue was not sensitive, rather it is to try to assign to it a sense of proportion. In that context it could well be said that the commitment of Catholics to the King, as is demonstrated in regimental command, and elsewhere, is nothing more than the manifestation of a shared political outlook with their Protestant comrades. There was, for the laity with which this study is concerned, no alternative political position other than those of support for the Parliament or neutralism. A 'Catholic' view, aside from these three options, did not exist, unless the notion of a Catholic conspiracy, pushed so hard and to such lengths by Parliament, is swallowed.

The Catholics were an identifiable group within society by virtue of their religious observance: non-attendance at the Anglican church marked them out as recusants, whether or not they participated in Masses celebrated by secular or regular clergy. The rigorous penal laws against them came much later in the century, and, the rantings of extreme sectaries aside, the most effective weapon by which the Catholic 'community' could be whittled away lay in the education of children by Protestant teachers. So long as it was possible for Catholic parents to send their offspring into Europe, or enjoy the services of priests as tutors, the survival of Catholicism, if not its expansion, was guaranteed. The Catholic clergy were the real targets of infrequent bouts of persecution, and the association of the clergy with sedition was certainly clear in the minds of many Protestants. What does not seem to have been the general case was the unequivocal popular association of sedition and treason with the lay Catholics at large. It was certainly more than hinted at by Protestant writers: 'The Church of Rome teaches disloyalty and rebellion against Kings and leads her people into all conspiracies and treasons against states and kingdoms,' thundered White.[8] In 1610 Donne pinpointed the Jesuits as instruments of rebellion: 'From you have come the subtle whisperings of rebellious doctrines, the frequent and traitorous practices, the intestine commotions, and the public and foreign hostile attempts.'[9] This kind of vituperation, given new impetus by Gunpowder Plot, could have been of only limited popular application, however its burden was maintained and developed by subsequent polemicists. The very lack of a sequel to 1605 made it difficult for Rome's professed enemies to constantly represent the local Catholic presence as a potential instrument of rebellion. The attacks on 'popery' in the late 1620s and 1630s, fuelled as they were by events in Europe, were yet an extension of the original premise to

take account of alleged shifts towards Rome within the organisation and observance of the state church. By the time civil war
came the 'papist' enemy was both Catholic and Anglican, the
anti-popery campaigners having taken on the church hierarchy
with the intention of modifying it or destroying it in the interests
of an incomplete Reformation. The attack on popery was so wide
that Laudian and other, moderate, Anglicans as well as observant
Catholics could all be caught up in its anger: by the time such men
came to fight side by side for the King (thereby giving their
enemies further proof of their collaboration) they had already
been driven into a near identity of interest in their resistance to
Puritanism. There was nothing 'popish' about Laud's church, any
more than Catholic rites smacked of Laudianism. The success of
Parliament's anti-popery measures lay in the association of
inherently seditious Catholicism with socially acceptable Laudian
revisionism. The inexactitude in the use of the word 'papist' by
1642, the necessary consequence of the extension of an old,
vilifying campaign against Catholics, enabled Parliament to
denounce the King's most Protestant followers as well as their
Catholic colleagues in one easily memorable and familiar insult.
The word became part of the vocabulary of denunciation,
alongside 'malignant' 'cavalier' and 'incendiary'. Nor was it a word
that could be thrown back in the faces of its users.

It is one thing to be aware of the truth concerning the Catholics,
another to impugn base motives to those who professed to regard
them as potential or actual traitors. Too many educated men, and
not all of them Puritans or Parliamentarians, viewed the Catholic
presence as a threat, partially realised in Gunpowder Plot, possibly to be realised in the wake of the Irish Rebellion of 1641. If
informed opinion did distinguish between the 'Jesuitical Catholics' and the rest, nevertheless, the image of the Jesuit was in
itself a sufficiently ogre-like caricature to keep very much alive
the sinister reality of a minority religion at variance with a state-
sanctioned church. In terms of English history, the fear of that
minority faith and its practitioners took a very long time to die.
The residual antipathy towards Catholics may yet reveal itself in
unlikely places, as for example, when an historian comments
upon the fact that in 1639 Catholic peers and gentry contributed
money to the King's war against the Scots: 'The chance given by
the Bishops' Wars to the Catholics to take up the pose of the

King's most loyal subjects was one many of them embraced with alacrity, but it did neither them nor the King much good.'[10] Professor Russell's assessment is a fair reflection of what some contemporary Protestants would undoubtedly have thought: that the Catholic support for the King against the Scots was a front, a facade, intended either to further their own communal interests (Russell) or some general devilish conspiracy (Pym *et al*). It presupposes a Catholic response to events as a community acting as a single group within society. It precludes the stronger probability that the Catholic response was a genuine indicator of widespread individual and familial loyalty to the Crown. The repeated assertions that the Catholics were a persecuted minority fail to explain, if that were so, whence came the money which Catholics poured into royal coffers in 1639 and to an even greater extent in 1642 and afterwards. When civil war broke out large advance instalments of recusancy fines were paid over to the King, representing a not inconsiderable reservoir of money available to the recusants. It is hard to accept the notion of persecution on the one hand, and that of a financially viable, socially and economically acceptable and occasionally politically active Catholic laity on the other. Recusancy did impose a burden upon Catholic families, but it was an outgoing that could be budgeted for; it might be irksome and in some cases harsh to pay out fines for the privilege of staying apart from the state church, but it was not unendurable. Such a level of persecution does not provide sufficient motive for adhering to the King's cause in expectation of thereby having it lifted entirely.

If Catholic Royalism is seen as a perplexing phenomenon of the Civil War there is clearly a need for historians to explain it. All explanations which rest upon perceived Catholic self-interest assume a state of affairs that did not prevail, and a collective Catholic purpose that runs close to Parliament's conspiracy theory of Catholicism. If, on the other hand, there is nothing in the motivation behind Catholic Royalism to distinguish it from Protestant Royalism – if Catholic Royalists are indistinguishable from their Protestant counterparts in social, economic and military terms – then concentration upon Catholics as a special case has two consequences. It perpetuates the myth of the mid-seventeenth century that was for good reason assiduously developed by Parliament and, more significantly, it diverts scholarly attention away from study of the origins and principles of Royalism *per se*. It is one thing to recognise that many articulate Protestants regarded Rome with suspicion, if not hatred, quite another to assume from that, that Catholic Englishmen and Welshmen have to be seen as members of a seditious minority simply because there were those who claimed them to be so. The Catholics' problem was that, though they were by and large no different from their Protestant neighbours, published literature implied otherwise. If it is properly supposed that Protestant Royalists were motivated less by self-interest than by conscience and principle, there is no reason to assume otherwise of Catholic Royalists, though with this caveat: that those Catholics who took up arms for the King or in other ways supported his cause may well have felt themselves to be the public image of their co-religionists. That the prominent role taken by some of them from 1642 was an affirmation of what had always been the case for the Catholic laity, loyalty to the Crown in no way different from that of Protestants. When Catholic commanders excelled in action, as many of them did, they were held by certain eulogists to be representative of a loyal Catholic people, against whom fought a large number of the King's Protestant subjects in arms for Parliament. The Civil War merely exemplified the palpable truth that observance of the old religion did not equate with rebellion and treason, unless and only if the observer held that the King's cause was itself treasonable. For those who thought in that way, the Catholic presence in arms was proof both of a Catholic conspiracy and of the extent to which popery had crept into the fabric of national institutions, the monarchy not excepted.

The case for Catholicism as synonymous with loyalty to the Crown was put vigorously by Matthew Pattenson in 1623 in a book which he dedicated to Charles as Prince of Wales. Pattenson presented for consideration 'the portraicture of a Roman Catholick, by the infallible characters of devotion, order, obedience, and the humilitie of the professors thereof'.[11] Pattenson's argument was taken up and disseminated during the Civil War years by men such as Edward Walsingham, concerned to punch home the lesson of the wars, that rebellion and treachery were the hallmark of the Puritan and Protestant dissenter:

Yf you look back to former ages [wrote Pattenson] yow shall find that from the Saxons to King E.6 To be a Catholick, was never taken as a barr to loyaltie; neither was ther ever anie opposition fownd in the essenc and nature of loyaltie, and the grounds of the Catholick faithe.

And good reason; for that religion, which most aymeth at mortification of the body, and best armeth hym to combat with sinn: and disposeth best the consciences of men, to peace and dew obedience; and is approved by experience of all ages, least to embroyle and endanger with practices, and treasons: must needs (of all indifferent men) be esteemed more consonant and agreable, to allegiance and fidelitie . . .[12]

We Catholics, Pattenson insisted, 'prefer a Monarchie: Calvin, Wolfius & Swinglius, an Aristocracie . . . Yet the Catholicks, and our English protestants agree in this (as in many other weightie matters) that princes ar not to be deposed . . .'[13] As Jean Bede wrote in 1612 in *The Right and Prerogative of Kings*, to deny royal authority was to fall into heresy.

Pattenson was at pains to compare and contrast Catholics with Protestants in the matter of loyalty to the Crown: "The Catholicks obey ex conscientia, and absolute; the Protestants conditionaliter and with a quatenus, and onelie for pollicie and gouvernement.'[14] Catholics would not hinder the succession of a Protestant monarch, he insisted, any more than they would seek to depose a ruling prince. Calvinists, however, 'hold the contrarie'. Charles was being warned against the Puritans and their intentions 'while this great controversie of religion dependeth in England undecided'.[15] The Puritans required to be policed rather than the Catholics with their patient adherence to their father, the King.

It was Pattenson's purpose to have the laws against Catholic clergy repealed, and it was in his interest and in that of his argument to stress the loyalty of ordinary Catholic men and women. But he could do so on safe ground, since in 1623 the most that could be argued against the Catholics turned upon events in Elizabeth's reign and Gunpowder Plot. If the congregations in Anglican churches heard the homily which denounced rebellion, it became increasingly less easy to assume that it could apply only to Catholics:

How horrible a sin against God and man rebellion is, cannot possibly be expressed according unto the greatness thereof. For he that nameth rebellion nameth not a singular or one only sin, as is theft, robbery, murder, and such like; but he nameth the whole puddle and sink of all sins against God and man; against his prince, against all men universally; all sins I say, against God and all men heaped together nameth he that nameth rebellion.[16]

Puritan reformers and their supporters who might claim to see ordinary Catholics as potential incendiaries in the state could not by 1642 avoid the identical charge laid against them: 'a principle not easy to cure, which is the judgement and conscience of a man, whereunto obeyeth at length his will and affection, whatsoever for a time he may otherwise dissemble outwardly'. Rebellion, when it came, as far as Royalists were concerned, came from Parliament and not from Catholics, and it had been the dissenting element in church and state which had dissembled for so long. There was no need for Royalists to pry into the religious persuasion of loyal men: the fact of support for the King in the face of rebellion was sufficient. It can be argued that the Civil War, though it heightened anti-Catholic sentiment in some, in others went some way towards laying it to rest. Catholic and Protestant Royalists stood and fought side by side as, in days of peace, they had rubbed along in routine social and economic life. Of course, Professor Russell was right, the Catholics' involvement with the King in the end did them no good, but the same could be said of Protestants faced with sequestration, composition and sometimes exile because of their loyalty to the King: the Civil War did Royalists in general little good, but Parliament used it as a good excuse to turn the screw on Catholics in general, neuters being made to pay for their religion quite as much as Royalist Catholics.

For the King the Catholic problem remained sensitive. Apologists such as Symmons chose to interpret the King's acceptance of Catholic support as purely utilitarian and expedient: 'ignorant people', Symmons noted, 'take scandall' from the presence of Papists in the Kings Armies' (here Symmons employs the word 'papist' in its strict sense) and Anglicans 'are heartily sorry that there are any . . . because of their Religion':

Not that hereby any scandall is justly given by his Majesty, for we hold it not only lawful for him to make use of those of that Religion but also necessary, yea, it would be a sinne against God, if being assaulted by Theeves and Rebells, he should not use the meanes for his own Preservation, and imploy for his own defence, all those whom God hath submitted under his Government for that purpose . . .[17]

Anyway, Symmons reckoned, if the Parliament could employ 'Papists from other Countryes to help them to destroy their Soveraigne' it was wholly acceptable for the King to 'permit Papists, his owne Subjects, to help to preserve him from such their violence'. The real scandal, for Protestants, which made them 'ashamed' was 'that Papists should out-goe any that beare the name of Protestants in duty and obedience to their King'.[18] Not only that, but the papists in arms for the King had a reputation as diehards, and their actions were to be held up as exemplary of what a true loyal King's soldier should be.

Lucy Hutchinson, describing the slaughter of the Queen's Horse at Shelford in 1645, observed that 'being all Papists [they] would not receive quarter, nor were they much offer'd it'.[19] At Marston Moor, and at Basing House, Catholic royalists sacrificed their lives with the very contempt for the process of dying which Symmons had insisted upon as one of the distinguishing features of a Compleat Cavalier. It is also true that there were a sufficient number of Parliamentarian officers and men ready enough to oblige Catholic, and other, Royalists who disdained to receive or ask for quarter. Lucy Hutchinson herself was upbraided by such a man for attending to the wounds of captured Royalists, 'his soule abhorr'd to see this favour to the enemies of God'.[20] It serves little purpose to rehearse the almost casual cruelties shown by one side to the other, except to make the point that if Lucy Hutchinson's critics could adopt such an attitude to Royalists in general, known Catholics must have suffered short shrift in the wrong hands. Colonel Cuthbert Clifton, who perished of ill usage in Liverpool Castle in 1645 was victimised as a Catholic as well as a Royalist. The point may be made by a simple comparison of the figures. Between 1642 and 1646 125 colonels were either killed or died, 20·7 per cent of the 603 commissioned in those years. The Catholic officers numbered 117 individuals, of whom thirty perished in the same period and are subsumed within the total number of fatalities. If Protestant colonels are considered alone, numbering 486 in all, then 19·5 per cent of them were dead by the war's end. The Catholic colonels lost 25·6 per cent of their complement. Over the period from 1642 until 1660 at least sixty-six of 117 Catholics died, were killed or were murdered, virtually 56 per cent of them all. The Protestant figure is 41·3 per cent, 201 of 486 in all. Catholic losses in regimental command were high, and any view of the motivation behind their loyalty which might rest upon self- or communal interest has to explain these figures.

II

Three important panegyrics of Catholic Royalist colonels who met their deaths in regimental command exist in print, all from the pen of Edward Walsingham. Two, those of Sir Henry Gage (*Alter Brittaniae Heros*) and Sir John Smith (*Britannicae Virtutis Imago*) were published in England in 1644 and 1645 respectively, and were intended for a wider audience than a purely Catholic readership, as will be more than apparent. The third, that of Colonel Sir John Digby, intended to be entitled *Hector Britannicus*, remained in manuscript form until edited for publication in 1910 by Georges Bernard.[21] The Digby eulogy was accompanied by various verses alluding to all three colonels and to some other Catholic casualties of the war. The important thing about all three works is that Walsingham took pains to present his heroes as exemplars of the Compleat Cavalier, to point the moral that Catholicism and loyalty were wholly compatible – indeed, intertwined – virtues. In the case of Colonel Sir John Smith, who had been knighted for his rescue of the royal standard at Edgehill when the standard-bearer, Verney, lost his life, Walsingham was present at Smith's deathbed.

He expressed in a mild manner that his death was now within a period, and conjured me by all the love and respect I owed him, to certify his dear Mother that he died with a quiet conscience, and a resigned mind, hoping likewise that she would not take his death with too much heaviness, but rather rejoice that she had a son to shed his blood for his Sovereign. A truly Christian and heroic speech which though but short, comprised the very elixir of true fortitude, loyalty and piety.

There is every reason to suppose that Walsingham did not embellish his subject's dying words: firstly, because nothing in them was peculiarly a Catholic sentiment and they might have been spoken by any dying Royalist; and secondly, because Walsingham did not put into the mouth of a dying Sir John Digby any deathbed speech at all, since he, Walsingham, was not present when Digby died. The use of the vehicle of a man's dying words to promote a case was not unusual: writers often created speeches that were presented as the words of living men, to convey a mood or a case. Walsingham, who appears to have been strict in his manner of eulogy, saw no need to add lustre to his portraits by attempting spurious last words. He was more concerned with the way in which his heroes, in their lives, exemplified the principle of loyalty to the King that he and other Catholic writers wished to emphasise to a non-Catholic readership. Only in verse did he let himself go, but no more so than any other contemporary poet or poetaster:

> This is brave Sir John Smith say they:
> Who hath for Valour won the day:
> Hee pawned his life for Charles his King:
> At Alsford in that bloody fight:
> England shall still his prowess ring:
> And blazon forth his Valours might:
> His vertues shall registred lie:
> In God's eternall Memory.

Smith came of a Warwickshire family with a long recusant history. He had soldiered in Europe and then for the King against the Scots, and, as with Digby, Walsingham drew attention to his overt loyalty at that early stage. At the battle of Newburn, when the rest of his troop scattered, Smith, serving as lieutenant under Digby, fought, disarmed and took prisoner Sir Archibald Douglas. He showed himself equally fearless at Edgehill, where he served in the regiment of Viscount Grandison as lieutenant-colonel. His knighthood preceded his elevation to a full colonelcy and the rank of Major General of Horse, in which capacity he was killed at Alresford on 29 March 1644.[22] Clarendon mentioned in passing that Smith was a Catholic, and concentrated upon his soldierly skills: 'from the beginning of the war to his own end [he] performed many signal acts of courage'.[23] Smith was not, therefore, a hero created by Walsingham but a Royalist who, as a Catholic, exemplified the ideal of devotion to the King. The same was abundantly true of Sir John Digby.

He and Smith were of similar age; both were in their late thirties when the Scots war broke out. Digby, a younger son of Sir Everard Digby, who had been executed for his part in Gunpowder Plot, did not carry with him the taint of his father's treason. He had been knighted in 1635 when serving under the Earl of Lindsey, and was a cornet in 1639 against the Scots. Walsingham presented him as 'this Mirrour of Men' and 'might

an English Scipio have hym stil'd'. Like Symmons's Compleat
Cavalier, Walsingham's Digby was held up for example:

if you contemplate and view Sir John Digbie, you shall see in generall a
vertuous and compleatly civill gentleman a valiant souldier, and an
expert commaunder, but if you please to break as it were this perfect
glasse of his Life into sondry particles, the skilfull warriour and officer
shall see his owne pourtraiture in hym lively expressed, the learned
scholler, the civill bachelour, the refined traveller, and accomplished
gentleman, in regarding hym may fruitfully observe what they are, or
should bee.

Whilst on an embassy to Venice with the Earl of Portland, Digby
drew attention of himself as a 'civill, courteous and well bred
Cavalier, a name among them and forraine nations of singular
esteeme and honour'. Such a commendation of the 'Cavalier'
might not have cut any weight amongst xenophobic Parliamentarians, but Walsingham here, as Symmons elsewhere,
sought to present the word as implicitly honourable to be known
by.

At Newburn, where Sir John Smith performed so well, Digby
was unhorsed and taken by the Scots, and when asked by their
commander who he was, answered, 'my name . . . is Digby, then
saith hee I believe you are a papist and I have maid a resolution to
give no quarter to any papist'. To which Digby is alleged to have
replied, 'Sr I am a Roman Catholique and so am resolved to live
and dy: at which resolute answeare the coronell admiring said Sr
because you are so gallant and noble a gentleman, the least haire
of your head shall not bee touched.' Walsingham here presents
his case, in which Catholicism and breeding, worth and resolute
loyalty are wholly compatible, and proceeds to build upon it
deftly. That he did not need to fabricate in order to do so was no
small help, though, as for the exchange of words, they must be
taken as they stand and wholly uncorroborated. In all respects, as
Walsingham sought to show, Digby was a very perfect Christian
soldier, and there were plenty alive at the time who could have
disputed it if there had been grounds for so doing. Thus in his
treatment of enemy prisoners Digby showed himself
punctiliously correct: 'By his favourable, courteous and gentile
usage, hee wrested deserved praise from the mouths of the . . .
prisoners which hee tooke, for they released highly extolled their
entertaynement acknowledging they had fallen into the hands of

a gallant Enemy.' Having established Digby's papist credentials, Walsingham did not dwell upon them, but presented his subject as a paragon of 'all good christians and loyall subjects', not hesitating to say that Digby expressed faith to God and duty to the King, 'his Viceregent on Earth'. The subsuming of the Catholic gentleman within the Royalist cause was carried to its fullest extent by Walsingham in this panegyric of Digby, who died of wounds on 16 July 1645 after lingering in great pain for thirty-one days. At the end of his survey of Digby's life, Walsingham presented his subject not as an exemplar of Catholic loyalism but as very much the Compleat Cavalier:

Sr John Digby late valiant Major Generall of his sacred Maties forces in the West (under the right Honble L. Generall Goring) sprung from noble and renowned Ancestours, embellished with the most radiant gemmes of Vertue, Learning Education and Valour, which shined in the whole course of his life, like a bright Sunne having enlightened this our little world of England with his bright rayes, overshadowed at Taunton in Sommerset shire with a ruddy or rather bloody cloud set at Bridgewater in the west . . . by a noble death in defense of his Soveraigne Liege King Charles; and shall, wee hope rise againe in the East of a blessed and endlesse Eternity in company of all the Saints and those glorious Martyrs, who having washed their stoles in the sacred blood of the Immaculate Lamb, have dyed them in graine with the rich Cochenell of their owne blood and togeather with them shall sing an immortall and victorious Poean and in triumphe to this never dying Generall Christ Jesus under whose Royall Standard of the holy Crosse hee so manfully and vertuously fought during his life.

It is by no means necessary to accept or be impressed by the writer's apparent hyperbole, wholly in keeping with the time at which he wrote, to perceive precisely what it was that Walsingham sought to do. As with Digby and Smith, so with Colonel Thomas Morgan of Heyford in Northamptonshire ('Since Morgan's Vertue, Modestie, Renowne / His Learning, mildleness [*sic*], Honour weare the Crowne / His prudence, Wisdome, Justice win Heav'ns goale'), these men were presented as equals of their Protestant comrades in resolution, status, loyalty and obedience. Such an assertion of Catholic laymen as reliable subjects of the Crown was made all the more possible by the rebellion of a large part of Protestant England and Wales. Elsewhere Walsingham could pick at random from amongst the King's dead commanders, and bring them together in a single 'Posy', as:

> Witnesse Carnarvon, Digby, Smith and Gage,
> Beaumont, Eure, Morgan, Markham, who wage
> Warre for their King, and nobly dying live
> Never to dy and *us Example give*.[24]

If it was true, in Royalist eyes, and as the author of *An Elegie On the Death of . . . Sir Charles Lucas* claimed in 1648, that 'There's no true Subject, save the Cavaliere' then clearly, and for some Protestants, the Catholics' part in the war had rid them of the taint of allegations over preceding decades. Sir Walter Ralegh's 'bonds . . . wrought out of iron' that should ideally bind subject to prince were clearly more powerful than any Catholic antipathy towards a Protestant monarch and a Protestant state church.

III

The presence of Catholics in the Royalist armies did occasion some mutterings amongst certain Protestant Royalists, and some evasiveness. The duplicitous Lord Savile (who was an exemplar for no one) let it be known that 'I hate Papists so much as I would not have the king necessitated to use them for his defense, nor own any obligation unto them'.[25] Colonel Richard Dacre expressed himself very carefully when taxed with the Catholic presence by Lieutenant Colonel Hutchinson of Parliament's Nottingham garrison: 'if he could be convinc'd that the King first entertein'd Papists into his Armie, and that the Parliament had none in theirs, he would never fight more on his side'.[26] Dacre, a cavalry colonel in the army of the Earl of Newcastle, knew very well not only how many Catholic fellow commanders he had (including his own Catholic relations) but also how early Newcastle had begun to recruit them. He did not need a rebel to 'satisfie [him] in that' but was quite prepared to spin out conversations for tactical advantage. He was later killed in action at Marston Moor. Even the Queen was careful in the way in which she promoted the interests of her Catholic field officers. In July 1644 she wrote to the King on behalf of Major Sir John Cansfield, who later became colonel of her own Horse regiment.[27] The letter concerned a commission to Cansfield's brother-in-law (it is not known who he was) which Cansfield himself could not solicit from the King 'on account of his religion' but he 'has served you so well, and will do so yet, that you should not refuse so small a thing'.[28] Cansfield was clearly an open and known Catholic: the Queen therefore recommended to her husband that the commission should pass through the hands of the recipient's near relation Colonel Sir Thomas Tyldesley, whose Catholicism was covert in the Oxford army, though widely known of in his native Lancashire. The extent to which Catholic officers and others openly displayed their religion cannot be assessed, but evidently some were more circumspect than others. That may have been a reflection of personal inclination and disparate views as to what was best for the cause in which they fought. But the problem is exemplified in Clarendon's account of the rivalry between Colonels Sir Arthur Aston and Henry Gage, already partly alluded to.[29] Clarendon's account [30] was coloured by his detestation of Aston and apparent approval of Gage, so that the rivalry between them is made to appear entirely of Aston's creation. Gage had been appointed successor to the wounded Aston as governor of Oxford against Aston's advice, whereupon the latter:

sent to some lords to come to him, who he thought were most zealous in religion and desired them to tell the King from him 'that, though he was himself a Roman Catholic, he had been very careful to give no scandal to his majesty's protestant subjects; and could not but inform him, that Gage was the most Jesuited papist alive; that he had a Jesuit who lived with him; and that he was present at all the sermons among the catholics; which he believed would be very much to his majesty's disservice.

Clarendon considered that Aston was lying, 'So much his passion and animosity overruled his conscience'. But Aston's words to the delegation of peers zealous for Protestantism (they are not named) touch upon the critical aspect of Catholic Royalism, its public profile in terms of religious observance. Moreover, Aston resurrected by imputation the image, widely entertained amongst Royalists as well as Parliamentarians, of the treacherous Jesuit. He also, by inference, associated himself with the anti-Jesuit secular Catholic clergy in a feud as old as Aston was himself. Royalists might accept a Catholic presence but would have been wary of Jesuit associations with the cause, and in *A Discourse Discovering some Mysteries of our New State* of 1645 Sir John Berkenhead was at pains to distinguish Catholics motivated by pure loyalty from those influenced by the Jesuit clergy. As Aston knew, there was a distinction to be drawn between attending Mass and attending a sermon.

Aston's attempt to have Gage removed failed with the King, but what he said caused Charles to let it be known to Gage that he must exercise 'discretion in his carriage'. When Gage was told this, he said that:

> he never had dissembled his religion, nor ever would; but that he had been so wary in the exercise of it, that he knew there could be no witness produced, who had ever seen him at mass in Oxford, though he heard mass every day.

Further, that he had only once attended a sermon, to which he had been invited by Aston's daughter and which was at her lodging. Gage concluded that this had been done at her father's behest to entrap him. This last remark of Gage's may have been nothing more than an attempt to blacken Aston, though Clarendon did not seem to think so. Both men died in arms, Gage of a mortal wound on 12 January 1645, Aston when Cromwell took Drogheda in 1649. Their rivalry had no consequence for the King's war effort, but is significant in that it demonstrates the discretion expected of Catholic officers in the Oxford army, so close to the person of the King. It is not therefore surprising to find that where regimental command was concerned, the greatest concentration of Catholic officers lay in the north, in Lord Newcastle's virtually autonomous command. Of 117 Catholic colonels, no fewer than forty-nine (41·8 per cent) originated in the six northernmost counties, which produced 122 colonels in all: 40 per cent of those were Catholics. The following list gives the counties, the total number of colonels in each, and in parentheses the number of Catholics comprised within each county total:

Yorkshire	52 (15)
Lancashire	21 (13)
Northumberland	17 (9)
Cumberland	15 (3)
Durham	14 (8)
Westmorland	3 (1)

Lancashire should be excluded: by the time Newcastle's authority was established there, in May 1643, most of the county's regiments were already formed under the direction of the Earl of Derby. Some of those regiments went south, others in 1643 drifted across the Pennines to Newcastle's field army. When Prince Rupert arrived in Lancashire in 1644 he may have recruited two to three new regiments, but no more. Newcastle himself did not recruit in Lancashire, and those regiments from that county which joined him in the spring of 1643 had a high Catholic percentage of field and other officers. Some regiments – those of George Middleton, William Bradshaw, John Preston and the Protestant John Gerlington – remained with the earl: others, or parts of them, went south with the Queen in June 1643 (hence the Lancashire basis of her Lifeguard regiments). Others, those of Molyneux, the Gerards and Tyldesley, had gone south in the autumn of 1642. Of the other five northern counties, Newcastle had authority over four of them from the summer of 1642, and with the exception of Westmorland, which contributed little in the way of fighting troops to the Royalist cause, it can be seen that three of those counties contributed forty-six colonels of whom twenty-one (45 per cent) were Catholics. Even without consideration of lesser field ranks, it is abundantly clear that Newcastle made no bones about accepting the high-profile association of Catholic gentry with his army from its very inception. Yorkshire came under his authority in December 1642 by agreement with the leading Royalist gentry. He found there regiments already on foot and he raised others, as Slingsby's case has shown.[31] The Catholic contingent among the Yorkshire colonels was small compared with that in Northumberland (52·9 per cent) and Durham (57·1 per cent), at 28·8 per cent. Some Yorkshire Catholics had been commissioned before December, but not, it would seem, by the Lord Lieutenant, the Earl of Cumberland: John Belasyse, for example, a closet papist, marched away from Yorkshire with his regiment in August 1642. It is impossible to say with any certainty that the recruitment of Catholic colonels in Yorkshire postdated Newcastle's arrival, but, given his track record farther north, it is a strong probability. No other general acting for the King created a corps of regimental commanders with such a significant Catholic element: it could not have happened farther south, and reflects Newcastle's own indifference to a loyal man's religion, as well as the very clear readiness of northern Catholics to associate themselves with the King's cause and, perhaps equally pertinently, with the Queen's own army. The geographical factors affecting regimental recruitment, and the question of the distribution of Royalist colonels across England and Wales, will be discussed subsequently.[32] What was certainly true was Parliament's view of Newcastle's army as a 'popish army', not because every member of it was either a Catholic or suspected of being one, but because command rank did not depend upon any other qualification than the ability to fulfil a commission. The Commons in London had more than enough correspondents in the north, as well as northern MPs at Westminster, to be kept aware of the Catholic presence in Newcastle's army in very specific terms indeed. The point cannot be stressed too strongly that these Royalist commanders – Catholic as well as Protestant – were known; for each of them there was likely to be someone clearly on the other side or acting as a correspondent or informant who knew them personally. If history resurrects such men and dusts off their names and reputations 300 years on, that should not obscure the evident fact that in their own day and time they were very visible figures indeed. However any Royalist accepted unquestioningly the rightness of what he was doing, it was in the nature of the war that he took an enormous personal risk: in that respect there was absolutely no difference between Protestant or Catholic commander, unless the Catholic risk be seen as a degree more pronounced, given the attitudes of the enemy.

Newcastle's recruitment of Catholics into high command levels in his army was sanctioned by necessity and by the royal prerogative. It is probable that the earl would have accepted in full John Cowell's definition of the prerogative, which, published in 1607, provoked then some disquiet: 'that especial power, preeminence or privilege that the king hath in any kind, over and above other persons and above the ordinary course of the common law, in the right of his crown'.[33] The King's right to make use of his Catholic subjects in his own defence was based upon his prerogative right as well as upon present need; indeed, had necessity not constrained him and his commanders to make use of them, nevertheless the King would have been entitled to call upon such help if only in order to affirm the broad basis of his support. To condemn the King for employing papists, as his enemies did, and to question the wisdom of it, as some of his own supporters did, was to dispute 'the mystery of the king's power': the Royalist case for using Catholic help was straightforward, and the best exposition of it remains that contained in *Eikon Basilike*, whether or not the words are those of Charles himself. As with Dacre at Nottingham, so with the Eikon, the employment of papists by Parliament is held to pull the rug from under the feet of Puritan critics, 'those who least of all men cared whom they employed, or what they said and did, so they might prevail'. Further:

> It is strange that so wise men, as they would be esteemed, should not conceive that differences of persuasion in matters of religion may easily fall out where there is the sameness of duty, allegiance, and subjection. The first they owe, as men and Christians, to God; the second they owe to me in common, as their King. Different professions in point of religion cannot, any more than in civil trades, take away the community of relations, either to parents or princes.

The cause why the King looked to his Catholic subjects was the 'foul and indelible shame' of those rebellious Protestants who forced him to it. The papists did 'but their duty', which his enemies had manifestly failed to do, and it was a matter of sorrow only that papists should 'have a greater sense of their allegiance than many Protestant professors' whose principles seemed to be more akin to 'the worst Papists' (the Jesuits). Catholics' loyalty was not a cause for wonder; their commitment surprised few, but contrasted markedly with the falling away from allegiance of those who had most reason to show themselves loyal. And what man 'disputed with by swords' points' would entertain scruples as to the private beliefs of those willing to fight off those swords on his behalf?[34] This was an argument that could make no headway with those committed to the detestation of Catholicism, but it must make an impact upon those, then and now, who recognised that the fundamental principle of Royalism was allegiance. The Catholic presence in the Royalist armies was welcomed if not made broadcast. It was not the manifestation of any Catholic position towards the war, but a reflection of a common sense of duty shared by Catholic and Protestant gentry alike. Thus whilst historiography requires consideration of the Catholic presence, the conclusion of such study should be that it must be subsumed within a broader study of Royalist principles and beliefs. If not, then it must be shown that Catholic Royalism differed in essentials from Protestant Royalism. It is improbable that that could ever be demonstrated.

IV

Of 603 identified Royalist colonels of the years 1642 to 1646, 117 (19·4 per cent) were Roman Catholics. None of them was a priest, though Colonel John Digby (George Digby's brother) died as one in 1664, and Colonel Sir John Cansfield was father and brother of Jesuits. Comprised within the 486 Protestant colonels is a group of eighteen officers whose religious persuasion may have been towards Catholicism, and two of that number, Sir Marmaduke Langdale and John Wilde, converted to Rome after 1649. In neither case is it possible to say with any certainty that the outward conversion reflected a reality of belief held during the years 1642 to 1646. Langdale, Wilde and the other sixteen require to be examined as a distinct group within the Protestant contingent, since some were alleged to be papists when they were commissioned, or else there is reason to think they were Catholics before 1642 or after 1646.

The ease with which the term 'papist' was thrown about in the 1640s has been noted. It was applied both to known Catholic recusants and to others who, quite apart from siding with the King, showed support for or conformity with Laudian reform in the church. Indeed, anyone known to favour episcopacy in its unreconstructed form could have been accused of 'popery'. In many cases the charge was untrue – Sir Thomas Aston is an example – but there remain those over whose career a question as to their religious persuasion still hangs. If in any of these cases it could be shown conclusively that allegations were justified, then the ratio of Catholic to Protestant colonels would stand a chance of rising towards a ceiling figure of 133. Beyond that it would be impossible to go, and the true figure for Catholics might well remain at 117.

It is of course recognised that within the figure of 486 Protestant commanders (inclusive of the eighteen to be considered) there must have been those who, like Henry Jermyn, were indifferent to religion. Yet indifference could be concealed behind outward conformity to the Anglican Protestant rite and probably often was. After all, absence from church made a man a recusant: recusancy and Catholicism were not necessarily synonymous. What differentiates 117 officers from 486 is the fact of professed Catholic belief on the part of the minority, with or without evidence of recusancy, rather than the fact of committed Anglicanism on the part of the majority. If only eighteen of the majority of colonels have some doubt attached to their Anglicanism, that serves to show that the vast majority of the King's commanders were his co-religionists as distinct from Puritans, reformers, sectaries and others. As would be expected, in the eyes of Parliament's more excitable propagandists, all who fought for the King necessarily fought against Protestantism. In September 1644, for example, the author of *A Nest of Perfidious Vipers* could arraign the Earl of Lindsey, dead two years, at an imagined gaol delivery: 'Thou understandest already what it is to fight against the true protestant religion, the parliament's privileges, and the subject's rights, under a feigned pretence of maintaining them.' Lindsey's undoubted valour 'was a crime, and so is the valour of all rebels valiant crimes'. He and others 'fight valiantly for the protestant religion, as it stood established in the reign of Queen Elizabeth's sister'. The King's forces were commanded by 'a crew of flying dragons, that have . . . double faces, that can soon face about, be here and there, and every where to do mischief, plunder, ravish, fire, and the like'. None of the King's generals or commanders could escape the accusation of opposing Protestantism. Even Prince Rupert, whose personal and familial credentials were religiously impeccable, was accused of aiming at becoming 'King of Ireland, or King of his Majesty's best subjects the Irish rebels, the papists, Jesuits and others'. The Marquess of Hertford could be judged by the company he kept: 'Does not Endymion Porter fight for the protestant religion? Does not Digby fight for the protestant religion? Yes, papists do fight for the protestant religion . . . to fight [it] away from us.'

Parliament's propaganda recognised the fact of Catholic commitment to the King and used it in an attempt to drown Royalism in a deluge of anti-papist vilification. The Parliament was, anyway, in an impregnable religious position. Whatever the debates within its ranks, Parliament's armies were led by men of undoubted Protestant credentials. For the King and his supporters to accuse Parliament of employing papist soldiery as if it were an excuse for the King to use papist commanders was a weak and untenable argument even if it were true that Parliament courted and employed foreign, Catholic, mercenaries. The threat from Roman Catholicism was not vested in what Lucy Hutchinson called 'the lewder sort' but came from a conjunction of Catholic belief with social and political influence. Neither side's leaders were much bothered about what their rank and file might or might not believe, so long as they fought well. The King's cause was distinguished from that of his enemies by the presence in influential command and advisory roles of men known to be or suspected of being Catholics. The Royalist party in arms was, for those who looked for such things, the most terrible manifestation of the imagined Catholic terror. Of course, Protestant Royalists demonstrated a Laodicean attitude by working alongside Catholic Royalists, but that was not to be indicative of any new tolerant English attitude. The King's enemies were, for the most part, profoundly shaken by Catholic Royalism, which seemed to justify old fears and anxieties. The more extreme Catholic-baiters need no longer look to the Queen, 'the old French madam', and her household for evidence of the popish threat. They need no longer target officers of state and other officials. They did not need to flog for all they were worth the innovations in the state church. However discreet the King may have wished to be, the names and the faces of the Catholic enemy were publicly known and were many: the long-brooded-upon conspiracy could be enumerated in personal terms, and if some Protestants were caught up in the anti-papist diatribes, then they must have been papists at heart. Parliament's religious categorisation had the weight of simplicity and embattled tradition behind it. The Royalist attitude, as it appeared, was innovatory and alarming.

The alleged Catholicism of some Royalist commanders may have been no more than the result of effective anti-Royalist lies. Determining the truth in any single case is not helped by the tendency amongst Restoration Catholic writers to claim for their co-religionists men who clearly were never Catholics: Slingsby and the Earl of Derby are examples. One of the King's most eminent and brilliant cavalry commanders, Sir Marmaduke Langdale, was seen as an exemplar of the true Catholic Royalist. In fact, when Langdale's reputation was at its height, he was a genuine conforming Protestant of possibly Puritan leanings.

Aubrey recorded Langdale's own account of his conversion to Catholicism, which occurred in Italy during the 1650s:

When Sir Mermaduke Langdale was in Italy, he went to one of those Magi, who did shew him in a Glass, where he saw himself kneeling before a Crucifix: He was then a Protestant; afterwards he became a Roman Catholick. He told Mr. Thomas Henshaw R.S.S. this himself.[35]

Conversion in exile was not unusual, and if what Aubrey wrote was a true account of Langdale's experience, the matter would seem to be cut-and-dried. Whatever he was in the 1650s, he was by his own admission a Protestant prior to then, though he came of an East Riding family with recusant associations. Langdale was forty-four when war broke out. He had become widely known during Strafford's presidency of the Council of the North as a difficult, predictable opponent of the King's officials. Before then he had soldiered in Europe in the armies of the Queen of Bohemia, and he had for a time been comrade-in-arms to Sir John Hotham. Hotham in 1642 and 1643 showed that he feared Langdale and any association with him. This was a view shared by the Royalist colonel Sir Edward Osborne, who had suffered from Langdale's enmity in the 1630s. Yet the man's capacities were such that the government sought to win him over by appointment as a deputy lieutenant and, with fine irony, as sheriff of Yorkshire in 1639 charged with collecting Ship Money. King Charles himself reprimanded Langdale for his dilatoriness in that duty of his shrievalty. Yet nothing said against him at the time implies that he was a Catholic. Slingsby, who admired him, depicted him as the 'faithfull and indefatigable' commander which he became in the King's cause:

. . . our Northern Horse . . . were not much inquisitive & hitherto shew'd a mind indifferent wt way they went so they follow'd their General; & such an army had Caesar, of whom they write, yt he would be so severe and precise in exacting discipline, as he would not give ym warning of ye time either of Journey or of battle, but kept ym ready, intentive, & prest to be led forth upon a sudden every minute of an hour whither soever he would.[36]

Slingsby's Langdale led his troops by personal example, 'lighting from his horse and leading ym on foot many times with his head bare, whether ye sun did shine, or ye clouds did pour down rain'. In 1648 Sir Thomas Fairfax considered Langdale so dangerous as to be worth a £1,000 price on his head after his escape from custody in Nottingham Castle.[37]

Langdale's last fight as commander of the Northern Horse brigades was at Sherburn in Elmet in October 1645, when George Digby's poor generalship led to a major defeat. Rallying his men at that battle, Langdale was reported to have said to them, 'For mine owne parte, I will not have you upon any designe, but where I will lead you myselfe.'[38] All reported speeches must be treated with caution but in this instance the tone accords well with Slingsby's view of Langdale.

In 1658 Charles II advanced Langdale to the peerage as Baron Langdale of Holme on Spalding Moor. By then his military role had gone into eclipse, commensurate with his fierce Catholicism and his support for the idea of a Spanish alliance against the Republic. He excused himself from Charles II's coronation on the grounds that his plundered estates could not afford the means to maintain the dignity of his peerage. One of the most eminent Royalist soldiers of 1642–48 had faded progressively into shadow. Langdale's own children, however, regarded him with fear. When he lay dying, so it was reported, his eldest son could not find the courage to warn his father of impending death: Langdale thus died without a priest.[39]

How far Langdale's conversion to Catholicism may be taken to indicate a tendency towards Rome in the 1640s is impossible to say. It seems unlikely, and the evidence must be taken at its face value, though it deprives Catholic Royalists of 1642–46 of a legendary soldier in their ranks. Less eminent, but another case of conversion to Catholicism, was Colonel John Wilde, who made the break with his Protestant past in 1650. Wilde's father, Sir John Wilde, sheriff of Shropshire in 1642 and an active Royalist Commissioner of Array, lived to initiate composition proceedings for his estate in 1645 which dragged on into 1649. At no time was there any allegation against father or son as papists. In 1651, however, information was lodged against Colonel Wilde as an active Royalist conspirator who had recently become a Catholic.[40] The informer did not throw the hint of popery around loosely, and whether it was well founded or not, it shows that Wilde had previously been known as a Protestant.[41]

Langdale and Wilde properly belong amongst the 486 Protestant colonels. A group of sixteen remains, for each of whom there is some reason to suspect Catholicism but nothing in the way of hard evidence. Often the implication is indirect, as with Henry Mordaunt Earl of Peterborough, Sir Robert Strickland of Thornton Bridge in Yorkshire and Sir John Lucas of Shenfield. Mordaunt was the son of a father who had publicly abjured Catholicism and become openly conformable to the Church of England, even to its Puritan wing. There were some, however, who regarded that conformity as suspect.[42] Henry Mordaunt became openly Catholic after 1660 and, like other Catholic peers, exercised high office under Charles II and James. II. He died in 1697 unreconciled to the *coup* of 1688. Nothing in his record between 1642 and 1646 implies Catholicism, unless his abandonment of Parliament when his father fell terminally ill may hint at it. Strickland also came of a Catholic background, and his wife was a recusant. Though covert Catholicism was no barrier to it, Strickland had served in Parliament in the 1620s and represented Aldborough in the Long Parliament. It was his Trained Band regiment which the King called to its colours in May 1642 as a guard for himself at York, but Strickland himself was probably still at London, for the regiment came in under the command of Edmund Duncombe, who was knighted. At some stage in the summer Strickland abandoned the Commons and returned to Yorkshire. His son, Thomas, was already in arms (and was to be knighted after Edgehill). Late in 1642, or early the next year, Strickland was knighted and received a new commission in March 1643. Though he surrendered in 1644 when York fell, he made no attempt whatsoever to compound for his estate, though his son did so for his own personalty. From 1660 until 1670 Strickland lived in retirement, Sir Thomas becoming a public figure and a known Catholic. Indeed, he went into exile in 1688 with James II.[43] Though the failure to compound is suggestive, it is likely that Catholicism passed from Strickland's wife to their son, and that Sir Robert was a conformable Anglican.

The case of Sir John Lucas is more dramatic. His brother, Sir Charles Lucas, shot at Colchester in 1648, was never said to be a papist. Sir John himself, advanced to the peerage in 1645 as first Baron Lucas of Shenfield, compounded without difficulty, though he made a meal of it: 'we found Sir John Lucas' estate so much obscured that to discover it we had to make many journies',[44] the Essex officials reported: they ran into opposition in their work, 'all men decline assisting . . . it contracts the greatest odium upon us'.[45] Popular feeling in favour of a known Catholic Royalist peer after 1646 would seem most unlikely. When war was imminent in 1642, however, Lucas's residence at Shenfield was ransacked by pro-Parliamentarian mobs in much the same way as the Essex home of the overtly Catholic Earl Rivers (subsequently a Royalist colonel) was plundered. What is also suggestive is that, when the siege of Colchester was laid in 1648, the family burial vault was broken into by regular New Model troops and the remains of Lucas's mother and sister were strewn about the chapel. Some of those godly soldiers chose to adorn their hats with bones and hanks of hair.[46] Such an obscenity might well have been visited upon a Catholic Royalist family, but it may also mark the vindictive hatred felt for Sir Charles Lucas, who commanded in Colchester.

Edward Chisenall of Chisenhall in Lancashire, commissioned by Prince Rupert in May 1644, was very probably a Laudian. Sir Charles Dallison of Greetwell in Lincolnshire had recusant associations and favoured toleration, but his writings suggest indifference. Charles Gerard, though stigmatised as a 'grand papist', had probably shrugged off his Catholic familial associations, as his post-Restoration career suggests. He, however, and Colonel Edward Grey or Gray of Chillingham and Cowpen in Northumberland, both attached themselves in exile to the pro-presbyterian alliance policy of the Queen Mother. That is not in itself proof of Catholicism on their part, though vaguely suggestive. Grey was the fifth and the youngest of the sons of a Northumberland knight, and his estate, valued at £60 per annum in 1642, he mortgaged to provide himself with funds for the war. He showed himself to be one of the most indefatigable plotters of the 1650s, underwent several spells in prison, and almost came to be transported to the West Indies in 1656. Sir Arthur Hesilrige considered that there was 'not a man in the north of England that hath done more mischief' and that he was 'most active and dangerous'.[47] One of Grey's brothers was the son-in-law of Colonel William Huddlestone of Millom in Cumberland, knighted by Newcastle in 1644. Huddlestone compounded for his estates without difficulty, though there was some recusant element in his family: his nephew(?) Major Edward Huddlestone was probably a Catholic, his mother certainly a recusant. Another

Cumberland colonel was Sir Thomas Dacre of Lanercost, a dilatory Ship Money sheriff like Langdale. Dacre petitioned to compound in April 1647 at two-thirds, which seems to be an admission of Catholicism on his part. His mother was a recusant. That he did not compound before 1652 may have been due to lack of the funds to do so. In 1648 he was listed amongst the Cumbrian delinquents sequestered in his country, but was not, by the county officials, styled a recusant or papist.[48]

Three other north country men were possibly Catholics: Jordan Crossland of Newby in Yorkshire was the father of two sons who became seminary priests. His property in Lancashire was sequestered on the grounds of his Catholicism, but he strenuously denied it. He compounded in 1649 on a sixth, and his wife compounded on her own account without difficulty for having been in Helmsley Castle garrison with her husband. If Crossland was a Catholic, he was capable of concealing it, and his composition proceedings suggest he was at least recognised as a conformable Protestant. John Eden of Windlestone in Durham had appeared before High Commission in 1633 on a charge of cohabitation, which sometimes indicated a secret marriage outside the rights of the Church of England.[49] Eden's brother, Robert, and nephew, also Robert, were active Royalist soldiers but experienced no difficulty in compounding as Protestants. Sir John Mallory of Studley in Yorkshire was knighted by King Charles in December 1641 as a sign of favour: Mallory was almost certainly a Straffordian in the Long Parliament, where he and his father represented Ripon. He refused to sign the Protestation in the Commons, and was almost certainly in the King's entourage when it left for York in February 1642. By early August that year he had a regiment on foot and training in Yorkshire, and was preferred to the governorship of Skipton Castle by the Earl of Cumberland. There, though not inactive, he sat out the war and found no difficulty in compounding for his own delinquency as well as for that of his father, who died in 1646. The suggestion of covert Catholicism is slender.[50]

In the remaining four cases, only one is worthy of any serious consideration. Thomas Lunsford attracted the label of papist alongside all the other taunts thrown at him. Neither he nor his brothers were Catholics. Nor, very probably, was Henry Wait, Muster Master of the Yorkshire Trained Bands and deputy governor of York from 1642. He may have been a Gloucestershire man. His wife, a recusant as well as a delinquent, had property there.[51] Henry Howard, a younger brother of Charles Viscount Andover and a son of the Catholic Royalist Thomas Earl of Berkshire, ought, by familial tradition alone, to have been a Catholic. Yet when he surrendered and sought to compound he stated that he had taken up arms in defence of the Protestant religion and had become disillusioned. That could have been special pleading, but no one challenged it, and he proceeded to composition.[52]

Colonel Sir Edward Bishop of Parham in Sussex, a 'great malignant' goaled in 1644 after he had surrendered Arundel Castle, was described in 1650 by the Committee for Advance of Money as a recusant.[53] There is nothing in the extant composition proceedings to suggest that this was true, and none of the Sussex Parliamentarians, who clearly mistrusted Bishop, made allegations against his religion. A massive fine of £12,300 set in 1644 was cut down to £4,790 by 1646, but Bishop made no attempt to pay it. He claimed that his estates were encumbered by debts left by his father, Sir Thomas the first baronet, at his death in 1626: that, rather than any reluctance to take oaths, may explain non-payment. It is also worth noting that his younger son Henry, a Royalist plotter in the 1650s, though known as a Royalist, was never alluded to as a papist. Bishop died in 1649. Proceedings to recover the fine, intended to defray Sir William Waller's wartime debts, ceased, since the dead man had been tenant for life. The charge against him therefore postdated his death, and there is no clear indication of the information on which the London committee made its charge. If the family could have been shown to be recusant, proceedings could have been commenced against it irrespective of Bishop's death. They were not. For a time in 1645, and later, Sir Edward was goaled in the Tower, and if he was a staunch Anglican Protestant he may have declined to attend services at which Presbyterian divines officiated. Had this been the case, it might technically have made Bishop a recusant without there being any Catholic basis for his action. Of course, the London committee's charge may merely have been unfounded: but their information had to have come from somewhere.[54]

Alleged papists whose cases require some scrutiny make up

slightly less than 3 per cent of all colonels, and account for under 4 per cent of the 'Protestant' contingent within the overall figure of 603. There are other cases, not worth pursuing, in which the allegation of popishness was manifestly absurd. Yet, in all attempts to define the religious persuasion of laity figures in this period, express statements of principle are so rare as to be inapplicable in any general sense. It would be impossible to categorise the 486 Protestants as pro- or anti-Laudians, though clearly there must have been some who opposed Laudian reform without dissenting from the established church or siding with the Parliament in 1642. Slingsby had trouble with the ritualism of Laud's church, but he did not associate himself with those who had similar reservations and who went so far as to howl down episcopacy and Laud together. Probably he was representative of the majority of the Protestant colonels, but who is to say? If, as has been suggested, for the Royalists the war was not a religious war – at least, not for most Royalist laymen – then to look for some form of uniform Royalist Protestantism may be pointless. Reduced to drawing conclusions from the fact of outward conformity, it is only possible to say that in the broadest terms the King's colonels were for the most part his co-religionists. Very few Royalist laymen were concerned to go any further than that until a handful of them discovered that their particular Protestantism had been betrayed by the King's use of Catholics: and such men appeared to have discovered their troubled consciences only, it would seem, when defeat seemed likely and imminent. In 1642 Royalists were primarily motivated by loyalty to the King and the inherent obligation upon them to defend his person against rebels. That no more makes Royalists into Laudians than the fact of rebellion makes Puritans out of Parliamentarians.

V

Nothing distinguishes Catholic colonels from those collectively termed Protestants other than the fact of their Catholicism. The social make-up of the 117 Catholic commanders shows an expected correlation with the findings arrived at for the colonels as a whole.[55] The *nobiles minores* provided 67 per cent of all colonels; within the Catholic group they accounted for 65 per cent, sixty Gentlemen and sixteen Knights. The *nobiles majores* accounted for a further 29 per cent of the Catholic presence:

there were eleven baronets, eight peers (including Lords Crawford and Aston of the Scottish peerage and Viscount Molyneux of the Irish), and fifteen heirs or other male representatives of the Catholic peerage in general. For seven individuals there is no positive evidence as to social status at commission but one of these, George Boncle, was knighted in 1645.

The Catholic peers who held regimental commands were Lords Andover, Carnarvon (covert but known) and Morley and Mounteagle, with John Savage second Earl Rivers and John Paulet fifth Marquess of Winchester. The latter's rank depended upon his authority in his fortified mansion at Basing in Hampshire, where he was ably assisted by other Royalist commanders. Winchester's house had been searched for arms in 1641, where sufficient for 300 horse and 1,200 foot were reportedly found: these were sold off to Protestant purchasers.[56] When Basing fell to Parliament in October 1645 in a welter of bloodletting the marquess was taken away to London, where there was debate in the Commons as to whether he should be tried for his life.[57] Earl Rivers had succeeded to the title of his maternal grandfather in 1639, in which year he had royal protection for his religion. By his wife he was related to Lord Morley and Mounteagle, and his son-in-law was Colonel John Scrope of Bolton in Wensleydale, a Catholic and illegitimate son of the Earl of Sunderland. Rivers's estates lay in Cheshire and in East Anglia, predominantly Suffolk and Essex, and it was his Essex mansion which was ransacked by an anti-Catholic mob in 1642. As with so many peers, Rivers's active command terminated when he was called to the Oxford parliament in 1644, but his 'black regiment' had already done good service and would continue to do so in defence of Donnington Castle under Lieutenant Colonel John Boys, a Kentish Protestant of some military experience.[58] The earl's war ended in Bristol in 1645 – he was reckoned an associate of Prince Rupert[59] – and he petitioned to compound on the articles for the port's rendition. He may have abjured his Catholicism. He was required to clear himself of accusations of recusancy in 1649.[60]

Other Catholic noble families were represented in regimental command by untitled males. The ramifications of the Howard of Naworth family and its connections have been noticed,[61] as has the commitment of the Somersets (Earls of Worcester), the

Digbys (the Earl of Bristol and his sons: Colonel John Digby was a known Catholic, his elder brother George was said to be one but it is doubtful), and the Eures of Malton. Colonel William Eure was killed in action at Marston Moor in 1644. Colonel Henry Arundell succeeded to his father's barony of Arundell of Wardour in 1643 after the death of the second Lord in action at Stratton. For a time the third Lord Arundell served as commander of the Lifeguard of the Marquess of Hertford, in which capacity he fought at Lansdown in July the same year.[62] Colonel Sir John Smith, eulogised by Walsingham, was brother to Charles Smith first Baron Carrington in the English peerage and first Viscount Carrington of Barrefore in the Irish, both creations of 1643. In all these cases, except that of the Eures of Malton, the colonels were but part of a profound familial Royalism. The same was true also of Colonel John Belasyse, the second son of Thomas first Viscount Fauconberg of Henknowle, who also fought for the King but in no command rank. So far as is known, Colonel Belasyse was already a covert Catholic in 1642, though his father is said to have converted to Rome whilst in exile after 1644. The viscount was succeeded by his grandson in 1653, who contracted a marriage with a daughter of Cromwell and seems to have enjoyed the Protector's favour. His uncle, since 1645 Baron Belasyse of Worlaby, plotted incessantly against the regime to which his nephew gave more than merely tacit support.

The Ango-Irish Catholic peerage which had rallied against the Catholic rebels in Ireland was represented in regimental command in England by two heirs: Oliver FitzWilliam and Patrick Barnewall. Other than these, the 'Irish' involvement in regimental command was limited to Colonels Donnell, Grady and O'Neill. The precise origins of Donnell and Grady are unclear, they may well have been native Irish gentlemen and certainly were both soldiers of some experience. O'Neill was a native Irishman. All three were Roman Catholics. O'Neill and Grady appear to have come into England from Ireland with some troops in 1643 or later: Donnell, FitzWilliam and Barnewall exercised command over forces raised in England and Wales. None of the five was a Confederate though all were Catholics. Apart from a handful of officers in the lower command levels, this is the sum total of Irish Catholic involvement in the King's regimental command structure during the First Civil War.

Colonel Barnewall, killed in Ireland early in the 1650s, was a signatory of the petition drawn up in August 1644 by officers of Wilmot's army following the latter's disgrace. When, in 1646, the King conferred upon Colonel Barnewall's father the title of Viscount Barnewall of Kingsland in the Irish peerage, it was partly a recognition of the son's loyal services in England. (A fellow signatory of the 1644 petition had been Colonel Thomas Weston, the probably Catholic son of Richard Weston first Earl of Portland, who ultimately succeeded as fourth Earl: Thomas Weston's mother was a Waldegrave.) Colonel Barnewall enjoyed the King's 'great esteeme and favour' in 1645.[63] Colonel Oliver FitzWilliam was the heir of Thomas first Viscount FitzWilliam of Merrion, who was killed or died in arms for the King in Ireland. Oliver, who became second Viscount in or around 1650, had territorial interests in Staffordshire, and his links with England were more pronounced than those of Barnewall. His first wife was a Brereton from Cheshire, a recusant; his second from the Royalist Penruddocks in Wiltshire. FitzWilliam's brief period of regimental command in England – he had served under Ormonde in Ireland since 1642 – fell in the mid-part of 1645, and whether or not he formed his own regiment and thereby fulfilled his commission is unclear. At the Restoration Charles II advanced him to the Irish earldom of Tyrconnell. In 1647 FitzWilliam was admitted to compound for his English estate without difficulty, but he was expelled the country by the Council of State in 1651.[64]

The Catholic baronets included some eminent commanders. Sir William Widdrington of Great Swinburn in Northumberland had been knighted in 1632 and advanced to a baronetcy ten years later. In 1643 he became the first Baron Widdrington of Blankney in Lincolnshire, which came to him through his marriage. Widdrington's Catholicism was widely suspected; it was deeply ingrained in his family but covert in him. He represented Northumberland in the Short and Long Parliaments. In the former he denounced the Scots as rebels, and in the latter voted in favour of Strafford: he spent some time in the Tower for laying violent hands upon a fellow MP. When Newcastle came into Yorkshire in December 1642 Widdrington was president of his council of war as well as a serving colonel. He was excepted from pardon by Parliament in 1646, and was killed in action at Wigan Lane in 1651. Through his mother he was connected with the

Royalist Curwens of Workington, and a cousin, Sir Edward Widdrington, likewise created a baronet in 1642, served alongside him as a cavalry colonel. Sir Edward Widdrington of Cartington in Northumberland was an overt Catholic, and was likewise denied the opportunity to compound for his estates, spending the years after 1648 in exile.[65]

The family commitment of the Vavasours of Hazlewood in Yorkshire, headed by Colonel Sir Walter Vavasour, created a baronet in 1642, was considerable. Sir Walter's wife was the Catholic daughter of Thomas Belasyse first Viscount Fauconberg; he and his brother-in-law John Belasyse fought side by side at Selby in April 1644, when a major defeat was inflicted upon the Yorkshire Royalists by Sir Thomas Fairfax. Vavasour had contributed money to the war against the Scots in 1639 and raised and led two troops of horse in that war: 'young Sir Walter Vavasour' had come fresh from the 'Germyne Wars' to serve the King.[66] After the defeat at Selby he went into Europe, though perhaps not until after York had fallen in July 1644. His regiment passed to Colonel Francis Hungate of Saxton in Yorkshire, another known Catholic, who was killed in arms at Sherburn in Elmet in 1645.[67] Three of Walter's brothers were in arms for the King: William served as major of the regiment, Thomas as major in the Lancashire-based regiment of the Catholic colonel Sir William Bradshaw (and was killed at Marston Moor in 1644), whilst John, who became lieutenant-colonel under Francis Hungate, was also killed on Marston Moor.[68]

Sir Richard Tempest of Stella in County Durham succeeded as third Baronet in 1641 and served as a colonel in both civil wars. In 1648 he was reported to be 'commaunder in chiefe of [the] Bushoprig'.[69] He did not attempt to compound. Through his mother he was related to Colonel Richard Tempest of Bolling Hall in Yorkshire, the son of a knight. Tempest of Bolling was commissioned in 1644 by Newcastle when the latter was reorganising his forces to face the Scottish invasion: prior to that, he had been a Commissioner of Array and a prisoner in Manchester for a time. Colonel Tempest of Bolling was not a Catholic and experienced no problems in compounding for his activism twice, for the First Civil War and for the 1648 rising. Thereafter he sold his property and went into Europe, where he died in 1657.[70] A third Tempest, John of Old Durham, was a known

Catholic when preferred to regimental command by Newcastle, probably in 1644, when he was barely twenty-one. He fought also in 1648. His father, Sir Thomas, had been Attorney General in Ireland.[71]

Away from the north country the role of Sir Edward Stradling, baronet, and his brothers has already been noticed.[72] At Strensham in Worcestershire was the principal seat of Sir William Russell, created a baronet in 1627 and when War broke out in 1642 Recorder of Worcester. He was instrumental in gaining the city for the King, became sheriff of his county for the second time in 1642 and was commissioned as a colonel in May 1643, though he did not perhaps fulfil his commission until the following year. Russell was admitted to compound at a third, and in 1651 summoned to take an Oath of abjuration.[73] At Grace Dieu in Leicestershire Sir John Beaumont, second baronet, and his mother were reputedly the pivotal figures in a recusant enclave. In July 1641 it was charged against them both that they 'and others, mostly recusants, violently resisted the constables when attempting to collect the subsidies' and that they had fortified their mansion.[74] As a colonel, Beaumont became for a time governor of Worcester, and was killed in action in Gloucestershire in September 1643.[75] The familial Catholicism was vested in his brother and heir Sir Thomas, also a Royalist activist.[76] Colonel Sir John Beaumont had been very forward in the King's service, and in 1640 had been major of Sir John Paulet's 'unruly regiment' when it was stationed in Derbyshire.[77] As a Catholic he was expelled from command that same year.

Colonel Sir Thomas Haggerston of Haggerston in Northumberland served under Lord Newcastle against the Scots in 1640, and had been an active collector of the Catholic subsidy the previous year. His baronetcy was conferred in August 1642, and Newcastle commissioned him to raise a regiment in April 1643 but he and his son Thomas, the regiment's lieutenant-colonel, were both captured in a seaborne raid in May. Haggerston refused to abjure, did not compound, and his property went up for sale.[78] During the Scots war, an officer was billeted at Haggerston Castle, 'a poore meane house with thick walls (somewhat castle like) and a flatt roofe' but

It was a house indeed, and naught els, for the master of it, fearing least the army beeing to encampe thereabouts, would, like an inundation, sweepe all his stocke and provision away with it, for prevention hee had wholly dissfurnished his house and left it empty and naked both of furniture and foode, and him selfe and family were retyred to Barwick, and hee had put himselfe in the earle of New Castle's troops, yet hee was a man [of] 7 or £800 per annum.[79]

Haggerston's foresight in 1640 was not repeated in 1643. His house was ransacked by the Parliamentarian Captain Shafto when Haggerston was captured, and goods worth £800 still on the premises were taken away.[80]

Sir Richard Fleetwood of Ellastone in Staffordshire was one of the earliest baronets created by James I, in July 1611. A 'professed delinquent and Papist', his house was plundered in June 1643 and he himself taken prisoner in January 1644. He did not compound.[81] Sir William Dalston of Cumberland and of Heath Hall in Yorkshire was MP for Carlisle in the Long Parliament when he was created a knight and a baronet in February 1641: his father, Sir George Dalston, knight, was still living. Sir William admitted to having been commissioned by Newcastle to raise a cavalry regiment but denied fulfilling it, though he was in the garrison of Carlisle (of which citadel his family were hereditary constables) in 1644/45. His attendance at the Oxford parliament may have interfered with his active military role, which according to him was initiated in November 1643.[82] Parliamentarian officials in Cumberland treated him as a papist delinquent. He coumpounded at a third as an MP, but his father settled at a tenth, though he too was a sitting member of the Commons in 1642, representing Cumberland.[83]

The family association of the Vavasours of Hazlewood with the King's cause, four brothers in arms and two dead in the field, is shown also by the Middletons of Leighton in Lancashire, a family which also illustrates the interconnection of Royalist and Catholic families. Colonel Sir George Middleton was knighted and made a baronet at York in July 1642 when appointed to the commission of array for his county. His second wife was a daughter of George Preston of Holker in Lancashire, and Preston's son, also called George, was killed in action in March 1644 serving as Lieutenant-colonel to his kinsman John Preston of Dalton in Furness. The new lieutenant-colonel of Preston's regiment when it became part of the Northern Horse brigades was Francis Middleton, Sir George's brother. Edmund Ludlow, who knew Francis

Middleton, alluded to him as a papist.[84] The mural monument at Saxton Church in Yorkshire commemorating Francis Middleton notes that he was uncle to Colonel Francis Hungate, who took over command of Vavasour's regiment after April 1644. John Preston's regiment at Newark in October 1644, where Francis Middleton was noted as its commander, probably contained elements of Sir George Middleton's old cavalry troops, Sir George having abandoned his command after Marston Moor and gone into Ireland. The likelihood is that Francis had served as lieutenant-colonel to his brother prior to Marston Moor, where they both fought. Sir George Middleton was admitted to compound on the articles for the rendition of Dublin, his Catholicism notwithstanding, though throughout the 1650s he was never trusted by the government.[85] Another branch of the Middletons, that of Stockheld Park in Yorkshire, was represented in regimental command by William heir to Sir Peter Middleton, knight, likewise a Royalist delinquent who died in 1645. Colonel William Middleton's brother Matthew was killed on Marston Moor as major in his brother's regiment. Colonel Middleton was the son-in-law of Henry Constable Viscount Dunbar, lieutenant-colonel to the cavalry regiment of Sir Edward Widdrington, who was killed defending Scarborough in 1645.[86] Three of the sons of John Middleton of Middleton Hall in Westmorland were killed in arms as field officers and the third son, Colonel John Middleton, fell at Hopton Heath in March 1643. Colonel John Middleton's brother William served as lieutenant-colonel in the cavalry regiment of the Protestant sheriff of Lancashire Sir John Gerlington: both he and Gerlington were killed during the Northern Horse march to the relief of Pontefract in March 1645.[87] Sir John Gerlington's widow, Katherine, remarried to a Catholic, Adam Bland of Kippax in Yorkshire, who had served successively as major to Sir Walter Vavasour and Colonel Francis Hungate.[88]

Catholic colonels fared no better and no worse than their Protestant comrades in the distribution of wartime honours. Three new peerages were created, for Sir William Widdrington (1643) and for John Belasyse and Edward Somerset (1645). All three were rewards for service and went to socially suitable recipients: Widdrington was a baronet and married to the Thorold heiress of Blankney in Lincolnshire, whence derived his title; Belasyse was the younger son of a Royalist peer; and Somerset was anyway heir to the earldom and marquessate of Worcester. Four new baronetcies were bestowed upon Catholic colonels, those of Bryan O'Neill, an Irish career soldier from Dublin, and Sir Edward Waldegrave, knight, in 1643, and those of John Preston of Dalton in Furness in 1644 and John Knightley of Offchurch, Warwickshire, in 1645. Knightley was the son of a known and convicted recusant[89] and was related through his mother to Colonel Sir John Pettus of Norwich, who had been made a knight and baronet in 1641. By his own marriage Colonel Knightley was connected with the Lewkenors of Sussex, two of whom, Anthony and Christopher, were colonels in the West Country. Indeed, for a time Knightley served under Colonel Sir Christopher Lewkenor who was knighted in 1644 and had been MP for Chichester in the Long Parliament.[90] It is possible that Knightley assumed command of Lewkenor's regiment when the latter attended the Oxford parliament. The baronetcy intended for Knightley in 1645 was not confirmed until 1660.

Ten colonels secured knighthoods between 1642 and 1646, some of whom have been noticed: John Cansfield (1644), George Boncle (1645), Henry Gage (1644), Gilbert Gerard (1643), John Smith (1642), Thomas Tyldesley (1643). Of the others, Colonel Richard Poore, knighted at some date between the outbreak of war and February 1645, when he was killed, remains obscure. He had been dismissed from the army in 1640 because of his Catholicism, and he may have been a Wiltshireman, although a man of the same name and rank was cited as an Irish rebel in 1659.[91] Colonel William Courtenay of Bogatt in Hampshire had similarly been dismissed from the army in 1640, and in 1642 was major under Colonel Sir John Beaumont, the recusant owner of Grace Dieu in Leicestershire. Courtenay's knighthood in April 1644 followed upon his promotion to a full colonelcy in George Goring's army.[92]

Henry Lingen of Sutton in Herefordshire seems to have been a covert Catholic, though his Parliamentarian adversaries the Harleys of Brampton Bryan had no doubts as to his 'popery'. He was knighted by the King on 6 July 1645 at Grosmont, and ended the war as governor of Goodrich Castle, where 'Lingen fought until the walls were beaten into rubble about his ears . . . only capitulating when they completely collapsed'.[93] He was Herefordshire's equivalent of John Arundel of Trerice, known as

'Harry for the King', though he had not the sons that Arundel had to take into war with him. In May 1642 he began mustering his Trained Band company in the King's interest, and in the autumn was with the Somersets in South Wales, serving in the army there forming. When the King reorganised following the disastrous collapse of Edward Somerset's military endeavours at Highnam in March 1643, Lingen, recently exchanged, was commissioned as a colonel and appointed sheriff of Herefordshire for a second term. His delinquency and suspect Catholicism were particularly noted by Parliament, perhaps owing to the extreme hostility of the Harleys of Brampton Bryan, and the fine first set in 1646 was at a half, subsequently cut to a third. Nothing deterred Lingen. He was wounded in arms in 1648, suffered a second fine at a sixth, and in November that year was engaged in a plot to seize Hereford.[94] By his marriage Lingden was brother-in-law to Colonel Sir Walter Pye of the Mynde in Herefordshire, who as late as August 1642 was looked to by the Parliament, but Pye became lieutenant-colonel to Sir Arthur Aston and from July 1643 a commissioned colonel like Lingen.[95] To take the familial connections in Royalism further, Pye had married the sister of Timothy Tyrell, Charles Gerard's nominated governor of Cardiff in July 1645, and Tyrell's own marriage made him the son-in-law of James Ussher, Archbishop of Armagh, whose son, Colonel James Ussher, was killed at Lichfield in 1643.[96]

Only one of the knighthoods which came the way of Catholic colonels went to a commander in Newcastle's northern army, that bestowed upon Robert Clavering of Callaly in Northumberland. The earl's willingness to commission Catholic officers did not extend to scattering wartime honours amongst them, though he enjoyed the viceregal powers of knighthood and did, indeed, knight Clavering himself in 1642. John Preston's baronetcy and Sir William Widdrington's peerage were beyond Newcastle's powers of creation, though he may well have recommended both men to the King. Robert Clavering was the heir of Sir John Clavering, knight, who was also a committed Royalist. Through his mother Clavering was related to Sir Thomas Riddell the Catholic commander of Tynemouth, who had been knighted by Charles I in 1639 when Riddell was Town Clerk of Newcastle. Bitter political antagonisms within Newcastle as much as Riddell's colonelcy and Catholicism drove him into exile, where he died, denied pardon by Parliament.[97] Clavering's knighthood followed upon his commission but preceded the 'many engagements' in which he 'eminently served his late Majesty'. Langdale, who said that of Clavering, also attributed the victory at Adwalton Moor on 30 June 1643 to the performance of the forlorn hope which Clavering commanded. Langdale's judgement emphasises that Clavering was a commander of considerable flair, as the deficient historical record would seem to indicate.

Clavering's military association with the Marquess of Montrose, and his operations behind enemy lines in February and through to June 1644, have been traced elsewhere.[98] In the latter month he and Montrose parted company, and Clavering struck south from Newcastle upon Tyne through enemy-occupied territory, intending to reach York before Prince Rupert engaged the Scottish and Parliamentarian armies on Marston Moor on 2nd July. He failed to arrive in time, and may have had trouble *en route*, for he died at Kendal in August. He was twenty-six.[99]

When Clavering died, command of his regiment passed to his former lieutenant-colonel, John Forcer of the Harbourhouse in Durham. Forcer, a 'notorious' recusant, was the brother-in-law of Colonel Sir Thomas Riddell and was linked with Clavering by more than a shared faith. Forcer commanded the regiment within the Northern Horse brigades from August 1644 until the brigades' destruction in October 1645. Langdale had a high opinion of Forcer, as he had had of Clavering. The Catholic profile of the field officers of Clavering's cavalry regiment was maintained by Forcer. His lieutenant-colonel was John Sayers, a recusant from Yarm on the Tees (who was killed in action at Naseby in 1645) and the regiment's major was Thomas Craithorne of Craithorne in Yorkshire, who had been dismissed from the army in 1640 because of his religion.[100] Clavering had also raised a regiment of foot in which the Catholic command presence was negligible. Though he remained colonel to his death in 1644, actual command probably lay with James Swinhoe, a Northumberland Protestant, who became full colonel when Clavering died. Swinhoe's father, Colonel Gilbert Swinhoe of Chatton, was alleged in 1645 to be leading a guerilla band of 'Moss troopers and thieves of Tynedale' against the occupying Scots, and died in prison in London in 1646. His son compounded for his inheritance in 1649 after involvement in the

1648 rising.[101]

The main Catholic representation in regimental command came from the ranks of the *nobiles minores*, and predominantly from untitled gentlemen. Residual Catholicism and recusancy were a gentry phenomenon, but these men drew upon themselves more than the usual attention of central government and its agents by their active adoption of rank and part in the King's struggle. It remains hard to envisage what it was they hoped to gain, if the notion of self-interest be accepted. It is also difficult to explain why such men infrequently gave up their involvement as the war turned against the King, which might have been advisable if their motivation was largely selfish. Moreover, family involvement, which is marked amongst Catholic as well as Protestant colonels, hazarded far more than an individual life. For many it was a mark of pride that sons and brothers were involved with them in the King's cause. The Stradlings, the Arundels of Trerice, the Somersets, Howards and Vavasours in this respect were no different from the Slingsbys, Comptons, Grenviles, Dallisons and Eyres. Loyalty to the King involved more than the mere individual adherent: as the 'publike father' drew his subjects about him in his defence, so Royalist heads of families expected the same of their own immediate kin. The colonels, Catholic or Protestant, were the most visible aspect of something far-reaching and familiar.

VI

In certain areas of the country commitment to the King by Catholics willing to accept his commission entailed immediate personal risk and danger to property and possessions. The powerful appeal of the royal cause alone can explain why Norfolk, Essex, Kent and Home Counties Catholics left everything behind to follow the armies. What possible self-interest could have taken the octogenarian Sir Edward Waldegrave away from his Norfolk and Kent properties, what degree of ambition have led the Registrar of the Consistory Court of Norwich, Stephen Knight, to follow him when he went?[102] The same question could be asked of Colonel Thomas Beddingfield, another Norfolk Catholic, who was taken prisoner when his regiment was destroyed in 1643, and spent the ensuing two years in prison in London. He and his father, Sir Henry, had drawn attention to themselves by things unspecified they were reported to have said at the time of the breaking out of the Irish rebellion in 1641, but there is no suggestion in their case, any more than in that of Waldegrave, that they were forced out of their county by anti-Catholic, let alone anti-Royalist, pressures.[103] The same degree of choice which can be posited in their actions was probably present for John Godfrey of Norwich and Hindringham, who was killed in arms as a colonel in distant Gloucestershire in 1644.[104] (His brother Francis served as lieutenant-colonel under John Belasyse and then under Belasyse's successor from April 1644, Theophilus Gilby,[105] and was killed with the Northern Horse in October 1645.)

A number of Catholics abandoned their homes and property in 1642 in order to associate themselves with and to become part of the King's marching army elsewhere in England. In doing so, they did as much as many Protestant Royalists. Samuel Tuke left Essex to serve in the Duke of York's regiment of horse, of which he became colonel, fighting under Newcastle until 1644 and then in the West Country. This 'wise and virtuous Catholic gentleman' had extensive military experience in Europe, continued in arms long after 1646, and earned a reputation in exile as a duellist: 'soe deadly . . . is that Collonels hand'. Though whilst in exile some affected to regard him as 'an atheist, but a great oracle', Tuke's Catholicism was constant, and in 1660 he 'harangued' (to quote John Evelyn) the House of Lords on behalf of his co-religionists whilst recounting to the peers the events at Colchester in 1648, where he had fought.[106] Charles Finch abandoned Kent, where his family was widely known for its recusancy, to serve as major under the Hampshire Catholic Richard Manning, who was a papist relative of Edmund Ludlow.[107] Manning's regiment fought farther west still, and when he was killed in action at Cheriton in 1644 Finch became colonel. As late as January 1646 Colonel Finch was still in arms and professing obedience to Ralph Hopton.[108] Richard Thornhill of Ollantigh in Kent quit the county in 1642, accepted command under a fellow Kentishman, the Protestant Sir William Butler, and, when Butler was killed at Cropredy in 1644, became the regiment's colonel. Thornhill was the son-in-law of Sir Bevil Grenvile, but how much influence that had on his early and decisive Royalism is unclear. At the war's end he went into voluntary exile and did not attempt to compound.[109]

It may be felt that those Royalists who abandoned home and

estate when war began, to travel a great distance to associate themselves with the King, evinced a significant degree of loyalty. Waldegrave, Beddingfield, Godfrey, Finch, Thornhill and Tuke must have known that their property would be seized and probably plundered, and rents diverted to the enemy's cause. They broke with their familiar domesticity and social routines, their absence eloquent of their loyalties. Their known Catholicism made them, anyway, men to be watched during the uncertainties of 1641 and 1642; they could not contribute in any anonymous way to the royal war effort, and they knew it. The sacrifice of virtually everything for some ill defined and dimly perceived benefits in the long term defies reason, unless it be supposed that Catholicism induced in such men a recklessness and spirit of disdain for their worldly possessions. Of course they were not alone: Protestant Royalists in counties likely to fall under Parliament's immediate control likewise made the journey to where resistance was forming and in need of them. When Waldegrave, Beddingfield and Godfrey quit Norfolk, Sir Jacob Astley and his son did likewise, as did Richard Crane, Sir Dru Drury of Riddlesworth (who was commissioned in August 1643) and others who served in various ranks in the King's armies. No doubt they made whatever dispositions they could of their property to safeguard it as best they might but recourse to lawyers, trustees and paperwork must have signalled intentions.

Counties such as Norfolk, Suffolk, Essex, Hertfordshire and Middlesex were abandoned to the Parliament by the organisation of the Royalist war effort, which concentrated upon the north, the west, the Midlands and Wales. Other counties formed debatable land, where one side or the other might achieve control either early in the war or as a result of campaigns. In Hampshire the Marquess of Winchester stayed put as Basing House, where he commanded during a long and bloody siege. Colonels Manning, Sir William Courtenay, William Chamberlain and Sir John Mill served elsewhere. Chamberlain, from Nash in Hampshire, was serving under Wilmot in August 1644 and a signatory of the petition to the King of that month. He ended the war in the garrison of Truro, but was denied composition because of his recusancy and his refusal to adjure, and was only finally admitted in 1653.[110] Sir John Mill of Newton Berry was killed somewhere during the war as a commanding colonel, perhaps dying in

Oxford in 1644.[111] Sir William Courtenay of Bogatt fought from 1642 until 1645 in Somerset and the west, ending the war as governor of Farringdon in his native county.[112]

Northern England was the heartland of Catholic Royalism in arms, the emergence of Catholic regimental commanders condoned and even encouraged by Newcastle and, briefly, by the Earl of Derby in Lancashire. The geographical patterns of regimental command are discussed elsewhere.[113] without distinction between Catholic and Protestant colonels. Nevertheless, the distribution of the former requires comment. The places of origin of 113 of the 117 colonels are known: forty-nine of them (43·3 per cent), as has been shown, originated in the six northernmost counties of England. If the Irish (five) and Scottish (three) Catholics are omitted, then northern England provided 46·6 per cent of all Catholic colonels commissioned between 1642 and 1646 whose ordinary place of residence at the time of commission can be identified. The remaining fifty-six were drawn out of twenty-nine counties, making often a token representation from shires as far apart as Gloucester (two), Lincoln (one), Dorset (two) and Buckingham (one). The figures demonstrate not only the widespread nature of Catholic Royalism, but the distinction to be drawn between that part of England where their involvement was encouraged and the remainder where it was only condoned. The case for a communal Catholic response, bearing in mind that these figures deal only with high-profile regimental command, stumbles in the face of the fact that, outside the north, Catholic colonels were infrequently to be met with. Only one of twenty-four colonels originating in Somerset was a Catholic: one in twenty-one in Lincolnshire, two of twenty-four from Devonshire. There were none at all from Nottinghamshire, Shropshire, Hertfordshire, Suffolk, Huntingdonshire and Cambridgeshire, though those six counties produced forty-eight commissioned colonels in all.

In those counties of England where Catholics were thin on the ground, the Catholic gentry would anyway have been noticeable. All the more so when they responded to the King's call to arms, and prepared either to raise forces in their locality or to go elsewhere with perhaps a small local following. For many a Parliamentarian the local Catholic gentleman forming his regiment was the immediate and visible token of the hitherto vague and formless papist conspiracy. It took courage for Richard Conquest of Houghton Conquest in Bedfordshire to appear openly and in arms for the King: this 'most dangerous and malignant papist' was leading his regiment in Buckinghamshire as late as November 1644.[114] In the contested ground of Gloucestershire the wealthy Sir John Winter, former secretary to the Queen, early personified the Royalist cause in his county from his power base in the Forest of Dean. A blood relation of the Somersets across the Severn, and son-in-law of Lord Howard of Naworth, his Catholicism was notorious from Lydney to London, and he quickly assumed ogreish proportions. His commission as a colonel came as late as September 1643, and in March 1644 he was made Colonel General of his county: in September that year he distinguished himself in battle against Edward Massey, standing 'stoutly upon his guards, with a fire-pike in his hands'. He was driven from the Forest in February 1645 at the battle of Luncoate, firing his own house as he fled.[115] Winter and Colonel John Slaughter in Gloucestershire were the Catholic contingent of the county's thirteen colonels. Beyond the Severn into Monmouthshire and Wales what Clarendon called the 'Catholic interest' faded abruptly away. In Monmouthshire the power of the Somersets provided three Catholic colonels out of seven. In Glamorganshire three of four were Catholics, but those three came of a single family, the Stradlings of St Donats. In the whole of the rest of Wales, which provided thirty colonels in all, not one of them was either a recusant or a suspected Catholic. Even allowing for the fact that Wales is a special case,[116] and that this study is concerned only with a specific command level, Catholic Royalism was very much an English phenomenon, at its most pronounced north of the Trent.

The Duchess of Newcastle recorded that her husband had been criticised for having 'Roman Catholics and Scots in his army' but that 'he answered them, that he did not examine their opinions in religion, but looked more upon their honesty and duty; for certainly there were honest men and loyal subjects amongst Roman Catholics, as well as Protestants'.[117] Honesty and duty were not, however, sufficient in themselves. It was Newcastle's precept to provide officers for his army 'known to be gentlemen of large and fair estates' who drew upon their own revenues 'to serve and support them in their public employments'.[118] This was not Newcastle's rule alone, but mere recognition of the fact that the King's war effort had to be at least partly if not wholly self-supporting, and that, in the initial organisational stages at least, the resources of the officers were essential. The development of assessments and other forms of regular income from communities where the King's writ ran necessarily followed on from this: but the funds available to regimental commanders were there and to be used before Treasurers at War came to collect and disburse tax and other moneys. In Newcastle's army at least were a large number of Catholic gentlemen whose loyalty was beyond dispute and whose resources matched it: in other words, and like their Protestant colleagues, they put their money where their lives were. That is a profound commitment indeed.

Colonel, later Major General, William Webbe was a Catholic and a diehard. He fought at Cadiz in 1626[119] and soldiered in Europe thereafter. He may have been a Wiltshireman by birth, but at the time war broke out in 1642 he appears to have been a rootless career soldier. Clarendon thought him 'an excellent officer, bred up in Flanders in some emulation with colonel [Henry] Gage'.[120] Webbe was crippled in action at Newbury in October 1644, but could still ride and fight. At the war's end he was Major General of the Horse to Ralph Hopton. Hopton's army was breaking up in a turmoil of spreading indiscipline, its morale shot and the majority of its commanders eager to reach a treaty of surrender with Sir Thomas Fairfax. Some officers were simply making their way to the enemy lines and handing themselves over. Only Webbe refused to countenance surrender so long as Hopton declined it: 'only major general Web . . . always professed against it'.[121] Almost twenty years later two Royalist gentlemen approached the Duke of Albemarle with a petition in favour of Webbe. The old major-general was suffering still from the wounds of Newbury and in desperate need of relief for his great wants.[122]

The Duchess of Newcastle recalled observing to her husband how many had shown themselves willing to appear for the King 'and at the noise of war endeavoured to be commanders'. She wondered 'what advantage they could make by their employments', to which 'My Lord smilingly answered, that for the generality, he knew not what they could get, but danger, loss, and labour for their pains'.[123]

Notes

1 The phrase is taken from the title of an anti-papist tract of 1673 by Peter du Moulin, *The Great Loyalty of the Papists to K. Charles I (Of Blessed Memory) Discovered*. Du Moulin's thesis was that the rebellion of 1642 was the work of Jesuits aiming at subverting the Protestant church by the overthrow of its head, Charles I. How seriously anyone took Du Moulin's rantings is impossible to say, but the anti-Catholic hysteria of the later seventeenth century was fuelled by such nonsense, which further obscured the material part played in the King's cause by Catholic laymen.

2 Sutherland, *Hutchinson Memoirs*, p. 57.

3 Paul Hardacre, *The Royalists during the Puritan Revolution*, The Hague, 1956, p. 51. My emphasis.

4 Symmons, *Vindication of King Charles*, p. 79.

5 D. C. Peck (ed.), *Leicester's Commonwealth*, Athens, Ohio, 1985, p. 66.

6 Russell, *Fall of the Monarchies*, p. 88.

7 Macray, *Clarendon's Rebellion*, II, pp. 318–9.

8 J. White, *A Defence of the Way to the True Church*, 1624.

9 John Donne, *Pseudo-Martyr*, 1610, preface.

10 Russell, *Fall of the Monarchies*, p. 217.

11 P.D.M. (Matthew Pattenson), *The Image of Bothe Churches*, Tournai, 1623, p. 277.

12 *Ibid.*, p. 392.

13 *Ibid.*, p. 396.

14 *Ibid.*, p. 395.

15 *Ibid.*, p. 400.

16 *Certain Sermons or Homilies*, 1899, p. 609.

17 Symmons, *Vindication of King Charles*, p. 79.

18 *Ibid.*

19 Sutherland, *Hutchinson Memoirs*, p. 163.

20 *Ibid.*, p. 99.

21 Georges Bernard, Life of Sir John Digby, *Camden Society*, Miscellany XII, 1910, and for what immediately follows unless otherwise referenced.

22 Newman, *Royalist Officers*, p. 348. HMC, *Thirteenth Report*, Portland Mss, 1891, p. 84.

23 Macray, *Clarendon's Rebellion*, III, pp. 337–8.

24 My emphasis.

25 J. J. Cartwright, Papers Relating to the Delinquency of Lord Savile, *Camden Society*, Miscellany VIII, 1883, pp. 5–6.

26 Sutherland, *Hutchinson Memoirs*, p. 109.

27 See above, Chapter Two.

28 M. A. E. Green (ed.), *Letters of Queen Henrietta Maria*, 1857, pp. 249–50.

29 See above, Chapter Three.

30 Macray, *Clarendon's Rebellion*, III, pp. 441–2.

31 See above, Chapter One.

32 See below, Chapter Five.

33 John Cowell, *The Interpreter*, Cambridge, 1607.

34 Catherine Mary Phillimore (ed.), *Eikon Basilike: the Portraiture of his Majesty King Charles I*, Oxford, 1879, pp. 123–4.

35 John Aubrey, *Three Prose Works*, ed. J. Buchanan-Brown, Fontwell, 1972, p. 99.

36 Parsons, *Slingsby Diary*, pp. 145–6.
37 Gardiner, Hamilton Papers, pp. 149, 175–6.
38 Newman, *Marston Moor*, p. 143, where the Pontefract relief ride is also covered.
39 Ellison Gibson, *Crosby Records*, p. 273. Newman, *Royalist Officers*, pp. 221–3 unless otherwise referenced.
40 HMC, *Thirteenth Report*, Portland Mss, 1891, p. 588. Newman, *Royalist Officers*, pp. 412–3. CCC, p. 978. CAM, p. 1284.
41 *Ibid.*
42 Coates, Young and Snow, *Private Journals*, p. 345.
43 Newman, *Royalist Officers*. pp. 361–2. HMC, *Mss in Various Collections* VIII, Wood Mss, 1913, p. 58. CCC, pp. 113, 138, 176.
44 CCC, p. 315.
45 *Ibid.*
46 HMC, *Twelfth Report*, Beaufort Mss, 1891, pp. 27–8.
47 Newman, *Royalist Officers*, pp. 167–8.
48 *Ibid.*, pp. 98–9. CCC, pp. 72, 124, 233, 1560.
49 Newman, *Royalist Officers*, p. 119.
50 Brunton and Pennington, *Long Parliament*, p. 236. Newman, *Royalist Officers*, p. 244. CCC, pp. 113, 1119. Spence, *Skipton Castle, passim*.
51 Newman, *Royalist Officers*, p. 395. Dore, Brereton Letter Books, II, p. 532.
52 See above, Chapter Two.
53 CAM, p. 508.
54 CCC, pp. 42, 91, 849.
55 See above, Chapter Two.
56 Coates, *Journal of Simond D'Ewes*, pp. 68, 102.
57 Whitelocke, *Memorials*, I, p. 526.
58 Newman, *Royalist Officers*, p. 39. Hovenden, Visitation of Kent, p. 40. CAM, pp. 727–8, 1392. CCC, p. 102.
59 HMC, *Thirteenth Report*, Portland Mss, 1891, p. 269.
60 Newman, *Royalist Officers*, p. 331.
61 See above, Chapter Two.
62 Newman, *Royalist Officers*, p. 6.
63 *Ibid*, p. 17.
64 *Ibid.*, p. 133. Coates, *Journal of Simond D'Ewes*, p. 120.
65 Newman, *Royalist Officers*, pp. 410–11. CCC, pp. 2416–8. HMC, *Twelfth Report*, Appendix, IV, Rutland Mss, I, 1888, p. 504.
66 HMC, *Twelfth Report*, Rutland Mss, I, 1888, p. 505.
67 Newman, *Royalist Officers*, pp. 204–5. CCC, p. 141.
68 Newman, *Royalist Officers*, pp. 387–8. HMC, *Twelfth Report*, Rutland Mss, I, 1888, p. 505.
69 Gardiner, Hamilton Papers, p. 227.
70 CAM, p. 931. Newman, *Royalist Officers*, p. 368.
71 Newman, *Royalist Officers*, p. 367. CCC, p. 204.
72 See above, Chapter Two.
73 Newman, *Royalist Officers*, p. 321. CCC, pp. 52, 425, 652.
74 HMC, *Fourth Report*, I, House of Lords Mss, 1874, p. 88. *Lords Journals*, IV, p. 316.
75 Newman, *Royalist Officers*, p. 20.
76 CCC, pp. 1109, 1187.

77 HMC, *Twelfth Report*, Appendix, II, Cowper Mss, 1888, pp. 256–8.
78 Newman, *Royalist Officers*, p. 172. CCC, pp. 318, 2558.
79 Hodgson, Aston Journal, p. 16.
80 CCC, pp. 902–3.
81 CAM, p. 1358. Newman, *Royalist Officers*, p. 134.
82 Newman, *Royalist Officers*, p. 100. CCC, pp. 107, 960–1, CAM, p. 424.
83 CCC, p. 124.
84 Firth, *Ludlow Memoirs*, I, p. 110.
85 Newman, *Royalist Officers*, p. 254. CCC, pp. 29, 99, 176.
86 Newman, *Royalist Officers*, p. 295.
87 *Ibid.*, and for Gerlington, *ibid.*, p. 153.
88 *Ibid.*, p. 32.
89 HMC, *Fifth Report*, I, House of Lords Mss, 1876, p. 9. CCC, p. 3147.
90 Newman, *Royalist Officers*, pp. 232–3. CCC, p. 216. See also CCC, pp. 1215–6, 2044.
91 Newman, *Royalist Officers*, p. 300. Firth, *Ludlow Memoirs*, I, p. 317.
92 Newman, *Royalist Officers*, p. 88. HMC, *Fifth Report*, 1, House of Lords Mss, 1876, p. 47.
93 Hutton, *War Effort*, p. 199.
94 Newman, *Royalist Officers*, p. 235. CCC, p. 140. 'A short account of the rebellion in North and South Wales', *Cambrian Quarterly Magazine*, I, 1829, p. 72.
95 Newman, *Royalist Officers*, p. 309. Long, Symonds Diary, p. 195.
96 Timothy Tyrell was a Buckinghamshire man, Gentleman of the Privy Chamber to Charles I, knighted at Oxford 1643. See Newman, *Royalist Officers*, p. 382.
97 Newman, *Royalist Officers*, p. 313. Hodgson, Aston Journal, p. 9. CCC, pp. 2037–8.
98 Newman, *Marston Moor*, pp. 26–7.
99 Newman, *Royalist Officers*, pp. 73–4.
100 *Ibid.*, pp. 139–40. For Sayer, *ibid.*, p. 333, and for Craithorne, *ibid.*, p. 91.
101 Newman, *Royalist Officers*, pp. 364–5. CCC, pp. 42, 127.
102 CCC, p. 114.
103 Newman, *Royalist Officers*, p. 21. Coates, *Journal of Simond D'Ewes*, p. 180. CCC, pp. 115, 174. HMC, *Fifteenth Report*, Hodgkin Mss, 1897, p. 100.
104 Newman, *Royalist Officers*, p. 159.
105 Gilby was a Protestant, the son of a knight of Stainton in Lincolnshire. See below, Chapter Five.
106 Newman, *Royalist Officers*, p. 380. Knowles Middleton, *Relazione d'Inghilterra*, p. 115. S. H. de Beer (ed.), *The Diary of John Evelyn*, Oxford, 1959, p. 408.
107 Firth, *Ludlow Memoirs*, I, p. 83.
108 Newman, *Royalist Officers*, p. 131. CCC, pp. 2346, 2676–7.
109 Newman, *Royalist Officers*, p. 370. CCC, pp. 102, 368.
110 Newman, *Royalist Officers*, p. 67.
111 *Ibid.*, p. 256. CCC, pp. 485, 1833.
112 Newman, *Royalist Officers*, p. 88.
113 See below, Chapter Five.
114 Newman, *Royalist Officers*, p. 81. F. A. Blaydes (ed.), The Visitation of the County of Bedfordshire . . . 1634, *Harleian Society*, XIX, 1884, p. 97.
115 Newman, *Royalist Officers*, p. 419. Coates, Young and Snow, *Private Journals*,

p. 391. Long, Symonds' Diary, p. 205.

116 See below, Chapter Five.

117 C. H. Firth (ed.), *The Life of William Cavendish Duke of Newcastle*, 1906, p. 137.

118 *Ibid.*, p. 99.

119 HMC, *Manuscripts in Various Collections*, I, Wiltshire Quarter Sessions Records, 1901, p. 104.

120 Macray, *Clarendon's Rebellion*, III, pp. 411–13.

121 *Ibid.*, IV, p. 141.

122 Newman, *Royalist Officers*, p. 401. G. D. Squibb, Wiltshire Visitation Pedigrees, 1623, *Harleian Society*, CV, CVI, 1954, p. 208.

123 Firth, *Newcastle Life*, p. 139.

CHAPTER FIVE

'The smoke and the fire'
The geographical origins of the King's colonels

I

This chapter is concerned with the county origins of the King's colonels, and is an elucidation of the accompanying maps and table. It is also a discussion of the role of the county as a military entity, most particularly in 1642. The concentration upon the county is justified by the fact that the King's resort to arms relied upon the creation of Royalist activist groups within as many counties of England and Wales as could be achieved. If they were not, at least initially, intended to provide him with troops, they might at least occupy and distract the forces of the Parliament. County emphasis was inherent in the Commission of Array, which provided a legal basis and sanction for loyalist activism. Study of the course of the Civil War between 1642 and 1646 shows at one and the same time how meaningless county boundaries were in the context of march and counter-march, and how real distinctions between counties were in terms of civilian organisation and military administration. Counties may have associated, but they cannot be shown to have merged: rather, to have submerged their differences for a specific and narrow military purpose.

All Royalist regiments, without exception, had an original county association, drawing their recruits for the most part from one, sometimes two contiguous, counties. By the same token, those colonels commissioned directly into regimental command often shared that association. Thereafter, for many regiments, the county link became more tenuous as they moved away with the course of the war, and recruited to make up depleted numbers in other parts of the kingdom. Impressment, enrolment of captured enemy rank and file, and the appointment of 'foreign' officers and commanders gradually transformed Royalist regiments into at least regional if not national formations. But in acknowledging that process the original fact remains, and is that marker by which subsequent change may be judged.

All serving colonels, it goes without saying, had an ordinary place of residence at time of commission or promotion, and in most cases (569 of 603, or 94·3 per cent) it is possible to specify both county and town or township of origin. Gentlemen and others commissioned in their counties, whether or not they subsequently marched away, were known loyalists within their county communities. Those colonels who came by their rank during the course of the war and often on active service were clearly promoted on the grounds of their county status, but that does not invalidate the identification of them with their county. A single case may clarify the point. Randolph Egerton of Betley in Staffordshire marched away from his county in 1642 as a captain in the regiment of Charles Gerard, under whom he served throughout the war, and through whom he advanced to the rank of colonel and major-general.[1] His command rank clearly rested upon his record as a subordinate regimental officer, but his initial commission as a captain went to him as a known and willing Staffordshire loyalist. These are the grounds on which Egerton, and others like him from other counties, can be classified according to their county origins. On the other hand, career soldiers long domiciled abroad may have had only tenuous, familial links with their county of origin if they did not have land and property and a house to which they resorted. Such a case is that of Colonel Robert Broughton, the younger brother of Sir Edward Broughton of Marchwiell in Denbighshire. The family was wholly Royalist: Sir Edward's sons, Edward and Robert, exercised subordinate field command in the King's armies, but their uncle Robert, who came over from Ireland with his regiment in 1644, was a fairly typical example of the peripatetic soldier for whom it would be difficult to ascribe any normal place of residence. Broughton cannot be classified as a Denbighshire colonel, though his familial link may be taken notice of as a further extension of the family's overt Royalism.[2] It also serves to underline the gentry origin of a professional soldier.

Table 1 requires some preliminary remarks. The figures are given in three columns. The first gives the total number of colonels ordinarily resident in each county, whether commissioned directly or promoted during the war. The second column gives the number of Roman Catholics subsumed within the county total. The third column is introduced for comparative purposes and as a further guide to county activism: it represents all officers, from colonel downwards, who petitioned in 1662–63 as indigent because of their wartime services. The source for these figures and the problems associated with it has been fully discussed elsewhere.[3] Only twenty-six colonels alive at the Restoration petitioned for financial relief, so the third column is concerned primarily with subordinate regimental and troop or company ranks. Of those twenty-six, twenty-three sent in their petitions as from London and Westminster, tending to indicate that either place was their normal residence. That may have been so in 1662–63, but at least nineteen of them can be shown to have been domiciled elsewhere when the war broke out in 1642.

Table 1   *Geographical distribution of regimental colonels*

County or area of origin	Total No. of colonels	No. of RC colonels in column 1	No. of indigent officer claimants of all ranks petitioning 1662–63
Yorkshire (all ridings)	52*	15	523
Somerset	24	1	309
Devonshire	24	2	208
London/Middlesex	22	1	1005
Cornwall	22	5	351
Kent	22	2	75
Lancashire	21	13	150
Lincolnshire	21	1	148
Northumberland	17	9	169
Shropshire	16	0	102
Staffordshire	15	3	82
Cumberland	15	3	94
Nottinghamshire	15	0	80
Durham	14	8	224
IRELAND	13	5	0

Dorset	13	2	113
Hampshire	13	5	65
Gloucestershire	13	2	51
Wiltshire	12	2	99
SCOTLAND	12	3	0
Cheshire	11	2	60
Warwickshire	11	2	40
Essex	11	1	41
Buckinghamshire	11	1	34
Northamptonshire	10	2	35
Oxfordshire	9	1	48
Worcestershire	9	1	97
Norfolk	8	4	29
Herefordshire	8	1	113
Suffolk	7	0	20
Caernarvon/Anglesey	7	0	18
Derbyshire	6	1	71
Leicestershire	6	1	39
Surrey	6	1	51
Sussex	6	3	26
Bedfordshire	6	1	13
Denbighshire	6	0	56
Glamorganshire	6	3	60
Monmouthshire	5	3	73
Carmarthenshire	4	0	74
Rutland	4	1	11
Cambridgeshire	4	0	18
Montgomeryshire	4	0	28
Flintshire	4	0	36
WESTERN EUROPE	4	?	0
Westmorland	3	1	46
Huntingdonshire	3	0	8
Berkshire	3	1	31
Hertfordshire	3	0	12
Pembrokeshire	2	0	24
Merionethshire	2	0	15
Radnorshire	1	0	7
Breconshire	1	0	17
Cardiganshire	1	0	4

* The figures for Yorkshire by riding are: West, 25; North 17, to include York; East, 10.

This fact warns of the need for caution when the figures for

London and Middlesex are considered, whether applied to the indigents of the Restoration, or to the alleged place of residence of serving wartime colonels. The designation of the capital city may be as misleading as it appears to be enlightening. Clearly, every effort has been made to locate a colonel's usual county and place of residence accurately, but the London and Middlesex figure remains problematical.

Included in the table are the numbers of colonels whose origins were in Scotland or Ireland (twenty-five) or Western Europe (four), accounting for 4·8 per cent of all colonels, or 5 per cent of those who can be classified geographically. The King's regiments were invariably commanded by English and Welsh colonels, and most of those who came with regiments from Ireland in 1643 or 1644 were emphatically not Irish, whether native or planter. The table emphasises, also, the extent to which Englishmen were predominant in regimental command, adding a further dimension to the embattled notion of the English Civil War.

The table is discussed in detail below, and the patterns which the figures show is plotted on map 1. The importance of Yorkshire, Lancashire, Devon and Cornwall to the King's war effort has long been recognised. The showing for Kent, Somerset and Lincolnshire is perhaps surprising and requires to be addressed. So, too, does the relatively poor showing of Wales, long regarded as some kind of Royalist heartland. The seven counties of Yorkshire, Somerset, Devon, Cornwall, Kent, Lancashire and Lincolnshire provided between them almost a third of the King's colonels. The counties of Wales accounted for 6·3 per cent of the total. If, to the seven leading counties, are added those which contributed between eleven and nineteen commanders each, then twenty-one English counties provided 62 per cent of all commissioned colonels. The Welsh contribution, in contrast, was often less, county for county, than that of certain English counties effectively under Parliament's control from the inception of the war.

The distribution of the twenty-one English counties as plotted on map 2 presents a complex pattern embracing much of the north, much but by no means all of the West Midlands and Marches, a solid bloc of south-western and western England, with isolated outliers of activism in the cases of Kent, Essex and, apparently, Buckinghamshire. That county, however, should be seen as the eastward limit of a Royalist bloc in which Oxfordshire and Northamptonshire marginally miss inclusion in the 11–19 category. To the east of Buckinghamshire and northwards of London are six low-yielding counties, as would be expected, as well as Essex.

Berkshire's low tally causes that county to intrude into what might otherwise have been a high-yielding band of counties reaching from Cornwall in the far west to Buckinghamshire in the east, and from Hampshire in the south to Gloucestershire in the north. Hampshire marks, more or less, the limit of Royalist eastward movement that never broke through to tap latent Royalist support in Kent. Berkshire therefore forms the northernmost of three counties, the others being Surrey and Sussex, in which Royalist impact was minimal. However, the high activism of Kent as it is expressed in regimental and subordinate command permits another conclusion: that Berkshire, Surrey and Sussex were more effectively controlled by Parliament because they were less inclined anyway to support the King than Kent appears to have been. That said, the relatively high number of indigents claiming from Surrey and Berkshire in 1662–63 cannot be ignored. It might also be pointed out that Surrey and Sussex, with twelve colonels between them, provided only one less than the contiguous North Welsh counties of Denbigh and Caernarvon.

Brigadier Peter Young used to be fond of saying that, if London had been where Birmingham is, Kent would have been Royalist. The number of colonels from Kent represents those who felt strongly enough to abandon their homes and to associate themselves with the King's war elsewhere in England. Such men would have been more than the nucleus of concerted county action had Kent been in a position to accept direct Royalist aid in 1642. The same point might be made of Essex when it is contrasted with its East Anglian neighbours, Suffolk and Norfolk. Kent and Essex have to be seen as counties in which gentry support for the King was not insubstantial, and is represented by thirty-three colonels and 116 inferior officers, all or any of whom may have led rank-and-file troops across Parliamentarian territory when they themselves made their move westwards. It is impossible to be sure how large was the iceberg of which they were unmistakably the tip, but the events of 1648 in both counties

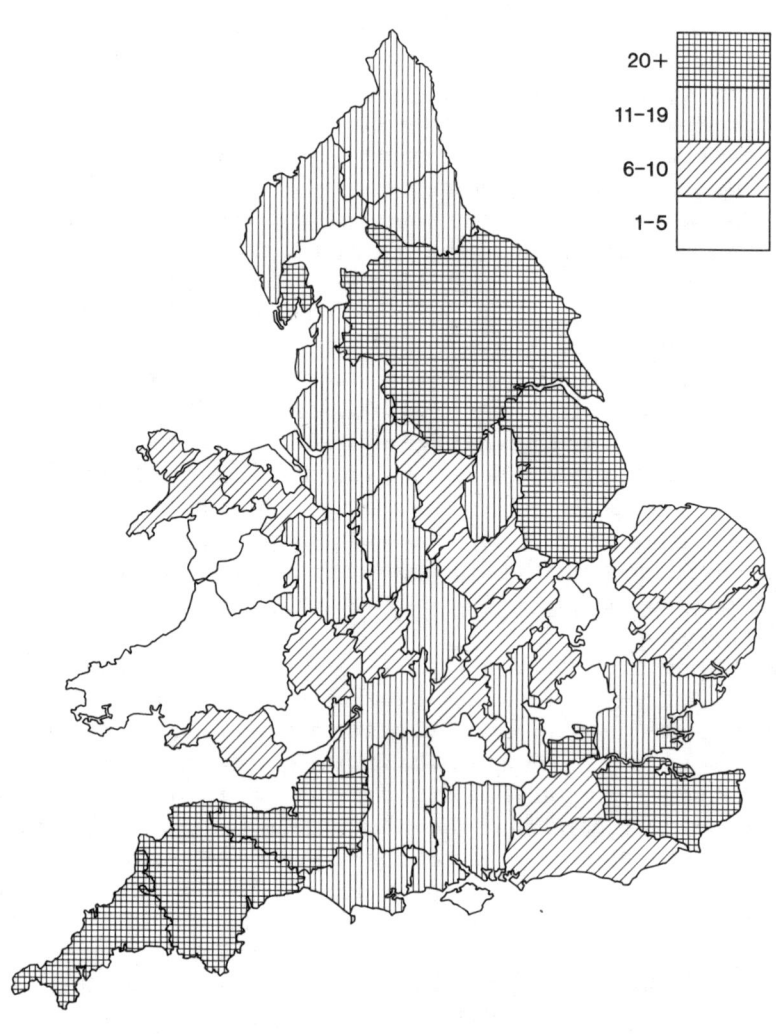

1 *The distribution of colonels by county*

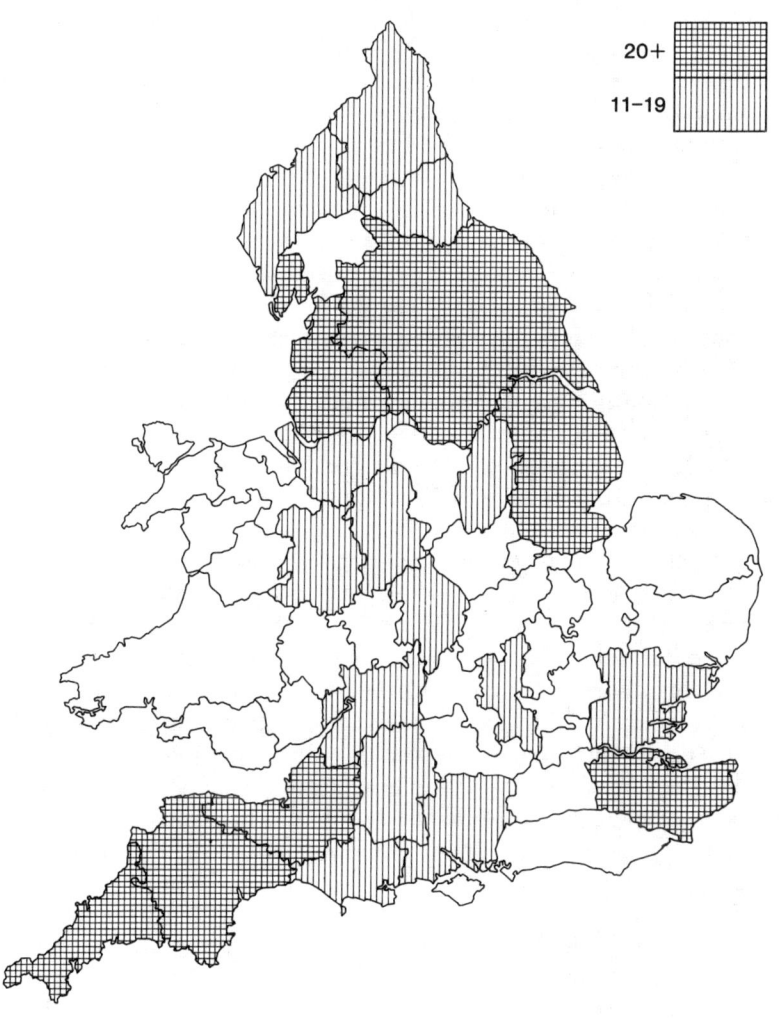

20+

11-19

2 *A limited and an extended Royalist heartland, 1642–46*

are suggestive.

In the view of Lucy Hutchinson, in 1642 'Every County had more or lesse the civill warre within it selfe'. That this was so she attributed to interventionism in the form of the King's Commission of Array and the MPs sent down from Westminster to their seats to enforce the Militia Ordinance.[4] The first of the King's Commissions of Array was sent down into Warwickshire from York on 6 June. Dr Hutton, in his seminal study of twenty counties in Wales, the Marches and the West Midlands, concluded that in those counties, with the exception of Herefordshire, 'local Royalism does not seem to have existed before the actual declaration of war'[5] which came on 22 August when the King's standard was raised at Notthingham. Mrs Hutchinson was graphically emphatic: 'Before the flame of the warre broke out in the top of the chimnies, the smoake ascended in every country.' Further, less precisely as to date, she noted that 'Some Counties were in the beginning so wholly for the Parliament that the King's interest appear'd not in them; some so wholly for the King that the godly [including, presumably, herself and her husband] were forc'd to forsake their habitations'.[6] Both Dr Hutton and Mrs Hutchinson, in all other events most unlikely bedfellows, agree in supposing that war was introduced into the localities from outside, as some contagion spreading out simultaneously from Westminster and York. The source of the Royalist infection 'must lie somewhere in the maelstrom at York', Dr Hutton observed,[7] where, by processes the historical record does not reveal, the King and his advisers were planning war. Nor will Dr Hutton allow that, in the counties which he studied, there were any divisions along partisan lines. On the contrary, he affects to believe that they 'were closing ranks' and had been since 1641, against the traditional enemy, the Catholic threat exemplified by developments in Ireland.[8] Dr Hutton's judgements are not lightly to be challenged, but the notion that partisanship emerged coincidentally with, or in the wake of, the outbreak of war itself is hard to accept. If there was a resurrection of anti-Catholic anxiety, it is more likely to indictate general floating anxiety within comunities indicative of political polarisation than simply the reworking of an old and tired obsession. The country was in a state of political tension for the whole of 1642, if not earlier, which tension arose from the beginnings of division within communities that reflected the realities of division at the centre of government. War in August gave names to enemies, but in the heightened fears of that year Catholics were still a good standby target, especially if they were far enough off.

II

The King's decision to go to war against the Parliament was taken in May. The instrument by which he intended to raise regiments for his campaigns was the Commission of Array, which began to be issued in early June and which was directed to named gentry in each designated county. Dr Hutton concedes that 'The men on the whole were accurately chosen.'[9] It has earlier been suggested that extensive informal canvassing of support must have taken place before the commissions were drawn up to be sent out, giving the King the names of likely and certain activists and a general idea of the extent of potential support in any given county. Dr Hutton's view that one or two men from each went to York to advise the King is very likely to have been the case, but before they made such a journey they must necessarily have informed themselves. It follows that men willing to be known as the King's friends were ascertaining the minds of their peers, certainly in May, probably as early as March. Whilst the evidence of activism in some counties must postdate 22 August, Royalism as a force was more or less developing months earlier. It cannot have been otherwise.

The named Commissioners of Array were men expected to secure their counties and the Trained Bands in the King's interest. The Array was the machinery by which counties were to be prepared for war, but it did not initiate partisanship so much as depend upon its existence. The development of sometimes armed neutrality movements in the summer of 1642 in some counties has been taken as a sign that unwillingness to fight was the common response of the nation at large. Historiographical preoccupation with neuters has always seemed to have more to do with the predilections of historians, preferring to see resort to force as an aberrant phenomenon, who appear to feel that neutrality movements were pillars of moral rectitude. Such movements have to be seen as indicators of developing partisanship rather than as a sign that the county elites were closing ranks against war. War was not imposed upon the counties but arose from within them, for, had it been otherwise, there could have been no war. Neither the King nor the Parliament possessed the means of coercion: they were reliant upon argument and exhortation until their supporters were animated enough to provide the men and the means to translate the political stalemate into armed confrontation. To raise armies, particularly for the King, required the active commitment of leading gentry, men who knew what the outcome of their efforts would be. It is irrelevant if the duration and bloodiness of the war they unleashed appalled them, as it is equally irrelevant whether they expected either a short war or mere gesturing. These men acted for the most part from principle, and if they are to be denied any moral integrity it must be denied also to the neuter movements. The fact that some of these were armed implies an intention to use force against the partisans of either side. If they were not prepared to do so, their neutrality lacked conviction and it is not to be wondered at that events drove them effectively and rapidly from the scene. Whether those movements which were to emerge in 1645 in parts of Royalist-controlled England may be akin to the earlier neuter groupings is debatable: what is certain is that later 'peace' movements were prepared to use force and had to be treated accordingly. The plain fact was that there were enough influential men in many counties who accepted, however reluctantly in some cases, that resort to arms to resolve the political crisis in government was necessary. One is tempted to wonder what solution the neuters might have offered as an alternative, if it were possible to discern a programme in what were intrinsically localist movements of narrow self-interest.

When the King arrived at York in March 1642 he had a considerable entourage but nothing remotely resembling a military force. York itself was to remain an open city during his stay there, and for some time afterwards. As the decision for war was taken, and the the Commissions of Array drawn up, Royalist and Parliamentarian sympathisers and partisans continued to rub shoulders in the city's streets and in the King's Manor. Parliament heard news from York, some false, some true, almost as soon as it happened. In May the King summoned to its colours, as a response to Trained Band musterings in London, the militia regiment of Robert Strickland, MP, to serve as a guard. This regiment was one of several which the King activated at that time, as

Slingsby recorded:

ye King being at York, gave commissions for ye severall Regiments of foot of ye Trainbands for Yorkshire, & to myself one amongst ye rest dated ye 11th May 1642 . . . and in ye Citty I received an order a little after from ye King to take 20 of a company to do ye duty of a soulgier, & to be a guard to ye King's person during ye time of his Abode at York.[10]

Slingsby gives no indication but that the King's intention was to use elements of each band in turn as Lifeguards. However, in the raising of the bands the King revealed a clear and partisan intent. Slingsby noted that there was some reluctance amongst the bandsmen to do 'ye duty of a soulgier', for he 'perceiv'd a great backwardness in ym & upon Summons few or none appear'd'.[11] Quite wrongly, historians have taken this as evidence of antipathy towards the King's cause, a general, obviously widespread, perhaps national, hostility, first manifesting itself in the militia. In fact Slingsby himself provided the clue by which the backwardness he noted can be explained. He expressly stated that he had received a commission from the King to command as a Trained Band colonel, not that his regiment was called to its colours. It has already been noticed that Strickland's regiment was mustered and brought in by Edmund Duncombe from near Pickering.[12] The King was actually selecting trustworthy commanders for existing bands, bypassing their original colonels if there was doubt as to their loyalty. Earlier in 1642, when the Earl of Newcastle had been intended to govern Hull, the Trained Bandsmen of Colonel Sir Philip Stapleton were called up, but command of them was given to Sir Thomas Metham. Stapleton was MP for Boroughbridge and hostile to the King; Metham was an elderly East Riding Catholic who had fought against the Scots and was known to be sympathetic to the King.[13] This process of replacing militia commanders went on everywhere in 1642, nor was it only the King's policy. Such interference with bands that were no more than civilian forces meeting together for drill and conviviality more or less irregularly aroused resentment, which, in men unused to military discipline, explains their 'backwardness' more readily than anything else. Where Trained Bands and their original colonels remained together, there was no lack of readiness: Conyers Darcy took the bridge at Burton on Trent with his Yorkshire bandsmen, not with a volunteer regiment.

The Yorkshire Trained Bands were, therefore, partly demoralised before they were sent against Hull in July. Strickland's regiment, which bore the brunt of a fierce sally from the town, broke up in the field and probably never reformed. Strickland, its nominal colonel, may not have been with it, though he was later commissioned as commander of a volunteer regiment. The fiasco before Hull would have completed the process by which the King came to be convinced of the need for a volunteer army. Local militia, if reliably led, could do duty well enough within their counties, but a marching army had to be based upon other premises than that of traditional county association. The Commission of Array empowered its agents to create a fighting army made up within specific counties, and the process of appointing loyal colonels to bands tested the militia's suitability. Subordinate, company commanders might be more immediately effective in determining reliability and allegiance than a new commander. No fighting army could be built upon such a foundation, and this was quickly recognised.

III

The King's military plans were formulated in the north: the creation of his marching army in August and September 1642 was based upon Cheshire and Wales. The strong northern representation amongst the King's colonels appears to be at variance with the fact of his search for soldiers elsewhere. The north is not only remarkable for its high Roman Catholic activism: the whole area, with the exception of Lancashire, was effectively no partaker in the King's war to the south, though it was almost solidly controlled by his supporters. Northern England and the principality of Wales are areas of contradictions which require to be addressed, and discussion should perhaps adhere to the priorities which the King established on his journey from London to Edgehill which accounted for much of 1642.

In the north, the two weak areas were Westmorland and Lancashire, though Westmorland's apparently poor showing in regimental command (when contrasted with that for Rutlandshire, for example) probably concerned no one at the time other than profoundly committed local Royalists. The balance of activism in the north-west was more than made good by Cumberland, whilst Westmorland was vulnerable to its south once Lancashire fell under Parliamentarian sway in spring 1643. To see the county as a military no-man's-land buffering Cumberland from Lancashire would be about right, though it might do injustice to the three colonels and forty-six indigent claimants of 1662–63 who came from there. Colonels Sir Henry Bellingham and Sir Thomas Sandford stood upon their guard in their native county, Bellingham adventuring south to sit in the Oxford parliament, but otherwise neither was particularly active until the Scots burst into Cumberland in 1644 and concentrated loyalist minds on the defence of Carlisle, and by that time Sandford had given up.

Lancashire was plunged rapidly into partisanship in June 1642 by the energy of Lord Strange, whose influence the King looked to benefit from without the necessity of supplementing local Royalist efforts. The county produced commanders of real quality – Charles Gerard, Thomas Tyldesley, Viscount Molyneux, for example – and they were rapidly drawn away to serve with the King's marching army. Between November and May 1643 Lancashire fell into enemy hands, though not by any means easily: there were at least seventeen actions in the county over those months, and the collapse which came may be attributed partly to the way in which the King used Lancashire as a source of men, leaving Strange to fend for himself as best he could. No serious attempt was ever made to recover Lancashire for the King, though it might well have happened by default if Prince Rupert in 1644 had actually won the battle of Marston Moor. Those Lancashire regiments which extricated themselves from the wreckage of the battle of Whalley and crossed the Pennines to join Newcastle effectively terminated their links with their county. Newcastle himself, though he threatened the enemy at Manchester from his position of strength in July 1643, chose to concentrate his attentions upon those counties to the south of Yorkshire, if that is a fit way of describing his strategic indecisiveness in the summer of 1643. Royalist generals wrote Lancashire off, and more or less did the same with Westmorland. Nevertheless, five of the six northernmost counties of England responded vigorously to the King's cause, and those four which came immediately under Newcastle's control in 1642 provided amongst them a not inconsiderable number of regiments and active commanders. Quite how far their performance may be seen as a major part of the King's war effort is, however, debatable. Newcastle's generalship was virtually autonomous. His army in the north-east was raised with a specific and narrow initial purpose, to control territory and to prepare for the Queen's arrival from Europe. Because of this, there was from the beginning no co-ordination between the northern army and those to be raised farther south. The projected dual advance on London in the summer of 1643, though it came to nothing, and may merely have been an idea in a mind or two, would have been the only single opportunity to create and pursue a combined strategy. The successes of the northern army, its size and its reputation did nothing whatsoever for the King farther south, in the Midlands and in the west. It did not even tie down forces which might otherwise have been used against the King. Wales, with its fewer colonels and apparent lack of activism, materially assisted the King with infantry, whilst the northern army sent the merest trickle of reinforcements south. Newcastle, whatever his merits, clung resolutely to his northern base, so much so that he virtually invited his own destruction. Had he punched his way, as he could have done, into Lincolnshire and on into the heart of the Eastern Association counties in the aftermath of his victory at Adwalton Moor – a battle won by the courage of Royalist commanders – he might well have prevented the Scottish invasion which wrecked him in 1644. Although his wife and biographer conveys the view that such a southward march was intended but prevented by the situation in Yorkshire, there is nothing of resolution in Newcastle's attitude after 30 June 1643. His army, considerable and effective as it was, expanded in auspicious circumstances as it had been, seemed to promise much but performed little. Its losses in men were light before the abortive siege of Hull in September 1643, though its turnover in regimental commanders was, as everywhere, high. It was never involved in a war of march and counter-march as were Royalist armies elsewhere but, after wiping the slate clean of early, minor, reverses, rolled on inexorably until it stopped where it had begun, north of the Trent. Its expeditions into Lincolnshire and Derbyshire were propitious but never followed up. The majority of the northern colonels were commissioned, recruited and fought on home territory. The quality of many of them was undeniable, but the fact was that it was easier to be a Royalist commander in the north-east and north-west than it was to come out of Kent, Essex, Norfolk and Suffolk, let alone Hampshire, Surrey and other debatable territories. The worth of the northern commanders was demonstrated at Adwalton Moor, at Marston Moor, and in the campaign against the Scots in the winter of 1644, when they had their backs to a wall largely of their general's own construction. They fought hard and died hard, and many of them continued the war in the campaigns of southern armies: but quite as many of them laid down their arms in 1644, and the conviction is inescapable that there was more kudos than risk in regimental command under Newcastle until 1644 put men to the test.

The considerable number of colonels originating in the north must be held to demonstrate two, apparently, divergent tendencies. In the first instance, a pronounced level of commitment to the King which Newcastle acknowledged by his distribution of commissions. Yet the proliferation of such commissions indicates that Newcastle was consciously creating an army which would reflect upon his own grandeur. It will never be possible to say how many colonels who owed their commissions to him fulfilled them to the extent of creating full-strength regiments, but the likelihood is that there was more show than substance to his army. That does not devalue individual commitment but it puts in another context Newcastle's undoubted shrewdness when it came to choice of commanders. He made them and he kept them by him. What he seems to have failed to do – and this impression is derived from admittedly scant surviving evidence – was to achieve a clear merging and integration of his own north-eastern army and its Cumbrian elements with that of the Yorkshire Royalists. The reluctance with which the latter viewed any plan to leave their native county when Hull remained unreduced effectively hamstrung Newcastle. Even had he seriously proposed to march south, he could not be sure that his army would follow in its essential entirety. His command over the Yorkshiremen was nominal and by agreement: over his original army it was absolute. This factor, Yorkshire Royalism's inherent local preoccupations, may be the factor which prevented any follow-up to Adwalton. It is far more likely than is the idea that Newcastle was afraid to submerge himself and his army in any general fusion of forces directed against London. He was too loyal to let that matter to him, and he bent more willingly to Prince Rupert's authority in 1644 than had the Earl of Lindsey in 1642. There is no doubt that Parliament feared the 'popish army', but here the Parliament was taken in by the show of the thing. Those at Westminster were also guilty of putting too high an estimate on the Fairfaxes, though of course they had no choice, since the Fairfaxes *were* Parliamentarianism in Yorkshire. Newcastle thrashed them at Seacroft Moor in March 1643 before routing them decisively at Adwalton. A decisive push south could well have rolled up the Eastern Association, Cromwell and all, but it would have had to be immediate. In military terms, Parliament's alliance with the Scots was premature, and the single long-term contribution which Newcastle made to the war may have been the ultimate embroilment of Parliament with the Scots. In terms of any direct contribution from the north to the King's war, Newcastle's only constructive act was to send some northern regiments south and, though not by design, to have recruited commanders who from 1644 on fought tenaciously with other armies in other threatres.

The root of the northern army's failure lay in Newcastle's lack of strategic consciousness. He permitted a distinction to exist between his army of the north-east and the army which the Earl of Cumberland had begun to raise in Yorkshire. For a county which provided the highest total number of regimental colonels and regiments, Yorkshire's part in the King's war effort was largely marginal. Newcastle allowed it to be so.

To assess the north's contribution to the King's war in terms of regiments raised and sent south to fight elsewhere is no easy matter. The King drew freely upon Lancashire's forces: the regiments of Molyneux, Tyldesley and the Gerards were drawn away in 1642. If any of them went back at all, it was only to recruit anew. As for the Yorkshire regiments which fought in the south, all of them that did so before July 1644 had left their county before Newcastle took control there, in December 1642. With one certain exception. Pennyman's, Belasyse's, Eure's, Duncombe's (not the Trained Band regiment of May 1642), and those of the Colonels Frank Wortley (the baronet's son and heir), Brettridge (the baronet's son-in-law), Mauleverer, Holtby, Hilliard and Richard Cholmeley formed no part of Newcastle's command, though Eure may have returned north late in 1643, and Duncombe did return to recruit. It can be no mere chance that when Newcastle was required to send troops along with the Queen as a guard in June 1643, troops which he knew the King would not send back – 'the King . . . was pleased to keep [them] with him for his own service' is the Duchess's phrase[14] – the one full-strength regiment the earl let go was a Trained Band commanded by Conyers Darcy. The rest of the Queen's escort of about 4,000 men was made up largely of Lancashire units, some of which formed her future Lifeguard regiments, and parties of commanded men under Colonels Henry Percy and Thomas Pinchbeck. Neither of these men had served in Newcastle's army but they appear to have accompanied, or preceded, the Queen from Europe. Pinchbeck was a career soldier, and at his death in action at Newbury in October his regiment passed to Henry Bard.[15] Whilst the Queen's escort did form a worthwhile accession of strength for the King, it did not much diminish the integrity of Newcastle's forces which remained behind, and it did not interfere with his campaign into the West Riding which culminated at Adwalton Moor within three weeks.

The earl could not take his army south with the Queen; he could not leave the north with the Fairfaxes unsubdued and he would have encountered resistance from the Yorkshire Royalists had he tried it. Technically, after 30 June, there was nothing in the way of an advance south save Hull and Yorkshire's hesitancy. The earl came under no discernible pressure from the King to move south. The independent command which he had enjoyed since June 1642 was never to be disputed by anyone. The earl's gesture in sending away 4,000 or so men with the Queen was not, given the campaign he proposed to launch, niggardly: but his contribution before then almost certainly was. Rumoured movement of Northumbrian cavalry in the summer of 1642 aside, only one of Newcastle's colonels can be shown to have taken his regiment south in 1642, Edward Grey of Chillingham and Cowpen in Northumberland. Grey fought at Marlborough in Wiltshire and at Winchester in Hampshire in December 1642 and, his regiment wasted, rèturned north to recruit. Newcastle kept him in the north, and commissioned Grey's major, Ralph Hebburn of Hebburn, to raise his own regiment as its colonel. He, too, remained in the north.[16]

To regard Yorkshire, the north-east and the north-west as a Royalist stronghold from 1642 until 1644 is wholly justified: like all strongholds, its army did garrison duty. There was considerable active support for the King, and it was the heartland of Catholic Royalism. It was an area in which Parliament's friends were unable to mount an effective challenge until the Scottish invasion gave them the edge they needed. Four of the five counties came readily and easily under Newcastle's authority – no other Grandee could have said so much – and in the fifth he established control by invitation and sheer weight of numbers, the county elite largely supportive if not actually active. That the counties concerned were therefore exceptional in the general Civil War experience of England and Wales goes without saying. Even Cornwall, quite properly seen as a Royalist county, had to be fought for, and Royalist success there was by no means guaranteed in 1642. All the remaining areas of Royalist activism as plotted on map 2 were consistently fought over; control everywhere was precarious and, where it was sustained, may be seen as a measure of the quality of the commanders responsible. There was jealousy of Newcastle amongst the King's advisers, envy and perplexity. It was wholly justified.

IV

In the collapse of Lancashire the Parliamentarians of Cheshire played a not inconsiderable part. It is arguable at least that without intervention from the south, and the withdrawal of good troops by the King, Lord Strange (Earl of Derby, as he had become) could have held his own. Cheshire was the northernmost of a band of West Midland and Marcher counties which formed a spine of activism in regimental command which linked the north with the south-west of England. This area, and Wales, have been the subject matter of Dr Hutton's *Royalist War Effort* and anything said of it might well become a rehearsal of his views, so persuasive are they. Nevertheless, there are points at which his arguments might be developed or questioned: but any discussion recognises that Dr Hutton's penetrating mind has been there first.

Cheshire itself provided eleven commissioned colonels between 1642 and 1646, including those associated with the city of Chester. There were sixty inferior officers who claimed to be indigent at the Restoration. Shropshire (sixteen, 102) Staffordshire (fifteen, eighty-two), Warwickshire (eleven, forty) and Gloucestershire (thirteen, fifty-one) make up that band as plotted on map 2. The counties of Worcestershire (nine, ninety-seven) and Herefordshire (eight, 113) fell outside the King's earliest recruitment drive, as, indeed, did Shropshire and Gloucestershire. Hereford, Worcester and Gloucester nearly fell into Parliament's hands in the weeks before Edgehill; Gloucester city was quite irretrievably lost to the King. All three were debatable ground for much of the war. Royalist activism as it is expressed in regimental command was a somewhat later development than in the counties immediately to the north, or the Welsh counties. Several of these were raising regiments before the process was under way in Shropshire and Herefordshire. Yet the eventual contribution of all the English Marcher shires outstripped that of the principality, and both Herefordshire and Worcestershire were only slightly lower than their neighbouring English counties. If figures for Hereford, Shropshire, Cheshire and Monmouth are combined, then these four counties provided forty colonels and 348 indigent officers. The entire principality accounted for thirty-eight colonels but 339 indigents.

Dr Hutton has observed that the King 'does not seem to have realised the potential of Wales'.[17] The implicit assumption behind that remark is the conventional view of Wales as some Celtic Royalist heartland. Seven Welsh counties provided fewer commanders than Suffolk and Norfolk, and five fewer than Huntingdonshire and Cambridgeshire, four English counties in which Parliament's writ ran uncontested. Further, four Welsh counties provided 60·5 per cent of all the principality's colonels and a good half of the Restoration claimants. If there was an area of Wales in which Royalist activism was pronounced, it lay within those particular counties: Glamorgan in the south and, in the north, Caernarvon with Anglesey, Denbigh, Flint. Even within these, the true picture of commitment was less clear-cut than mere figures might suggest.

Dr Hutton has shown that when Charles came to the northern March to recruit in September 1642, commissions to raise regiments had already gone out in August to named gentry. They had been directed into Flint, Denbigh, Caernarvon, Brecon, Montgomery, Glamorgan, Pembroke and Carmarthen, and this was before any English Marcher counties other than Cheshire were activated. These initial commissions show the King's intention to resort to Welsh help, but only seven colonels were involved. Pembroke and Carmarthen were the domain of Colonel the Lord Carbery, who was eventually to become Lieutenant General in south-west Wales perhaps most notable for not actually raising a credible field army to make good his rank. Carbery's service has been assessed by Dr Hutton,[18] who has demonstrated the earl's reliance upon diplomacy and guile to win the area for the King – in itself, perhaps, a laudable approach. It has also been shown that, once a concerted Parliamentarian military push was launched from Pembroke by the able Rowland Laugharne, Carbery's scattered forces were easily rolled up. It seems that the earl relied upon existing militia units and that he made no effort to create volunteer regiments. The number of colonels located in south-west Wales clearly attests to this. Lord Carbery, the first commissioned commander of August 1642, raised a foot regiment which he sent to the King under the actual command of his brother, Henry Vaughan, the MP for Carmarthenshire. Colonel Vaughan was knighted by the King, and returned to Wales in 1643 to serve as major-general to his brother.[19] Both men were resident Carmarthenshire gentry, in which county only two other colonels can be shown to have been commissioned: Howell Gwynne of Llanbrayn[20] and Colonel Henry Crow, whose association with the county is somewhat tenuous. It is possible that Crow was a career soldier: he certainly fell out with his superior, Carbery, on military matters, though he could not prevail against him.[21] In Pembrokeshire only two local gentry can be shown to have been commissioned, Roger Lort[22] and the MP for Haverfordwest, John Stepney of Prendergast.[23] Carbery presumably also drew into his war effort the Cardiganshire gentleman Francis Lloyd, the MP for Carmarthen and Comptroller of the Household to Charles I. Lloyd was knighted at Oxford in March 1643 and was there in the parliament in 1644 before he again returned to Wales, so his service, like that of many MP colonels, was disrupted.[24] If these men represent the full extent of Lord Carbery's attempt at regiment formation, it is hardly surprising that his efforts were overturned by Laugharne. Unless Crow be so accounted, there does not seem to have been any influx of professional soldiers to stiffen

Carbery's troops. When, in April 1644, it was almost too late, Colonel Herbert Price marched down from Brecon to support Carbery[25] but, finding the situation quite beyond repair, turned rapidly round and went home. Price himself had been one of the first to be commissioned in August 1642. He was MP for Brecon and a natural candidate for command in his county. He was also his county's sole regimental colonel. No further commissions followed that solitary paper of August 1642.

This disappointing evidence of military activism at senior command level in south-west and mid-Wales is a true picture of Radnorshire and Merionethshire as well. Neither county was sent a commission in 1642. In Radnorshire, where such Royalist activism as there may have been was broken by the Earl of Stamford's forces in late 1642,[26] the only local colonel appears to have been Robert Martin of Radnor, who was commissioned under the Great Seal not long before Stamford sent troops against Radnor.[27] As for Merionethshire, Colonel William Price, the county's MP, was commissioned at some time, but Symonds noted him as a Denbighshire resident in 1645.[28] A more active figure was William Salusbury, appointed to the Commission of Array there in 1642 but probably also resident outside Merioneth, which he had represented as MP in 1620, when he was styled as of Ruge within the county.[29] Salusbury proved to be a tenacious governor of Denbigh, which he surrendered only when directly commanded to do so by the King in September 1646.[30] Radnorshire and Merionethshire at most provided three colonels, and certificates originating from those counties in 1662–63 from inferior officers totalled only twenty-two. If this be taken as a true measure of involvement, Carmarthen's seventy-four claimants would show the influence of some organisation under Carbery.

Given the fact that Wales and Royalism have long been held to be synonymous, and the assumption (for that is what it is) that the King recruited there in September 1642 in recognition of that fact, how is this dearth of military activism to be explained? Dr Hutton may be right in asserting that the King failed to realise Welsh potential, but if that was so, then clearly that potential was never tested. Was it there? Poverty, which Dr Hutton has advanced to explain the apparently poor Welsh showing, may well have worked against gentry involvement in expensive regimental command: it is also possible that lack of money and necessary parsimony prevented Carbery from creating anything like an effective army and inclined him towards negotiated victory. For the fact is inescapable that Wales as a whole provided company and troop commanders and contributed to the war effort in the form of footslogging infantry. Welsh Royalists in arms were more likely to be wage-earners than payrollers. It has been shown[31] that Wales did not contribute on any scale to the cavalry forces which the King raised. Not one of the commissions of August 1642 to Welsh gentry were for cavalry regiments, Hanmer's dragoons were roughly mounted infantry, and no subsequent cavalry commissions were issued. Wales was the source of infantry, recruited into companies if not regiments, and drafted into existing regiments, the colonels of which were invariably not native Welshmen. It must be on this resource of manpower that the idea of Welsh activism rests, rather than on the creation of gentry-officered regiments with a distinct Welsh identity.

Some 44 per cent of all Welsh colonels came from the north Welsh counties, Caernarvon/Anglesey, Denbigh and Flint. The quality of the commanders from these counties was by no means uniform, either. There were side-changers among them, one of three from Flintshire as well as an activated Trained Band colonel, John Aldersey. The King set recruitment going in these counties by direct commissions to named resident gentry, and in September Flint and Denbigh associated themselves with Cheshire and Shropshire in a co-operative alliance which owed much to the tireless work of the future Shropshire colonel, Frank Ottley of Pichford.[32]

The integration of the North Welsh war effort with that of England inevitably drew Caernarvon in. In each of these counties, as elsewhere, the King commissioned resident local gentlemen whose sympathies were widely known in August 1642. For Caernarvon, the choice of John Owen of Clenennau was inevitable: a soldier of wide experience, he was to become one of the most distinguished commanders of the war years, an inveterate plotter against the Parliament and the Republic, a man marked for execution in 1649 but reprieved. His regiment was not ready for service at Edgehill, but he led it at Bristol in July 1643 and was severely wounded in the action in which Slanning,

Trevanion, Buck and Grandison were killed. He was knighted in 1644. Leaving his original regiment in England, which went on to fight at Naseby, he returned to North Wales, recruited a second, and served as governor of Conway, to the immense irritation of John Williams, Archbishop of York.[33] Other colonels followed in Owen's wake, but none of them, except for Hugh Wynne,[34] can be regarded as particularly active. William Thomas of Aber went over to the Parliament in 1643, and John Bodvell (technically of Anglesey) an MP and for long considered to be hostile to the court, had his service disrupted by attendance at the Oxford parliament.[35] There were only eighteen indigent claimants from Caernarvonshire and Anglesey in 1662–63, markedly fewer than from Carmarthenshire and only one more than the figure for Brecon. The figures of inferior officers for both Denbigh and Caernarvon have to be combined to match that for Carbery's home county. There is no apparent reason why it should have been so.

Denbighshire, like its western neighbour, owed its initial activism to the King's choice of a strong and dominant local gentleman, Sir Thomas Salusbury, baronet, who had been MP for the county in the Short Parliament but had been displaced in the elections for the Long Parliament by the future rebel Sir Thomas Myddleton. Salusbury's loyalty, so he said himself, was based upon a rational consideration of the King's claims and promises, though whether this makes him a convert (and, if so, from what?) as Dr Hutton claims[36] is conjectural. Salusbury's industry, once commissioned, was prodigious. He raised an infantry regiment to full strength, 1,200 men, in time for Edgehill: 'poor Welsh vermin, the offscouring of the nation', sneered Parliamentarian propaganda, betraying a healthy racism ordinarily inflicted on the Irish. Salusbury's mysterious death in 1643 deprived the King of a profoundly committed North Welsh supporter and, as with Owen in Caernarvonshire, those that followed after him were a somewhat mixed group.[37]

The MP for Denbigh, Simon Thelwall, had Royalist relations in the brothers John and Anthony Thelwall of Plas Coch. John, High Sheriff of the county in 1643, commanded in England the following year. Anthony, the first to march away from the county, served as lieutenant-colonel under Sir Edward Fitton of Gawsworth in Cheshire, and took command of the regiment when Fitton was mortally wounded in August 1643: he was himself killed in action in the ensuing year.[38] Of the remaining county colonels, Ravenscroft changed sides, as has been noticed,[39] and William Wynne of Llanfar was killed in action at Wem in October 1643.[40] The most tenacious of them, however, was Robert Ellice or Ellis, a soldier of experience like Colonel Robert Broughton, but more closely associated with his native county. Ellice took Chirk Castle in January 1643, was captured in Cheshire in March, promptly exchanged, and defeated at Wrexham in November. Joining Prince Rupert in 1644, Ellice fought successively at Bolton, Liverpool and Marston Moor.[41]

The leading Flintshire Royalist commissioned in the King's recruitment drive was Sir Thomas Hanmer, a man who also, and perhaps importantly, owned property at Isleworth in Middlesex. Hanmer's abandonment of the King in 1644 has been cited[42] and may have stemmed from affronted dignity, self-interest or a genuine lack of commitment. He was still apparently recruiting in January 1643[43] and remained county-based as if he were some mere militia commander. An altogether different calibre of Royalist was Roger Mostyn of Mostyn, Bulstrode Whitelocke's nephew: 'a gentleman of good parts and mettle . . . well beloved there'. Mostyn went away from Flintshire to fight as a captain at Edgehill, became a colonel and governor of Flint Castle in 1643, and in 1645 journeyed to Ireland to try to recruit his depleted regiment.[44] Other Flint colonels as committed as Mostyn were Thomas Davies of Gwysaney, intended for service in Ireland, who commanded as Colonel General in Flintshire and Denbighshire under Lord Capel from 1643;[45] and Roger Whitley of Aston, who, like Mostyn, accepted a captain's commission under Charles Gerard, and rose to full colonel in South Wales before moving back to Shropshire with Sir William Vaughan.[46]

Assumptions about the degree of partisanship within counties should take account of the men who, like Mostyn, Whitley and Egerton of Staffordshire, marched away in 1642. They, by accepting company or troop command in formed regiments, began the process of cross-county assimilation which made a volunteer army. By marching away they not only demonstrated their degree of commitmènt, or thirst for action, but left behind them in their counties men whose sympathies may not have been matched by their activism. This can be illustrated by consideration of events in Staffordshire and Cheshire in the early months of war. From both these counties the King drew marching regiments during September – at least four, perhaps five. In the wake of the departure of the more active partisans, both counties lapsed into watchfulness.

V

In Staffordshire Lord Paget, commissioned as a colonel by the King,[47] and his brother Colonel Thomas Paget were recruiting in August. Thomas Paget had either been intended for Irish service, or had returned specifically to assist his brother.[48] Lord Paget's own regiment was drilled and ordered by a Lincolnshire soldier, Richard Bolles, who became effective commander and actual colonel by the time of his death in action in Hampshire in 1643.[49] The success of Paget's efforts drew the King into Staffordshire from Nottingham, entering the county on 16 September before pushing on into Shropshire to activate the Marches and North Wales. Dr Hutton has shown that after Paget's diligent quarrying for troops, always intended to march away, the county fell into a comatose state and no further commissions appear to have been issued.[50] However, in November cavalry forces under Sir Francis Wortley entered Staffordshire on a recruiting drive: it was probably upon Wortley's arrival that Dud Dudley, an illegitimate son of the Lord Dudley, turned activist and accepted a commission as major under Wortley.[51]

Wortley's presence in Staffordshire on no more than a routine recruiting drive was accompanied by allegations of unruliness and plundering. It was certainly a catalyst. Dudley, who in time became a colonel, cannot have been the only sign of welcome which Wortley encountered. An isolationist element in the county's leadership, alarmed by the baronet's arrival and what it portended, planned to raise a county defence force to preserve the integrity of Staffordshire's boundaries. Both King and Parliament could have seen such a development as a challenge. The King certainly did, and sent back into Staffordshire a newly commissioned colonel, Thomas Comberford,[52] to raise his regiment and resist the isolationists. This inaugurated the second assertion of Royalist activism: to this period probably belong the colonelcies of Devereux Wolsely, the son of Sir Richard Wolsely, a Commissioner of Array,[53] and Sir Richard Leveson of Trentham, the former MP for Newcastle under Lyme and, like Wolsely's father, a commissioner.[54] The proposed county defence force was clearly to be superseded by a Royalist force intended to be largely county-based. Appeals for assistance to Leicestershire, where Colonel General Henry Hastings was operating, resulted in the return to Staffordshire of, probably, Colonel Sir John FitzHerbert of Norbury, who had quit the county to march with Fitton's Cheshire regiment in September,[55] and certainly Colonel John Lane of King's Bromley, who was to be severely disfigured in battle in September 1644.[56] If the war was carried back into Staffordshire in the winter months of 1642–43 it was taken there by Staffordshire men whose partisanship had initially led them away. Leveson and others fell into line, though he, William Whorwood of West Bromwich[57] and Ralph Sneyd of Keel, the MP for Stafford,[58] tended to remain county-based when Lane, FitzHerbert and others were again drawn away. The events of the war beyond the county's boundaries merely accentuated a militarisation which remained essentially the creation of Staffordshire men. Staffordshire's experience was by no means unique in the Midlands and much of England, and all considerations of attempts by 'county communities' to keep war at bay should take account of the role of the county partisan in resistance to that. There was nothing unanimous in a county's apparent tendency towards neutrality or isolation: in Staffordshire a handful of armed Royalists put paid to such a drift.

The King drew three regiments from Cheshire for the Edgehill campaign, those of Sir Thomas Aston, the Catholic Earl Rivers and Sir Edward Fitton of Gawsworth.[59] Fitton, the brother-in-law of Colonel Ralph Sneyd, would die of wounds in Somerset before a year was out.[60] Rivers's regiment does not seem to have returned to Cheshire, where it was largely raised, but Aston and his men did return, much as Lane and Comberford went back to Staffordshire, drawn by a deteriorating military situation, though the circumstances for Aston were less propitious. He had to contend with regular Parliamentarian troops led by the extremely able Sir William Brereton, the county's MP.

Royalist control in Cheshire has been attributed to the direct intervention of the King and his army in September 1642.[61] Before that there had been manifestations of the isolationist tendency noticed in Staffordshire, but when Charles arrived in the county from Shropshire on 23 September he found more than 4,500 men in arms on his account. Apart from Aston's, Rivers's and Fitton's regiments, which he would draw away with him, some 2,000 men had been raised by Lord Cholmondeley and Colonel Richard Egerton of Ridley.[62] To recruit freely on such a scale requires the security of control to achieve it. The King's arrival recognised the success of his sympathisers, just as his departure effectively weakened them. The similarity between Cheshire and Staffordshire lies in this: that after the most active partisans had fulfilled their obligations, both counties experienced a damaging period of inactivity in which Royalist sympathisers actually did very little, perceiving, perhaps, the shift of war away from them with their own marching regiments.

The sequence of events in Cheshire following the King's departure has been established and lucidly interpreted by Dr Hutton.[63] As in Staffordshire, the failure of the county's resident Royalist leadership to make good depleted manpower laid them open to the threat posed by the neuter tendency which, more vigorously than in Staffordshire, overran much of the county in December 1642 and forced the Royalists, based in Chester, to negotiate a local pact at Bunbury in that month in which they agreed to stand down their soldiery. Part of the blame for the Royalist humiliation in Cheshire must lie with the links established between them and the Earl of Derby, who, as Lord Lieutenant of the county, had pushed his nominee, Bridgeman, to the forefront of military affairs. There was a leadership vacuum to be filled, and Derby sought to fill it: the association implied a notional military back-up from Lancashire which did not materialise. Dr Hutton's generous view of the Bunbury treaty, that it gave the Royalists a breathing space and may have been entered into by them for that reason, would not seem to be justified. Apart from Egerton's regiment in Chester itself, and some militia units the reliability of which was never tested, for they were never used against the neuter forces, Bridgeman, the future colonel Francis Gamull, MP for Chester, and other leaders had no means of making good the control they were steadily losing. The neuter forces, composed of volunteers, demonstrated conclusively that the Royalist writ could no longer be made to run uncontested beyond Chester itself and its environs. The Bunbury accord, denounced by the Parliament, signalled to it that the Royalist weakness could be exploited, at the same time as it showed that the neuter movement was not pro-Parliamentarianism in masquerade. In January Sir William Brereton took the war into his county: almost a fortnight behind him, Sir Thomas Aston set off to do the same. On 28 January at Nantwich and on 13 March at Middlewich Aston was so decisively beaten that he was recalled south, and stayed there until he was killed. The neuters went over to Brereton.

The collapse of effective Royalism in Cheshire was inherent in the failure to make good depleted manpower after September 1642. Chester, from February under the rigorous eye of Colonel General Sir Nicholas Byron, and its western hinterland formed what was left of virtually undisputed Royalist Cheshire. This is why subsequent colonelcies within the county were all associated with the need to garrison Chester: Francis Gamull's command of a city regiment, John Marrow of Brombrough in the Wirral, who took over Cholmondeley's cavalry and was killed in 1644, and Marrow's successor in that same, original, regiment, Colonel Robert Werden, who earned himself a violent and desperate reputation.[64] The solitary attempt to recruit a fresh regiment within the county was made in May 1643 by Colonel Thomas Leigh of Adlington, and ended in unmitigated disaster. He was driven from his home and estates by, it was alleged, his own tenantry, and died in Chester garrison in 1644.[65] His son and heir, who served as the regiment's lieutenant-colonel, was apprehended on a secret visit to Stafford and gaoled in Coventry until his exchange could be effected. Another son, Peter Leigh, served away from the county and was taken at Naseby in 1645.[66] The county's best native-born soldier, Sir Arthur Aston, did not set foot in it during the entire course of the war.

The case studies of Staffordshire and Cheshire, both counties crucial to the development of the King's army in 1642, demonstrate how the formation of that army tended to draw away the best and most active King's men. In both counties those left behind failed to make good the loss of soldiers, and both counties offered ample scope for internal dissent and external pressure. The true pattern there, and elsewhere, was the emergence of partisans during the late summer of 1642, followed by a period of inactivity, leading in turn to resurgent activism unwelcome to, and uncontrolled by, those Royalists remaining at home. In such circumstances the hinterlands of the King's marching armies could be described as anything but secure, and what often passes for Royalist territory was often debatable ground.

VI

The King came into Staffordshire, and eventually to Cheshire, from Nottingham, where he had raised his standard. Lucy Hutchinson believed Nottingham was one of those counties which showed itself largely to be for the King: 'All the Nobillity and Gentry and their dependants were generally for the King'. She recollected how, when the Bishops' Wars broke out, 'the gentlemen of the Country sett . . . forth two troopes, one all of Gentlemen, the other of their men' who waited upon the Earl of Newcastle into the north 'at their owne charges'.[67] Nottinghamshire figures in the second rank of counties which provided colonels for the King, but the figure of fifteen conceals the fact that these came of only nine county families. Four Nottinghamshire colonels were Byrons, three others were Cavendishes, including Newcastle himself, whose principal seat was at Welbeck, and the Stanhopes provided a further two. Of the remaining cases, all but two can be shown to have been commissioned at the latest by April 1643. In that month William Stanton of Stanton was appointed to command a regiment of foot the war service of which is obscure, but Stanton himself was in Newark garrison at the surrender in 1646.[68] The pivotal figure in the Nottinghamshire recruitment drive seems likely to have been the Earl of Kingston. He, as has been noted, hung back from committing himself to activism, though his loyalty to the King was not because of that in doubt. Kingston's own commission was dated 25 March 1643. Less than two months later he became Lieutenant General responsible for Lincolnshire, Rutland, Huntingdonshire, Cambridgeshire and Norfolk but he was captured, and killed, before he could begin to make any impression beyond Lincolnshire. To the earl's brief period of command may be attributed the activism in Nottinghamshire of, as well as Stanton, Isham Perkins of Bunny,[69] Sir Gervase Eyre, who was a friend of Kingston's (and who died in Newark garrison in 1644),[70] and Sir John Digby of Mansfield Woodhouse. Digby had been knighted by the King in July 1642: his Royalism was well established, but he seems to have acted as a militia commander as late as January 1643, when his presence with sixty men in Mansfield was noted by an informer.[71] The only Nottinghamshire colonel active as early as the Byrons and Newcastle's family was another Mansfield gentleman, Thomas Blackwell. He was kinghted at Oxford in December 1642, and had led a regiment away from the county to the King's marching army, with which he served constantly.[72] Under differing circumstances, the Nottinghamshire pattern was somewhat akin to that of Staffordshire and Cheshire: the movement away of partisans, a period of quiescence, and then resurgent activity centring upon the example of a leading Grandee. No other Nottinghamshire gentlemen can be shown to have been commissioned after April 1643, nor were any promoted to command rank, though several held subordinate field ranks in various regiments.

If it could be said with any justification that the Royalist potential in Wales was never realised, such a conclusion would be beyond dispute in the case of Lincolnshire. As plotted on maps 1 and 2, the county appears to be a major extension of the solid Royalist bloc of the north. The figures are impressive: twenty-one colonels native to the county, and 148 indigent claimants in 1662–63. Yet from 1642 until 1646 Lincolnshire remained, if not at the constant mercy of Parliament, then at best debatable ground over which the advantage tended always to lie with the Eastern Association. It is also true that if the Earl of Newcastle had not, in December 1642, put a garrison into Newark on Trent under the Scottish Catholic, Colonel Sir John Henderson, Lincolshire could well have been written off by the King's supporters. Newark acted not only as a major garrison barring routes north, setting the seal, as it were, upon Newcastle's garrisoned counties, but also as a base from which to launch campaigns into Lincolnshire.

In March 1643 Newark forces under Henderson and detachments from the north under Lieutenant General Charles Cavendish struck at Grantham. On 11 April they routed Willoughby of Parham's Parliamentarian forces at Ancaster Heath, and drew upon themselves the attention of the Eastern Association. The Grantham attack coincided with the appointment of the Earl of Kingston to field command, and the latter's promotion to become Lieutenant General in Lincolnshire and related counties in May seems to have been part of an attempt by the King to cut into the Eastern Association from the north. The Parliament reaction to the battle at Ancaster Heath seems to have turned upon their perception of it as the first sign of a southward march by the northern Royalists, though such a thing was not then (or subsequently) seriously contemplated by Lord Newcastle. In May, therefore, and in response to orders from London, Eastern Association forces gathered at Sleaford to move against Newark, which had been unsuccessfully assulted in February. The concentration of enemy troops in the Sleaford vicinity is an indication of the limit of the Royalist inroad after Ancaster: Cavendish and his men still held Grantham, which they had seized in March, and the ensuing battle on 13 May was far more of a stalemate than Edgehill had ever been, but it did block further Royalist expansion.

Subsequent events in the county were even less propitious for its emergence as Royalist territority. General Cavendish, detached from the Queen's escort to deal with Gainsborough, was killed in action against Cromwell on 28 July. That was three days after the Earl of Kingston, captured when Gainsborough fell to the Parliamentarians, was killed by Royalist gunners on the Humber. Although the Eastern Association troops fell back after the fight at Gainsborough, and eventually retired into the Isle of Ely, the Earl of Newcastle's offensive did not amount to anything like a concerted push into Lincolnshire. When, in August, he was persuaded or coerced into concentrating his field army in a wasteful siege of Hull, the Eastern Association crept back and, on 11 October 1643, won the decisive battle for Lincolnshire at Winceby near Bolingbroke Castle. The Royalists defeated at Winceby were led by the Scot, Henderson, and Colonel Sir William Widdrington, a Northumbrian detached from Newcastle's army to exercise overall command in the county. Although, in the wake of Prince Rupert's relief of Newark in March 1644, there was some resurgence of Royalist activity, Lincolnshire was effectively lost. Its loss might have been felt the harder had it been gained in the first place.

The county gentlemen who received commissions as colonels, rather than those (five of twenty-one) who were promoted to the rank, can be shown to have made their appearance either in 1642, when activists anyway, and almost everywhere, were busy organising for the King, or in the period between the Ancaster campaign begun in March 1643 and the battle of Winceby seven months later. How many owed their rank to the brief authority of the Earl of Kingston is quite impossible to say. When Kingston was captured on 20 July 1643 he was using Gainsborough as an organisational base, but he does not seem to have had much strength there. Willoughby's capture of the town was by no means a walk-over. The loss of Kingston's command structure, however, was so serious that it obliged the Earl of Newcastle to send Charles Cavendish against Gainsborough immediately, with the resulting death of his Lieutenant General in action. So presumably, between May and July, Kingston had not been entirely dilatory and the safeguarding of the county had effectively fallen to him. To this period can be ascribed the colonelcies of Maurice Bawds of Somerby, who was to be killed at Naseby in 1645;[73] Robert Dallison of Greetwell, who was fighting out of Newark garrison in 1644 and 1645, and who had been drawn out of Lincolnshire by Newcastle in 1643;[74] Ralph Eure of Washingborough, the county's only Catholic colonel, who was also drawn north by Newcastle;[75] Sir William Pelham of Brocklesby, who was mortally wounded at Marston Moor and whose son, Edward, was his lieutenant-colonel;[76] and Philip Welby of Gedney, who was taken prisoner on 24 July 1643 and gaoled in London until 1649.[77] Of these men, only Pelham can be shown to have associated himself with the King's proceedings at York in the summer of 1642, 'being his saruant . . . and so bound by his oth'.[78] When Pelham was dead his son abandoned the cause, but the regiment's original major, Adrian Scroop of Cockerington, had long since moved on to lieutenant-colonel in Lord Forth's regiment before becoming a commissioned colonel in his own right. Scroop's career is not readily untangled: he and his father, Sir Gervase, fought at Edgehill, where both were severely wounded, but they may well have been gentlemen volunteers rather than officers in a specific regiment. It is likely that the son moved into Forth's regiment after Edgehill, and his majority under Pelham may well have been a temporary attachment to help recruit and train a new regiment. Whatever the case, as a colonel in his own right Scroop fought in the West Country in 1644 and earned himself a reputation as a brutal enemy. He surrendered in Exeter garrison in 1646.[79]

Although Scroop's colonelcy was two years ahead, he was one

of those committed partisans of 1642 whose activism took them away from Lincolnshire immediately. Richard Bolles, who went into Staffordshire to command in Paget's regiment, was another. Thomas Dallison of Laughton became colonel of Prince Rupert's Horse in 1642 and came close to returning to his county only when Rupert relieved Newark in 1644; he was to be killed at Naseby a year later.[80] Theophilus Gilby of Stainton marched away as lieutenant-colonel in the Yorkshire regiment of John Belasyse, under whom he served until Belasyse was sent north to command in York in January 1644. At that point Gilby took over Belasyse's command, and served under Wilmot. He was one of the signatories of the petition to the King in August 1644. After Naseby, where he fought, Gilby went eventually into Newark garrison, where his former commander, Belasyse, became governor, and was knighted there by the King in October 1645.[81] Gilby's younger brothers, Anthony and Emanuel, left Lincolnshire when he did. Anthony Gilby became lieutenant-colonel to John Digby in Nottinghamshire, and spent the war years attached to Newark,[82] whilst Emmanual joined William Eure's Yorkshire cavalry as major.[83] Gervase Holles of Grimsby, the historian of his family,[84] accepted a captaincy under Sir Lewis Dyve, fought at Edgehill and in December was sent back into Lincolnshire to recruit a foot regiment of which he was to be the colonel. Like Dallison, Eure and Pelham, Holles was drawn north by Newcastle, and served under him until April 1644, when the King intended him for the governorship of Lyme Regis.[85] Two Lincolnshire colonels whose commissions may date to late 1642 served mostly in their county, Farmery of Heapham and Charles Dallison of Greetwell, the apologist.

Matthew Appleyard of East Halton, the brother-in-law of Sir William Pelham, was a career soldier and on the strength of his familial relationship might have been a natural appointment to the rank of major in Pelham's regiment, which went to Scroop. When Pelham was recruiting, however, Appleyard was in Ireland serving as lieutenat-colonel in the regiment of his fellow Lincolnshireman, Sir Charles Vavasour of Skellingthorpe, baronet. In the summer of 1643 Appleyard arrived in England with the knowledge of the Parliament, which ordered him to Hull, there to take up a pre-war post in the garrison. His return, however, was to prepare the way for the arrival from Ireland of Vavasour and the regiment, which finally left Dublin in mid-October. At Bristol there was a mutiny. Vavasour resigned his commission and retired to Oxford, where he died in March 1644. Command fell to Appleyard, who imposed his authority on the troops and led them, for example, at Leicester in May 1645, where he was knighted for his part in the storm. He was the youngest of six sons of an East Yorkshire country gentleman, and his marriage to a Pelham, though it drew him into Lincolnshire, hardly improved his situation. He chose to describe himself as a soldier of fortune and, when required to compound, acknowledged an estate of £160 in ready money. He paid a fine of £20. Yet the knighthood of 1645 stood him in good stead. At the Restoration he was once more in Yorkshire, a JP and Deputy Lieutenant in the East Riding, and from 1661 MP for Hedon.[86]

Lincolnshire's colonels were all of gentry status, Appleyard at one extreme from the Earl of Lindsey and his sons at the other. The cement which held men of such varying fortune together was that of their service to the King, and the evidence for Lincolnshire as it is expressed in terms of regimental command and military service in general indicates a county far more so committed than Nottinghamshire, or any of the Midland shires. The way in which the war was waged drew attention away from the county in 1642, but the military activity of 1643, though it went against the Royalists in the end, has incidentally shown that there was a reservoir of potential activists still to be drawn on. If the figure for indigent claimants petitioning from London is discounted, Lincolnshire's total of such men made it the eighth county in importance in sub-regimental command. As with all counties, the London figure must conceal additional Lincolnshire men. If 82 per cent of indigent colonels who petitioned from London can be shown to have resided elsewhere, Lincolnshire's true indigent figure may have exceeded 200.

VII

All the counties so far considered, including those in mid-Wales, were fought over more or less intensively: their contribution in terms of regimental commanders and other officers varied. Kent, not the scene of any serious fighting until 1648, ranks as the fourth most important county in terms of colonels. Nor did these come from a mere handful of committed families, though the

Slingsbys produced three, and the Coverts of Maidstone two (John Covert succeeding his brother Thomas when the latter died in 1643).[87] It is possible that the Coverts were drawn into arms by their relationship to the Gorings, since Colonel Thomas Covert, who was commissioned in August 1643, was George Goring's brother-in-law, and Goring exerted himself to have Thomas's brother succeed to the regimental command. Such a consideration may have influenced Covert Royalism, as indeed, the links of the Slingsbys with the Stuart court may have drawn them in. Nineteen Kent families produced twenty-two colonels, the same proportion as that for Lincolnshire (eighteen, twenty-one) and that for Somerset (twenty-one, twenty-four).

What is also true of Kent is that its colonels came predominantly from the *nobiles minores*: seventeen of the twenty-two were either knights or gentlemen. The peerage was represented by William Compton of Erith (son of the Earl of Northampton) and Richard Spencer of Orpington, uncle of Henry Lord Spencer, who was killed in action in 1643.[88] Spencer was commissioned in July 1643 and was captured in Gloucestershire that same year when commanding his regiment.[89] Of three resident baronets two, William Butler of Teston and Edward Deering of Surrinden, have already been mentioned.[90] The third was, without doubt, the most eminent of the county's commanders, Sir John Mayney of Linton, whose hazardous Civil War career was partly recorded by his friend, Sir Henry Slingsby. Mayney was advanced to his baronetcy in 1641, appointed to the Commission of Array for Kent in 1642, and joined the King's army as a volunteer before Edgehill, where he fought under the Earl of Northampton. He then rode with Charles Gerard before returning to Kent secretly to raise money. Early in 1643 – he may have been with the Queen briefly in Holland – he arrived in the north, where the Earl of Newcastle appointed him to command a newly formed regiment. In all likelihood, this was the one being raised by the Kent colonel Guilford Slingsby, who was mortally wounded in January that year. Mayney ended the war much as he had begun it, serving as a Reformando under Charles Gerard in 1645, his brigade wrecked whilst he lay at Newark recovering from wounds. When Rupert was disgraced, and Charles Gerard appeared amongst those who challenged the King at Newark, Mayney was caught up in the affair and went into Europe. He returned to Kent in 1648 in time to take a command in the rising and to fight at Maidstone.[91]

Pre-war links between Royalists are as often hinted at as apparent, and a Mayney–Slingsby connection is suggested by both men turning up in Yorkshire within a month or two of each other. Similarly, John Boys of Bonnington, the eldest son of Sir Edward Boys, became lieutenant-colonel in the Cheshire-based regiment of the Earl Rivers, who enjoyed extensive estates in Essex. Boys was serving in Ireland as late as May 1642, but by November at the latest had risen from his Irish captaincy to rank under Rivers, whose regiment he came to command with distinction in 1644, in which year he was knighted as defender of Donnington Castle in Berkshire.[92] There must have been some connection between Richard Thornhill of Ollantigh and Sir William Butler of Teston which drew Thornhill to serve as lieutenant-colonel in Butler's regiment. Thornhill's father-in-law was Bevil Grenvile, which family connection ought to have drawn Thornhill farther west. He succeeded to the command of Butler's regiment after the latter's death in action in 1644 at Cropredy Bridge.[93] Should any links be inferred between the obscure Kent officer Charles Finch and the equally obscure Hampshire colonel Richard Manning, beyond that of their mutal Catholicism? Yet Finch went into Hampshire and served as Manning's major. When Manning was killed at Cheriton in 1644, Finch rose to a full command.[94] Presumably Finch went where the action was, and that may well have been true of Sir Anthony St Leger of Ulcombe, who went into Sussex to serve as a field officer in the regiment of the Catholic John Apsley of Pulborough. At some point in 1644 St Leger went into the regiment of the Monmouthshire professional, William Pretty, but managed to avoid being caught up in Pretty's cashiering in 1645, and continued to serve as a full colonel.[95]

Obscurity often surrounds the service of known colonels, though ordinarily something in the historical record permits an informed judgement as to where they went and what they may have done. Guilford Slingsby and Sir John Mayney were exceptional in their move into the north, though both, perhaps, preceded the Queen from Europe. Oxford and the King's western armies became the ultimate base for Kentish soldiers. Sir Thomas Bosville of Aynsford died in Oxford garrison in May 1643.[96] Edmund Chapman of East Greenwich petitioned at the

Restoration as an indigent colonel, and he had been in Pendennis Castle at its surrender.[97] Philip Froude or Frowd of Gillingham compounded on the articles for the surrender of Exeter.[98] Andrew Mennes of Chislet, a younger brother of the naval commander Sir John Mennes, saw out the war serving in the Oxford garrison and, in 1648, went from Kent to Colchester after Maidstone had fallen to the Parliament.[99] Colonel John Heath of Brasted compounded upon the articles for the rendition of Oxford. He was a younger son of Sir Robert Heath, the loyal Chief Justice of the King's Bench who died in exile in France in 1649. Colonel Heath's elder brother, Francis, was involved in the 1648 rising in Kent and, like Mennes and others, made for Colchester.[100] With the exception of Bosville, who must have been commissioned before May 1643, it is impossible to know whether these more obscure commanders were appointed direct to regimental command or rose by promotion like St Leger, Boys and Thornhill. The material does not exist to permit a definitive history of the King's regiments akin to that of Firth and Davies for Cromwell's army.

Kent activists were constrained by the circumstances in which they found themselves to abandon their county if they were to serve their King in arms. From Nottinghamshire, Staffordshire, Cheshire, and other counties, the King drew away the most active of his supporters in the preliminaries to Edgehill. In many such counties periods of inertia ensued: vacuums were created. In the case of Somerset, however, events took a different course, ironically because of the initial success of the Commissioners of Array under the direction of the King's Lieutenant General, the Marquess of Hertford.

Somerset and Devon, with twenty-four colonels drawn from within the county gentry, were second only to Yorkshire in this respect. If the indigent officer figures are also considered, then the 309 certificates originating from Somerset in 1662–63 were inferior in number only to those from Yorkshire (523 from all Ridings) and Cornwall (351) and well ahead of the fourth highest county, Durham, with 224. Of course, such figures conceal imponderables. Not every officer petitioned as an indigent, because not all of them were, and many were dead anyway. The certificates originating from London and Westminster must conceal original county affiliations. Thus the indigent total can be only minimum figures. Then again, some certificates, but arguably very few, may have been fraudulent: it was only to sift out the few remaining improper claims that a list of claimants was published at all.[101] The number of indigents must also include men commissioned in 1648, 1650–51 and later. Allowing for all these caveats, the indigency figures for any county are better than a rough guide to county activism, and in Somerset's case they show that there, as in Cornwall and Durham, there was no lack of men willing to accept a command in the King's interest. Yet, on the other hand, the period in which recruiting of regiments in Somerset largely took place – the latter part of 1643 – was a time in which Royalist control of the county was virtually complete. The time was propitious, rather as it had been for the Earl of Newcastle in the north-east in 1642. Yet Somerset, unlike the counties under Newcastle's control, but very much like Lancashire, was a source of men and commanders for armies elsewhere. The lack of a sufficiency of regular troops within Somersetshire is shown by the commissioner's resort to the *posse comitatus* in 1644 and, quite unequivocally, by the spread of anti-Royalist Clubmen in 1645.[102]

On 8 August 1642, at Marshalls Elm, Hertford's Array men met and put to flight Parliament's militia. It was not a battle between rival armies but a clash of partisans: when it was fought, the Array was drawing men to its colours, but if more than one or two regiments were actually in the process of formation by the time of Marshalls Elm the evidence does not suggest it. The victors in that auspicious encounter were in the process of creating armed forces, and the consequence of their victory should have been to increase their appeal. The armed neuter movement which responded, however, disrupted the Array's progress, scattered its leadership and drove Hertford and the majority of them clear out of the county. Royalist organisation was nipped in the bud, and many months were to elapse until those thus dispersed returned on the back of Cornish arms and overran their native county in June 1643. True organisation of Royalists in Somersetshire lay almost ten months on from the outbreak of war. By that time the needs of the western armies of the King predominated: Somerset was merely a source of man-power, and with very few exceptions all those regiments recruited in the county drifted away.

Royalist control in Somerset came under threat, theoretically, in May 1644 when Parliament established itself again in north-western Wiltshire, a much fought-over county. March and counter-march of rival armies in that year plunged Somerset into the realities of war, and additional recruitment of existing regiments (whether Somerset in origin or from elsewhere) must have taken place. In January 1645, however, a drive for recruits was initiated by the Somerset general Ralph Hopton of Wytham, not with a view to creating new regiments within the county, but to make good depleted manpower in existing regiments of his field army. Recruitment and impressment on a wide scale provoked reaction: the Clubmen of 1645, militarily worth nothing in the field against regular troops, had a free hand because, outside the Royalist garrisons, no field forces existed to oppose them. The situation of Somersetshire in the months before the crucial battle of Langport on 10 July 1645 may be compared with the experience of Cheshire in 1642 after the activists had quit the county: a vacuum had come into being which in Somerset was filled by the Clubmen as, in Cheshire, it had been filled by a neuter movement. Such Royalist partisans as there were found themselves confined to their garrisons, as had been the case in Cheshire. It is one thing to say of the Clubmen that they were war-weary, non-partisan country folk reacting against the degradation of war, and quite another to perceive the thrust of their actions. The Somerset Clubmen were specifically, and for much of 1645 unequivocally, anti-Royalist; though they were not gathered together to be so, they nevertheless became the auxiliaries of the New Model Army which broke Goring's ill disciplined forces at Langport and effectively destroyed Royalist control of the county. The link between the Clubmen of 1645 and the neuters of 1642, who also effectively did the work of Parliament, remains to be established, but both phenomena show that Somerset's Royalism was tenuous and found its fullest expression away from the county in the King's fighting armies. Although the men that remained behind – Sir John Stawell, Sir Edward Rodney and others – were no less committed than their more numerous comrades who fought elsewhere, they had not the resources in regular troops to maintain their ascendancy once it was seriously threatened. The experience of many Somerset colonels was not unique to them: the shift of war took them away and they left behind them counties in which their cause was ill maintained precisely as a result of the need to wage a war of campaigns that could not be county-based. What may be said fairly of Somerset could be said of many counties: there was widespread Royalist activism, but it was finite, and when in obedience to the King's proceedings it expressed itself within the structure of mobile campaigning armies, Somerset's Royalist activism left the county behind.

The point has been made that the engagement at Marshalls Elm in August 1642 was a clash of rival partisans. Most of the leading Royalist figures in Somerset at the time are known, and most have already been touched upon elsewhere: Hopton, Hawley, Doddington of Barrow, the Stawells of Cothelstone and Lord Paulet of Hinton St George. What is not known is who precisely provided the muscle with which the Array trounced the militia at Marshalls Elm. In all probability they numbered among them almost all those who later became regimental commanders, and who might have become so sooner had the neuter movement not overawed them with sheer weight of numbers. It is virtually certain that amongst those present in a subordinate capacity at Marshalls Elm were John and Hugh Tynt of Chelvey, young men – the former barely twenty-four, the latter no more than twenty – who came back to their county in 1643 to form a regiment under John Tynt's colonelcy. At his composition Colonel Tynt stated that he had laid down his arms in January 1645, at precisely that point at which Hopton's recruitment drive was launched in Somerset. The younger brother, Hugh, in his turn said that he had surrendered in November 1644, by which date, clearly, their regiment was disintegrating for whatever reasons. Lieutenant Colonel Hugh Tynt, second-in-command of the regiment, admitted only to having served as a troop commander under Sir Francis Hawley of Buckland. It was by no means unusual – and the reason will be obvious – for a Royalist at composition to admit to an inferior rank, just as information laid against Royalists quite often, and for reasons equally apparent, alleged a rank superior to that actually enjoyed. Hugh Tynt's admission, however, hints at a not unfamiliar development of 1642: the first appearance of future field commanders in company or troop command in such regiments as were forming at that date. Examples from Cheshire, Lancashire and Wales have been given. Hawley's regiment was in existence in some form before Marshalls Elm: Hugh Tynt and his elder brother probably served in it, and were driven ultimately from their county along with Hawley. They returned in 1643, commissioned to recruit their own regiment (which remained a distinctively Somerset unit) on the strength of their proven partisanship.[103] The same circumstances may well account for the regimental commission to Edward Bisse of Spargrove and Thomas Bridges of Keynsham, who was to be sheriff of the county in 1644 and governor of Bath.[104] The indigency claimants show that both regiments were almost exclusively officered by Somerset Royalists.

Not all who left their county in 1642 returned, unless fleetingly. Robert Lawrence of Creech Grange went into Dorset, where his family had extensive interests, and became governor of Corfe Castle: he appears to have spent the war in that county.[105] William Helyer of East Coker waited until 1646 before he was promoted to a colonelcy in Exeter garrison, and Sir Walter Earle that same year referred to Helyer by what must have been an earlier rank of major.[106] The most significant of the group of Somerset commanders who fought away from their home county was John Stocker of Chilcompton, who in August 1644 was serving in a field command under Wilmot and set his hand to the petition to the King which followed Wilmot's disgrace.[107] Stocker did not petition to compound until May 1648, having fled into Wales when the war ended: by luck or judgement he appears to have avoided involvement in the Wesh rising of 1648, though he was to be in arms again in 1650–51.[108] The indigents who claimed in 1662–63 to have served under Stocker were men from Carmarthenshire, Wiltshire and Dorset as well as from his native county, enough of them to show that he fought a mobile war as colonel of infantry. Through his mother Stocker was related to the Capels of Hadham, which connection may have advanced him in the army, for he was otherwise, like Bisse of Spargrove, a very minor country gentleman indeed.[109] Of the others who left Somerset for the duration of the war, Roger Newborough of Barkley was so obscure that though of gentry status his precise identity remains to be established.[110] He was taken prisoner in December 1645 and not subsequently exchanged, so that his rank must antedate that month, but beyond the fact of his capture in Dorset nothing is known of his service.[111] Colonel Thomas Pigott of Brockley, like Stocker, served under Wilmot in 1644 in a field rank, probably as major in an untraced regiment, a rank he certainly held in April that year when at Wareham in Dorset with the Irish regiment in which he had soldiered in 1641–42. Through his marriage, it was reported, Pigott had acquired 'a gallant house and park with deer' in Wiltshire, but the indigents who claimed him as their commander were probably all from Somerset, including the regimental major, Adam Roche, who was himself a petitioner.[112] Both Roche and Pigott's second-in-command, Lieutenant Colonel Barret, ended the war in Oxford garrison, where Pigott himself may well have gone.[113] If Pigott was a regimental major as late as August 1644, then his promotion to command rank must have taken place in conjunction with Hopton's recruitment campaign in Somerset in January 1645. If this were not so, it would be difficult to account for the Somerset indigents claiming as their commander a man who had returned from Ireland in 1642–43 in time for the Bristol campaign but in an inferior field rank. Since the ranks of Roche and Barret support Pigott's entitlement to be regarded as a colonel, his regiment may be the only one recruited in its entirety, its realised complement notwithstanding, in Somerset in 1645.[114] Hopton was less interested in adding regiments to his army than in making good losses in extant regiments: Pigott's may therefore be unique.

There is, however, the curious case of George Trevillyan of Nettlecombe. When he came to compound, Trevillyan admitted that he had been a colonel, but denied that he had ever exercised his rank. Independent evidence taken in 1650 shows that this was a lie,[115] whilst that of indigent claimants does suggest he did not try very hard to recruit. Only a single Somersetshire officer, Captain John Trowbridge, claimed to have served under him,[116] and nothing is known of Trowbridge. If Trevillyan was activated by Hopton in January 1645, as Pigott very probably was, he was clearly less energetic than the other man, and the pressure of anti-Royalist populism may have told against him, though Nettlecombe was far enough away from the main areas of Clubmen activity. What makes Trevillyan's case so singular is evidence that in March 1643, when he was Keeper of Ivelchester prison, he was responsible among other things for the confinement of a Royalist soldier, John Sheppard, accused of sheep stealing. Sheppard's misdemeanours were still the subject of enquiry in 1647–48, by which time Trevillyan had ceased to be Keeper because of his deliquency.[117] In respect of his office of Keeper in 1643, Trevillyan at the least collaborated with the Parliament and its officials: he was not an early partisan of the King, though his latent Royalism may have been discovered once Somerset was overrun in June and Royalist authority established for the next eighteen months. If Trevillyan had been commissioned, like others, in 1643, he could not have got away with so little effort. If he was appointed to recruit in 1645, that would explain the poor performance, whilst also showing the dearth of reliable gentry available to Hopton that year in his native county.[118]

Of the regiments commissioned in Somerset during 1643 only two, those of Lord Paulet and Francis Doddington, lost their original county associations in so far as those were expressed in the officer complement of a regiment. The regiments of John Coventry of Barton, Robert Phelips of Montacute, Edward Stawell of Cothelstone, the Wyndham brothers of Kentsford and their uncle, remained, like those of Bisse and Bridges, largely county-affiliated. Paulet was commissioned to recruit in May 1643 when he was almost sixty. His son and heir, an obvious candidate for involvement and perhaps command, was on active service in Ireland at the time and returned to England too late to take part in his father's proceedings. Lord Paulet may have been a reluctant commander: he certainly passed his role on to his son-in-law Richard Cholmeley, a Yorkshireman who had been serving in the West Country since 1642.[119] He may well have been Paulet's second-in-command anyway. In 1644 Cholmeley was killed leading the regiment at Lyme Regis, and command devolved upon Colonel Thomas Walker, in whose appointment Lord Paulet may have had a hand. If the evidence of indigent claimants be taken as a guide, Walker – unknown, unidentified – had more impact upon the regiment than his predecessors.[120] How seriously impaired the regiment was when Cholmeley fell is not known, but at the time Lord Paulet was in Oxford; Walker was sent from there to take over, and took with him an Oxfordshire man, William Knolles of Rotherfield, to serve as regimental major.[121]

Paulet's son and in 1649 successor in the title, Sir John Paulet, 'a bold hardy man', returned from Irish service as a full colonel late in 1643, and recruited and fought with his own regiment in Hampshire the following year. Service in Winchester and Exeter garrisons thereafter is reflected in the fact that this Somerset colonel was not cited by any Somerset indigents in 1662–63: his regiment was almost exclusively officered by men drawn from the counties in which it fought.[122] This was probably true as well of the regiment of Horatio Cary of Cockham, who began the war as a major, serving under Sir William Waller. When Somerset was overrun by the Royalists in June 1643, Cary defected to them and fought at the storm of Bristol in July. Prince Rupert took an interest in facilitating Cary's change of allegiance, and promoted him to regimental command. It is impossible to say that Cary, a Somerset man, raised troops in his own county, and his own origins may have been incidental. In 1662–63 there were eleven indigent officer claimants to cite him as their commander, of whom only one, Cornet John Champnes, sent in his certificate from Somerset. However, since eight of the indigents petitioned from London and Westminster, that may conceal a county presence.[123] Cary's second-in-command, Lieutenant Colonel William Rumball or Rumbold, transferred to the regiment from that of the Norfolk colonel Richard Crane, who commanded Prince Rupert's Lifeguards. Rumball had no previous association that can be traced with Somerset or Cary, though he had been a junior officer in Ireland in 1642 and Cary was a captain there in 1640–41. Rumball's earlier career had been as an officer of the royal household for at least fifteen years.[124] His appointment to back Cary up shows the extent of Prince Rupert's interest in the regiment and emphasises that the Somerset links were not important. Cary maintained his forces until the end of the war.[125]

If Sir Francis Doddington had been in the process of forming his own regiment in 1642, when he was a commissioner of Array, it was cut short by his capture in October and imprisonment until August 1643. To ascribe his commission to the latter part of that year seems reasonable, and Doddington proved himself both an inveterate Royalist and a bad enemy to the Parliament.[126] His war service is as well documented as recital of alleged atrocities perpetrated by him permits.[127] Yet at some stage Doddington lost his regiment and his command – to whom is not known – as is evidenced by the indigent claimants of 1662–63.[128] So active a commander, still alive at the Restoration, should have been called upon to authenticate the petitions of more than only two officers, and that he was not so cited indicates either that his regiment sustained very high mortality (which cannot be entirely ruled out) or that it passed to another whose identity is unknown, and cannot be guessed at.

Where there was continuity of command the regimental associations with a county could be preserved. Colonel Edward Stawell, a son of Sir John Stawell, began recruiting in 1642, completed in 1643, and led his regiment until severely wounded and captured at Alresford on 29 March 1644. With the single exception of a Surrey cornet, those who claimed as indigents in 1662–63, nine of them, were Somerset men. Stawell's major, however, was a career soldier from Europe, Robert Bates, and, as in the case of William Rumball of Cary's, there is no indication of a county link.[129] Edward Bisse of Spargrove died, or was killed in action, before 23 July 1644, whereupon his regiment was disbanded, presumably because it was not of sufficient size to preserve. Its Somerset associations were thus not broken.[130] Nor were they lost in the active regiments of Edmund and Frank Wyndham.

Edmund Wyndham had been expelled from the House of Commons as a monopolist in 1641. His court associations were strong – his wife had been wet-nurse to the future Charles II – and he was foremost amongst those who responded to Hertford and the Commission of Array in 1642. In that year he was sheriff of his county and became governor of Bridgwater by Hertford's appointment, but when he began to recruit his regiments seriously is not known. Again, 1643 seems to have been the time. The extent of his energy is well shown both by his own admission and by the evidence of the indigent claimants: eighteen horse officers, only one of whom, Cornet William Wake, came from beyond the county, eleven officers of foot, of whom four at most may have been outsiders, and a single dragoon cornet.[131] Wyndham's claim to have laid out £7,000 in war service was probably accurate, even if his total losses, set at £50,000, were rounded up. As far as Wyndham's cavalry regiment went, although it was obviously initially and heavily recruited in Somerset, it was planned for elsewhere. The lieutenant-colonel was a Dorset man, William Ancthill, who ended the war as governor of

Corfe in succession to Robert Lawrence,[132] and the first major was a Devonshire Royalist, Humphrey Sydenham, who had fought at Edgehill.[133] In time he was replaced by Robert Leversedge of Frome Selwood, a native of Somerset.[134] Lewin Buskin, who claimed as an indigent, was major in Wyndham's infantry regiment, and he was a Sussex man.[135] The structure of field command in Wyndham's otherwise almost exclusively Somerset regiments suggests that he fled from the county in 1642 and returned in 1643, equipped to recruit.[136]

Wyndham's younger brother Frank left Somerset at some date in 1642 and rode with the Gentlemen Pensioners at Edgehill in October, returning home in 1643, when he occupied Dunster Castle and was recognised as its governor by Lord Hertford. His regimental commission followed upon the governorship and, not surprisingly, the indigent claimants of 1662–63 who named him all certified from Somerset, though nothing whatever is known of Wyndham's subordinate field commanders. This, incidentally, was the same Frank Wyndham whose personal loyalty to Charles II was so profound, and who materially assisted the King's escape after the battle of Worcester in 1651, where Wyndham fought.[137]

The brothers' uncle, Sir Hugh Wyndham, ostensibly at the outbreak of war resident in Dorset, may materially have contributed to the development of Edmund Wyndham's regiments. There is a suggestion that Sir Hugh's permanent removal from Somerset may have been as late as 1650[138] and that he, himself a colonel, recruited heavily in the county. What is important is that two Somerset indigents (of eleven such) petitioned that they had served under Sir Hugh in the troop commanded by Lieutenant Colonel William Ancthill, the Dorset man who was Edmund Wyndham's second-in-command as well. Clearly, Ancthill either moved from Sir Hugh's command to the nephew's, or from the nephew to the uncle, although the former seems more likely. Ancthill would, in this sense, be to Edmund Wyndham's recruitment what William Rumball was to Horatio Cary's, an essential addition of experience. However, if Sir Hugh Wyndham recruited as heavily in Somerset as the indigent figures would suggest, when did he do it? If in 1643, at the same time as his nephew, he might well have brought Ancthill in from Dorset only to lose him to the other's regiment before his own could be readied. If Ancthill was replaced in Sir Hugh Wyndham's it is not shown: the other field officer of that regiment, the Somerset man Major John Harvey of Chardstock, may have been promoted. He certainly had military experience from 1641 against the Scots.[139] The link between the separate regiments of Edmund and Hugh Wyndham is clear; the explanation of it remains open.

Three further colonels maintained strong county links: Stawell, Bridges and Robert Phelips of Montacute. Sir Thomas Bridges was named by eighteen indigents,[140] of whom no more than four came from elsewhere, petitioning from Dorset and London. Bridges's second-in-command, Lieutenant Colonel Rysley, does not seem to have been local and it is remotely possible that he was a Bedfordshire man.[141] As for Stawell, twenty-two indigents cited him,[142] of whom only three came from counties other than Somerset, though bordering on it. Stawell's second-in-command, Lieutenant Colonel Roger Powell, was probably an Oxfordshire man, and was killed in action during 1644, though when and where is not known.[143] In the case of Robert Phelips, who clearly recruited in his native county during 1643, eleven officers cited him, of whom four sent in their certificates from Wiltshire or London.[144] Both of Phelips's subordinate field officers were local: Lieutenant Colonel Andrew Overton of Babcary,[145] and Major John Morgan of Wells, whose brother William served in a similar capacity in the *posse comitatus* under Sir Edward Rodney.[146] Colonel Phelips's war service is patchily documented. He was governor of Ilchester in 1645, and appears to have been promoted to his command in 1643 from a field rank in another, unidentified, regiment. He was certainly serving as a Commissary General in January 1643 in the West Country. His brother, Edward, identified more closely with the anti-court politics of their father, Sir Robert Phelips, though he abandoned Parliament in 1642, sat in the Oxford parliament of 1644, and was actively raising men in that same year in the Somerset *posse*.[147]

There can be no doubt that Somerset was a good source of fighting commanders for the King, the most eminent of whom, Ralph Hopton, was one of the King's finest and most committed partisan generals. It was a county in which circumstances were for a time propitious for the raising of regiments, some of which were to lose their associations as a result of war service and changes in command personnel. Some of the Somerset regiments are also clear cases of the way in which outsiders could be drafted in at field command level to facilitate the training and preparation of volunteer formations. It was also a county in which there was considerable popular anti-Royalism which, even if defined as militant neutralism, in its effects was antagonistic towards the King's supporters. That may have been a reflection of circumstances, and there is no doubt that Royalist control was never disputed by 'neuters' after June 1643 until the military situation became so critical that the collapse of the King's forces within the county seemed inevitable.

VIII

Somerset was well activated for the King and, in terms of native colonels and regiments of strong county origins, contrasts with the case of Oxfordshire, for which nine colonels and only forty-eight indigent claimants can be identified. Given that Oxford was the King's headquarters from 1642 until 1646, however its hinterland was debatable territory, there does not seem to have been any recruitment drive comparable with that in Somerset or other counties such as Cornwall, Devon, Hampshire and Dorset. The Oxfordshire contribution was no better than that of Buckinghamshire and Essex and inferior to that of Kent.

The forty-eight Oxfordshire indigents by no means served exclusively in county regiments. The only solidly officered Oxfordshire regiment was that of Colonel Nicholas Selwyn, who was himself, though ordinarily domiciled in Oxford, of a Sussex family.[148] He was commissioned on 17 June 1643, probably on the strength of the fact that he had served as a lieutenant-colonel against the Scots in 1640. His commission, however, may not have been fulfilled in the sense intended. In November 1644 the Oxford city councillors recorded their unhappiness that Selwyn had been appointed to command their own regiment, being 'a stranger' who was 'never approved of' and 'never nominated' by them. More than that, Selwyn had affronted the mayor, physically assaulted him, and occupied his chair at a previous meeting.[149] What it is not possible to determine is whether the indigents who claimed Selwyn as their commander served under him by the original commision of 1643 or came under him in his capacity as commander of a formed city regiment. If the latter, then Selwyn clearly did not undertake a serious drive for recruits. That he did command a full structured regiment is, however, more than clear. His lieutenant-colonel, Francis Hall, came into that rank in January 1646, having previously been major, and before that an officer on service in Ireland.[150] Whether Hall was an Oxford, or Oxfordshire, man does not appear. His successor as major, Leonard Bowman, certainly belonged to Oxford.[151]

Of the county's other colonels few were cited by petitioners in 1662–63. Sir Charles Blount of Mapledurham served widely before he was accidentally killed at Oxford in 1644, but nothing is known of the composition of his regiment.[152] Edmund Chamberlain of Stratton Audley was commissioned as early as 9 December 1642 but there is nothing to show that he fulfilled the commission, there were no composition proceedings concerning him, and he passed anonymously and unscathed, it would seem, through the war.[153] Robert Keys, as has been shown,[154] deserted the King in 1644 with his regiment and was commissioned anew by Sir Thomas Fairfax. Thomas Napier of Cowley served under Lord Byron and claimed himself as an indigent in 1662–63, sending in a certificate from London.[155] David Walters of Godstow was High Sheriff in 1643–44 and commanded his cavalry regiment at Henley on Thames in September 1645: he certainly proved an active commander, but only three indigents named him in 1662–63 (none of them from Oxfordshire) and one, a Gloucestershire cornet, Robert Master, cited Walters as a major-general subordinate to Charles Gerard, a rank he only briefly held.[156] Gerard Croker of Steeple Barton was promoted from a troop command to a colonelcy between 13 December 1642 and 22 January 1643, a sure indication of early partisanship. Croker later served under Wilmot, but was spared involvement in Wilmot's disgrace and the petition of other officers, for he was taken prisoner in July 1644 and gaoled at Gloucester until November when released on parole. His health had apparently deteriorated, and though he found his way to Exeter garrison late in the war, he died in 1647.[157] Five indigents cited Croker, two of them from London and Westminster, though that may conceal other county links: three were Oxfordshire men, and Croker's second-in-command, Henry Harris, came from Churchill, near Chipping Norton.[158] He, like Croker, had been a captain at the outbreak of war, and was amongst those who signed the pro-Wilmot petition in August 1644.

Henry Wilmot, technically an Oxfordshire man from Culham,

has been discussed.[159] None of his officers who petitioned at the Restoration came out of Oxfordshire, but half of them were from the Welsh border, four petitioned from London and one from Surrey.[160] In Wilmot's case, however, these indigents, with one certain exception, might well have served under him during the Worcester campaign in 1651 and the original officers of his first regiment, if any survived to petition, may be concealed within other formations. At Wilmot's disgrace his own regiment ceased to be commanded by him: his second-in-command, Paul Smith, was not promoted to a colonelcy, and disbandment seems most likely. Smith, who was certified as indigent, was a professional soldier of European experience and had been promoted from a majority after Roundway Down in July 1643, Wilmot's spectacular victory. Not surprisingly, Lieutenant Colonel Smith set his hand to the petition of Wilmot's officers in August 1644, and that may have been his last military act, for thenceforth the record is silent concerning him.[161]

Oxfordshire compares poorly in this study with Somersetshire and many other counties. As plotted on map 2, it forms part of a broad band of low-yielding counties westwards of London, running from Sussex in the south to Derbyshire in the north. The indigent figures for those counties show variation, seventy-one petitions from Derbyshire (with the usual caveat) and only twenty-six from Sussex, though both counties provided half a dozen commanding colonels. Surrey's fifty-one indigents contrast strongly with neighbouring Berkshire's thirty-one, and all counties in this band pale beside isolated Kent and even Essex. As plotted on the map, Buckinghamshire's contribution is thrown into relief, eleven colonels and thirty-four indigents in 1662–63. This country was real frontier territory and debatable land, most strongly evidenced by the disaster which befell two local regiments in process of recruitment, those of John Denton and Sir William Smith.

Denton's was short-lived indeed: no indigents claimed to have served under him, and he himself was killed after his regiment was spoiled, on 9 August 1644.[162] Sir William Smith was Denton's brother-in-law, and based his recruitment drive around the Denton house at Hillesden, to the south of Buckingham. He had probably been commissioned to recruit late in 1643, and all the evidence shows that he entered upon the task with spirit: his officers were duly commissioned by February 1644, when 200 men were enlisted, and in March Hillesden was attacked by Parliamentarian troops intent upon wrecking Smith's embryo forces. Smith himself was taken prisoner and sent to London, where he made his escape in 1645, only to be recaptured.[163] Six indigents cited Smith as their commander, but only Captain William Lambert sent in his certificate from Buckinghamshire.[164] The others all certified from London, one of whom, Cornet Hugh Merchant, named the regiment's second-in-command, Lieutenant Colonel Hurter. Hurter was not a local man, nor an Englishman, though whether he was a Dutch or German professional is not known. What is important about his presence in Smith's forming regiment is that it shows Smith was in earnest, bringing in and paying a professional adviser and organiser. Hurter, Horther or Heitter (as he is variously named) does not seem to have transferred to Smith's from any other regiment, and he may well have been hired by Smith's rich father-in-law. When the regiment was wrecked, and Smith taken, Hurter himself was briefly a prisoner, Exchanged, he served in a field command on the Welsh border under the Devil of Shrawardine, William Vaughan, and was again captured at Rowton Heath near Chester in September 1645. Three indigents cited Hurter by name when they petitioned, but there is no discernible link between them and the officers of Smith's original regiment, which must have been utterly broken.[165]

Of the other Buckinghamshire colonels, the brothers Edmund and Henry Verney of Claydon were both promoted from subordinate ranks and fought outside their county. Edmund came back from Ireland in the regiment of Richard Gibson late in 1643, and succeeded to the colonelcy of John Marrow when the latter was killed in August 1644. Thus Verney became commander of what had originally been a Cheshire regiment, that of the Lord Cholmondeley. Edmund Verney perished when Cromwell stormed Drogheda in 1649.[166] His brother Henry returned from European service in 1642 to become second-in-command in the regiment of the Hampshire Royalist, Colonel Humphrey Bennet of Shalden. Bennet's force fought almost exclusively in the King's western armies, and the sixteen indigents who claimed under him came predominantly out of Hampshire, though in the course of the war Bennet gathered up a Durham lieutenant and a cornet,

Nicholas Aris, from Verney's native county.[167] Henry Verney's colonelcy, which clearly came his way by May 1644, may have been in succession to Bennet, who was captured in April. Neither of the Verneys was cited by indigents in 1662–63, and what became of Henry is not known.[168]

No indigents cited their services under Colonels Thomas Stafford of Tottenhoo, who was recruiting in December 1643;[169] Thomas Panton, who ended the war in the garrison at Truro;[170] or Philip Palmer of Dorney, the son of an officer of the King's household.[171] A lone indigent, a quartermaster, named as his commander Colonel Henry Sandys of Latimers. Sandys, who was mortally wounded at Alresford in March 1644, was father-in-law of Colonel Sir Edmund Fortescue of Fallapit in Devon. Fortescue's own regiment of infantry contained at least one indigent from Buckinghamshire, Lieutenant Henry Edmunds.[172]

The Tyrringhams of Tyrringham and Fulgrave produced two colonels, the brothers Sir John and William. The former, knighted in November 1642 when a Commissioner of Array, was recruiting in August 1643 around Bicester, and died at Oxford in May 1645.[173] No indigents named him, and only three – but two of them from Buckinghamshire – cited the younger brother. William Tyrringham was twenty-four in 1642. He had served briefly in Europe, had fought against the Scots, and in July 1643 was Adjutant General to Prince Rupert when he was probably a regimental major. Little is known of his war service beyond the fact of his full colonelcy, enjoyed at the latest in July 1645, and there is a possibility that he shared in Prince Rupert's disgrace that year, for he petitioned to compound in December.[174]

The most eminent Buckinghamshire commander, deriving from Wing in that county, was Robert Dormer Earl of Carnarvon,[175] who was killed in action at Newbury in September 1643. The evidence of indigent claimants shows that the earl's own regiment had no real links with his native county. Of thirteen claimants, only four certified from there, and the others sent in petitions from Lancashire, Yorkshire, Dorset, Northamptonshire, Wiltshire and London, evidence of the way in which specific commanders could draw to them activists from all over England.[176] Charles Gerard, for example, in his dual capacity as colonel and general, was named by more than sixty indigents, of whom only one sent in from Gerard's native county of Lancashire.[177] Caernarvon's Lancashire link came through his second-in-command, Lieutenant Colonel Alexander Standish of Standish, who, like the earl, was a Catholic.[178] What is curious is that after Caernarvon's death the regiment passed not to Standish but to Richard Neville of Billingsbear in Berkshire, the brother-in-law of the unjustly notorious Sir Thomas Lunsford.

The case of Neville, Standish and the Earl of Caernarvon's regiment illustrates the complexities of attempting anything approaching a formal regimental history of the King's armies. That Standish was second-in-command to the earl is made clear by the indigency claimants. Standish's presence in the regiment underlines its lack of Buckinghamshire links in the officer complement. That Richard Neville ultimately became commander of the regiment after the earl's death is also clear. Moreover, the evidence for Neville would seem to show that he was lieutenant-colonel in 1642, fought in that rank in June 1643 and was present at Newbury when Caernarvon fell. So at what point prior to Caernarvon's death can Standish have been second-in-command? Neville's field rank was clearly early. Those indigents who cited him in 1662–63 named, as inferior officers under him, the Buckinghamshire gentleman Thomas Panton and the Bedfordshire Catholic Richard Conquest. According to Lieutenant Henry Jewkes, who petitioned from Middlesex, Panton was major under Neville, and according to Quartermaster John Salvin from Durham, Conquest was a captain. As has been said, Panton in time became a full colonel. Conquest was a full colonel by November 1644 at the latest.[179] What is not to be known from the indigency claims is whether Neville is cited as a full or half-colonel, since no claimant named anyone as his lieutenant-colonel. Since the historical record is unforthcoming, and since no claimant listed under Caernarvon alluded to anyone other than Standish as second-in-command, the following explanation may be offered.

It is known that the King, on his recruitment drive in the late summer of 1642, drew away from Lancashire formed regiments and other partisans. Alexander Standish was probably among them. It was later alleged against him that in March 1643, when Caernarvon's regiment was in action with the King's western army, Standish was back in Lancashire and present at the burning of Lancaster.[180]

It is known that several Lancashire field commanders returned home in 1643 to recruit. At the time when Standish was thus employed, the evidence for Neville shows the latter to have been Caernarvon's second-in-command and to have remained so thenceforth. Standish must therefore belong to the early formative period of Caernarvon's regiment, and have preceded Neville in the rank. This does not explain what happened to Standish, or where he afterwards served, though he signed the August 1644 petition of Wilmot's officers and so was still a field commander at that date. He was captured at Langport, in Goring's army, in July 1645. Neville was also a signatory of the 1644 petition: perhaps Standish returned to the regiment after Caernarvon's death, when Neville's promotion opened a vacancy. Of course there are a number of imponderables, not least what became of Major Thomas Panton in the officer hierarchy under Neville. The resolution of such problems falls outside the scope of this study, but the case is highlighted to show the fluidity of regimental officer complements and the attendant problems of fragmentary evidence.

IX

No consideration of the geographical origins of the King's colonels should bypass counties where they were thin on the ground, and nowhere were they thinner than in Huntingdonshire, which produced three colonels and only eight indigents to claim from there in 1662–63. Since the county is synonymous with the Parliamentarian general Oliver Cromwell, it is worth noting that the Cromwells as a whole did not share Oliver's loyalties. Henry Cromwell of Ramsey and Upwood and his son James were both commissioned colonels for the King. A third member of the family, Gregory Cromwell, was an early partisan and was present in Chester with his family in September 1642. He was to claim himself as indigent at the Restoration.[181] A fourth, Thomas Cromwell of Great Staughton on the Bedfordshire border, and a younger brother of Colonel Henry Cromwell of Ramsey, served as major in the Duke of York's Horse under the Essex Catholic, Samuel Tuke.[182]

Henry Cromwell was an early partisan, noted in August 1642 with armed men in Cambridge to bring silver plate to the King. He was appointed to the Commission of Array in his county, and to recruit his own regiment on 5 May 1643. He brought in Gregory Cromwell as his major, who in 1662–63 petitioned from Norfolk, whilst two other indigents came from Lincolnshire and Cambridgeshire. As late as December 1645 Colonel Cromwell's regiment was in action in Dorset.[183] Henry's son, Colonel James Cromwell, who was captured commanding his regiment at Rowton Heath outside Chester in September 1645, probably had no connection with his father's regiment.[184] The indigent claimants citing James Cromwell show a northern tendency. Of six, two petitioned from Northumberland, two from Yorkshire and Lincolnshire, and two more as of London and Westminster. What is remarkable is that both subordinate field officers of the regiment, Lieutenant Colonel Muschamp and Major Husthwayte Write, certified themselves as indigent.[185] Edward Muschamp was a Northumberland man but, more important, had been major in the regiment of the Cambridgeshire Royalist Sir Richard Willys of Fen Ditton, who was disgraced with Rupert after the surrender of Bristol on 10 September 1645. James Cromwell succeeded Willys in the latter's regimental command, Muschamp was moved up a rank, and Wright, a Lincolnshire man and a very early partisan in that county, became major.[186]

The third of Huntingdonshire's colonels was Sir Lodowick Dyer, baronet, of Great Staughton, from which parish Major Thomas Cromwell also came. Dyer was commissioned in June 1643 but was still recruiting a year later. A solitary Lincolnshire indigent, Lieutenant John Greaves, cited Dyer and mentioned a Captain Barnard of the regiment. Dyer surrendered in August 1645 and nothing is known of his war service.[187]

Space does not permit a county-by-county analysis of the origins and geographical associations of the King's commanders. Specific counties have been examined in terms of their relation to the war in general, and the way in which activism was expressed in military command. By bringing into the analysis the evidence of the indigent officer claimants of the Restoration, a broader picture has been achieved. In the case of northern England and Wales, both areas were treated collectively rather than piecemeal, to submit to examination the historical reputation of each. It has been shown that the north generally contributed little to the overall war effort, though it added considerably to the number of men commissioned and in arms for the King. That paradox has been explained. For Wales, the country's legendary Royalism has been shown not to manifest itself in terms of regiments and regimental command, and the far greater importance of England in those terms was necessarily emphasised. Above all, this chapter has sought as often as possible to bring back from the sidelines and footnotes of historiography as many of the men who waged the King's war as the nature of the argument permitted. They had their counterparts nationwide, and there was not a county in England or in Wales that did not possess its partisans. That is why there was a civil war. Such men were willing to fight.

Notes

1 Newman, *Royalist Officers*, p. 120. Dore, Brereton Letter Books, II, p. 424. HMC, *Rawdon Hastings Mss*, p. 117. CCC, 18, 113, 120.
2 Newman, *Royalist Officers*, p. 44.
3 P. R. Newman, 'The 1663 list of indigent Royalist officers considered as a primary source for the study of the Royalist army', *Historical Journal*, 30 (4), 1987, pp. 885–904. Subsequently cited as Newman, 'List'. When the document discussed, *A List of Officers Claiming to the Sixty Thousand Pounds &c. Granted by His Sacred Majesty for the Relief of His Truly-Loyal and Indigent Party*, is referred to beneath it will be cited as *List*, followed by the column number alluded to. The document was not paginated.
4 Sutherland, *Hutchinson Memoirs*, p. 60.
5 Hutton, *Royalist War Effort*, p. 4.
6 Sutherland, *Hutchinson Memoirs*, p. 60.
7 Hutton, *War Effort*, p. 4.
8 *Ibid.*, p. 4.
9 *Ibid.*, p. 5.
10 Parsons, *Slingsby Diary*, p. 76.
11 *Ibid.*.
12 See above, Chapter Two.
13 Coates, Young and Snow, *Private Journals*, p. 127.
14 Firth, *Newcastle Life*, p. 23.
15 Newman, *Royalist Officers*, pp. 297–8. CAM, p. 1185, shows his son was killed in 1642.
16 Newman, *Royalist Officers*, p. 184.
17 Hutton, *War Effort*, p. 15.
18 *Ibid.*, p. 23.
19 Newman, *Royalist Officers*, p. 385.
20 Newman, *Royalist Officers*, p. 171. CAM, pp. 730–1.
21 Newman, *Royalist Officers*, p. 96.
22 *Ibid.*, p. 237. CAM, p. 1019. See also above, Chapter Two.
23 Newman, *Royalist Officers*, p. 359. CCC, pp. 39, 1715.
24 Newman, *Royalist Officers*, p. 137.
25 Hutton, *War Effort*, p. 74. Newman, *Royalist Officers*, p. 305. HMC, *Twelfth Report*, Rutland Mss, I, 1888, p. 511. CCC, pp. 360, 443, 2042–3.
26 Hutton, *War Effort*, p. 34.

27 CAM, p. 1022.
28 Newman, *Royalist Officers*, p. 306.
29 *Return, Members of Parliamant*, Part I, *1213–1702*, 1878, p. 455.
30 Newman, *Royalist Officers*, p. 325.
31 Newman, 'List', *passim*.
32 Hutton, *War Effort*, p. 24. Newman, *Royalist Officers*, p. 280.
33 Newman, *Royalist Officers*, p. 281. CCC, pp. 131, 1754.
34 Newman, *Royalist Officers*, p. 427.
35 *Ibid.*, p. 35. Hutton, *War Effort*, pp. 17, 136.
36 Hutton, *War Effort*, pp. 15–16.
37 Newman, *Royalist Officers*, pp. 324–5.
38 *Ibid.*, pp. 368–9.
39 See above, Chapter Two.
40 Newman, *Royalist Officers*, pp. 427–8.
41 *Ibid.*, pp. 121–2.
42 See above, Chapter Two.
43 Hutton, *War Effort*, p. 38.
44 Newman, *Royalist Officers*, p. 266. CCC, p. 60. Whitelocke, *Memorials*, I, p. 228.
45 Newman, *Royalist Officers*, p. 105. HMC, *Third Report*, Whitehall Dod Mss, 1872, p. 259.
46 Newman, *Royalist Officers*, p. 409.
47 Hutton, *War Effort*, p. 22.
48 Newman, *Royalist Officers*, p. 284. Long, Symonds Diary, p. 254. Coates, *Journal of Simond D'Ewes*, p. 168. HMC, *Fourteenth Report*, Ormonde Mss, I, 1895, p. 123.
49 See above, Chapter Two.
50 Hutton, *War Effort*, pp. 39–40, and for what follows unless otherwise referenced.
51 See above, Chapter Two.
52 Newman, *Royalist Officers*, p. 78, Fetherston, Visitation of Warwickshire, p. 35. CCC, pp. 89, 1016, 1960.
53 Newman, *Royalist Officers*, p. 420.
54 *Ibid.*, p. 231.
55 *Ibid.*, p. 132. CCC, pp. 295, 2283. CAM, p. 1358.
56 Newman, *Royalist Officers*, p. 221. CCC, pp. 112, 2784. CAM, p. 1252. Pennington and Roots, *Committee at Stafford*, p. 196.
57 Dore, Brereton Letter Books, I, p. 445.
58 Newman, *Royalist Officers*, p. 350. G. J. Armytage and J. P. Rylands (eds.), Pedigrees made at the Visitation of Cheshire, 1613, *Harleian Society*, LIX, 1909, p. 216. Coates, Young and Snow, *Private Journals*, p. 491. HMC, *Rawdon Hastings Mss*, p. 117. Pennington and Roots, *Committee at Stafford*, p. 29. CCC, pp. 90. 113. CAM, 433..
59 Hutton, *War Effort*, p. 23.
60 Newman, *Royalist Officers*, p. 131.
61 Hutton, *War Effort*, p. 38.
62 Newman, *Royalist Officers*, p. 121. Armytage and Rylands, Visitation of Cheshire, p. 97. CCC, pp. 100, 103.
63 Hutton, *War Effort*, pp. 38–9, 44–6.
64 Newman, *Royalist Officers*, pp. 148–9. CCC, pp. 104, 120, 217, 1438, Gamul. Newman, *Royalist Officers*, p. 247. Fetherston, Visitation of Warwickshire, p.

70. HMC, *Fourteenth Report*, Ormonde Mss, I, 1895, p. 124. HMC, *Tenth Report*, Kilmorrey Mss, 1885, p. 373. CCC, pp. 61, 100, 103, Marrow. Newman, *Royalist Officers*, p. 405. CCC, pp. 100, 103, 106, 122, 269. CAM, p. 85, Werden.

65 Newman, *Royalist Officers*, p. 229. CCC, pp. 1067–8.

66 Newman, *Royalist Officers*, pp. 229–30. CCC, p. 894.

67 Sutherland, *Hutchinson Memoirs*, p. 61.

68 Newman, *Royalist Officers*, p. 357. G. D. Squibb (ed.), Visitation of Notthinghamshire, 1662–64, *Harleian Society*, New Series, 5, 1986, p. 84.

69 Newman, *Royalist Officers*, p. 293.

70 Newman, *Royalist Officers*, p. 125. CCC, pp. 107, 2744. CAM, p. 1320.

71 CAM, p. 770.

72 Newman, *Royalist Officers*, p. 30.

73 *Ibid.*, p. 19.

74 *Ibid.*, p. 99. CCC, p. 1340.

75 Newman, *Royalist Officers*, p. 123.

76 *Ibid.*, pp. 289–90. CSPD, 1660–61, p. 13.

77 Newman, *Royalist Officers*, p. 402.

78 Lewis, Letters of Lady Brilliana Harley, p. 161.

79 Newman, *Royalist Officers*, p. 336. CAM, p. 868.

80 Newman, *Royalist Officers*, p. 100. CAM, p. 1485.

81 Newman, *Royalist Officers*, pp. 156–7. HMC, *Fifteenth Report*, Hodgkin Mss, 1897, p. 115.

82 Newman, *Royalist Officers*, p. 156.

83 *Ibid.*.

84 A. C. Wood (ed.), Memorials of the Holles Family, 1493–1656, by Gervase Holles, *Camden Society*, Third Series, LV, 1937.

85 Newman, *Royalist Officers*, p. 193. CSPD, 1660–61, p. 113.

86 Newman, *Royalist Officers*, p. 3. *Commons Journal*, III, p. 154. Newman, *Royalist Officers*, p. 387. CCC, p. 1879.

87 Newman, *Royalist Officers*, p. 90. CCC, p. 787. CAM, p. 467.

88 See above, Chapter Two.

89 Newman, *Royalist Officers*, p. 353.

90 See above, Chapters Two and Three.

91 Newman, *Royalist Officers*, pp. 250–1. CAM, p. 1330, refers to him, though he is incorrectly named.

92 Newman, *Royalist Officers*, p. 39. Hovenden, Visitation of Kent, p. 40. HMC, *Fourteenth Report*, Ormonde Mss, I, 1895, p. 132. CCC, pp. 102, 1859.

93 Newman, *Royalist Officers*, p. 370.

94 *Ibid.*, p. 131. For Manning see above, Chapter Three.

95 Newman, *Royalist Officers*, pp. 323–4, St Leger. Newman, *Royalist Officers*, p. 4. CCC, pp. 616, 868–9, Apsley. Newman, *Royalist Officers*, p. 305, Pretty.

96 Newman, *Royalist Officers*, p. 38.

97 *Ibid.*, p. 68. Hovenden, Visitation of Kent, p. 164. CCC, p. 2645.

98 Newman, *Royalist Officers*, p. 146.

99 *Ibid.*, p. 251. Hovenden, Visitation of Kent, p. 107.

100 Newman, *Royalist Officers*, pp. 183–4. Hovenden, Visitation of Kent, p. 163.

101 Newman, 'List', pp. 887–8.

102 The best recent assessment of Somerset during the Civil War, though it is in no way concerned with military matters, is in David Underdown, *Revel Riot*

and Rebellion, Oxford, 1985.
103 Newman, *Royalist Officers*, p. 382.
104 *Ibid.*, p. 43. J. J. Howard (ed.) *Miscellanea Genealogica et Heraldica*, new series, IV, 1884, p. 34.
105 Newman, *Royalist Officers*, p. 225. CCC, pp. 144, 240, 537. CAM, pp. 1376–7.
106 Newman, *Royalist Officers*, pp. 185–6. CCC, p. 125. Howard, *Miscellanea*, IV, p. 35.
107 See above, Chapter Three.
108 CCC, p. 427.
109 Newman, *Royalist Officers*, p. 359. Colby, Visitation of Somerset, p. 105. CCC, p. 1932.
110 Colby, Visitation of Somerset, p. 79.
111 Newman, *Royalist Officers*, p. 272.
112 *List*, column 106.
113 Newman, *Royalist Officers*, pp. 18, 316.
114 *Ibid.* p. 359. CCC, pp. 427, 1932. Colby, Visitation of Somerset, p. 105.
115 CCC, p. 2104.
116 *List*, column 132.
117 CCC, p. 83.
118 Newman, *Royalist Officers*, p. 378.
119 HMC, *Fifteenth Report*, Hodgkin Mss, 1898, p. 103.
120 Newman, *Royalist Officers*, pp. 71, 288, 396. *List*, columns 27, 103, 137.
121 Newman, *Royalist Officers*, p. 218.
122 *Ibid.*, p. 288. *List*, column 103.
123 *List*, column 24.
124 Newman, *Royalist Officers*, p. 320. CSPD, 1661–2, p. 53.
125 Newman, *Royalist Officers*, p. 64.
126 See above, Chapter Three.
127 Newman, *Royalist Officers*, p. 112.
128 *List*, column 40.
129 Newman, *Royalist Officers*, pp. 19, 357. *List*, column 123. CAM, p. 476. Firth, *Ludlow Memoirs*, I, p. 89.
130 Newman, *Royalist Officers*, p. 30. Colby, Visitation of Somerset, p. 8.
131 *List*, column 147.
132 Newman, *Royalist Officers*, p. 2. J. J. Howard and J. L. Chester (eds.), The Visitation of London, II . . . 1633–5, *Harleian Society*, XV, 1880, p. 21. J. P. Rylands (ed.), The Visitation of the County of Dorset, 1623, *Harleian Society*, XX, 1885, p. 6.
133 Newman, *Royalist Officers*, p. 365.
134 *Ibid.*, p. 231.
135 *Ibid.*, p. 51. Bannerman, Visitation of Sussex, p. 189.
136 Newman, *Royalist Officers*, p. 425. CCC, pp. 119, 342, 2615. CSPD, 1663–64, p. 13.
137 Newman, *Royalist Officers*, p. 426. CCC, 1417. *List*, column 147.
138 CAM, p. 1337.
139 Newman, *Royalist Officers*, pp. 178, 426. CSPD, 1660–61 p. 106.
140 *List*, columns 15, 16.
141 CCC, p. 554.
142 *List*, column 123.
143 Newman, *Royalist Officers*, p. 303.

144 *List*, column 105.
145 Newman, *Royalist Officers*, p. 280.
146 Newman, *Royalist Officers*, p. 263–4. Aubrey recorded a curious anecdote about Major Morgan; see *Three Prose Works*, p. 30.
147 Newman, *Royalist Officers*, pp. 294–5. CAM, p. 1159. Colby, Visitation of Somerset, p. 85.
148 Bannerman, Visitation of Sussex, p. 109. Newman, *Royalist Officers*, p. 337.
149 Hobson and Salter, Oxford Council Acts, p. 133.
150 Newman, *Royalist Officers*, p. 173. HMC, *Fourteenth Report*, Ormonde Mss, I, 1895, p. 122. Hobson and Salter, Oxford Council Acts, p. 133.
151 Newman, *Royalist Officers*, p. 39.
152 *Ibid.*, p. 33.
153 *Ibid.*, p. 67.
154 See above, Chapter Two.
155 Newman, *Royalist Officers*, pp. 270–1. Foster, *Admissions to Grays Inn*, p. 219. Dore, Brereton Letter Books, I, p. 187.
156 Newman, *Royalist Officers*, pp. 396–7. *List*, columns 53, 137. Clark, *Life of Anthony Wood*, p. 216.
157 Newman, *Royalist Officers*, p. 94. Whitelocke, *Memorials*, I, p. 201. *Ibid.*, II, p. 7.
158 *List*, column 34. Newman, *Royalist Officers*, p. 177.
159 See above, Chapter Three.
160 *List*, column 143.
161 Newman, *Royalist Officers*, p. 348.
162 *Ibid.*, p. 108. See above, Chapter Two.
163 Newman, *Royalist Officers*, p. 349. CAM, pp. 42, 1233. Whitelocke, *Memorials*, I, p. 311.
164 CCC, p. 67.
165 Newman, *Royalist Officers*, pp. 206–7. *List*, column 75.
166 Newman, *Royalist Officers*, p. 390. HMC, *Fourteenth Report*, Ormonde Mss, I, 1895, p. 123. See above, note 64 and text. Verney followed Werden, who was Marrow's immediate successor.
167 *List*, column 10, Newman, *Royalist Officers*, pp. 23–4.
168 Newman, *Royalist Officers*, pp. 390–1.
169 *Ibid.*, p. 354.
170 *Ibid.*, pp. 285–6.
171 J. J. Howard, *Miscellanea Genealogica et Heraldica*, new series I, 1868, p. 109. CCC, 2787.
172 Newman, *Royalist Officers*, pp. 141–2, 327. *List*, column 51.
173 Newman, *Royalist Officers*, pp. 382–3. J. Wilson (ed.), Buckinghamshire Contributions for Ireland, 1642, *Buckinghamshire Record Society*, 21, 1983, p. 39. See also CCC, p. 1009.
174 Newman, *Royalist Officers*, p. 383. *List*, column 133.
175 See above, Chapters Two, Three.
176 *List*, columns 22–3.
177 *Ibid.*, columns 52–3.
178 Newman, *Royalist Officers*, p. 355.
179 *List*, column 99. Newman, *Royalist Officers*, pp. 81, 271.
180 CCC, p. 21.
181 Newman, *Royalist Officers*, p. 95.

182 CCC, p. 90. Dore, Brereton Letter Books, I, pp. 84, 396.

183 Newman, *Royalist Officers*, p. 95. HMC, *Eighth Report*, Appendix, II, Manchester Mss, 1881, p. 59. *List*, column 34. Whitelocke, *Memorials*, I, p. 571.

184 I have suggested otherwise previously, see Newman, *Royalist Officers*, p. 95.

185 *List*, column 34.

186 Newman, *Royalist Officers*, pp. 268, 424–5.

187 *Ibid.*, p. 118. *List*, column 41.

CONCLUSION

King Charles I undertook a war against his Parliament in the knowledge that he had the support to do it. He had been driven into a political and constitutional corner, and this perception of his predicament in 1642 was not his alone. He made a direct and personal appeal to the political nation. It was answered by thousands who would thenceforth be known as Royalists or Cavaliers, Malignants or Incendiaries, according to the stance of the observer. The swift development of a Royalist party in arms in defence of the King demonstrates how profound the crisis in government had become. The English civil war was fought, predominantly, between Englishmen. I have endeavoured to show that for this reason alone historians cannot dispense with the term. The structure of English society was what made the King's war possible. Charles I drew upon traditional values of obedience and loyalty, implicitly believing in them as rallying calls quite as much as those who recognised their obligation to serve him in arms. Although the terms 'Royalist' and 'Cavalier' had currency before 1642, they assumed a new and more vigorous meaning thereafter when the notions upon which patriarchal society rested were transformed into armies.

Those who undertook military command in the King's service were no rakehells but invariably solid, comfortable, respectable and conservative gentlemen. They were men with the obligations of family and, often, property to consider. The imperative which led them to sacrifice such considerations in the almighty gamble of war must have been overwhelming in its meaning for them. It is no longer possible to suppose that the King's cause was espoused and maintained by self-interested courtiers and their hangers-on or reckless, landless adventurers of name and coat armour and small expectations in the world. The very idea that the Royalist party in arms from 1642 correlated with the royal court of pre-war years and was therefore narrowly based and inherently weak must be abandoned. The most notorious example of the lawless Cavalier archetype, Thomas Lunsford, is nothing but a propaganda construct. If any find themselves perplexed by the duration of the war and the repeated Royalist attempts at insurrection in its wake, it must be because they have failed to perceive that which ought to be an axiom for historians: the degree of real commitment and resolution shown by the King's 'servants' in the King's service.

I have argued that the King's appeal for support was couched in terms which relied upon an identification of interest between King and people. This was no matter of expedience. Charles I had reached the limit of his power to concede further to his Parliament without undermining the authority of the Crown which he would pass on to his successors. He appealed over the heads of the Parliament men to their electorate, and the war which he was enabled to wage was made possible by its response. The divisions within the Commons were mirrored in, or reflected, those throughout the country. The King's armies were largely commanded by voters: they were a crucial part of the political nation, and they sided against the representative body which they had almost unanimously welcomed in 1640.

The King's appeal transcended earlier political divisions and, quite as important, religious differences. The response of Catholics to the King had little to do with their religious faith and much to do with that continuing identity of interest which tied them to their Protestant gentry neighbours. They largely shared the values subsumed within the notion of service to the Crown. They reacted as did many Protestant loyalists, setting aside the grumbles of years of 'persecution' as others did the petty grievances nurtured during the Personal Rule. The King's appeal to arms went far deeper than mere exploitation of gentry self-interest. The King's armies which so rapidly emerged testify to that. Parliament's obsession with the 'popish conspiracy' betrays the extent to which it miscalculated in its dealings with, and expectations of, the King. Since the blame for war could not be assigned to Parliament's political ineptitude, it had to be seen as part of a general popish assault upon the English nation. Whether with irony or not, post-Restoration Protestant writers were not themselves averse to seeing Parliament's cause as Jesuited and priest-driven.

The King and his advisers were aware of the conflicting values of Catholic support. They sought to minimise its public face, appearing to suppose that Parliament's popish allegations required to be based in fact. The way in which Catholic and Protestant Royalists fought side by side for so long in a common cause may give cause to speculate just how far the myth of the popish conspiracy really had percolated. If the Royalist armies are anything to go by, differences in faith were shallow matters amongst laymen. They could only appear to deepen in the atmosphere of a country at peace within itself. Civil war, for the Royalists, created an attitude towards Catholics inherently more rational than Parliament's continued trumpeting of its own peculiarly Protestant insecurities. The King's cause would have been the weaker had he pried too closely into men's consciences.

I have not sought to argue that the King's commanders or his supporters in general were motivated by high political principles. The basis upon which Royalists took up arms was part and parcel of their view of the world and their part in it: the obligation which they conceived to lie upon them. This is not the same thing as a purely emotive response to events, although there is within the concept of service an element of the irrational which is of considerable importance. But wars are not sustained by mere emotive force. The prosecution of war and the impact of fighting must have forced anyone driven by purely gut loyalty to evaluate their actions. It is my contention that the experience of civil war created Royalism rather than that Royalism made civil war possible. The identification of interest between king and subject upon which the cause initially rested developed into something approaching an ideology which the King over the water, Charles II, strongly benefited from. Against that the coercive powers of the republican regime could not prevail. Historians would do well to pay attention to the potency of Royalism even if they do not go so far as to identify it as an ideology. Moral integrity was not the preserve of the King's enemies; indeed, the Royalists show a more consistent position than the supporters of Parliament may be felt to have done.

Parliament's victory over the King's men came in on the back of a Scottish, mercenary, army. The New Model, for all its muscle-flexing after 1646 and apparent politicisation, barely scraped a victory at Naseby, and its military reputation was based upon the defeat of already exhausted and diminished Royalist forces. Historiography, with its dominant interest in the New Model, has effectively put into the scholarly shade not only its Royalist enemies but its own provincial allies. A full redress of the historical balance will require not only a commitment to Royalist studies in the broadest sense, but also new research into those Parliamentary armies which faced the King's men at the height of their power. There were better generals than Sir Thomas Fairfax ranged against the King's servants, and better rank and file than those who fled before Prince Rupert at Naseby. Any evaluation of the Royalists in arms must entail a complementary study of Parliament's provincial armies and its Scottish allies.

In this study I have sought to restore to the King's commanders some of that significance which defeat and academic indifference have deprived them of. I have tried to show the extent to which the Royalists were part and parcel of the entire political nation, and not some curious amalgam of unrepresentative elements. By taking the idea of service as the basic principle underlying active Royalism, I hope I have shown that the King's war enjoyed widespread support; that, by definition, the proceedings of the Parliament met with widespread and persistent resistance. I have also argued that the King was more in touch with the political realities of 1642 than were his potential enemies, and that the scale of his support proves that. Parliament might attempt to portray Charles I as the Man of Blood, imposing war upon his people, but there were a vast number of his subjects who emerged from the 1640s convinced that the King (as a tract of 1660 put it) was 'A Martyr for His People'. Though we may stand aloof from such emotive judgements, it behoves us to remember that this was how contemporaries simplified complexities in order to cope with them and their implications. Ultimately I believe that allegiance was a straightforward and relatively simple matter – that it arose from inclination, temperament and other humours that will for ever defy precise analysis. The true extent of such commitment may best be judged by the actions to which it leads. The King's regimental commanders for the most part, and many subordinates and rank and file, in their service demonstrated the vitality and vigour of their commitment. Royalist studies must begin from the fact that such men saw something profoundly worth fighting for, and fought for it accordingly.

The reality of the fears and jealousies of the 1640s as they affected contemporaries cannot be known to us – at least, not without a concerted effort of the intellect, leavened with a pinch of imagination. If this study serves to remind us that Charles I lacked neither friends nor champions in 1642, and could count upon large numbers of the politically and socially influential to stand beside him, it will have achieved something. If it prepares the way for further exploration in the neglected territory of Royalist studies, it will have achieved its overall purpose.

INDEX

Royalist colonels are cited in this index according to their social status at time of commission.